FLESHLY TABERNACLES

Fleshly TABERNACLES

Milton and the Incarnational Poetics of Revolutionary England

BRYAN ADAMS HAMPTON

University of Notre Dame Press
Notre Dame, Indiana

Manufactured in the United States of America

Library of Congress Cataloging-in-Publication Data

Hampton, Bryan Adams.
   Fleshly tabernacles : Milton and the incarnational poetics of
revolutionary England / Bryan Adams Hampton.
       p.   cm.
   Includes bibliographical references and index.
   ISBN 978-0-268-03096-4 (pbk. : alk. paper) — ISBN 0-268-03096-0
(pbk. : alk. paper) — ISBN 978-0-268-08174-4 (ebook)
   1. Milton, John, 1608–1674—Criticism and interpretation.   2. Milton, John,
1608–1674—Religion.   3. Incarnation in literature.   4. Christianity and
literature—England—History—17th century.   I. Title.
   PR3592.R4H36   2012
   821'.4—dc23

                                                        2012025743

For Ceri, and for our children,
Isabel, Elijah, and Nate:

"Beatitude past utterance"

contents

Part III. Revolutionary Incarnations and the Metaphysics of Abundance

a c k n o w l e d g m e n t s

"a grateful mind / By owing owes not . . . , at once / Indebted and discharg'd." This work has been encouraged and sustained by many, and it is my hope that I have met their considerable generosity with a mind and heart brimming with gratitude. I know that none of them consider their involvement in the book as having incurred any debt, yet I am compelled all the same to celebrate their contributions.

Regina Schwartz and Michael Lieb initiated me into the mysteries of Milton studies with watchfulness and affection, permitting me to "imp my wing" on theirs. Ethan Shagan and Steve Long each challenged me, respectively, to think more historically and more theologically, and I find the project is much the richer for it, even though juggling so many balls proved to be a challenge. John Shawcross took an interest in my graduate work from the fortuitous moment I met him at the Milton Seminar at Chicago's Newberry Library; in his passing, many will affirm that his hospitality toward young scholars will remain unmatched. I have appreciated the literary conversations with and friendships of Glenn Sucich and Scott Huelin, whose steadfast presences during the trials of graduate school and a new academic career have sharpened my humanity and my intellect. The late Richard DuRocher crucially revived my fortitude after many months of despair. At the University of Notre Dame Press, Stephen Little ably guided my "skiff" through the perils of the publication process. My colleague Aaron Shaheen hospitably offered his experience and encouragement, and I owe a note of thanks to Maria denBoer for her "culling and sorting" while copyediting the manuscript.

Along the way, the following have offered their careful direction, much-needed annotation, or trenchant criticism of individual chapters or sections: David Ainsworth, Michael Bryson, Phillip Donnelly, Charles Durham, Richard DuRocher, Scott Huelin, the late Albert Labriola, Jeff Masten, John Morrill, Kristin Pruitt, Glenn Sucich, and Michelle White. Anonymous readers for the University of Notre Dame Press and elsewhere have challenged my conceptions of Milton, his milieu, and his work; their gracious bruising has shaped me into a more careful reader and a writer more skeptical of his own ideas. I extend my thanks also to fellow interlocutors and colleagues who have participated in the Early Modern Colloquium at Northwestern University, the Works-in-Progress program at the University of Tennessee at Chattanooga (UTC), and the Conference on John Milton at Murfreesboro, Tennessee. I also appreciate the fruitful conversations with my students (to whom I occasionally feel as if *I* should be paying tuition). Moreover, a UTC Faculty Summer Research Fellowship enabled the time to revise some of the manuscript.

The lion's share of gratitude and devotion belongs to my family, "my dearest and best possession," who offered encouragement and blessing by their mere presence even as they endured my absences.

Some of the material has been published in other venues. Chapter 4 appeared as "Milton's Parable of Misreading: Navigating the Contextual Waters of the 'night-founder'd Skiff' in *Paradise Lost,* 1.192–209," in *Milton Studies* 43 (2004). A shorter version of chapter 2 appeared as "Infernal Preaching: Participation, God's Name, and the Great Prophesying Movement in the Demonic Council Scene of *Paradise Lost,*" in *The Uncircumscribed Mind: Reading Milton Deeply,* ed. Kristin A. Pruitt and Charles W. Durham (Selinsgrove, Pa.: Susquehanna University Press, 2008).

Repairing the Ruins

Milton, the Poetry of Proclamation,
and the Incarnation of the w/ Word

*Since the Incarnation, God has been externalized. He was seen
at a certain moment and in a certain place, and He left behind
Him words and memories which were then passed on.*
—Maurice Merleau-Ponty, *Sense and Non-Sense*

These are only hints and guesses,
Hints followed by guesses; and the rest
Is prayer, observance, discipline, thought and action.
The hint half guessed, the gift half understood, is Incarnation.
—T. S. Eliot, *The Dry Salvages*

Revolutionary England was populated by immortals. Most dwelled in
the banality of their own day-to-day affairs without interruption, without incident, and within the sometimes-overlapping spheres of public
and private devotion. Prompted by mysterious, inner motions, a few of
these men and women defiantly struck their spades into the soured
ideological soil of the commons and wastes, thereby striking also into the
hearts of their oppressors; others paraded naked through the cramped

1

market streets of London, preaching the immediacy of the *parousia;* one scandalously entered Bristol in imitation of Christ's triumphal entry into Jerusalem. More simply, but no less dramatically, a significant number refused to take public oaths or doff their hats in the presence of earthly authorities. These gave testimony to the ascendancy and delicious unpredictability of the Spirit in a world magistrated and measured by the flesh, and heralded the coming of the kingdom of heaven. Still others took up arms in order to usher in and to secure their place within that chiliastic, revolutionary kingdom. All had a particular view of what that revolutionary kingdom might consist of: saints ruling as vice-gerents with King Jesus during the millennial reign; or an Eden raised in the wilderness of the *now,* where the poor have a share in the abundance of the treasury of the earth, or where the disenfranchised demolish the interpretive monopolies on the Law and the scriptures. None were surprised by sin, and a few even denied its pervasive or rapacious reality, proclaiming instead a narrative whose central chord reverberated, "to the pure all things are pure" (Titus 1:15), whether one is speaking about drunkenness or blasphemy, fornication or banned books. Revolutionary England was populated by men and women who saw themselves as earthen vessels housing a precious treasure, as fleshly tabernacles iridescent with the divine.

John Milton considered himself to be among these. During the turbulent years that saw the arrest, trial, and execution of Archbishop William Laud, the introduction of the Root and Branch petition, the signing of the Solemn League and Covenant between Scotland and Parliament, and the victory over the royalists, appeared Milton's small treatise *Of Education* (1644). In the role of schoolmaster, Milton boldly proclaims that "the end . . . of learning is to repair the ruins of our first parents by regaining to know God aright and out of knowledge to love him, to imitate him, to be like him, as we may the nearest by possessing our soules of true vertue" (*CPW* 2:366–67).[1] The trajectory of Milton's pedagogy may not seem very revolutionary; in fact, it may appear quite pedestrian. Consider this statement by the Moravian Jan Amos Comenius, a millenarian and elder contemporary of Milton's, who devoted himself to the task of Protestant educational reform:

all things are nothing without God. Yea, all our Pansophie [system of universal education] must be so husbanded, that it may perpetually spurre us forward to the seeking after God in every thing, and point us out the way where to find him, and also prepare our minds for the due embracing and acknowledgement of him; That by this meanes it may be as a sacred ladder for our mindes to clime up by all visible things, unto the invisible top of things, the Majesty of the Highest God . . . there at last to repose our selves in that center of rest, and end of all our desires.[2]

Milton's program of education is certainly not the same as Comenius's, but their *telos* of education is.[3] For Comenius, education is shaped by the realization that God is the Alpha and Omega—the beginning and the end of all things—and all knowledge must compel the human being toward a greater understanding of God's mystery and majesty. No doubt, Milton would agree with Comenius's conclusions, but the schoolmaster's added emphasis on the relation between *gnosis* ("regaining to know God aright") and *mimesis* ("out of knowledge to love him, to imitate him, to be like him") is compelling. What if we take Milton, already with a growing reputation for heterodoxy in the mid-1640s, at his word here? And what if his stated end has farther-reaching implications beyond the furrowed brows, anxious looks, and lusterless lessons of his pupil-nephews, beyond the cramped confines of a makeshift household classroom in the streets in Aldersgate, and even beyond Milton's own deeply held pedagogical suppositions? Repairing "the ruins of our first parents" is not just the exalted aim of Milton's educational program, but also the cornerstone of his Protestant poetics, politics, and hermeneutics. But what does this mean for Milton? How is it that we "know God aright," and what does imitating God "look like" in the world? In what ways do this godly knowledge and imitation affect how this revolutionary poet reflects on the ends of speech and language, ponders the holy office of the pulpit, interprets sacred scripture or secular texts, or engages in politics? What role does Milton's own work play in converting readers, in making and finding an audience "fit" to behold and imitate God in the world?

These are certainly not new questions in Milton scholarship. The tendency among some critics, however, is to address them either by severing them from the contextual strands of history and politics, or by firmly enmeshing them within these tangled webs without sufficiently admiring the intricacies of the theological filaments spun throughout the matrix of the revolutionary period. John Leonard remarks that in *Paradise Lost* Christ's name is "the central hidden name in the poem," but his claim is an accurate assessment of Milton's canon beyond his epic.[4] For Milton, these seemingly disparate questions about godly knowledge and imitation or about politics and hermeneutics focus around the Incarnation: the still center about which these issues turn. This book argues that these pressing questions cannot be adequately addressed until one grapples with Milton's sustained preoccupation with the Incarnation as a paradoxical symbol and as the seminal theological event, and until one grasps his peculiar heterodox Christology.[5]

Milton's Christology is most clearly articulated in his doctrinal treatise, *De Doctrina Christiana*.[6] But the doctrinal treatise is by no means the "final authority" on the matter. It represents just one of Milton's creative sorties with the Incarnation; moreover, we will find that the significance of Incarnational theology dwells in many works beyond those that directly invoke or engage it. Consequently, in what follows I hope to uncover and interrogate one neglected cultural episteme during the revolutionary period that I am calling "Incarnational poetics": the synchronic strategies of perceiving, representing, or appropriating the narrative and theology of the Incarnation in theories of preaching, in the praxis of textual hermeneutics, and in the revolutionary politics of seventeenth-century England, for the purposes of cultural confrontation and transformation. Through the creative interplay and dialectical tension between *kenosis,* the emptying of the Godhead at the Incarnation (cf. Phil. 2:5–11), and *pleroma,* the full revelation of the Godhead at the Incarnation (cf. Col. 1:19; 2:9), inspired preachers, godly readers, and political revolutionaries claim to be "fleshly Tabernacle[s]" (*PR* 4.599)—phenomenal ciphers for a noumenal reality that remains in apophatic hiddenness, but that erupts in kataphatic expressions into the world.[7] "God with us" (Isa. 7:14; Matt. 1:23) is the charged nexus and ethical disruption of the In/finite in self and community; it is the site for the tensive relationship and paradoxical reconciliation of tradition and iconoclasm in text and culture; and it is the eloquent translation of a transcendent God in a bustling political world of action and immanence.

The Word is made flesh—this is the electric moment of divine disclosure, at once full of serene beauty and stark terror, when he who made the creature became a creature, and when he that ruled the stars slept under them. John Milbank and Catherine Pickstock remark that "in a post-lapsarian economy, the Incarnation is the sole ground for the restoration of our participation in the divine understanding."[8] Milton would concur, as indicated by the first five lines of his great epic: while "the Fruit / Of that Forbidden Tree . . . / Brought Death into the World, and all our woe, / With loss of Eden," Milton finds hope in the "one greater Man" who will "Restore us, and regain the blissful Seat" (*PL* 1–5). Through the Incarnation of the Word, Milton rhapsodically glimpses the ruins of human creatures and the fallen world they inhabit in repair, and the picture of human participation in the divine gaze that bestows "[b]eatitude past utterance" (*PL* 3.62). At the Incarnation, Milton might argue, God condescends to participate in the human creature, so that the human creature might ascend to participate in God.[9]

But participation, whether initiated from heaven to earth or inspired from earth to heaven, is invariably linked to an interpretation, and any interpretation is inevitably manifested in a performance. George Steiner remarks that "interpretation is understanding in action"; "interpretation is, to the largest possible degree, lived."[10] Nowhere is Steiner's point more affirmed for Milton than in the Incarnation of the Son, who is the "Bright effluence," or outpouring, of that "bright essence" of the Father (*PL* 3.6). To be sure, Milton apprehends the Incarnation as God's radical act of hospitality, for the divine Word "Forsook the Courts of everlasting Day, / And chose with us a darksome House of mortal Clay" ("On the Morning of Christ's Nativity," 13–14). He thus believes that it is only in the Son's charitable embrace of human nature, and in Jesus's extraordinary life of participation in God through obedience and the exercise of virtue, that human beings see the glory of the divine shine forth as light breaking through a window. The philosopher Paul Ricoeur understands this point as well. Pointing to John 1:18, wherein the Beloved Disciple declares, "No one has ever seen God; the only Son . . . has made him known [*exēgēsato*]," Ricoeur insightfully remarks that the Son is the "*exegesis* of God."[11] Jesus, as true for John or Ricoeur as it is for Milton, is the interpretation or translation of God in action. The Incarnate Christ for Milton is the narrative picture of the "ruins of our first parents" in repair, for the Son not only "knows God aright," but also loves and imitates him perfectly in the world.[12]

But certain aspects of Milton's own theology of the narrative of the "Word made flesh" are revolutionary and heretical. The council that met at Chalcedon in the fall of 451 c.e. negotiated a tensive balance between two extremes: the Antiochene *Logos-anthropos* paradigm and the Alexandrine *Logos-sarx* paradigm. In the former "low" Christology, the humanity of Christ tended to be emphasized over his divinity, while the latter "high" Christology emphasized the mystical, transcendent, and particularly Greek concept of the Logos and generally assumed the primacy of Christ's divinity over Christ's humanity. Chalcedon determined that Christ had two natures, divine and human; these operate fully and equally in a single person through the hypostatic union without confusion, conversion, severance, or division. Russell M. Hillier has convincingly demonstrated the high Christology that Milton's soteriology and theology of atonement require, and the centrality of that orthodox paradigm as it shapes his notions of redemption and mercy. "In the cosmic narrative of Milton's poem the Son comprises the *sine qua non* of human salvation," and Hillier observes that the Son is "the Saviour of lapsed Creation, and the tireless sustainer of Creation's welfare." He concludes that for Milton the Son is more than an exemplary model of imitation and more than just a mere man raised to perfection. Concerned with highlighting Christ's "divine and consecrated nature" that is "set apart from humanity," Hillier wishes to steer us clear of Milton's "heterodox Christology" that "should not distract us from the compelling orthodoxy of his soteriology." As Hillier elaborates, Christ is the "external motive force" in human salvation, but humans, "if they so choose, can be made new creatures, liberated from sin and restored to

God's image by faith in Christ's salvific humiliation and exaltation."[13] My purpose is not to oversimplify Milton's theology, nor to ignore his points of orthodoxy. But what do we make of the other side of the equation — the "distraction" of Milton's heterodox Christology? If Christ perfectly mediates from above by his consecrated divine nature, what does Milton make of his equally perfect mediation from below? This book's central focus is on the *fruits* of that salvation: the equally compelling low Christology that pulses in Milton's theology, monist ontology, and poetic imagination, and how those fruits bear witness to the individual believer's choice to appropriate the narrative of liberation and restoration.

A more thorough treatment of Milton's doctrinal Christology, as it is delineated in *De Doctrina Christiana,* will appear a bit later, but for now we must content ourselves to say that in this work the mature Milton is dissatisfied with at least some of the conclusions reached at Chalcedon. Hillier appropriately emphasizes the consecrated nature of Christ that is necessary for human salvation and redemption in Milton's theology. But, as many readers appreciate, Milton characteristically defies categories. We might just as tenably characterize Milton's doctrinal position on the two natures of Christ as Antiochene, a low Christology that emphasizes Jesus's humanity and kindles Milton's thinking about the process of sanctification in the believer, after salvation has occurred. Moreover, his doctrinal treatise argues that Christ is subordinate to the Father, in that Christ shares the same substance with the Father, but not the same essence. As John C. Ulreich explains, the trajectory of the Incarnation for Milton is "actual in one Man, potential in all men" because the divine Logos appears to be equally available to believers.[14] Believers become the adopted sons and daughters of God insofar as they submit to and persist in the life of virtue and obedience. In *Paradise Regained,* the Father seemingly confers Sonship on Jesus by virtue of his virtue:

That all the Angels and Ethereal Powers,
They now, and men hereafter, may discern
From what consummate virtue I have chose

> This perfect Man, by merit call'd my Son,
> To earn Salvation for the Sons of men. (*PR* 1.163–66)

In *Paradise Lost,* however, Milton equivocates on this point. Following the Son's decision to volunteer for the mission to redeem humanity in Book 3, the Father declares that the Son is "Thron'd in highest bliss / Equal to God" (305–6); but, as Alastair Fowler notes in his edition of the poem, *De Doctrina Christiana* insists that "equality" can only denote something that exists between two different "essences" (*CPW* 6:274).[15] Therefore, the Father elaborates that the Son "hast been found / By Merit more than Birthright Son of God, / Found worthiest to be so by being Good" (*PL* 3.308–10). The point is reinforced in *De Doctrina Christiana* in the chapter "OF THE ADMINISTRATION OF REDEMPTION," wherein Milton speaks about Christ's humiliation and exaltation. Because of his *kenosis,* Christ was "RAISED TO IMMORTALITY AND TO THE HIGHEST GLORY . . . BY VIRTUE PARTLY OF HIS OWN MERIT AND PARTLY OF THE FATHER'S GIFT" (*CPW* 6:440–41). Christ's voluntary *kenosis* cannot be separated from the divine *pleroma* that raises him to glory, an intriguing theological pattern of emptying and filling that we will find occurring throughout Milton's canon.

Milton's description of this heavenly man of virtue has some affinities with the heretical theologies of Origen (ca. 185–254 C.E.) and Paul of Samosata (200–275 C.E.), for whom the doctrine of human perfection through obedience and adoption was a theological truism. Like Origen's writings, Paul's works were consigned to the flames. But his unorthodox ideas are preserved in the work of his contemporary opponents, Eusebius and Athanasius, and Thomas Aquinas directly castigates Paul's heterodox Christology in *Summa Contra Gentiles.*[16] The official synodal letter from Antioch, preserved by Bishop Eusebius, accuses Paul of refusing "to acknowledge that the Son of God came down from heaven" and of asserting instead that "Jesus Christ was from below."[17] That is, Paul argued that Christ was a normal man characterized by extraordinary divine participation, which appears to be partly in harmony with the mature Milton's poetic account of the "perfect Man" who regains paradise, as well as the Christ explicated in the systematic theology. *De Doctrina Christiana* reasons that Christ "declares [John 10:38; 14:10, 20–21; 17:21–22] that he and the Father are one in the same way as we are one with him: that is, not in essence but in love, in communion, in agreement, in charity, in spirit, and finally in glory" (*CPW* 6:220). Such a conclusion about human praxis and the potential for divine participation leads Milton to assert that "the ultimate object of faith is not Christ, the Mediator, but God the Father" (475). Under an Antiochene formulation, the human nature that Christ assumes is complete and independent, therefore allowing Christ to genuinely develop, to grow in knowledge and virtue, and to struggle with temptation. Against the Socinians and in line with Hillier's conclusion, Milton emphatically states that Christ was not "a mere man" (419), but potentially, everyone is Christ—a position that resonates in the writings of Milton's radical contemporaries as well. Tracing those connections, where human perfection is the trajectory, will occupy the last third of this book.

Like the Independent preacher John Everard, the Digger Gerrard Winstanley, and the Quaker James Nayler, Milton would have his readers believe that the Incarnation is not a singular event of antiquity, celebrated by some on Christmas Day. Ranters and Seekers, Diggers and Quakers, Fifth Monarchists and some Anabaptists—many of those identified with these revolutionary groups in early modern England—aver that the Incarnation is primarily understood, rather, as a present eruption and charged manifestation within the life of the individual believer, such that faithful believers become windows of the divine. While historians and literary scholars of the period have rightly focused their efforts on examining the explosion of radical theologies of the Spirit, Christology ought to occupy a more central place in both our construal of Milton's work and thought, and also the vibrancy of the nonconformist sects during the Interregnum. These Christologies generated and shaped particular brands of anticlericalism, theories of reading and language, and political agendas. For Everard, Winstanley, and Nayler, the Incarnation is a recurring event in their hearts, one that is multiplied exponentially as their fellow believers "incarnate" God in their everyday lives.

We must be careful, however, to refrain from saying that Everard, Winstanley, Nayler, and Milton share precisely the same Christology. None of them, save Milton, ever methodically delineates his Christology, and it is likely that the Digger and the Quaker never read a systematic theology. But Incarnational theology is deeply embedded in their work, in the dozens of crackling sermons that Everard leaves behind and in the flurry of pamphlets produced by Winstanley and Nayler. Yet we will find that there are several points of contact between the four of them that the following chapters will address more fully:

1. They share a fierce animosity toward what they consider a "Wordless" clergy who fail to embody and perform Christ in the world.
2. They share some aspects of a low Christology that tend to accentuate the humanity of Christ.
3. They share the view that believers who incarnate Christ are "adopted" as God's sons and daughters in a similar way that Jesus is adopted as God's Son: because of his perfect obedience, rather than because he is the preexistent, second member of the Trinity.
4. They share the view that believers who incarnate Christ, through their own obedience and their cultivation of virtue by the sacrifice of the Son and by the Spirit of grace, can achieve perfection in this life.
5. They share the conviction, quite startlingly, that as a result of this perfect incarnation, the realms of proclamation, hermeneutics, and politics are ineluctably shaped by ontology—a sublimated mode of being-in-the-world.

Milton has scruples about the fourth point, the prospect that the perfection of the saints can be achieved in this life. Sin is an ever-present and highly destructive reality for Milton. In *De Doctrina Christiana* he flatly declares that "complete glorification is unattainable in this life," for it "consists in [the] eternal and utterly happy life, arising chiefly from the sight of God" (*CPW* 6:514, 630). But his unequivocal statement here is complicated by his philosophical monism, in which all material substances that emanate from God are purified inasmuch as they participate in God through their acting according to their form or created end. Throughout this study, we will see that for Milton the proper end for the human being is participation in God through grace and the exercise of virtue in the world. Stanley Hauerwas asserts that any "ethic of virtue centers on the claim that an agent's being is prior to doing."[18] Milton, I think, would agree with the tenor of Hauerwas's ontological ethics. For him, the Son comes to realign humanity's "being" not only by his death, but more specifically by the narrative possibilities of his Incarnate life, by which Jesus demonstrates the fulfillment of the human *telos*. In the figure of Jesus, God interprets the human creature, as the human creature interprets God. As Michael explains to fallen Adam, if he but exercises "Faith / . . . Virtue, Patience, Temperance, . . . [and] Love, / By name to come call'd Charity," he shall "possess / A paradise within thee, happier far" than *unfallen* paradise (*PL* 12.582–84, 586–87). The Son embodies this inner paradise, and Milton advocates that it can and must belong to faithful believers as well. But that inner paradise is not self-contained or selfishly enjoyed—the Incarnated Christ within must break forth into the world, as the reformed and regenerated self necessitates the reformation and regeneration of church and state. Consequently, because of their own inner transformations and their belief in their own perfect incarnations, Everard demolishes the monopoly on scriptural interpretation and proclamation held by the professional clergy; Winstanley begins to dig up the commons on St. George's Hill in the spring of 1649; and Nayler marches into Bristol in the fall of 1656 in imitation of Christ's triumphal entry into Jerusalem. Theory and theology *are* praxis; clearly, for these revolutionary figures interpretation is, as Steiner asserts, "understanding in action."

For Everard, Winstanley, Nayler, and Milton, Jesus is the model exegete of God; he understands or "reads" God in the "immediacy of translation" in his private acts of devotion and in his public deeds of virtue. Thus the poet's educational program to "repair the ruins" in his students is incarnationally inflected. Milton's paradigm of reading turns on the mutually reinforcing axes of theory and praxis in a hermeneutical circle. How does one know God "aright"? Through the window of the Incarnation. What must follow? One's imitation through obedience.

The more one imitates Christ, the more the ruins are repaired in the self and the world, which subsequently renders a person capable of receiving more of the divine illumination, and so on.

Importantly, for Milton the activity of reading itself is *poiēsis,* a kind of "making," or rather "remaking," of the ruined divine image implanted in the human creature. Like many of the church fathers, from Irenaeus to Athanasius to Aquinas, or like his older contemporary John Donne, Milton understands Genesis 1:26–27, wherein God implants his divine image into the human creature, Christologically. By "this Image of God," Milton explains, "is meant Wisdom, Purity, Justice, and rule over all creatures. All which being lost in *Adam,* was recover'd with gain by the merits of Christ" (*Tetrachordon, CPW* 2:587). Milton's understated "with gain" merits our uncommon interest. Those two words suggest that all the capacities of the divine image, repaired in the human creature through grace and in one's active participation in Christ, exceed even unfallen Adam's. Reading, for Milton, is thus closely tied to pilgrimage — one's journey in this world toward greater participation in the "life more abundant" that the Beloved Disciple describes (John 10:10). Thus, the wide range of reading he recommends in his proposed course of study in *Of Education,* which is to say the reading he himself enjoyed in the years after his matriculation from Cambridge, "makes" or "fashions" his own students into incarnated citizens of the *civitate Dei.* But they are also citizens, repaired "with gain," of the wider commonwealth: "I call therefore a compleate and generous Education that which fits a man to perform justly, skillfully and magnanimously all the offices both private and publike of peace and war" (*Of Education, CPW* 2:378–79).

The study of poetry, tragedies, and classical orations plays a critical role in the moral formation of both earthly and heavenly citizens, for these help prepare students to finally "contemplate upon moral good and evil." The current university system, Milton objects, trains "young unmatriculated novices" in the rigors of logic or metaphysics (*CPW* 2:375). Although the students may have left their alma mater for their lofty careers in law or the ministry, they remain "unmatriculated novices" in Milton's eyes precisely because the education they have received has miserably failed to "repair the ruins." Their university education unsuccessfully prepares their minds and souls to discern the nature of wisdom, and to distinguish the thorny relationship between the good that is "so involv'd and interwoven" with the evil in the world (*Areopagitica, CPW* 2:514). Such a failure leads to ruined praxis in the world: corrupt courts filled with unfit lawyers who are ungrounded in "the prudent and heavenly contemplation of justice and equity," and bullying pulpits occupied by preachers who are "ambitious and mercenary, or ignorantly zealous" (*Of Education, CPW* 2:375).

We might imagine that in addition to the philosophical works of Plato, the plays of Sophocles and Euripides, the poems of Hesiod, or the orations of Cicero, Milton would include his own treatises, poems, and epics as part of his educational program. Mindele Ann Treip notes that Milton's didactic impetus in his oeuvre seeks to "enlighten and instruct fallible man, to comfort and offer hope, and, in the moral sphere, to lead him to the kind of self-understanding and acceptance of individual responsibility which alone can provide a foundation for restoration."[19] In the course of this study, we will find that Milton, too, is involved in the Incarnational *poiēsis* of his readership, and we would do well to remind ourselves of Milton's invocation to Urania that his epic "fit audience find, though few" (*PL* 7.31).[20] He is ceaselessly searching for and making fit readers: those who would become like Milton, faithfully incarnate Christ, and repair the ruins of the divine image.

In Milton's England, however, the usual task of repairing and remaking that divine image in others fell solemnly upon the shoulders of preachers—God's most visible spokesmen for and embodiments of the Word on earth. From an early age Milton envisioned a distinguished career in the church. At the end of his studies, however, as William Laud's star was fixed in the constellation of Charles I's personal rule, Milton confesses with scorn and great disappointment that he has been "Church-outed by the Prelats" (*CPW* 1:823). Despite his admission, however, Treip discerns an intriguing connection between the ambitions of Milton's work and those of homiletics, a nexus between the pen and the pulpit that has been undervalued but not unnoticed by other scholars.[21] Jameela Lares notes that Milton recognized an intimate connection between writing and preaching, observing that many scholars ignore Milton's collapse of the aims of poetry and the pulpit. In his *Reason of Church Government* (1642), for instance, he closely aligns his poetic gifts with the office of the pulpit: "These abilities, wheresoever they be found, are the inspired guift of God rarely bestow'd . . . and are of power beside the office of the pulpit" (*CPW* 1:816).[22] Similarly, *De Doctrina Christiana* states further, "EXTRAORDINARY MINISTERS are sent and inspired by God to set up or to reform the church both by preaching and by writing" (6:570). Milton's use of the word "EXTRAORDINARY" ought to be noted here because traditional preaching is one of the "ordinary" means of infusing grace into the hearts of congregants in the early modern period.[23] We might profitably question what Milton means by "writing," but his establishing a crucial link between the pulpit and the pen to reform and transform those who encounter his texts has tantalizing possibilities for his poetry as well as his prose. For Milton, the aims of the preacher and the poet are very similar:

> To imbreed and cherish in a great people the seeds of vertu, and publick civility, to allay the perturbations of the mind, and set the affections in right tune, to celebrate in glorious and lofty Hymns the thrones and equipage of Gods Almightinesse, and what he works, and what he suffers to be wrought with high providence in his Church, to sing the victorious agonies of Martyrs and Saints, the deeds and triumphs of just and pious Nations doing valiantly through faith against the enemies of Christ, to deplore the general relapses of Kingdoms and States from justice and Gods true worship. (*Reason of Church Government, CPW* 1:817)

In this conflation, Milton clearly perceives that his prose and poetry are given to the proclamation of the Word through an Incarnational *poiēsis:* forming, reforming, and transforming the individual as well as the state, leading Lares to conclude, "it was easier to get the never-ordained Milton out of the pulpit than it was to get the pulpit out of Milton."[24] Although Milton confesses that he was "Church-outed by the Prelats," he continued to see his writing as emanating from his "Church-outed" pulpit. The connection between pen and pulpit becomes even more pronounced when we consider that for Milton and his contemporaries the activities of reading and speech were not radically disjoined. Commenting on the fairly novel practice of silent reading, Roger Chartier explains that "in the sixteenth and seventeenth centuries, the implicit reading of a text, literary or not, was construed as a vocalization and its 'reader' as the auditor of read speech."[25] Writer is speaker; reader is hearer. Chartier's comment seems especially germane to Milton when we consider that much of his poetry, composed in his blindness, was precisely intended to be recited and heard. Moreover, after Milton's blindness is complete in 1652 and he can no longer read to himself, words do not belong to the whiteness of the page, but are enfleshed in the voices of those who read to him. Since the Word occupies an important place in his work, this reciting and hearing results in nothing less than what we might term the "poetry of proclamation." Given Milton's penchant for identifying himself as God's ideal spokesman and interpreter, the poet-preacher would appreciate his revolutionary readers inscribing themselves as his congregation of faithful hearers, poised to repair their own ruins through the Incarnation, and become "doers" of the Word (James 1:22), if not *his* words, in the world.

But what are the precise relations between Milton's poetry of proclamation, an Incarnational hermeneutics of transformation, and his revolutionary readers' appropriation of the text? What occurs in the self during the liminal moments between the hearing and the doing, and in the ongoing conversation between the text and the reader? What must happen for texts to "convert" readers? How is "textual conversion" related to spiritual conversion? If Milton is a kind of preacher, how exactly do his texts convert English readers? How do hearers and readers "embody" narrative? What are the practical—and political—consequences that follow from incarnating a narrative whose theological trajectory is earthly perfection?

Addressing these questions will be the larger task of this book, but in order to erect a framework for doing so, we might briefly turn our attention to two thinkers, one ancient and one contemporary. The paradigms that Augustine and Paul Ricoeur develop for describing the encounter between the "horizons" of text and reader lend themselves to our considering the possibility that the activity of reading, whether in a premodern, early modern, or postmodern frame of reference, occurs within an "incarnational" matrix. Texts not only become "embodied" through the narrative of a reader's life, but also project a new "horizon" of the self that acts in the world. Augustine and Ricoeur will thus help us to peel back the intricate layers of Milton's poetry of proclamation and its Incarnational *poëisis*—the textual process of "making" hearers, readers, and doers of the w/Word—as well as to untangle the Gordian knot of preaching, reading, and performing the Word in Milton's tumultuous England. Consequently, we will see aspects of Augustinian and Ricoeurrian Incarnational hermeneutics reverberating in the chapters that follow.

For Augustine self-knowledge is intricately bound to textual knowledge. We might consider the *Confessions* to be Augustine's voyage of self-knowledge through the pleasures and detours of various texts that call him to actively appropriate them: pagan epic poetry, Manichean myth, Ciceronian rhetoric, and Skeptic or Platonic philosophy. In Book 11, Augustine comes to see the narrative of his own life as "distended" in several directions, "scattered in times whose order I do not understand. The storms of incoherent events tear to pieces my thoughts, the inmost entrails of my soul."[26] The various texts to which Augustine is exposed structure the fragmented experience of the ego; they shape desire, order thoughts, interpret events, and offer pictures of possible worlds for the self to inhabit, appropriate, or reject. Michel de Certeau comments that it is only recently that reading has become largely "a gesture of the eye." For millennia, reading was accompanied by the "murmur of vocal articulation," and de Certeau argues that the combination of eye and voice led to a more radical interiorization of the text: the reader "made his voice the body of the other; he was its actor." The modern "withdrawal of the body," however, "puts the text at a distance."[27] De Certeau's observation bears out in Augustine's early education, where students were encouraged to "relive" the text as it was "*absorbed* at the earliest occasion."[28] Augustine thus incarnates what he reads. The texts of his early education—Homer, Virgil, Cicero, Sallust, Terence—played a crucial role in the formation of his identity. He became that which he read because what he read was what he imitated as a model of action.

The text for him is thus more than an aesthetic object to be admired, contemplated, or critically dissected. Certainly, the young Augustine is given over to the delights of this kind of reading. But the text is also a keenly powerful force to be treated with caution, as admiration leads inevitably to contemplation, which then yields to action. Hermeneutics for Augustine thus appears to have a dual function: it not only helps him to understand and sift through the claims and traditions that various Greek and Roman texts make upon his life, but it also serves to aid in his emancipation from those claims and traditions. Yet, as Gerald Bruns observes, this liberation comes not from Augustine's adopting a different hermeneutic, but by his "entering into an alternative history."[29] Or, we might differently say, his liberation comes by his "entering into an alternative flesh." Texts seem always involved in the business of proclamation and conversion for Augustine as they shape desires, actively inhabit memories, and entwine themselves in the incarnated narratives of one's life.

While Augustinian hermeneutics is consciously Christocentric, in no place does Paul Ricoeur explicitly secure or consciously derive his philosophical hermeneutics in or from an understanding of the Incarnation.[30] Yet there are striking parallels between Ricoeur's hermeneutical project and Augustine's evolving sense of identity as readers "appropriate" the world of the text. For Ricoeur, "what must be interpreted in a text is a *proposed world* which I could inhabit and wherein I could project one of my ownmost possibilities. That is what I call the world of the text, the world proper to *this* unique text."[31] Like Augustine, Ricoeur posits that texts proclaim ontological possibilities and that texts are always in the business of converting their readers.

Ricoeur understands the hermeneutic task as a dialectic between an original event, in which something is said by someone about something (*noesis*), and the subsequent meaning, in which something said continues to say something (*noema*). The event of discourse "freezes" words or sentences, but the original moment fades and disappears. In the latter, meaning escapes or eclipses the initial event of the utterance, its circumstances, and the intentions of its authors; in some sense, it explodes the world of the author, as the audience expands to include anyone who can read. Consequently, when speech-discourse passes into written-discourse the text is "decontextualized" only to be "recontextualized" by readers in disparate circumstances.[32] The movement from speech to writing thus effects what Ricoeur terms "alienating distanciation" (*Verfremdung*): the temporal, cultural, and/or conceptual gap between the said and the saying. Distanciation produces the conditions for interpretation; understanding seeks not to bridge the gap, as if to "get back" to the original world behind the text, but to overcome our sense of alienation by discovering the world projected *in front of the text*.[33]

Ricoeur wants to spur readers beyond the "desert of criticism," which aims at dissecting the text in a Cartesian mode, to the recognition that texts are revelatory; that is, texts disclose and potentially transform our horizons of understanding. We do not seize the text; rather, as Augustine discovered, the text seizes us. Hans-Georg Gadamer, Ricoeur's frequent interlocutor, describes this disposition of a "listening" hermeneutic as a "fusion of horizons." Elaborating on the metaphor of horizon, Gadamer explains that our own hermeneutical assumptions are conditioned by our "effective-historical consciousness," or the circumstances of our being-in-the-world. Those circumstances are our current "horizon" of perception. "The horizon," he explains, "is the range of vision that includes everything that can be seen from a particular vantage point. . . . A person who has no horizon does not see far enough and hence overvalues what is nearest to him." On the other hand, "to have a horizon" means not being limited to what is nearby but being able to see beyond it.[34]

Similarly, texts offer readers opportunities for enlarged visions of the self and the world when the horizon of the text and the horizon of the reader fuse. The process requires from readers an implicit moment of trust or faith in the text to express, disclose, and address. Understanding always involves a creative reconfiguration. As in Augustinian hermeneutics, in which the self is caught in the hermeneutical circle between self-alienation (a kind of *kenosis*, or emptying of the self) and textual appropriation (a kind of *pleroma*, or filling of the self), Ricoeur maintains that there is a critical "unmasking" moment after distanciation and prior to appropriation, which alienates us from ourselves. We are dispossessed by the text in the same moment that we are possessed by the text. Self-understanding for Augustine and Ricoeur begins with the "detour" of internal critique, which Ricoeur sees as closely allied with a hermeneutics of suspicion in a Marxist or Freudian tradition. Ricoeur, however, does not want us to dwell in suspicion, but to retrieve our faith in the text to transform and enlarge the self. "As a reader, I find myself only by losing myself. Reading introduces me into the imaginative variations of the *ego*. The metamorphosis of the world in play is also the playful metamorphosis of the *ego*."[35] In this way, a work participates in re-creating its audience and potentially sets them free from their illusions. In Augustinian and Ricoeurrian hermeneutics there is a real sense in which readers must, as Anselm states, "believe in order to understand."

Milton understood that texts make powerful claims upon the minds and hearts of their readers. It is from within the assumptions of this Incarnational hermeneutics, wherein the self is alternately emptied (*kenosis*) and filled (*pleroma*), that Milton reads texts and envisions the appropriation of his own writing. Nicholas Wolterstorff describes this textual paradigm as an "action model" of the text, as opposed to the modern Cartesian "aesthetic model."[36] Milton was raised and educated in an era that prized the value of this kind of mimetic reading, and it has strong moorings in an Augustinian hermeneutic. As prophet, polemicist, and "Church-outed" preacher, he certainly saw the rapier thrust of much of his prose as piercing the English nation. Whether he is defending divorce or working systematically through the major tenets of Christian doctrine, he frequently solicits readers to listen and to be open to the viewpoints he espouses in his texts because he poses himself as a reasonable and virtuous man who is worthy of our trust. He encourages his students and revolutionary readers to use that knowledge to understand themselves as "repaired" creatures before God, to achieve their *telos* as human beings by their divine participation, and to allow the Spirit and the scriptures to seize upon them to "illumine in [them] what is dark."

In an attempt to illumine the rich and varied confluences of the *kenosis* and *pleroma* of the Incarnation in Milton's England, this interdisciplinary study traffics in the disciplines of literature, early modern and postmodern theology, language theory, and hermeneutics, as well as dramatic and civic ritual theory. The inherent jeopardy in any thematic approach is that the overriding structure can lead to the tendency to neglect the development of an individual's ideas over time, thus losing the trees for the forest, so to speak. Milton possessed a restless mind, and that is precisely part of the pleasure of studying him in his turbulent milieu. In the chapters that follow, I do not intend to argue comprehensively for a stable unity of thought underlying Milton's work, and several scholars have fruitfully interrogated such an assumption.[37] The youthful Milton of 1629 who depicts the Incarnation in the "Nativity" ode cannot seamlessly be equated with the mature Milton who systematically explicates the Incarnation in *De Doctrina Christiana* several decades later, nor the writer of *Of True Religion* (1673) in the twilight of his years. The first is probably Trinitarian and orthodox; the second is anti-Trinitarian and theologically eclectic; and the third fertilizes the *radix* of "heresy" as reasoned "choice."[38] Milton certainly changed or modified his positions on a number of issues during his distinguished career; his theology of the Incarnation may be one of them. I am convinced, however, that the *significance* of the Incarnation as aesthetic symbol, theological event, and narrative picture of humanity's potential is not. Pursuing that thread is the major aim of this book, as we examine the Incarnational poetics of Milton's milieu—the creative interplay between the octaves of *kenosis* and *pleroma,* an emptying and a filling that are integral to the theology of the Incarnation itself. This Incarnational dynamic resonates within a chorus composed of the following timbres:

1. An Incarnational aesthetics wherein emptiness and fullness provide an underlying structure for Milton's poetry, much of which is built upon a series of pairings, or dyptichs, including poems as wide-ranging as the "Nativity" ode and "Lycidas," "L'Allegro" and "Il Penseroso," *Comus* and "Arcades," and *Paradise Regained* and *Samson Agonistes.*[39]

2. A theory of the material world that is comprehended within an Augustinian *methexis,* or participation, in the divine. For Milton, a post-lapsarian material world is severed from this participatory

framework, and to remain in this state is a negatively construed *kenosis*—the evacuation of meaning in language and other forms of human making. The Incarnation fully partakes of and partici-pates in both the material and the spiritual realms; it is thus the means by which this negative *kenosis* is redeemed and achieves a *pleromic* fullness of meaning through divine participation.

3. A Miltonic impulse toward proclamation, the trajectory of which is shaped by a general hermeneutics of transformation. This her-meneutic assumes an embodied practice of reading that is preva-lent in the seventeenth century, and that leads to the confrontation of the reader's self through a process of alienation (emptying) and reappropriation (filling) in light of divine truth as revealed in the narrative of the Word made flesh.

4. A conversion of the reader by means of this transformational her-meneutic toward a narrative of the Word made flesh that accentu-ates an understanding of Jesus's Sonship, and subsequently a be-liever's sonship or daughtership, through adoptionist theology. This theology of adoption is strongly inflected by merit and the prac-tice of godly virtue, which is one of the principal avenues by which humans participate in the divine.

5. A vibrant perfectionist strain, coupled with a low Christology, that accentuates the frailty of Jesus's humanity without draining the full-ness of his divinity—two elements that Milton shares with many in the radical milieu of revolutionary England. Incarnating Christ in this radical milieu is an act of cultural alienation (emptying) and retrieval (filling) for the purposes of national, ecclesial, and politi-cal transformation.

In the chapters that follow, I have tried to maintain a roughly chro-nological organization in discussing Milton's work. We might usefully divide this study into three parts, which correspond to three converg-ing avenues of investigation: preaching, reading, and politics. Part I delineates the role preaching plays as the locus of divine disclosure and the primary vehicle of repairing the image of God in man. Chapter 1 reflects on the Incarnational aesthetics of the 1645 *Poems of Mr. John*

Milton, and establishes the "Nativity" ode and "Lycidas" as companion poems that both harness the preaching potential of the symbol of the Incarnation and banish a Wordless clergy. Chapter 2 accounts for Milton's prevailing anticlericalism by situating the demonic council scene in *Paradise Lost* within the historical phenomenon of Puritan "prophesying," wherein a group of nonconformist ministers gathered to deliver sermons on the same scriptural text. In this instance, the demons dissent from participating in the divine gaze—an alienation and diminution of being that refuses to be retrieved into God's Being—as they deliver infernal sermons on the Name of God. This framework enables us to reflect on the place of rhetoric and dramatic performance in the pulpit, a bitterly contested issue among early modern Protestant divines, the nature of fallen and unfallen "language games," and Milton's thoughts regarding a participatory, incarnational theory of language as he satirizes a Wordless clergy.

Part II examines Milton's incarnated reader, with chapter 3 examining the radical hermeneutics and perfectionist strain of Milton's Christology and theological monism in *De Doctrina Christiana.* Here I reframe Milton's doctrinal understanding of the hypostatic union of the divine and human natures in Jesus through an Augustinian-Ricoeurrian hermeneutics of transformation. The human Jesus as reader "listens" to and "cooperates" with the interior "text" of the divine Logos, and is transformed by it—a potential that Milton and his fellow congregation of believers can and must imitate. Chapter 4 considers Milton's evolving role as poet-preacher and his focus on the relationship between this perfection of godly virtue and the exigencies of textual discernment. Distrustful of the sermonizers, Milton prefers a form of preaching that blends poetry, proclamation, and incarnation: the parable. As a genre the parable is a hermeneutical crucible where only select hearers/readers understand its message. In particular, I demonstrate how Milton participates in the homiletic tradition of the medieval exemplum by examining how this poet-preacher transforms an epic simile into a parable on the dangers of misreading. In chapter 5, we then turn to Milton's final dyptich in *Samson Agonistes* and *Paradise Regained,* as we examine how one particular virtue shapes the hermeneutical journeys of the protagonists. Temperance, understood by Milton primarily as self-restraint rather than moderation, is the hermeneutical lens that aids Samson and Jesus in discerning the nature of "true" transcendence, differently conceived in each work, from the simulacrum of that transcendence. Paradoxically, their devotion to temperance leads to a different kind of excess that shapes and characterizes the "kingdom of God."

Finally, part III demonstrates some of the practical consequences of incarnating Christ during the revolutionary decades of the English nation. John Everard, Gerrard Winstanley, and James Nayler bear out the trajectory and consequences of Milton's Christic preacher and reader, resulting in a radical metaphysics and economy of abundance, and bringing judgment upon the metaphysics and economies of lack and scarcity they see operating in the world around them. Chapter 6 yokes together the sermons of the Independent preacher John Everard and the prophetic pamphlets of the Digger Gerrard Winstanley, both of whom revive the hermeneutical abundance of the allegorical interpretation of scripture, a discipline of reading long scorned by the Protestant community because of centuries of perceived abuse by Catholic exegetes. In doing so, Everard abolishes the monopoly of reading and interpreting held by the professional clergy, and Winstanley abolishes the tyrannical powers that selfishly hoard the "common treasury" of the earth. Finally, chapter 7 understands the Quaker James Nayler's entrance into Bristol in 1656, in imitation of Christ's entrance into Jerusalem, within the neglected context of civic pageantry: the elaborate procession of the monarch through a city, but here performed by Nayler during a time when there was no king. Nayler's passing by the almshouse, the market district, and the monument of kingly power called the High Cross "redeems" these places of marginalization and scarcity by offering a different economy infused by the abundance of the Inner Light. His subsequent downfall offers us a picture of those who refuse to participate in the dynamics of his incarnational "language game" and allows us the opportunity to ponder the limits of incarnation during a time of national strife and revolution.

part i

Proclaiming the Word

chapter 1

"Such harmony alone"

The Incarnational Aesthetics of the 1645 *Poems*
and the Proclamation of the Word

And all their eyes still fixed, hoping to find once more,
Being by Calvary's turbulence unsatisfied,
The uncontrollable mystery on the bestial floor.
                        —W. B. Yeats, "The Magi"

The Incarnation is the site of serene beauty and stark terror, flashing
illumination and darkened vexation: How is it that an infinite Being
stoops its head under the lintel of the starry sky to dwell in the cracked
clay of a finite creature? In the Incarnation, the "manger contains the
world" in order that "weakness might become strong, strength become
weak."[1] In the Incarnation, the fiery glory of God shimmers as the sun
through a lattice. And while the angelic hosts thunder in sonorous praise
at that moment, the babe's mother and father, along with a handful of
curious onlookers, bow in the argent darkness and remain in silence.

Milton understood that silence at the birth of the Word—the
speechless infant Christ—ought to be the appropriate response. When
it comes to explicating the Incarnation, he warns that it is "much better for us to hold our tongues and be wisely ignorant" (*CPW* 6:424),
echoing Raphael's injunction to Adam to "be lowly wise" in matters

celestial. In this chapter I want to turn our attention to Milton's poetic rendering of the Incarnation in "On the Morning of Christ's Nativity. Compos'd 1629." Very few things indeed are said about the still, small center about which the poem turns, the "Heav'n born child, / All meanly wrapt in the rude manger" (30–31). In fact, as J. Martin Evans observes, unlike other sixteenth- and seventeenth-century poets writing on the nativity, Milton "never addresses the child directly"; rather, "Jesus is consistently referred to in the third person."[2] Instead, the Incarnation of the Word in Milton's ode initiates a fierce flurry of action around the resting infant in a kind of ontological ripple effect: personified Nature quietly retreats in "her naked shame" (40); kings cease from battle (59–60); the stars "Stand fixt in steadfast gaze" (70); the sun stops in its course (79); the "old Dragon under ground" is bound in "straiter limits" (168–69); the oracles are struck "dumb" and the false gods are banished (173–228). This flurry of action suggests that at least one dimension of Incarnational *poiēsis* for Milton involves performance: the actualization of the Word in the world. But what does this Incarnational performance entail? And what role does Milton's poetry of proclamation play in its actualization?

In order to address these questions, I invite us to read "On the Morning of Christ's Nativity. Compos'd 1629" with its companion poem in mind: not Milton's abandoned 1630 poem on the Crucifixion, "The Passion," as is commonly assumed, but "Lycidas." This may seem like a very odd pairing indeed. What, after all, does a 1637 lament about the drowning of a college friend have to do with a hymn on the Incarnation? What do they have in common? 1645: the publication of *Poems of Mr. John Milton, both English and Latin, Compos'd at Several Times. Printed by his true Copies.* More precisely, Milton's "Nativity" ode and "Lycidas" function as "book ends" of the poems proper in the English collection, *A Maske* excluded, and are therefore organically linked.[3] But these poems are even more closely related than simply marking the physical boundaries of Milton's volume of poems. Moreover, one finds that many of the 1645 *Poems*, English and Latin, display peculiar movements between *kenosis* and *pleroma*, between emptiness and divine fullness, in what could be described as an Incarnational aesthetic.

I propose that we approach and understand the relationship between these two poems as we approach and understand metaphor: the radical joining of two seemingly disparate horizons, out of which is unleashed "the power . . . to redescribe reality," as Paul Ricoeur writes.[4] At the heart of such power, "such harmony alone" ("Nativity" ode, 107) for Milton, is the Incarnation: the radical joining of two disparate natures, divine and human, out of which emerges a powerful new "reality" for believers. These poems present disparate horizons — date of composition (1629, 1637), genre (hymn-ode, pastoral), and occasion (meditation on birth, meditation on death). But we see in their pairing a joint venture characteristic of proclamation: a hermeneutic of suspicion, which attempts to unveil, empty, and banish the idols of a Wordless clergy; and a hermeneutic of retrieval, which attempts to fill and recover the possibilities for language and the actualization of the Word in the world. As Ricoeur states, "the idols must die — so that symbols might live."[5] Those idols, we will find, include not only the corrupted clergy, but also the idols of self and language.

All "Passion" Spent: Milton's "unfinish't" Poem and the Incarnational Aesthetics of the 1645 *Poems*

The subject of Book One, Chapter Fourteen of *De Doctrina Christiana* concerns "Of Man's Restoration and of Christ the Redeemer." In part, Milton defines "redemption" as "THAT ACT BY WHICH CHRIST, SENT IN THE FULNESS OF TIME, REDEEMED ALL BELIEVERS AT THE PRICE OF HIS OWN BLOOD" (*CPW* 6:415). We will engage more fully Milton's own Christology in chapter 4, but his linking redemption here specifically with the spilling of Christ's blood at the Crucifixion is common enough among his contemporary Protestant systematic theologians. What is curious about this chapter in Milton's "dearest and best possession" (121), however, is his willful neglect to provide any commentary whatsoever on the nature of the "PRICE OF HIS OWN BLOOD." Milton simply lists a dozen or so scriptural references, and then abruptly drops the subject only to take up a new one that he exposits at length: the "great mystery" (421) of the Incarnation.

This theological circumlocution finds its counterpart in the poetry as well. Milton's 1629 "Nativity" ode celebrating the Incarnation is a tour de force for a young man flexing his precocious poetic muscles. But many scholars agree that his poem "The Passion," commemorating the suffering and death of Christ and presumably written during the Lenten season of the following year, is a consummate poetic failure. Milton's editorial supplement to the poem, in which he confesses the subject of the Passion narrative to be *"above the years he had, when he wrote it"* and expresses his dissatisfaction with the attempt, certainly invites critics to "[lift] the hem of the bard's singing robes to reveal the clay feet beneath," as one scholar eloquently puts it.[6] The *Milton Encyclopedia*, for instance, comments that the eight proem stanzas are technically "competent," but "quite simply, do not go anywhere."[7] E. M. W. Tillyard pointedly states that the poem's "failure is complete," arguing that the poet's "puerility has supplanted youthfulness."[8] More recently, Michael Schoenfeldt describes the poem as a "pathetic attempt at a Passion poem," asserting that Milton "sounds like Crashaw on a bad day."[9] Barbara Lewalski fairly characterizes the poem as "painfully self-referential," although we might construe that Milton's desire to experience a "holy vision," "pensive trance," or an "ecstatic fit" ("The Passion," 41–42) indicates his hope of escaping self-consciousness.[10] Lewalski concludes that the occasion was "perhaps the first time Milton fell so far short of meeting the demands of his poetic subject."[11] Yet Milton evidently thought this particular shortfall worth preserving for posterity, including it in both the 1645 and 1673 *Poems*. But why?

Some scholars attribute the poem's presence in his oeuvre to Milton's repeated gesture in his work toward autobiography.[12] But perhaps another answer to this question may lie in the postscript. In this section I want to address what many believe to be Milton's most conspicuous poetic failure, and the poem that many scholars assume is the natural companion to his masterful "Nativity" ode. Both conclusions are permissible. But arriving at these conclusions perhaps neglects Milton's overriding preoccupation with the potential of the Incarnation as both event and ongoing occurrence in his life. I contend that the poet himself may have considered "The Passion" to be a theological and hermeneutical success, a position that we may find reflected in the Incarnational aesthetics of the 1645 *Poems*. In what follows, I invite us to think about the significance of two terms in the postscript that are pregnant with theological meaning: "*nothing satisfied*" and "*unfinish't*." The first summons to mind Christ's death as "satisfaction" for sins, as stated in the Thirty-Nine Articles, and the second echoes by contradiction Jesus's last words on the cross. Milton's use of these terms in the postscript may partially account for his circumlocution of the Passion and Crucifixion and his sustained engagement with the theological and hermeneutical possibilities of the Incarnation.

Having inherited the tradition from Paul, which was elaborated upon by Anselm, many Reformed theologians understood the spilling of Christ's blood as accomplishing the act of Atonement: Christ's death pays back the personal debt owed to God as creditor that humanity incurred at the Fall. John Calvin, for instance, avers that through his voluntary death Christ is made "our substitute-ransom and propitiation. And hence, mention is always made of blood whenever scripture explains the mode of redemption: although the shedding of Christ's blood was available not only for propitiation, but also acted as a laver to purge our defilements."[13] Similarly, Martin Luther explains that through Christ's office of priest and mediator, his "blood has obtained for us pardon forever acceptable with God. God will forgive our sins for the sake of that blood so long as its power shall last and its intercession for grace in our behalf, which is forever."[14] This "pardon" that Luther mentions carries with it the implication that without the blood of Christ human beings are under the penal consequences of God's wrath, which must be "satisfied" before forgiveness can be extended.

Questions 12–14 of the Reformed Heidelberg Catechism address the issue, stating that "God demands that His justice be satisfied," and that "no mere creature can sustain the burden of God's eternal wrath against sin." The agony that the Son endures on the cross to satisfy the penal consequences of the Father's wrath demonstrates the depths of his vulnerability and obedience. Thus, the creedal statement that Christ "descended into hell"—previously understood by Catholic theologians as the "harrowing of hell"—is reinterpreted by Reformed divines as that crucial moment when the Atonement is completed at the cost of the Son's agonizing abandonment by the Father and his subsequent desolation on the cross. As Debora K. Shuger points out, Bishop Joseph Hall, who is Milton's interlocutor in his early anti-prelatical tracts, figures Christ's "inward torments" as "apprehension of thy Father's wrath" that "pressed thy soul, as it were, to the nethermost hell." Similarly, the separatist Henry Jacob argues that suffering the "horrors of Gods fierie wrath" is "equal to *Hell*: So we affirme, Christ was in *Hell* even in this life."[15] Consequently, Jesus's last words, "It is finished," recorded only in the Gospel of John, mark the end of his hellish suffering and desolation. Moreover, Article 31 of the Church of England's Thirty-Nine Articles, published in 1571 and republished in 1662, emphasizes the finality of Christ's sacrifice on the cross: "The offering of Christ once made is the perfect redemption, propitiation, and satisfaction for all the sins of the whole world, both original and actual, and there is none other satisfaction for sin but that alone."

Despite this sense of finality, however, popular Calvinist piety often urged participation in and identification with elements of the Passion narrative. Shuger thus remarks that the Atonement was seen as a "mimetic opportunity" in which the devotional self is bifurcated and narratively fashioned as both the torturer whose sin makes the individual complicit in the act of the Crucifixion and as the victim who is persecuted like Christ at the hands of the ungodly or who offers himself or herself up to God for immolation. Early modern Passion narratives thus provide a "primary symbol" for "speculation on selfhood and society," she explains, and produce "a specific version of Christian selfhood—a divided selfhood gripped by intense, contradictory emotions and an ineradicable tension between its natural inclinations and religious obligations."[16] We find this to be the case with several early modern devotional verses on the Passion and Crucifixion, including George Herbert's "The Sacrifice," or "The Crosse," John Donne's "Good Friday, 1613, Riding Westward," and Richard Crashaw's "Upon the Body of Our Blessed Lord." These poems imagine the physicality and spirituality of Christ's suffering, a suffering that the poet's consciousness intrudes upon as alternately the guilty party who is its causal agent and as the self who desires to be sacrificed.

Milton's proem—the site where we might expect these elements to appear—demonstrates almost none of these impulses. There seems to be no indication that the poet feels the weight of the Father's wrath demanding satisfaction; there is no self that identifies with the torturer; there is no sense that by his sin he is complicit in Christ's death; and the only self-recrimination the poet seems to muster is his lack of readiness to address the subject. What dominates the proem stanzas is the poet's sense of loss: "For now to sorrow must I tune my song," he states in the second stanza, pleading for supplication that "Night, best Patroness of grief," might "Befriend" him, for "Heav'n and Earth are color'd with my woe, / My sorrows are too dark for day to know" (7, 29, 32–33). The poet's vague melancholia, as Sigmund Freud might regard it, paralyzes his ego rather than frees it for the process of mournful expression and progression toward an event like the Resurrection. The young Milton communicates his desire to circumvent this paralysis by imagining his spirit as presently being transported by Ezekiel's chariot. But even the hoped-for escape is nullified; "holy vision," "pensive trance," "anguish," and "ecstatic fit" pull the self in disparate directions rather than sublimate its grief. This confusion is reflected in the shifting images and motions of his earthly "return": from the "sad Sepulchral rock" into which the poet is gazing, to his ascent on "viewless wing" to "Mountains wild," or the "gentle neighborhood of grove and spring" (43, 50–52).

As we explored in Ricoeurrian hermeneutics, "what must be interpreted in a text is a *proposed world* which I could inhabit and wherein I could project one of my ownmost possibilities. That is what I call the world of the text, the world proper to *this* unique text."[17] The Passion and martyrdom of Christ, culminating in the Crucifixion, remains for Milton a distant and alienating text that leads the ego, like Christ on the cross, to a *kenosis* characterized by abandonment or desolation. For Milton the Incarnation is the site of teeming possibility for the self, a place of *pleroma,* recuperation, and appropriation. Milton

consciously envisioned his revolutionary writing as intended for readers to appropriate and incarnate in their lives, and the Incarnation
thus promises more narrative possibilities for Milton's "self" than the
narrative of suffering and martyrdom. Put another way, Milton prefers
to be a living martyr, bearing witness to the narrative of transformation,
than a dead one.

The poet's "painfully self-referential" proem, as Lewalski characterizes it, and his theological circumlocution of representing the stages
of the Passion in either the poetry or the prose demonstrate his inability or unwillingness to participate, hermeneutically or theologically,
in the text. Hermeneutically, Milton is not "*satisfied*" with the scriptural
text of the Crucifixion, thus leaving his own poetic text "*unfinish't*."
Theologically, Milton may be implying that the Atonement is indeed
a "mimetic opportunity," but one that comes about not through the
reader's embodying the Passion narrative, but by harnessing the narrative potential of the Incarnation through the passionate life of virtue
and obedience. James Holly Hanford concludes that "the crucifixion
was not a congenial theme to him at any time. Even this early he seems
to have felt instinctively that man's salvation depends upon himself and
that he needs Christ as guide and model perhaps more than as a redeemer."[18] Hanford overreaches a bit; Milton may not have found the
Crucifixion to be a hospitable subject for poetry, but that does not necessarily imply that the poet thought Christ to be mere example. It may
be fair, however, to assert that the Jesus of Milton's brief epic regains
paradise not by dying—"It is finished" (John 19:30)—but by living:
"It is *unfinish't*." Consequently, Milton appropriates the Incarnation,
rather than the Passion, as a transformational text for himself.

Though he does not invoke Ricoeurrian hermeneutics, Richard
Halpern acutely observes that Milton "appropriates the occasion of
Christ's birth to announce his own poetic nativity and to anticipate the
maturation of his own powers." Halpern asserts that the infant Christ
of the "Nativity" ode, the first poem in the volume, provides Milton
with one possible narrative for his own future poetic career. William
Shullenberger agrees, suggesting that the powerful language of the ode

"registers Milton's own Incarnation as a poet, his accession to mature creative power."[19] These are indeed insightful comments, but Halpern and Shullenberger only gesture toward the Incarnational matrix within which Milton's poetic project is deeply embedded. Moreover, both critics ignore an important context for reading the "Nativity" ode and understanding the trajectory of Milton's poetic career which, as I am arguing, is explicitly tied to an evolving sense of a ministerial vocation with a *telos* of conversion: the publication of the 1645 *Poems*. In doing so, their analysis of the poem is necessarily one-sided, for they fail to appreciate fully the Incarnational *poiēsis* of a poetic vision continually shaped by preaching and engaged in proclamation, as well as the Incarnational aesthetics that structure the volume itself.

Louis Martz comments that "Milton's original arrangement creates the growing awareness of a guiding, central purpose that in turn gives the volume an impressive and peculiar sense of wholeness."[20] What if one considers the possibility that the "central purpose" and "peculiar sense of wholeness" to which Martz points derives from Milton's sustained thinking about the aesthetic dynamics of *kenosis* and *pleroma* in the Incarnation? This is not to argue comprehensively that the Incarnation is at the heart of every, or even most, of the poems. It is, rather, to note the startling number of poems, both English and Latin, that internally resonate and shift octaves between emptiness and fullness, or between human weakness and divine strength—between the solitary notes of the poet's confessed "slow heart and hard breast" ("Sonnet III," 13), and the swelling movements of a "breast . . . aflame" with "mysterious impulse" when "Apollo himself comes" ("Elegy V," 11–14). *Kenosis* and *pleroma* appear to be integral aesthetic elements not only to the poetic identity being constructed, but also to the structure of the volume.

A brief look at the order of some of the poems may help illustrate my point. Immediately after the "Nativity" ode—placed first in the *Poems* as Milton's announcement of his poetic birth, as well as the play between *kenosis* and *pleroma* in the poems that follow—are the young Milton's early attempts at translating Psalms 114 (a paraphrase) and

136. The first obscures the biblical text's allusion to Jacob and instead begins by alluding to "*Terah's* faithful Son" ("Psalm CXIV," 1), Abraham, whose seminal individual strength in obedience offsets Israel's collective weakness or unsurety in the later events that the psalm evokes: the crossing of the Red Sea (7–9) or the crossing of the Jordan with the Ark of the Covenant (9–10). Abraham's solitary vow of obedience plants the "blest seed" of his countless children, but the cultivation of that seed is marked by the "long toil" and shaky confidence of the Israelites as they emerge into Canaan (1–2). The *kenotic* weakness makes possible their witness of YHWH's *pleromic* power, as all of creation is "aghast" at "the presence . . . / Of him that ever was" (1–2, 15–16). The trajectory of the psalm is continued in the language of praise in "Psalm CXXXVI," as the psalmist reflects on how often "His mighty Majesty" turns "with a piteous eye" toward his children and "Beheld us in our misery" ("Psalm CXXXVI," 90, 79–80). In his majesty God stoops toward the creation, and in his condescension "All living creatures he doth feed, / And with full hand supplies their need" (85–86).

These psalms declaring human weakness and celebrating divine omnipotence then lead into Milton's "failed" poem on the Passion, perhaps indicating the poet's resolution to be among the meek so that the majesty of God's presence shines through in the very act of abandoning the poem itself. Following this, in turn, is a trinity of poems that continue to juxtapose *kenosis* and *pleroma:* "On Time," "Upon the Circumcision," and "At a Solemn Music." In the first, Time devours its own progeny, which might lead a poet like Milton, still full of youthful anxiety that he might perish before his great poetic work is complete, to even more despair. But the poem ends by transcending the "mortal dross" that is the product and sustenance of Time's devouring womb, moving instead to an Eternity in which the saints (even those who are minor poets) sit "Attir'd with Stars" and sing the eternal poetry of "Truth, and Peace, and Love" ("On Time," 6, 21, 16). But in order for this *pleromic* triumph over "Death, and Chance, and thee / O Time" (22–23) to be complete, however, Milton must turn his countenance first to mourning and to a meditation on Christ's *kenosis* in his poem commemorating the first spilling of the meek Savior's blood:

For we by rightful doom remediless
Were lost in death, till he that dwelt above
High-thron'd in secret bliss, for us frail dust
Emptied his glory, ev'n to nakedness. ("Upon the Circumcision,"
   17–20)

Christ's *kenosis* will result in the believer's *pleromic* recovery of that "secret bliss" once enjoyed by the pre-Incarnate Christ. As Milton describes in the following poem, "At a Solemn Music," human weakness has severed participation in the "undisturbed Song of pure concent" (6). Presently, the poet laments how "disproportion'd sin" has "Jarr'd against nature's chime, and with harsh din / Broke the fair music that all creatures made / To their great Lord" (19–22). The perfect balance of the *kenosis* and the *pleroma* in the Incarnation will be the hinge between heaven and earth, the means by which "we soon again renew that Song, / And keep in tune with Heav'n, till God ere long / To his celestial consort us unite" (25–27).

Some of the Latin poems, too, display this theological aesthetic of emptiness and fullness. Milton empties himself of being worthy of the "excessive praise" of the Italian poets who write testimonial verses on his behalf, but in the next moment he allows himself to be filled by their praise as a way of honoring "the favorable judgment of distinguished men of intellect." Charles Diodati's dedicatory epistle, "To John Milton of London," celebrates the Englishman as one whose "endowments of mind and body move the senses to admiration, and yet through that very admiration rob every man of power to move, whose masterpieces urge all men to applause, yet by their grace, their charm rob of voice all them who would be happy to applaud." Milton's full potency as a poet and man of learning is simultaneously a litany of his contemporaries' poetic frailty and paralysis; his *pleroma* is their *kenosis*. Yet Milton's immense singularity is bound by the duty he owes to his weakened community of fellows, for by his endeavors he "probes the hidden mysteries of bygone days, restores whatever the distance of time has obscured, and covers all the intricacies of learning," thereby implicitly allowing all in their frailty to share in the abundant fruits of his merits.[21]

Yet in "Elegy VI" one discovers that it is in Milton's desire to "live sparingly" (59–60) and in weakness that allows him the singularity of vision and intellect that Diodati praises. In chapter 5 we will engage more fully Milton's thoughts on the virtue associated with living "sparingly," that of temperance, as it shapes his hermeneutics and the protagonists of *Paradise Regained* and *Samson Agonistes.* Presently, however, Milton explains to his friend Diodati that Bacchus and Apollo are not diametrically opposed as guiding deities of song. But the serious poet, "whose theme is wars and heaven under Jupiter in his prime, and pious heroes and chieftans half-divine . . . [and] of sacred counsels of the gods on high, and now of the infernal realms where the fierce dog howls," must turn from the fullness of his banqueting to enjoy the *kenotic* simplicity and temperance of the "innocent diet" (55–60). Such a poetic resolve toward *kenosis* leads ironically to *pleroma.* The bard, singer, or prophet who lives sparingly, as the examples of Homer, Orpheus, Tiresias, and the Jesus of *Paradise Regained* demonstrate to Milton, is he whose "hidden heart and . . . lips alike breathe out Jove" to excess (67–78). It is no surprise, then, that "Elegy VI" ends with Milton's indicating that he is writing a poem on the Incarnation:

> I am singing the heaven-descended King, the bringer of peace, and the blessed times promised in the sacred books—the infant cries of our God and his stabling under a mean roof who, with his Father, governs the realms above. (79–84)

Christ governs the realms above, but he appears also to govern the poetics of the 1645 *Poems.*

Barring the portrait frontispiece that Milton found either laughable or irritatingly disagreeable, the 1645 *Poems* thus seems to bear at least some trace of the "authorial imprint." One may legitimately cast doubt on the dating of some of the poems, which might be attributed either to Milton's desire to appear "*above the years he had*" in a precocious sense, or to Humphrey Mosely's additions as a publisher with a heavy-handed history of fashioning early modern poetic personas. But the placement of many of the poems, certainly not all, appears too measured to assign fully the volume's structural cadences and harmonies to the tone-deaf ears of publisher or printer.[22]

Stella P. Revard listens most sensitively to these cadences. She comments that the 1645 *Poems* is not just a single volume, but it is a "double book, comprising an opening volume of English poems followed by a volume of Latin poemata with its own separate title page, preface, and set of dedicatory poems." While it was not unusual for seventeenth-century poets to publish both English and Latin poems, Revard points out that in most collections the English poems follow the Latin poems. Always the poetic innovator and iconoclast, Milton reverses the order, thereby proclaiming the superiority of his English verse — and the English language — to his Latin. These English and Latin "horizons" function together in Milton's "double book" in the same creative interplay that we see between the terms in metaphor and between text and reader. Revard finds wonderful correspondence between the two volumes, arguing that the English volume begins in poetic infancy and ends with a skilled poet looking for "pastures new," while the Latin volume begins with the schoolboy Milton and ends with the fully matured poet; the last English poem, "Lycidas," written for Edward King as a pastoral lament, should be paired with the ultimate Latin poem, "Epitaphium Damonis," a poem written for Milton's friend, Charles Diodati, wherein Thrysis laments the death of Damon; finally, "L'Allegro" and "Il Penseroso," which occupy the structural and oppositional center of the English volume, should be paired with "Elegy I" and "Elegy VI," all poems concerned with the travails of poetic composition through the opposite horizons of celebration and solace, Bacchinalian drunkenness and Apollonian sobriety.[23]

Moreover, I would point out that at the heart of the volume, functioning as the "hinge" between the English poems and the Latin poems, is Milton's *A Maske, presented at Ludlow Castle* (1634). More will be said of Milton's virtuous Christic reader in the chapters that follow, but here we might be permitted to read the masque as an allegory of the pilgrim reader's hermeneutical journey. The virtuous Lady who embodies Faith, Hope, and Chastity (214–16) is beset by Comus's "dazzling Spells" that seek to convert her virtue to vice with the "power to cheat the eye with blear illusion, / And give it false presentments" (154–56). Like Milton's Jesus in the wilderness, who is subjected to the seductive narrative webs of Satan's temptations in *Paradise Regained,* this virtuous Lady is assaulted by "dazzling Spells." Unlike Jesus, however, the Lady is deceived; trusting the "honest offer'd courtesy" of this "gentle Shepherd" (323, 271), she follows him to the promised lodging, but thanks to the timely intrusion of her two brothers she resists a further fall. Her virtue tested, the masque ends in celebration with the attending Spirit delivering the epilogue to the audience: "Mortals that would follow me, / Love virtue, she alone is free, / She can teach ye how to climb / Higher than the Spherey chime; / Or if Virtue feeble were, / Heav'n itself would stoop to her" (1018–23). This is a fitting, though understated, image of the Incarnation itself, as heaven stoops to earth in order to enable earth to ascend, recalling Milton's depiction of the "Light unsufferable" who "Forsook the Courts of everlasting Day, / And chose with us a darksome House of mortal Clay" ("Nativity" ode, 8, 13–14).

Roger Chartier comments that "the form in which a text is presented for reading also plays a part in the constitution of its meaning"; further, "we must insist that there is no text outside the material structure in which it is given to be read or heard."[24] For Chartier and other historians of reading practices, the material construction of the text gives us clues as to how to read it. Leah S. Marcus also warns against our minimizing the aesthetic features of a printed book: "We need to view them instead as milestones in the process by which the printed book became identified with the *corpus,* carrying the life and spirit of the author."[25] For Milton, that life and spirit are centered on the Incarnation. We see in the structure of the 1645 *Poems* the fusion of poetic horizons at work throughout, the center of which is the life of virtue in a discerning reader of texts. Moreover, the 1673 second edition of the *Poems* culminates in a reprint of Milton's tract *Of Education,* whose central tenet is that the end of education is to "repair the ruins of our first parents." As we have seen, for Milton that process of repair occurs as one appropriates the Incarnation; his reprinting the tract for the 1673 volume, therefore, makes an implicit statement about the purposes of his own poetry. Milton is thus engaged not only in an incarnational *poiēsis,* as he profiles, fashions, and converts his "fit audience" of discerning congregants, but he also employs an incarnational aesthetic where form and content are one and the same. This is an aesthetic unity whose paradigm is the *kerygma* of the Word, where form and content display "such harmony alone."

Preaching and Performing the Word: Milton's "Nativity" Ode and "Lycidas"

We can bring these structural and vocational dimensions into greater relief by pairing the "Nativity" ode, as the first poem of the English volume, with its companion poem, the last of the English poems in the volume, "Lycidas." The birth of the Word in the former poem heralds judgment upon the Wordless preachers of the latter poem who fail to embody or perform its potential in the world. Milton's "vow of rigor," his critical unmasking of the idols of clergy, is at the same time a "vow of obedience" and listening to the symbol of the Word; as Ricoeur states, such "extreme iconoclasm belongs to the restoration of meaning."[26]

It is precisely this "restoration of meaning" through the destruction of linguistic, theological, or ecclesial idols that informs the vision of Milton and the Reformers at large, and it has its hermeneutical roots in the Incarnation of Christ, one particular hermeneut who was seen by the people as at once a rabbi with great authority and a dangerous iconoclast and blasphemer. Ricoeur's endorsement of a hermeneutics of suspicion, in the vein of Karl Marx, Friedrich Nietzsche, Sigmund Freud, or Jürgen Habermas, which serves to unmask economic power relations or projections of the human will or psyche, is reflected in Jesus's perpetual critique of the ossified religious practices and scriptural interpretations of the Pharisees. One of the tasks of hermeneutics, as Ricoeur sees it, is to develop a critical and "defiant" stance against the "distortions of human communication which conceal the permanent exercise of domination and violence."[27] Equally important to the biblical narrative, however, is Jesus's admonition in Matthew 5:17, "Think not that I am come to destroy the law, or the prophets: I am not come to destroy, but to fulfill." Such a statement belies a radical embrace and recognition of tradition, authority, and historical "situatedness," only to reconfigure them. Jesus's acknowledgment of tradition and authority parallels Ricoeur's endorsement of a hermeneutics of retrieval, in the vein of Hans-Georg Gadamer, which is characterized by a willingness to listen in order that a person might receive renewal and the disclosure of revelation.[28] Consequently, for Ricoeur the "task of the hermeneutics of tradition is to remind the critique of ideology that man can project his emancipation and anticipate an unlimited and unconstrained communication only on the basis of the creative reinterpretation of cultural heritage."[29] Jesus, Gadamer, and Ricoeur remind us that critique is itself part of a tradition; as Ricoeur remarks, critique "plunges into the most impressive tradition, that of liberating acts, of the Exodus and the Resurrection."[30]

We might construe the "Nativity" ode and "Lycidas" as performing "liberating acts" as well. This may well be more readily seen in the former poem than in the latter, especially when we consider J. Martin Evans's comment that the "Nativity" ode is about the reader's conversion. Evans observes that Milton's circumvention of direct address to the infant Christ in the "Nativity" ode is reflective of other notable absences in the poem, as Milton envisions his hymn to be the first sacrifice of praise: the wise men have yet to arrive (22–26); the shepherds are still in the fields (85–87); Mary just barely makes it into the poem (237); and the traditional animals of the manger scene, as well as Joseph himself, are nowhere to be seen. Moreover, as Evans points out, the reader only encounters the abstractions of Nature, Peace, Truth, Justice, and Mercy in the early stanzas, prompting Evans to conclude that not only is the scene "dehumanized," but also that Milton's poem reflects "the characteristically Puritan distaste for allowing any intermediary to intrude between the individual soul and its Maker," such that "we encounter the Christ child face to face."[31] Evans thus agrees with Richard Halpern that these absences reflect a deeply *kenotic* dimension to the poem. For Halpern, Milton's ode forgoes "epic expansiveness" to dwell in the lowly style of the ode; for Evans, Milton has emptied even himself from the poem.[32]

Yet Evans and Halpern neglect the theological dialectic between *kenosis* and *pleroma*. This dialectic is certainly present in Milton's poem, for the poet acknowledges the *kenosis* in the one who "chose with us a darksome House of mortal Clay" (14), as well as the *pleroma* in the "Light unsufferable" and "far-beaming blaze of Majesty" (8–9), and the "Infant God" who shows his "Godhead true" in banishing the pagan gods (16, 227). These critics' omissions of the latter dimension thus lead to an insufficient acknowledgment of the sense of alienation or distance Milton's absences create, the kind of alienation so crucial to proclamation and conversion. The *pleroma* of the infant deity complicates the *kenotic* immediacy of the scene upon which readers gaze. These absences do not create intimacy, as if the gap is closed by the mere removal of the traditional figures of the nativity scene, subsequently bringing the reader into direct illumination of the "thing-in-itself." Rather, these absences deepen the strangeness of the Incarnation, suggesting that no one, not even the *Theotókos,* can comprehend her sleeping babe — except through reading the narrative traces of his presence in the world, in the "ontological ripples" of the infant Christ's performance. Theologically, the *kenosis* cannot be comprehended except in relation to the *pleroma.*[33] "Milton's parallel *kenosis*," as Halpern puts it, ought thus to be accompanied by Milton's parallel *pleroma*, but the two critics nowhere affirm what this might entail.

Moreover, it is commonly assumed that Milton added the phrase "Compos'd 1629" to the title for the publication of the 1645 *Poems*, a supplement no doubt intended to inspire the reader's admiration for the author's precocious poetic talents.[34] Some scholars have argued that in adding the supplement, Milton politically "radicalizes" the ode.[35] James Dougal Fleming has recently argued against this tendency.[36] As Fleming confirms from manuscript and print sources, Charles I delivered his last speech to Parliament on 10 March 1628, and the turn of the year occurred on 25 March. All things considered, Fleming concludes, there was no need in 1645 for Milton to target an anti-Caroline audience, and the poem's headnote remains either non-Miltonic or politically and ideologically problematic.

But what if we shift our context for thinking about the poem's "radicalizing" tendency away from a mere political one to a theological matrix? By 1645, Milton already had a growing reputation for unorthodoxy. Edward Phillips records that during the days of Schoolmaster Milton (1640–46) student exercises on Sundays included their reading a chapter in the Greek New Testament, followed by their uncle's learned commentary, as well as their recording his dictation on "some part . . . of a Tractate which he thought fit to collect from the ablest of Divines . . . *Amesius, Wollebius, &. viz.* A perfect System of Divinity."[37] Presumably, these Sunday lectures formed the core of what would become *De Doctrina Christiana,* though it cannot be proven precisely which doctrines Milton was working through with his pupils in the early to mid-1640s.[38] I have sketched Milton's unorthodox "low" Christology in the introduction, with its perfectionist strain and adoptionist emphasis on virtuous participation in the divine. A more detailed accounting of it will occur in the third chapter, but here we might consider that the supplement "Compos'd 1629" effectively distances the orthodoxy of the young Milton of 1629 from the heterodoxy of the matured and increasingly radical Milton of 1645. Christ's *pleroma* is also Milton's *pleroma* as the man of obedience and virtue; the fullness of deity is the "fullness" of Milton's cooperation with the divine Spirit within. While Christ's birth into the world silenced the pagan gods and oracles and ushered in a new age, the symbol of his birth continues to proclaim that Milton, his fellow believers, and listening readers of the poem can and must inhabit and appropriate the Word's perfectionist potential in the world turned upside down.

The reader's conversion thus crucially hinges not only on Evans's *kenotic* immediacy of the "meanly wrapt" infant lying in a "rude manger" (31), the hermeneutical "laying bare" or demystification of the divine; it also rests on what we might term *pleromic* distanciation, a kind of hermeneutical agnosticism because the symbol overpowers the *cogito* and cannot be exhausted. Subsequently, converted readers can only "faith" the symbol of the Incarnation, for it liberates Milton and his fellow believers beyond their captive illusions of the self and the capacities of the divine to work in the world. The silencing of the oracles and banishing of the pagan gods may well reflect the young Milton's millenarian hopes that a new Protestantism would finally triumph over Rome and Charles I's Catholic sympathies, or the matured Milton's celebration of the defeat of William Laud and Charles's courtiers.[39] But their silencing and banishment also reflect the silencing and banishment of the idols of self. Evans suggests that the "Nativity" ode is "about the *reader's* conversion, the *reader's* dawning awareness of the new birth and its overwhelming consequences."[40] But before the reader can be "converted" with the rest of the world in the course of the poem, the reader must be alienated; or, to echo Ricoeur, before the world of the text can be appropriated, the world of the reader must be exploded.

The litany of alien pagan names—Lars and Lemures, Peor and Baalim, Thammuz and Typhon (176–226)—remind readers that once they gaze upon, appropriate, and perform the works of the infant Christ they will no longer be captive to the familiarity of the "old self." Like these gods, the old self becomes foreign and alienated, bound to "th'infernal jail" as "Each fetter'd Ghost slips to his several grave" (234–35), never to be freed or to rise again. Rather, the "new self" is summoned into existence by a new name and accompanied by a new *pleroma* of narrative possibility in the world as Milton and his fellow believers enact an apocalypse within through active participation. Even in the 1640s, some in the radical fringes were proclaiming a realized or personal eschatology. In his *Gangraena, or A Catalogue and Discovery of many of the Errours, Heresies, Blasphemies and pernicious Practices of the Sectaries of this time* (1646), the Presbyterian minister Thomas Edwards records that among the heresies of the sectaries is the belief "That we did look for great matters from one crucified at *Jerusalem* 6 hundred years ago, but that does us no good, it must be a Christ formed in us, the deity united to our humanity."[41] The New Model Army officer Joseph Salmon writes of "*the spirit of Antichrist that is in all of us*" until a person realizes "Jesus Christ to be come in thy flesh." Christ comes to judge the Antichrist and end his days, but the Antichrist is not the pope or the popish royalists; the kingdom of God has already come and Jesus has returned to bring "judgement in thee, and the end of the world to be in thee."[42] Realized eschatology is both the end and the beginning of the new self, and each person is his or her own preacher.

This new summoning recalls the moment of creation. The infant Christ's birth, which signals Milton's birth as a poet and man of virtue, is remarked by Nature herself, who "knew such harmony alone / Could hold all Heav'n and Earth in happier union" (107–8). The hypostatic union, the joining of heaven and earth in happy union, is celebrated by the angelic choirs whose beautiful song is equated with the music of the spheres at the moment of creation when the "Creator Great / His constellations set, / And the well-balanc'd world on hinges hung, / And cast the dark foundations deep" (120–23). Significantly, Milton's "hinge" occupies the structural center of the poem, "well-balanc'd" between the heavenly constellations in the preceding verse and the earthly foundations in the following line. The harmony of the hypostatic union at Christ's birth, those *pleromic* "unexpressive notes to Heav'n's newborn heir" (116), causes the "Crystal spheres" to "Ring out" (125) as at creation, a potent "holy Song" that might "fetch the age of gold" and cause "leprous sin" to "melt from earthly mold" (133–38).

Milton elsewhere writes of this divine harmony in the *Second Prolusion* with the disclaimer that the theory of the music of the spheres must not be taken seriously. Yet one wonders just how playful the young Cambridge student is being, for it becomes clear that for Milton the theory has poetic potential and symbolic gravity. Assigned to defend the Pythagorean theory of the music of the spheres as an academic exercise, he observes that Pythagoras himself claimed to have heard the divine harmony "alone among all men." Either the philosopher was a kind of demigod sent to "instruct mankind in holiness and lead them back to righteousness," Milton reasons, or "he was assuredly a man endowed with a full meed of virtue, worthy to hold converse with the gods themselves, whose like he was, and to partake of the fellowship of heaven" (*CPW* 1:238). Either way, Pythagoras's life of virtue entitles him to be worthy of divine kinship. Moreover, the fact that a person cannot hear it, argues Milton, reveals more about the darkened state of his or her own soul than about the validity of Pythagoras's theory. "The fault," he says, "is in our own deaf ears, which are either unable or unworthy to hear these sweet strains." Clearly, he favors the latter possibility and focuses on a person's unworthiness, for we are unable to hear the celestial harmony

> so long as we remain buried in sin and degraded by brutish desires; for how can we become sensitive to this heavenly sound while our souls are . . . bowed to the ground and lacking in every heavenly element? But if our souls were pure, chaste, and white as snow . . . then indeed our ears would ring and be filled with that exquisite music of the stars in their orbits; then would all things turn back to the Age of Gold, and we ourselves, free from every grief, would pass our lives in blessed peace which even the gods might envy. (*CPW* 1:238–39)

Without the conversion of a person's will and soul, and her or his appropriation of the infant Christ's performance, Milton indicates that readers can have no kinship with the divine, cannot hear the music, and cannot achieve the harmonious balance between heaven and earth as displayed in his poetic image of the "hinge" between heaven and earth ("Nativity" ode, 122). Their ears become more finely attuned as readers elevate their souls through cooperation with the "heavenly element," the divine Logos implanted within the human creature. Seemingly single-handedly, Milton's powerful man of virtue can miraculously return the world to the "Age of Gold" described in the *Second Prolusion*.

The stunned silence of the banished gods in the poem sharply contrasts with the thunderous divine music at Christ's birth, music that is re-created and continues to silence them in Milton's virtuous actions in the world. The celestial song at Christ's birth in the poem may well "fetch the age of gold" (135) with its extraordinary beauty, but that same harmonious beauty is also the "wakeful trump of doom" and "horrid clang" of judgment upon the world and "those ychain'd in sleep" (155–56)—those living who yet must awaken to redemption by destroying the idols of self. The "hideous hum" (174) of the old self that is "buried in sin and degraded by brutish desires," as Milton puts it in the

Second Prolusion, is outsung in the repeated acts of worship by the regenerate self, now cooperating with the Spirit in obedience, now appropriating and incarnating a different narrative, and now adding its voice to the "holy Song" of the "glittering ranks" (133, 114) of an angelic consort that is accompanied by the "exquisite music of the stars in their orbits." It is a song that may well find its fullest expression at the eschaton, when "Truth and Justice then / Will down return to men" (142–43) and the "dreadful Judge in middle Air shall spread his throne," as Milton describes at the end of stanza XVII. But the poet abolishes not only the idols of self in stanzas XIX–XXV, but all temporal constructions in the beginning lines of the next stanza: "And then at last our bliss / Full and perfect is, / But now begins" (165–67). Oddly, Milton collapses the future kingdom with a present apocalypse, for that bliss "Full and perfect *is*"—not "Full and perfect *will be.*" Catherine Belsey observes the poem's shifting verb tenses throughout and asserts that the "present begins to predominate" the poem. As the gods depart, the reader "is made a witness in the present," one who observes the past nativity scene in the present.[43] But her sense of "the present" is not radical enough, nor does she sufficiently account for what "the present" entails. The nativity is continually reenacted in every conversion and every act of "internal worship" through the life of virtue—through the realized or internal eschatology we examined a moment ago. The age of gold is now in the making, in the incarnation and performance of Milton's man of virtue; his making reflects the world's making, and is subsequently the world's unmaking and remaking through his faithful listening to the symbol of the Word, as well as his appropriating the potent proclamation of Milton's words.

These cosmic dimensions of making, unmaking, and remaking within the human creature—so resonant among many of the radicals in the 1640s—find more particular articulation within the religious life of the commonwealth when we pair Milton's "Nativity" ode with "Lycidas," a poem that has as its center the preaching of the Word. Though the poem was occasioned by the untimely death in 1637 of Milton's contemporary, Edward King, Michael Wilding notes that its original publication in King's memorial volume did not contain the superscription, which was added for the publication of the 1645 *Poems*: "In this Monody the Author bewails a learned Friend, unfortunatly drown'd in his Passage from *Chester* on the *Irish* Seas, 1637. And by occasion foretels the ruine of our corrupted Clergy then in their height." Wilding is right in reading the supplement as an apocalyptic political gesture, for the opening phrase of the poem's "Yet once more . . ." is an allusion to Haggai 2:6–7 and Hebrews 12:25–27, both of which announce the coming Judgment—the glory of the rebuilt Temple in Haggai and the advent of the *parousia* in Hebrews.[44]

To be sure, the last years of the 1630s witnessed an explosion of radical anti-prelatical pamphlets, as many denounced the idols of the clergy even as William Laud attempted to strengthen his grip in England—idols that must be shattered and false gods that must be banished.[45] The *Letany* of John Bastwick, published in 1636–37, overtly characterizes the prelates as idols. They dangerously overstep their authority, always desire more power, and threaten to "ruine kingdomes and demolish states, to invocate a plauge upon their dominions by their disloyalty to God and the King." Speaking of their great wealth, Bastwick depicts them as idols to which all of England must bow down: "Looke on them againe in their manssions, and behold the great adoration that they have given them of all men see them also in their courts, veiw the Statelinesse, severity of pride of their carriage and superciliosity you shall find no such reverence and veneration given to any of the Nobiles, nor to other the Kings Majesties most honorable Courts. . . . Looke on them I beseech you . . . seeing the great preParations that are made for them." Cities and towns entertain them and make "petitions to them with all submission," and all the gentry come "to worship the[m]," bringing sacrifices of "large and munificent presents and all maner of raritiers unto them, offering their service to them." Why such obsequious worship? Because, as Bastwick puts it, Laud and his prelates have "the keys of heaven, to shut out whom they will. They have the keys of hell, to thrust in whom they please. They have the keys also of our purses, to pick them at their pleasure. . . . They have the keys likewise of all the prisons in the kingdome, to infetter any at their beck." Despite such lavish worship, however, these are idols who bring not blessing, peace, service, or virtue to the world, continues Bastwick; rather, these are idols that bring plague and contagion, poverty and death. They oust or silence true ministers who "carefully and diligently feed their flocks, with the sincere Milke of the word," and replace them with pretenders "who are enemies of the Crosse of Christ, whose end is destruction, whose God is there belly, & whose glory is their shame, who mind earthly things."[46]

"Free-born John" Lilburne, arrested and imprisoned by Star Chamber in 1638 for possessing and distributing Bastwick's treatise, also addresses the idolatry redolent within the "false Ecclesiasticall State."[47] In one of his earliest anti-prelatical pamphlets, *A light for the ignorant* (1638), Lilburne compares the conditions of the true and false civil and ecclesiastical states. The latter is made of false prophets who themselves set up the idols of laws and ordinances that must be obeyed. Lilburne admonishes, however, that "whosoever obyes these or any of these breaks the three first Comandements, for in hearing & obeying these they hear & obey the Dragon, Beast, & Whore that sent them and gave them their authority and office." But, as Lilburne laments, these "poore Captivated slavish assemblies" lack the power to dissociate themselves without fear of punishment, for they are compelled to "submit to, and practise such ordinances, Lawes & administrations, as are the inventions of men and will worship, and so breake the second commandment [prohibiting idol worship]."[48]

Both Bastwick and Lilburne depict an England in fetters, spiritually and physically impoverished, and slavishly bowing down either to the power-hungry priests themselves or to their established ecclesiastical laws, all of which derive their authority from the "PRIOR OF CANTERBURY . . . WILLIAM THE DRAGON," as Bastwick puts it.[49] The Dragon who was cast out of heaven, depicted by John in Revelation 12, gives power to the Beast that rises from the waters in Revelation 13; both are doomed to judgment and destruction when the Word, called "Faithful and True," appears and draws a sharp sword of Judgment from his mouth (19:11–15). For the moment, however, the plague and black contagion spread by the idol and idle priests, imagery with which the physician Bastwick must have been overly familiar, afflicts England's body. This plague imagery is echoed in Milton's poem: "The hungry Sheep look up, and are not fed, / But swoln with wind, and the rank mist they draw, / Rot inwardly, and foul contagion spread" (125–27). Unlike Edward King, celebrated and lamented by Milton as the only ordained minister of the church humbly serving and fulfilling his vocation, these "Blind mouths! that scarce themselves know how to hold / A Sheep-hook" (119–20) are castigated by Peter. The innocence of the shepherds in the fields, guiding their flocks under the stars and following the "call" they receive from the angel to worship the newborn Christ, is no more in "Lycidas." The shepherds scorned by Milton in "Lycidas" heed not the call nor bend their knee in humility before their Incarnate King.

In *An Humble Remonstrance* (1640), Bishop Joseph Hall lauds England's "learned . . . grave, holy and accomplished Divines."[50] In his *Animadversions* (July 1641), Milton responds by acerbically attacking these "Blind mouths." They have "fed themselves, and not their flocks," and "with force and cruelty have . . . ruled over Gods people: They have fed his sheep . . . not of a ready mind, but for filthy lucre, not as examples to the flock, but as being Lords over Gods heritage." Their "false feeding" has resulted in the bishops' abundant wealth at the expense of "numberlesse soules" (*CPW* 1:726–27) lost and starving. Just months earlier in *Of Reformation* (1641), Milton derides the prelates' wealth and idol ostentation as a kind of false "incarnation" in the

> customary ey-Service of the body, as if they could make *God* earthly, and fleshly, because they could not make themselves *heavenly* and *Spirituall*, and the Soule, yea, the very shape of *God* himselfe, into an exterior, and bodily forme, urgently pretending a necessity, and obligement of joining the body in a formall reverence, and *Worship* circumscrib'd, . . . they be deck't it, not in robes of pure innocency, but of pure Linnen, with other deformed, and fantastick dresses in Palls, and Miters, gold, and guegaw's fetcht from *Arons* old wardrope, or the *Flamins vestry*: . . . the Soule by this meanes of over-bodying her selfe . . . shifted off from her selfe, the labour of high soaring any more, forgot her heavenly flight, and

left the dull, and droyling carcass to plod on in the old rode. (*CPW*
1:520–21)

In contrast to the Incarnation of the Word, where form and content
are inseparable and brought into "such harmony alone," here Milton
seems to be describing an incarnation where form is privileged over
content, flesh over soul. As Michael Lieb points out, Milton "invokes
the kenotic experience in order to point up the irreverence of the
prelates toward Christ." Rather than divesting themselves, Lieb observes, the prelates invest themselves—reflecting not the servanthood
of Christ, but the glory of the Lord.[51] Wordless priests don the idol
robes of the office of the Word, and the wealth of the exterior is not
mirrored by a wealth of interior virtue.[52] Instead of disciplining their
souls for the ascent, these priests join their bodies in a false union to
their "deformed" and "fantastick" vestments. The result is ossification,
the "over-bodying" of their souls; having only an eye to the flesh, "all the
inward acts of *worship* issuing from the native strength of the SOULE,
run out lavishly to the upper skin, and there harden into a crust of
Formallitie" (*CPW* 1:522). Their overburdened exterior chokes the simplicity of the gospel, prompting Milton to ask: "Tell me ye Priests wherfore this gold, wherfore these roabs and surplices over the Gospel?"
(*Reason of Church Government, CPW* 1:828).

If we return to the poem, we find Peter deriding these false priests
whose overwrought "flashy" but "lean" sermons "over-body" the spiritual content as well. The Laudian bishops, who admire the "fantastick,
and declamatory flashes" (*Of Reformation, CPW* 1:568) of the church
fathers, fail to deliver the simplicity or nourishment of the gospel:
"And when they list, their lean and flashy songs / Grate on their scran-
nel Pipes of wretched straw" (123–24). So, not only have the clergy
transformed themselves into living idols, encrusted in "Formallitie" as
Milton puts it in *Of Reformation*, but the clergy have also caused language itself to petrify. The power of the Word to transform and renew
its hearers through proclamation, a power that "stirres and moves, and
agitates the holy affections of the Congregation, that they slumber not
in a senselesnesse" or that "flings open the gates of Heaven" as John

Donne describes it, has ceased to dwell within their words.[53] In "Lycidas" their preaching is characterized as "wind" and "rank mist." This is the text that starving congregants appropriate and embody, only to be "swoln" and rotten within (126–27). Instead of bearing witness to others of the nourishing gospel, they can only bear witness to disease, spreading "foul contagion."

James Holly Hanford, remarking a century ago on the pastoral tradition in the poem, characterizes Peter's speech (108–32) as a "digression."[54] In a similar manner, many scholars assume that the death of Edward King is the impetus, and not the subject, of the poem. They reason that King's untimely death provided Milton with an opportunity to dwell, with characteristic anxiety, on his own poetic career.[55] But given Milton's headnote to the poem, my pairing the poem with the efficacious performance of the Word in the "Nativity" ode, and the similar imagery developed in the anti-prelatical tracts, we should consider Peter's speech and Milton's relationship to King of more central importance to the poem and to the swain's complex process of grieving and his desire for consolation.

With the advent of Peter, Milton converts the classical pastoral into a Christian pastoral, accomplishing the move he repeats on the epic scale with *Paradise Lost*. But Peter's speech is the catalyst for the poet's turn from melancholy to mourning in a Freudian sense precisely because of the new context. Freud's melancholiac displays "an impoverishment of his ego on a grand scale" because the loss of the love-object has become "transformed into a loss in the ego" that has been "altered by the identification" of the love-object with the ego itself. The mournful person, on the other hand, feels the same painful sense of loss, but recognizes that the loss of the love-object is not a diminishment of the ego, for "having shown that the love object no longer exists . . . all the libido shall be withdrawn from its attachments to this object."[56] In Ricoeurrian terms, Peter's speech is the text that transforms the poet's paralyzing grief, abiding sense of alienation, and unanswered questions to the poet's resolve to "Weep no more" (164), to appropriate mournfully the narrative of the life that was lost, and to begin the move to "Pastures new" (193).

Peter's denunciation of the clergy is framed by Milton's invocations to Arethuse (85) and Alpheus (133). In classical myth the beautiful nymph Arethuse, seeking to escape the river god Alpheus, who pursued her under the sea "by secret sluse" as Milton puts it elsewhere in "Arcades" (30), was transformed by Diana into a fountain. Her waters, however, eventually coalesced with the waters of Alpheus's river. Merritt Y. Hughes notes this framing device, significantly observing, though without further comment, that the sixteenth-century mythographer Natale Conti asserted that Arethuse's name means "virtue," while Alpheus's name means "imperfection."[57] Not to belabor the point, but if Conti is correct, then Milton's allusion is a fitting classical analogue for the dynamic union of divine virtue and human frailty in the Incarnation. The "Blind mouths" of the prelates, who "Creep and intrude and climb into the fold" like a "grim Wolf" and devour the flock seemingly without consequence (115, 128–29), stand in stark contrast to the virtuous Edward King, whose gentle clerical star was only just ascending.[58]

In point of fact, King's sympathies lay with the royalist and Laudian programs, and Barbara Lewalski notes that by 1637 these sympathies had been published in King's own court poems.[59] But as she also notes, Peter's scornful derision—ventriloquized by the "Church-outed" preacher and poet—does everything to separate King, whom Milton must have considered an active participant in and ardent proclaimer of the Word, from the English church. Milton's persona in the poem recounts with longing the times he and Lycidas would rise "Under the opening eyelids of the morn," spend their days driving their flocks to fresh pasture, and their evenings "Batt'ning our flocks with the fresh dews of night" (26, 29). Lycidas's untimely exit from the world accounts for the "heavy change" (37) lamented by Nature herself. Crucially, his death, like Christ's birth in the "Nativity" ode, sends ontological shockwaves through the world: the woods and caves, overgrown with thyme and vine, mourn (39–41); the willows and hazel copses will no longer be seen "Fanning their joyous Leaves" (42–44); the rose cannot bloom because it is afflicted with canker worms (45); the herds cannot prosper because they are threatened with the taint-worm (46); the "gay wardrobe" of the delicate flowers is destroyed by frost (47–48). We might understand these natural changes as emblems of the swain's interior state, and the disintegration of the simplicity and abundance of the pastoral world is reflected in the poet's Jobean questions that are ventriloquized through the lamentable voices of the many. The poet asks, despondently, "Where were ye Nymphs when the remorseless deep / Clos'd oe'r the head of your loved *Lycidas?*" (50–51). "What could the muse herself that Orpheus bore" have done to prevent his being rent "by the rout that made that hideous roar" (58, 61)? What does it matter that the shepherd-poet tends to his craft with "uncessant care" for a "thankless muse," when "blind Fury with the abhorrèd shears" (64, 66, 75) haphazardly ceases the poet's potential and work with a whimsical snip? Neptune dodges the question by sending Triton, his "herald of the sea" (89), to interrogate the "felon winds" for an answer; and Hippotades, the god of the winds, exonerates his servants only to blame "that fatal and perfidious bark" that carried him (91–92, 100). Camus is the penultimate speaker, and he, too, is filled with the same bewildering despair: "Ah! who hath reft . . . my dearest pledge?" (107).

Peter's denunciation follows, and the consolation he offers the poet-shepherd is not a straightforward answer to these piercing and melancholy questions. His denunciation, however, ought not to be read as one that simply castigates the poet and the various voices for raising the troubling questions in the first place, and one might just as fairly observe that Peter dodges the questions like Neptune before him by rhetorical "pyrotechnics" of a sort.[60] As Rosemund Tuve has argued, Peter's role is to shift perspective, and the various arcadian voices play a critical role in the "cumulative" sense of consolation.[61] The present tragedy of Lycidas's death, however, is the fulcrum. Peter counters the poet's paralyzing grief with the promised Judgment at the eschaton. Just as Christ's birth heralds the conversion of the world through the performance of the Word, Lycidas's death heralds the "heavy change" of the world through the clergy's glaring lack of performance of the Word; they are the cankerworms of the English church devouring everything they see through a negative *kenosis* without an accompanying positive *pleroma*. But the "two-handed engine at the door" (130) will deliver justice and final consolation. The passing of Peter's "dread voice" forces a "Return" (132) to the present moment from the imagined eschaton, which has caused the waters of Alpheus to shrink and the "Vales" to withdraw temporarily the "Bells and Flowrets of a thousand hues" (133–34). But the saturating melancholy has been transformed into an act of beautiful mourning through the shepherd's new capacity to behold the fragile splendor of the myriad of flowers (140–50) that decorate his "laureate hearse" (151). Like the poetry of the fallen angels, whose desperate beauty "Suspended Hell" (*PL* 2.554) and its torments for a brief moment, the beauty of the flowers here serves only "to interpose a little ease," and the poet-shepherd's "Ay me!" and "where'er thy bones are hurled" (152, 154–55) belie a sighing grief and lingering agnosticism. Peter's avoidance of the swain's question of theodicy is a brutal acceptance that there are, ultimately, no satisfying answers in the present. But one must live anyway.

The virtuous and promising Edward King may have drowned, but the English church killed him (and their "swoln" congregants) first. Lycidas is translated to heaven to hear the "unexpressive nuptial Song" (176), and the Orphic "gory visage" (62) of his flesh that was carried upon the water is sublimed to spirit as he becomes the "Genius of the shore" who "shalt be good / To all that wander in that perilous flood" (183–85). Ostensibly, Lycidas will protect those sailing the Irish Sea where he himself drowned. But we might profitably question why this "Genius of the shore" should succeed in protecting others when the Nymphs, Muses, Neptune, Hippotades, and Camus have so obviously failed. In short, he may not—suffering, injustice, hypocrisy, and death pervade the present pastoral world. In a sense, Peter's denunciation is itself a kind of "pleasing sorcery" that "could charm / Pain for a while or anguish, and excite / Fallacious hope, or arm the obdured breast / With stubborn patience as with triple steel" (*PL* 2.566–68). But the poet's return in "Lycidas" from Peter's eschatological reverie, like Alpheus's called-for "Return" ("Lycidas," 132), is one characterized by a transformed perception of that pain and anguish.

Peter's speech is the text that has reoriented the swain's horizon of being-in-the-world. The trajectory initiated by Peter's denunciation of the church and clergy finds its hermeneutical arc in the swain's hoped for resurrection like Lycidas.[62] The poem ends with the "uncouth Swain" looking to the *pleromic* future of "Pastures new" (186, 193), but it is a future that shapes the horizons of a new pastoral present—an immanence suspended over the transcendence Peter offers, rather than an immanence given to the desperate beauty of the void. This movement in the poem perhaps reflects what James K. A. Smith terms a "theological materialism" that not only "funds a proper valuation of immanence," but also participates in an "incarnational ontology," one that renders the material truly meaningful in its multiplicity, rather than a simple materialism that is "flattened" and "squandered into nothing."[63] A satisfying end to the troubling questions that the poem occasions may elude the poet. But the Orphic anxieties that Milton might have had as an ambitious poet, called by God to be the *vates* who sits "in order serviceable" like the "Bright-harness'd Angels" gathered about the infant Christ ("Nativity" ode, 244), and who dwells upon the potential for his own premature death—all must be set aside and ultimately outweighed by the justice and reconciliation at the eschaton and the incarnational ontology in the present. "God doth not need / Either man's work or his own gifts," the poet asserts in "Sonnet XIX," for "who best / Bear his mild yoke, they serve him best" ("Sonnet XIX," 9–10).

"*Lycidas* is dead, dead ere his prime" ("Lycidas," 8), but the significance of King's virtuous life, which is to say a nascent clerical life whose narrative was ineluctably shaped by his listening to the symbol of the Word, lives on. But more significantly, King's virtuous life serves as a model to aspiring young clergy entrusted with piloting the "wandering" ecclesial ship through the perilous floodwaters of the world. The "text" of King's life cries out for witness, and this is just what Milton does by writing the poem: "He must not float upon his wat'ry bier / Unwept, and welter to the parching wind, / Without the meed of some melodious tear. / Begin then" (12–15). Milton's bearing witness recalls Ricoeur's idea that texts call for a hermeneutics of testimony. Echoing Ricoeur, Donald G. Marshall comments that the "text's reality lies in our keeping it alive, in 'testifying' or 'witnessing' its truth through our own actions." We might say, along with Marshall, that Milton calls for others to look to the life of King, who himself embodied the narrative of the

Word, in order to "assum[e] responsibility to make the text speak again with power to affect present action."[64]

The "present action" of the "uncouth Swain" is to continue as a faithful shepherd, feeding his flock by Lycidas's example. Following his song the rustic gathers his reeds at sunset, and "rose, and twitch't his Mantle blue: / Tomorrow to fresh Woods, and Pastures new" (192–93). The clerical idols exposed, and anticipating their destruction when the "two-handed engine at the door / Stands ready to smite once, and smite no more" (130–31), Milton the "Church-outed" poet-preacher will take upon himself the burden of feeding his flock of readers. In his dual vocation, Milton might claim that his is not just any voice; he is, like other preachers of the early modern era, "The voyce. Christ is *verbum*. The word; not A word, but The word: the Minister is *Vox*, voyce; not A voyce, but The voyce, the voyce of that word, and no other," as Donne puts it. The preacher does not just deliver the Word, but is himself the *Verbum*, the embodiment of the Word in the speech and actions of his daily life. He is "a pleasing voyce, because he pleases him that sent him . . . and pleasing to them to whom he is sent by bringing the Gospel of Peace and Reparation to all wounded, and scattered, and contrite Spirits."[65] For Donne, the preacher is the *Verbum* and has the mission to infuse into his ruined and fragmented congregants the grace necessary for them also to become the Word. As we have seen in the Incarnational aesthetics of the 1645 *Poems,* and in the preaching dynamics of the "Nativity" ode and "Lycidas" in particular, Milton, too, endeavors to make his audience "fit" by admonishing them in his poetry of proclamation to listen to the symbol of the Word, and to incarnate its potential in their lives of virtue, in order that they might fetch back the "Age of Gold" and regain paradise.

In the following chapter, we will place more pressure on Milton's caustic criticism of a mercenary and Wordless clergy, figured in the demonic preachers of Book 2 of *Paradise Lost,* who have undergone a disastrous *kenosis* that describes and inscribes the culture of hell. In figuring the fallen angels as preachers, we uncover Milton's hope and conviction that the true Protestant preacher could incarnate the Word to bring about personal, national, and ecclesial revolution.

chapter 2

Infernal Prophesying

Unsaying God's Name in the Demonic Council Scene
of *Paradise Lost*

*Rhetorick is an art sanctified by Gods Spirit, and may be lawfully used
in handling of Gods word: there may be given . . . instances of all the parts
of Rhetorick out of the Scripture. And therefore the Art is to be approved,
and only the abuse thereof is to be condemned.*
— Richard Bernard, *The Faithfull Shepheard* (1609)

*Thy actions to thy words accord, thy words
To thy large heart give utterance due.*
— Milton, *Paradise Regained* (3.9–10)

When Satan is discovered by the angels Ithuriel and Zephon in Eden,
having already half-accomplished his task in his insidious whispering to
the sleeping Eve, he is brought before Gabriel to account for his presence. Satan first replies that he has escaped hell to "boldly venture to
whatever place / Farthest from pain" he can find, and blames God's carelessness in not securing "His Iron Gates" (4.892, 898). When Gabriel
mocks the "courageous Chief['s]" hasty flight from the pain of hell,
while his faithful rebel cohort still suffers, Satan replies that he has escaped to "spy / This new created World" in order "to find / Better abode,

and my afflicted Powers / To settle here on Earth" (4.936–940). Gabriel immediately draws attention to Satan's doublespeak: "To say and straight unsay . . . / Argues no Leader, but a liar trac't" (4.947–49).

Gabriel's provocative statement that Satan's speaking is at once an assertion and a negation suggests that his language is deceptive, full of half-truths, diversions, and illusions. This is made all the more intriguing when we consider that such language is not only "trac't" back to the perfidious leadership of Satan as a point of origin, but also that Milton directs his polemical career against the many pamphlets and "tracts" that in his opinion employ similar tactics by correspondingly false leaders.[1] Implicit in Gabriel's statement is the gesture toward a satanic semiotics in which language is divorced and in exile from the Presence of God. Milton recognizes the threat that satanic language, contemporaneously a saying and an unsaying, poses toward the divine gift of language. In this crucial scene, Gabriel as the "strength of God" and bearer of the divine Sign is juxtaposed against the Arch-Fiend, here for the first time directly called "Satan," the "enemy" or "accuser," in the poem by someone other than the narrator, and whose grammatical apposite is "liar" (4.950).[2] The Arch-Fiend comes not as Lucifer the "bearer of light," but as the bearer of "mournful gloom" (1.244) and a new semiotics of flux, hiddenness, and negation.

These dynamics of satanic language find one of their most sinister expressions in the demonic council scene of *Paradise Lost* when the newly vanquished demons assemble to debate their next course of action against heaven's King and the Anointed One. This scene has been approached from a number of provocative perspectives, and the general consensus has been to investigate the orations as reflections of political debates in English Parliament during the revolutionary years.[3] To my knowledge no one has approached the infernal speeches within the context of preaching, itself a very political endeavor. Thomas Cogswell argues that the Stuarts looked upon the pulpits as "a formidable platform for disseminating the royal line."[4] Jeanne Shami comments further that "[p]reachers were becoming more actively engaged in propaganda for and against public policies" even though the pulpit was "at best an unpredictable political tool."[5] Far from being the sword-tongued heralds of the new age, many early modern preachers (at least those who desired to keep their benefices and their ears as well) were often spin-doctors or ventriloquists disseminating royal policy. Milton left the ministerial path in part because of his refusal to swear an oath of allegiance to the king and Carolingian ecclesial policy. When we examine the discussions in hell within the context of preaching, we find that Milton's fallen angels follow suit as a congregation of dissenters who "dislodge, and leave / Unworshipt, unobey'd the Throne supreme" (*PL* 5.669–70). In their dissent they preach the gospel of the "liberty" of conscience and "freedom equal" from below (5.679, 793, 797), not the gospel of the newly raised Son. While Milton was sympathetic to dissenters generally, however, we will find that he is not sympathetic to these because the fallen angels fail his litmus test for pious dissent.

To be sure, Milton figures the fallen angels as dissenters. But how fairly can we characterize these dissenters as preachers and their speeches as sermons? The influential Puritan divine William Perkins explicitly links ministers with angels: "are they *Gods Angels*? therefore they must preach Gods word," and, "Art thou therefore an *Angell* of God, then magnifie the Spirit of God, and not thy self in thy preaching of his word."[6] In his *Animadversions* (1641), Milton addresses the various obligations of the truly inspired preacher and heavenly messenger:

> there is no imployment more honourable, more worthy, then to be a messenger, and Herald of heavenly truth from God to man, and by the faithfull worke of holy doctrine, to procreate a number of faithfull men . . . ; arising to what climat so ever he turne him, like that Sun of righteousnesse that sent him, with healing in his wings, and new light to break in upon the chill and gloomy hearts of his hearers, raising out of darksome barrennesse a delicious, and fragrant Spring of saving knowledge, and good works. (*CPW* 1:721)

Milton's ideal preacher, as the "Herald of heavenly truth" who provides others with a clearer perception of God and who brings "healing in his wings," shares many of the duties that are ascribed to angels in the seventeenth century. As Joad Raymond thoroughly demonstrates, angelic activity is wide-ranging and includes offering assistance, interpreting and executing the will of God, inspiring praise, presenting models of imitation, extending healing, and comforting the distressed. Moreover, in the revolutionary decades, nonconformist preachers often validated their theological beliefs, framed their political agendas, and carried out their polemics by aligning themselves with angelic authority.[7] Jameela Lares comments that the "seventeenth-century mind . . . accepted angels as types of preachers," and she proceeds to examine the angelic speeches of Raphael and Michael delivered to Adam as sermons.[8] Angels and ministers had the supreme duty of proclaiming the "good news": the eruption of the divine into the world at the Incarnation.

Even more, many Protestant preachers figured themselves not only as angels, but as "incarnations" or embodiments of the Word acting in and speaking to the world. Heiko Oberman explains that the Reformation sermon, with its emphasis on individual and corporate transformation, is an apocalyptic event.[9] Whereas the medieval Catholic sermon was heavily centered on preparing the audience by way of the explication of doctrine, the Reformation sermon was the "*decisive* encounter with the Holy One himself. . . . It does not call man *out* of his sinful situation to the unassailable safety of the sacred but reaches man *in* his worldly situation: Jesus Christ becomes present under the veil of the preached Word, *outside* the cathedral, on the steps."[10] Not only is God disclosed or revealed through preaching, but so is the new nature of the self in Christ and its operations as a "being-in-the-world." In this way, preaching is conceived as a verbal sacrament. Martin Luther certainly has this sense in mind when he exults, "Yes, I hear the sermon; but who is speaking? The minister? No, indeed! You do not hear the minister. True, the voice is his; but my God is speaking the Word which he preaches or speaks."[11]

Consequently, there is precedent within the early modern period and within Milton studies for thinking about angelic speech in terms of preaching. But we ought to be more suspicious on Milton's behalf if we are to regard angels as preachers and preachers as incarnations. The "Church-outed" poet-preacher well knew that these angelic preachers have their demonic counterparts not only in hell, but also on earth. As

Milton repeatedly charges in his prose, the task before his revolutionary readers involves discerning the incarnational performance of the true reader and preacher from that of the satanic pretender and dissembler. Both William Perkins and Jameela Lares, however, neglect the infernal counterparts to heavenly ministers who deliver sermons bearing the "good news" to their captive audiences. Consequently, this chapter critically addresses these omissions and creatively revisits the cultural context of preaching. The first section of this chapter considers how Augustine, Milton, and Perkins describe a theory of language and a praxis of preaching that is grounded in the doctrine of participation. Importantly, language theory for them implies also a metaphysics and a theology, which are radically redefined by the dissenting angels in their speeches in Book 2 of *Paradise Lost*. The political and oratorical dynamics of this scene are reminiscent of the Great Prophesying movement of the late sixteenth and seventeenth centuries, wherein a panel of nonconformist ministers gathered to deliver a series of sermons on the same text of scripture and then publicly discuss them. By the 1640s, prophesying became standard practice among many of the "mechanick preachers" in the sects, partly out of distrust for the perceived monopoly on the scriptures by university-trained clergy.

In the second section, I argue that these infernal preachers deliver sermons on the same "text": the Name of God. As Russell Hillier observes, the fallen angels "rewrite history to forget God's Messiah and his victory" in their "Christless propaganda." They "blank the Son's name with an indefinite title" and "reduce his initiative to instrumental means by metonymy or synecdoche" in an attempt to erase the Son's significance.[12] As dissenters from divine rest, and as champions of the liberty of individual conscience and exegesis, the restless demons play language games that attempt to "unsay" the Name of God. Their dissent marks a pernicious self-alienation or *kenosis* that refuses to be retrieved into the *pleroma* of divine participation, at least as long as God is the agent to do so. Their linguistic attack on the Name is also a metaphysical assault on God's essence, and the performative manifestation of that "bright essence" in the Anointed Son (*PL* 3.6). In the assay, the fallen angels loosen the Name from its mooring as defining Presence—a move that uncannily anticipates some poststructuralist assumptions about language and meaning. Here, I do not intend to flagellate poststructural theory. Rather, my purpose is to argue that for Milton the Logocentrist, the demonic break from Presence is one that he deems malevolent in his poem, and one that has consequences for the "form of life" that takes shape in the culture of hell that Milton represents in the poem. While a preacher like John Donne advocates that in preaching God is made "*Deus noster;* Ours, as we are his creatures; ours, as we are like him, made to his image," the preaching that emerges in hell also renders God "*Deus noster*," but a God subject to the fallen angels' own making, or unmaking, as we shall see.[13] Instead of fulfilling what promises to be a proliferation of meaning through the freedom of individual reading, however, Milton demonstrates that satanic language games paradoxically inscribe the fallen angels within a calculus of vapid sameness and a form of life whose performance is characterized by aggression and violence, manipulation, and self-interest.

"Son of Thunder": Incarnation, Performance, and the Doctrine of Participation

In the *Marrow of Sacred Divinity* (1630; 1642) William Ames states that divinity "is of all Arts, the supreme, most noble, and the matter of peece, proceeding in a speciall manner from God," and that the "Ministry is an Eclesiasticall function whereby a man being chosen out doth dispense holy things of speciall right." Regarding this special calling of a minister, William Perkins asserts in *Of the Calling of the Ministerie* (1605) that "a true *Minister,* one that is a right Angel, & a true Interpreter, is no comon or ordinarie man, but thin sowne, one of many, *nay one of a thousand.*" The true minister "is *Gods interpreter* to the people" and "the *peoples interpreter* to God, by being able to speake to God for them. . . . In which respects, he is properly called, *Gods mouth* to the people; by preaching to them from God, and the *peoples mouth* to God."[14] Not only does Perkins again conflate preachers with angels here, but also he draws an implicit connection between the Incarnate

Christ and the preacher. Just as the Incarnation provides an exegesis of God, the preacher who incarnates the Word functions as the nexus for divine-human communication. Such assumptions lead Donne to exhort, "Be thou *Verbum* too, A Word, as God was; A Speaking, and a Doing Word, to his glory, and the edification of others."[15] Proclaiming is, therefore, a kind of *poiēsis,* a "making" and incarnating. The speech of God both stands in the pulpit in the figure of the preacher and infuses the world sacramentally through the words of the sermon.[16]

It is not too much of a stretch to say that popular preachers, such as Donne or Bishop Launcelot Andrewes, who exuded charisma, could wittily turn a phrase, or could stir the passions of their audience, were to the early modern world what rock stars are to contemporary culture. Broadsides announced the details of their forthcoming engagements, young men and women met there or accompanied each other on the way, verbal quarrels or the occasional fracas ensued over points of doctrine, and members of every social class often departed abuzz with excitement and devotional zeal. William Haller aptly describes this age of the sermon as the "vital rage for utterance," and early modern audiences displayed their own vital rage for hearing them.[17] Many Puritans not only heard several sermons on Sundays, but also gave ear to four or five sermons during the week, and they discussed them at length during their times of work and leisure.[18] Moreover, we need only to look to the popular Puritan phenomenon of "gadding" to sermons—the practice of English parishioners of traveling several miles to another parish in order to hear a particularly striking preacher—to confirm the point.[19]

As Bryan Crockett surmises, the sermons delivered at Paul's Cross by the most prominent divines, for instance, attracted audiences as large as six thousand. Because these sermons were usually about two hours in duration, preachers had to rely on every rhetorical device and dramatic tactic in their performative arsenal to keep the crowds from becoming unruly.[20] Preachers at such large sermon gatherings were frequently met by laughter, jabbering, or other disruptive behavior from the audience, in just the same manner as acting companies in the playhouse; apparently, crowds had no scruples about physically removing from the pulpit those ministers whose preaching fell woefully short.

With so much riding on capturing the attention of the crowd—no less than their salvation as well as the preacher's own livelihood, if not bodily health—and such crafted attention paid to one's performance, it is no wonder that the pulpit and the playhouse contended for the same audience until the 1583 ban on Sabbath day theatrical productions.[21]

But preachers themselves were deeply conflicted over the extent to which "man-made" eloquence and dramatic performance ought to enter into the preaching of the Word.[22] Do a minister's study of classical rhetoric and his dramatic performance in the pulpit aid the Holy Spirit in moving the congregation, or do they compromise the integrity of the Spirit's work by relying overly much on the preacher's own academic preparation and personal charisma? I shall argue in this section that their debates ultimately revolve around the doctrine of divine participation. Over "what," we might imagine Milton and his contemporaries asking, is language and the preacher's performance in the pulpit "suspended": over the One in whom, by whom, and through whom all things move and have their being (Acts 17:28); or over the void, the "dark unbottom'd infinite Abyss," where "all life dies, death lives, and nature breeds, / Perverse, all monstrous, . . . / Abominable, inutterable, and worse" (PL 2.405, 624–26)?[23] If the first, then language and performance can be construed as "icon"—something that refers beyond itself and is "pointing to that which is transcendent and inviting one to complete the sign with the experience of the thing itself (God)." If the second, then language functions as "idol"—wherein "the world is enjoyed as an end in itself, substituting for God."[24]

This distinction is a crucial issue for Milton. Repairing the "ruins of our first parents" involves a strong sense of the Platonic doctrine of participation (*methexis*, "sharing"). Language plays an important role in the process, argues Milton, especially the language emanating from the pulpit. In *The Reason of Church Government*, Milton scorns the prelates for neglecting the supreme duty of "healing our inward man" (*CPW* 1:837). They fail not just because they have traded the "pure, spirituall, simple, and lowly" gospel for the advantages of "worldly degrees of authority, honour, [and] temporall jurisdiction" (1:766). For Milton, their failure to heal and to minister to the inward man is also a result of their spiritually impoverished language, a "fast and loos" language full of equivocation, "falshood and dissention" (*The Tenure of Kings and Magistrates, CPW* 3:232, 235). John Spittlehouse, who fought for Parliament against the king at Newark, expressed the militant anticlericalism that many shared: the established clergy, foisted upon the parish, were the "very fountains of atheism and antichristianism."[25] Their "fast and loos" language reflects their own "antichristianism," their own failure in personal governance and discipline, and their lack of divine participation. The result for the community is disastrous: a plague of spiritual maladies, sloth, and disorder. It is as if a physician were to assume the pulpit, as Milton offers the analogy, gather all the sick into the chapel, and then do nothing but lecture them on sickness. "[A]nd so," Milton denounces, "without so much as feeling one puls, or giving the least order to any skilfull Apothecary, [they] should dismisse 'em from time to time, some groaning, some languishing, some expiring, with this only charge to look well to themselves, and do as they heare" (*The Reason of Church Government, CPW* 1:756). Without their own inner regeneration and journey toward sanctification, their language and congregation have an improper end.

The doctrine of participation and the ends to which human beings put language are important issues not just for Milton, the poet-preacher engaged in spurring his congregation of readers to obedience and to the cultivation of virtue, but also for Augustine. Augustine was the seminal patristic figure in the early modern period, frequently cited by Catholic and Protestant preachers alike. Even the most radical Protestants, "who on principle rejected human authority, used Augustine more than any other writer, save Paul."[26] Early modern divines not only looked to Augustine's *On Christian Doctrine* for a general account of the nature and function of language, but students aspiring to the ministry also scrupulously studied the work because it helped define the parameters for the use of rhetoric in the construction of sermons. Their debates on the proper scope of rhetoric reflect Augustine's own ambivalence toward the use of rhetorical theory in preaching. Like Milton, the question with which Augustine often finds himself wrestling is this: What is the value of pagan literature to the Christian? The study and use of classical rhetoric is included under this rubric, and the answer Augustine consistently gives is that Christians can legitimately participate in the study of pagan literature through a limited "hermeneutics of hospitality": non-Christian literature ought to be welcomed, but by no means should it be given the best seat in the house, so to speak.[27]

While Augustine believes that the study of rhetoric is important for the aspiring preacher, it is crucial to note at the outset that Augustine does not relegate preaching to a "subset" of rhetoric. He, like many early modern preachers, believed that the ultimate power to move an audience to obedience, introspection, and godly behavior lay not in the clever use of the orator's tricks, but in the decisive piercing of the Word through the moving of the Spirit. True eloquence in a preacher is derived from prayer and personal piety. The ecclesiastical orator is able to move his audience "more through the piety of his prayers than through the skill of his oratory . . . he is a petitioner before he is a speaker."[28] The English divine Richard Bernard echoes Augustine: "Begin the Prayer before thou read the Texte, after the custom of Ancient fathers, as *S. Augustine* testifieth, and as religious reverence bindeth us. Prayer must be the Proeme."[29] The preacher's practice of praying, both as a prelude to his own encounter with the scriptures and as the means through which his congregation may be made "fit" for their reception of the Word, is of prime importance. Prayer properly aligns the preacher's heart, and it is therefore an act of charity that fulfills the two greatest commandments to love God and to love one's neighbor. For Augustine, true eloquence and true reading derive from this rule of charity.

Augustine admonishes the preacher to pray that "God may place a good speech in his mouth."[30] That "good speech" is the subject of Book Four of Augustine's *On Christian Doctrine,* and we will discover in a moment that the Incarnation, God's own Good Speech, explicitly undergirds his theory of rhetoric and the ends of language. Augustine begins with a disclaimer that he will not, as some of his readers apparently had hoped, "give the rules of rhetoric which I learned and taught in the secular schools." The reason for Augustine's demur appears to be that he does not want to be responsible for disseminating rules that could be used in the employ of evil and the propagation of falsity. Strangely, however, Augustine's refusal does not arm the "good man" with these rules either. Augustine assumes that his readership is already well versed in the rules of rhetorical art; as he sees it, his job is to clarify to what end rhetoric is to be used.[31] He acknowledges that rhetoric is a vital and necessary avenue of study for preachers. "Should [the pagans] speak briefly, clearly, and plausibly," he objects, "while the defenders of truth speak so that they tire their listeners, make themselves difficult to understand and what they have to say dubious? Should they oppose the truth with fallacious arguments and assert falsehoods, while the defenders of truth have no ability either to defend the truth or to oppose the false?" For Augustine, rhetoric is employed in a spiritual battle to move the hearts and minds of men and women toward the knowledge of God, and subsequently spur them to conversion and virtuous action in the world. Thus, eloquence and the rules of rhetoric function in the same way for Augustine as signs in language: rhetoric does not draw attention to itself for its own sake, but points to the Beauty of the God behind it that grants truth and life.[32] He is able to affirm the use of rhetoric as long as it satisfies this condition of participation, and he declares, "[L]et everyone who is a good and true Christian understand that truth belongs to his Master, wherever it is found."[33]

Given this endorsement, many divines devoted long hours to academic study in order to have at their command not just the rules of rhetoric, but also a vast storehouse of knowledge, from philosophy to economics to geography, all of which might function as supplements to their exegesis. Among the disciplines that the minister must master, Richard Bernard includes the study of logic and rhetoric, for the "diversity of knowledge in severall things which a man brings with him, to the reading of the Scripture, are as many candles to give light to see in to his text." In *The Faithfull Shepheard* (1609) Bernard discusses the proper preparation and delivery of a sermon. He asserts that by logic "we see the method of the Spirit, we behold the arguments, the coherence, the scope; by it wee collect doctrines, confirme them, enlarge the proofs, gather thence consequently apt uses, and urge them by reason upon the Hearers." Without logic the preacher's words will fall on deaf ears or fail to take root; without "Knowledge of Rhetoricke" the preacher

will not be able to understand the fullness of scripture's tropes and figures, and his effectiveness in moving his audience will be compromised.
Consequently, for Bernard there is little room for impromptu preaching; the preacher's sermon must be carefully researched, prayed over,
and written out before he assumes the pulpit. Yet Bernard gratefully acknowledges that the gift of "godly eloquence" is given to some, and that
"[n]o man, neither will any wise man condemne eloquence, or forbid by
any good meanes, to attaine to the gift. . . . All men must order their
words with discretion, much more in that place a Minister."[34]

Other preachers in England were more divided about eloquence
and the use of rhetoric and extra-biblical material in their sermons.
George Herbert, for instance, advocates that a preacher "procures all attention by all possible art." Extra-biblical knowledge is not to be discarded: "They say, it is an ill Mason that refuseth any stone: and there is
no knowledg, but, in a skilfull hand, serves either positively as it is, or
else to illustrate some other knowledge." Moreover, Herbert advises
that preachers choose "moving and ravishing texts" upon which to ex-
pound, but cautions that the "character of his Sermon is Holiness."[35]
Like Herbert, John Preston, Donne's successor at Lincoln's Inn and
master of Emmanuel College, insists that ministers "use all the Arts,
Sciences, and Knowledges that we can" in preparation. Unlike Herbert,
however, he argues against a preacher's using that knowledge in public,
for fear that it could obscure the plain sense of the gospel: "humane
Wit and Eloquence is so farre from setting forth the excellencie of the
Word, as it obscures the excellencie of it."[36] Preston's cautious demurral
is Bartimaeus Andrewes's slippery slope. He caustically upbraids those
preachers who "thinke Christ too base to bee preached simply in him
selfe . . . and thinke that Christe commeth nakedly, unlesse clothed with
vaine ostentation of wordes" or think that "he must be glosed out and
printed with the froth of Philosophi, Poetry or such like."[37] At stake for
Andrewes is proper worship, for "clothing" Christ in eloquence leads to
a kind of verbal idolatry; the danger that the study and deployment of
rhetoric, philosophy, and poetry pose is that these disciplines compete
with the very beauty and power of the Word in whose service they are
supposed to be employed.

During the decades of the revolution and the Interregnum, Andrewes's caution becomes full-scale prejudice by Ranters, Seekers, and Quakers who attacked the professional clergy trained in rhetoric. The antinomian Army chaplain William Dell, friend of John Bunyan and the regicide John Okey, observed that it was the untutored and the unlearned apostles who shook the world. A man's learning will add nothing if the Holy Spirit is not present: "No man is sufficient for the work of the Ministerie, by any naturall part and abilitie of his own, nor yet by any acquisite part of humane learning and knowledge, but onley by this power of the Holy Ghost."[38] Echoing John's apocalyptic warning in Revelation 13:18 against taking the mark of the Beast, Dell preached that the universities, which are the nurseries of the Antichrist's "School-Divinity" and "His IMAGE, *that is, the Church of the* Bishops *and* Presbyters," imprints Antichrist's mark through human erudition, the "fleshly wisdom, Rhetorical Eloquence, and Philosophical learning" that keep England's people enslaved as citizens of the kingdom of the Beast.[39] The separatist minister Samuel How remarked that "knowledge of Arts and Sciences, diverse Tongues, much reading" did nothing to help the preacher "to understand the *mind* of God in his Word." Because humanistic study is a "*rudiment* of this world" Christ's mysteries will be obscured rather than revealed. For How, resorting to human learning in the pulpit dangerously treads on the "*sincere word*" and evokes the duplicity of the Serpent in Eden who beguiled Eve and who now infects and putrifies one's mind "from the *sincerity* that is in Christ."[40]

Thus, we might see in these objections an echo of earlier politically charged debates about the nature and function of church aesthetics, revitalized during the reign of Charles I through Archbishop William Laud's campaign to "beautify" the churches as an aid in devotion. Milton, too, participates in this debate using language that is strikingly similar to that of Bartimaeus Andrewes. Attacking the outward adornment of the prelates, he objects "he that will cloath the Gospel now, intimates plainly, that the Gospel is naked, uncomely, that I may not say reproachfull" (*The Reason of Church Government, CPW* 1:828). In Andrewes's and Milton's responses, we might detect a "distrust of artistry congenial to the antisacramental, anticeremonial temper of the stricter English Calvinists."[41] As How reminds his readers, echoing Isaiah 53:2, "*Jesus Christ was without form, or beauty, or any such thing wherefore he should be desired.*" To clothe Christ in human learning is to behold the "*smokey power,* and *glory,* flowing *from the Kingdome of Sathan.*"[42] Such distrust of beautifying the gospel leads Andrewes, How, Dell, and Milton to ardently pose: Is not Christ proclaimed sufficient?

Though certainly no radical William Perkins sounds much like How or Dell when he warns against the preacher's temptation to "beautify" the gospel unnecessarily. In *Satans Sophistrie Answered by Our Saviour Christ* (1604), a sermon on Christ's temptation in the wilderness, Perkins exposes the sophistical tricks of Satan and implicitly likens the Adversary's enticing Christ toward worldly glory and riches in the third temptation to the preacher's desire to use rhetoric for the wrong reasons. The preacher must be wary of the opulence that Satan offers, for in their "beholding of beauty," some are incited to desire the external signs, or "wares" as Perkins puts it, that have been laid open rather than the God who is the source of Beauty. He agrees with Augustine that the language and performance issuing from the pulpit must participate in the God who is the Giver of language.

The preacher's use of rhetoric or extra-biblical materials in his sermon can be a precarious endeavor. Perkins zealously points out the dangers of "cunning" satanic language and biblical exegesis loosened from its moorings in divine participation by a preacher who is a "Diuel," who "disputeth like a subtill Sophister," and who uses beauty to sway his audience as he "cast[s] a mist before their eyes, and beguile[s] them with his subtill fallations."[43] The Devil well knows, Perkins asserts, that the scriptures are the "onely engine for the battery of his kingdom." He seduces aspiring ministers from "eat[ing] the bookes of God" and "digest[ing] them in his understanding" by delighting them with the beauty of non-Christian literature. He warns that "even in Gods church the Diuel works mightily in this way, by stealing away the affections of yong students from the Bible, and ravishing them with delight in the writings of men; for thus he keeps them from the fountaine of truth, that they either fall into error themselves, or be less able to discerne and confute it in others."[44] As John Morgan observes, an individual person's faulty comprehension of the scriptures or the tangential disciplines that contribute to their exegesis "would likely affect only his own chances of salvation. . . . But in a minister this deficiency *created* the failing of ineffective preaching, and thus affected the eternity of the whole congregation."[45]

Unlike How or Dell, however, Perkins does concede that the preacher is permitted to use rhetoric. One of the reasons Christ went into the wilderness was that "he might returne againe with greater authoritie and reuerence to preach the Gospell."[46] Paradoxically, then, the study of eloquence forges the minister's resolve not to be persuaded by its charms, allows him to discern its proper scope, safely filter it, and temperately disseminate it to his congregation. In *Areopagitica*, Milton makes a similar claim about the province of books: "He that can apprehend and consider vice with all her baits and seeming pleasures, and yet abstain, . . . and yet prefer that which is truly better, he is the true warfaring Christian" (*CPW* 2:515). Perkins's "warfaring" reader/preacher does not shy away from the trial of extra-biblical learning and the study of rhetoric, but he recognizes that his eloquence should point, as one of Augustine's signs, to something beyond itself: the transforming Presence of God. The preacher's eloquence becomes one of the most effective signs pointing to God because the preacher himself as creature and sign has been renovated by his participation in the Signified. He is able to present clearly that light to others, as his single transformation efficaciously brings about the regeneration of another through a kind of holy violence.

Thus, much more is at stake for Perkins, How, and Dell than simply the question of whether or not rhetoric ought to be used in the pulpit. Giving assent to Augustine, all seem to argue that the central issue is one's own performance and incarnation in the world as a sign that points to either Christ or Antichrist. The display of human learning in the pulpit appears to be one fulcrum. As Perkins concludes, it is a minister's "dutie to seeke to be as unlike the Diuell as possibly we can," for if we are seduced away from the service of God by satanic performance, "we become euē diuels incarnate."[47] Will one embody the narrative of the Incarnate Son, whose divine participation and performance point to his Father, or will one be subject to a devilish incarnation that undermines Christ's Incarnation and all it entails?

Turning to Milton, we find that he shares Augustine's and Perkins's thoughts on "true eloquence." More like Augustine than he is the separatists How and Dell, Milton is ambivalent about the use of rhetoric in the pulpit. Even though he confesses he is not "utterly untrain'd in those rules which best Rhetoricians have giv'n," Milton decidedly separates himself from the goats, or the "carnal rhetoricians," as Stanley Fish puts it. The poet-preacher declares that "true eloquence" is "none but the serious and hearty love of truth"; for him, the true preacher and reader is one "whose mind so ever is fully possest with a fervent desire to know good things and with dearest charity to infuse the knowledge of them into others" (*Apology against a Pamphlet, CPW* 1:949). As Fish observes, Milton holds to the belief that "eloquence and the love of truth *are* one and the same"; "eloquence is known by its relationship . . . to an inner state."[48]

The unity between linguistic eloquence and this "inner state" to which Fish gestures is derived from Milton's doctrine of participation as well as his philosophical monism. Stephen M. Fallon argues that as early as the divorce tracts (1643–44) Milton is "intent on separating his audience into wise monists and blind dualists," and I suspect that something similar is going on in the *Apology* (1642) as well.[49] As Fallon points out, many of the metaphors that Milton uses in the prose works to argue against dualism are those that depict "outsides-without-insides": husks without kernels, carcasses without souls, customs without meaning. Milton uses this latter example of a ceremonial-outside-without-meaningful-inside to blast the prelates "who are in words [like] the Fathers, but in their deeds the oppugners of the faith" (*CPW* 1:952). For the prelates, outward ceremony through ritual and liturgy is conducive to inward spiritual growth: the outside (body) shapes the inside (soul). Milton's implicit argument throughout the tract is that this perpetuates a dualist aesthetic and spirituality, for their insistence on outward ceremony and liturgy is form without content, words without the Word, and the material without the spiritual. "For the monist," Fallon

observes, "the one substance is both outside and inside."[50] The prelates are rendered by Milton as outsides-without-insides, "Sermon-
actor[s]" instead of "true Sermons"; or, better yet, true preachers are "a
true Poem . . . and patterne of the best and honorablest things" (*CPW*
1:890), like the Son who is the *sermo* of God. Perhaps Milton's desire
for a clergy that are "true Sermons" is akin to Donne's exhortation to
preachers, "Be thou *Verbum* too, A Word, as God was; A Speaking,
and a Doing Word, to his glory, and the edification of others" (*Sermons* 8:52).

Milton's nascent monism in the anti-prelatical tracts allows us
to see that his aesthetics is his metaphysics is also his theology. While
he may at times be inconsistent in his application, this unified vision
underpins his thoughts on the nature and function of language, his
theories about rhetoric and performance, and his praxis of preaching.
Christ is the eloquent "speech" of God, for he is God's "new language"
to humanity (Heb. 1:2); or to recall Paul Ricoeur, Christ is the perfect
"exegesis of God." As will become more evident in subsequent chapters, Milton the talented linguist demonstrates that he is also fluent in
the Son's "new language" of virtue, for he aspires to be God's perfect
exegete in and through his own actions. If the great poet "ought himselfe to bee a true Poem . . . and patterne of the best and honorablest
things" (*CPW* 1:890), then the same holds true for preachers: the faithful preacher is he who bears the mark or "patterne" of the truest "Poem"
or "Sermon": the Incarnation. In the preacher's embodying the narrative of the Word by his practice of virtue, he also functions as God's
eloquent Speech and charitably "infuses" the knowledge of the "good
things" of God's Good Speech into his congregants. In Milton's *De
Doctrina Christiana,* this charitable infusing by the preacher has its
analogue in the creation of Adam. Clarifying his position on a monis-
tic, integrated view of body and soul in the human creature, Milton
states that "the whole man is the soul, and the soul man: a body . . . or
individual substance, animated, sensitive, and rational." When God
breathes life into Adam (Gen. 2:7), we are to understand this breath
not as "a part of the divine essence, nor was it the soul, but a kind of
air or breath of divine virtue, fit for the maintenance of life and reason

and infused into the organic body" (*CPW* 6:318). God is thus the first Preacher who infuses and animates the human body with life and reason, here closely aligned with divine virtue itself, into Adam, his first congregant.

For Milton the beauty of rhetoric and one's performance in the pulpit hinge on the doctrine of participation. Sever that connection, Milton would have us believe, and satanic performance in the pulpit and in the world is all that remains: "Ambiguous words . . . to sound / Or taint integrity" and "calumnious Art / Of counterfeited truth" to hold and entertain our ears (*PL* 5.703–4, 770–71). As David Loewenstein ably demonstrates, part of Milton's multifaceted attack on the Presbyterian ministers in *The Tenure of Kings and Magistrates* (1649) is directed against these "prevaricating Divines" perverting the ends of language by saying one thing and doing another (*CPW* 3:232).[51] Theirs is a sophistical language and politics of equivocation and flux; like Satan they "say and straight unsay." In their rhetorical performances, Milton asks, do preachers bear true witness to the Speech of God, whom the Father calls the "Son of my bosom" and "effectual might," and who has "spok'n as my thoughts are, all / As my Eternal purpose has decreed" (*PL* 3.169–72)? Or, do the preachers dissemble and manipulate "with clov'n tongues of falshood and dissention" (*The Tenure of Kings and Magistrates, CPW* 3:235), and rely on the thunderous "affected zele of thir pulpits" (*History of Britain, CPW* 5:449)? If the former is the case, then what follows is "[b]eatitude past utterance" (*PL* 3.62): blessing, charity, community. If the latter is the case, then what remains is neither eloquence nor, to be clear, speech. To Milton, it *is* nothingness: a saying that is simultaneously an unsaying that cannot even properly be called beauty in the lowercase. It is an illusion, a nonperformance that is a reflection of the void, as we will see in a moment when we will turn our attention to the infernal preachers of hell.

Hearing the sermons of preachers who are satanic dissemblers and nonparticipants produces not the internal fruits of salvation (Rom. 10:13–14); instead, it produces nothingness, for the bellies of the "hungry Sheep" in their congregation are "swoln with wind" and "rank mist"

("Lycidas," 125–26). Milton's attack against the preaching of the Word-less clergy is thus tied to the doctrine of participation, and much more is at stake for him than just a few hours wasted in listening to a bad sermon. To dissemble and deny the fruits of the "good news" in one's preaching is serious business, for "in the seventeenth century, hearing the word of God, even almost in terms of the auditory reception itself, was thought to be crucial to salvation" itself.[52]

The fiery Puritan divine Stephen Denison, whose preaching style apparently approached something akin to theatrical performance, claims that the minister should be a "son of thunder" in order to take full advantage of that hearing. But it was generally acknowledged that even a preacher whose performance lacked such dramatic flair could effect grace in his hearers.[53] Peter Lake adds that many Protestants believed that "[e]ven a carnal and corrupt minister, so long as he preached only the unvarnished word, could transform and convert souls through his preaching."[54] By Lake's account, preaching approaches the status of a sacrament in Protestant theology, for preaching is the "infusion" of grace (recall that Milton's preacher "infuses" the knowledge of "good things") into the receiver. The Word itself transformed the hearer, regardless of the preacher's performance in the pulpit or in his life. Milton would agree that it is one's encounter with "the quick and pearcing word" that "enter[s] to the dividing of their soules" that ultimately transforms the hearer (*The Reason of Church Government, CPW* 1:827). But he would have deep reservations that the way the preacher conducts his life is irrelevant. On the contrary, the preacher's life must be a "true Sermon," and those called to the ministry must always be ministers. As George Herbert puts it, "after a man is once Minister, he cannot agree to come into any house, where he shall not exercise what he is, unless he forsake his plough, and look back."[55] For Herbert and Milton the message of the corrupt minister who does not actively participate in the narrative of the Word is greatly diminished, if not completely compromised; he is a sign that is dangerously free-floating from the Signified to which his life must give testimony. Unite the minister's holy life to the "unvarnished" proclamation of the Word and there exists ineffable power to engender the fruits of holiness and salvation.

Consequently, the point I want to stress here is that these reflections on the proper end of rhetoric are intimately bound not only to a theory of language, but also to a metaphysics and a theology. In the premodern and early modern worlds, someone could not "do" language theory without also "doing" metaphysics; language theory was a venture into both metaphysics and epistemology. Ancient philosophers and language theorists were concerned not only with the verbal structure of language and how a particular utterance gives meaning, but also the philosophy of the mind and soul that understands language and attempts to grasp the reality that language discloses. Reflection on the use of rhetorical theory and human learning in the pulpit thus pivotally implies a metaphysics and, necessarily so for Augustine, Dell, How, Perkins, and Milton, a theology.[56] Satanic language amounts to a desperate beauty without regard to its connection to the Good or the True; it is an external sign unmoored from a correspondingly Good/True/Beautiful Signified, and set adrift upon the void.

If we return to Augustine for a moment as we conclude this section, it is not surprising to see that the doctrine of participation and the wonder of the Incarnation form the core of his metaphysics and theology. These in turn inflect his broader theories of language, his thoughts about rhetorical theory, and his praxis of preaching. Perfectly participating in both the material and spiritual realms, Christ is the Logos in the logos, the union of the spirit and the letter, and the fusion of interior intention and external performance. Consequently, Christ's preaching is a genuine rendering of the essence of God, the reality of the world God created, and the human person's place in it.

The character and unity of Christ reveals for Augustine that the primary purpose of human language, in or out of the pulpit, is to divulge the contents of one mind to another, to expose desires and the will (as in the *Confessions*), or to convey information for the purpose of teaching (as in *On Christian Doctrine*). While Christopher Kirwan asserts that Augustine's general views of language were "mainly unoriginal" and that they followed "a tradition that was already several hundred years old," Kirwan's assessment fails to account for their dynamic theological nuances.[57] Consider this compelling and illuminating passage from *On Christian Doctrine*, in which the bishop of Hippo explicitly argues for an Incarnational theory of language:

> How did He come except that "the Word was made flesh, and dwelt among us"? It is as when we speak. In order that what we are thinking may reach the mind of the listener through fleshly ears, that which we have in mind is expressed in words and is called speech. But our thought is not transformed into sounds; it remains entire in itself and assumes the form of words by means of which it may reach the ears without suffering any deterioration in itself. In the same way the Word of God was made flesh without change that He might dwell among us.[58]

Just as the Mind of God conceived the Eternal Word, whose power is to create through divine speech *ex nihilo* and which descends into the material world by taking on corruptible human flesh without itself being corrupted, so also does entire human thought conceived in the mind "descend" into words that we might utter them through speech. But for what purpose?

Augustine describes Christ as the "Cure" who "received sinners to heal and strengthen them." Just as a physician binds wounds, "so the medicine of Wisdom by taking on humanity is accommodated to our wounds, healing some by contraries and some by similar things." Although Augustine does not make the analogy between human words and the Word explicit in this or the following sections, having already made the connection in the previous section, it is fair that we apply the various aspects of the Incarnation to human words. Consequently, just as Christ is the "Cure" for the sickness of sin, human words have the capability of being curative and restorative. Just as Christ's resurrection demonstrated "how He was willing to give His life for ours when He had power to take it up again," human words have the capacity to serve our fellow human beings in personal sacrifice.[59] Just as God's Word in divine utterance is synonymous with action (a speech-act par excellence), human words should move oneself and others to charitable action.

All these analogies, therefore, congeal into a picture of the church for Augustine, which participates in the Eternal Mind and Word of God: "For the Church 'is His body,' [Eph. 1:23] as apostolic teaching asserts, and it is called His bride. Therefore, He binds His body, which has many members performing diverse offices, in a bond of unity and charity which is, as it were, its health. He exercises it in this world and cleanses it."[60] If Augustinian language consists of signs that point to something other than themselves, then signs must ultimately and covenantally point to God. In the *Enchiridion* Augustine writes, "speech was given to man, not that men might therewith deceive one another, but that one man might make known his thoughts to another. To use speech, then, for the purpose of deception, and not for its appointed end, is a sin."[61] In *Paradise Regained* the sophistical Satan, relying on the "persuasive Rhetoric / That so sleek't his tongue, and won so much on *Eve*" (*PR* 4.4–5), reluctantly compliments Jesus that his inward thoughts and outward speech and action are one and the same. For How and Dell, the use of rhetoric is already tainted with the contagion of participating in the kingdom of Antichrist. For Augustine, Perkins, and Milton, the preacher who uses language and rhetoric deceitfully is unambiguously "satanic." His is the language of separation and exile: from knowledge of himself and his thoughts, from the congregation to whom he preaches, and from knowledge and participation in God. But more profoundly, satanic language denies on a fundamental level the Incarnation and all that follows according to Christian theology: healing, hope, unity, charity. It is the word without content, which, finally in Augustinian terms, must be "no-thing-ness"; it is simultaneously a saying and an unsaying. This, we find, is precisely what the demons accomplish as they deliver their own sermons on the Name of God, and it is to their hellish exegesis and language of exile that we now turn.

Wittgenstein in Hell: The Infernal Prophesying of God's Name

Despite the ambivalence of preachers toward rhetoric and human learning, the structure of the sermon by learned clergy was modeled, more often than not and with modification, on the classical rhetorical tropes and divisions. Jameela Lares observes that in his *De Formandis Concionibus Sacris* (1553; English translation, 1577), Andreas Gerardus Hyperius (1511–64) almost singlehandedly formulated what would become the standard parts of a typical Protestant sermon: reading the text, invocation, introduction (*exordium*), announcement of the subject and divisions (*propositio sive divisio*), treatment of the subject (*confirmatio*), argumentation (*confutatio*), and conclusion (*peroratio*).[62] Furthermore, Hyperius had regulated how the *confirmatio* fell into distinct categories or sermon "types," derived from 2 Timothy 3:16–17: doctrinal (to teach correct doctrine), redargutive (to reprove incorrect doctrine), and correction and instruction (to urge virtuous action and habits). Hyperius adds a fifth type that is important, as we will see, for Milton's demonic preachers: consolation, as derived from Romans 15:4.[63] Of these sermon types, Lares argues that Milton most often prefers the redargutive and consolatory sermons. The latter, she observes, is "present in *Paradise Lost,* even from the beginning, as a counterpoint to correction, and the epic ends on at least a provisional note of consolation."[64] As William Perkins states, "Our dutie is, to labour to bee setled and assured in our conscience that God is our God: for first in this assurance is the foundation of all true comfort."[65] Consolation for Perkins derives from the Name of Names as the secure anchor of hope as one navigates the troubling waters of spiritual existence.

The demons, however, have lost that anchor. Despite their desperate search for it, there is no real comfort for the spiritual reality they face. The "infernal councilors are *not* attempting to investigate reality," John M. Steadman emphatically writes, "but to argue the merits or demerits of a proposed course of action. . . . Political orators rather than philosophers, they are concerned less with knowledge than with persuasion and dissuasion."[66] Steadman is only partially right: the demonic orators are certainly concerned about persuading their peers toward a course of action, and there is no question that politics resides in their speeches. Where Steadman errs is in his assertion that the devils are not concerned with "reality." Conversely, in this section I argue that the demons must come to grips with the novel, tortured reality that confronts them in their separation from the anchor of the Name of Names *before* they can decide what to do next.

These angels are newly fallen, tossing upon the furious waves of hell's lake, licked by the "livid flames" and "o'erwhelmed / With Floods and Whirlwinds of tempestuous fire" (*PL* 1.182, 76–77). The anguish of this new reality and their desire for comfort are what motivate Satan to gather his cohort together in the first place, even though his brave rhetoric masks his pain: "So spake th' Apostate Angel, though in pain, / Vaunting aloud, but rackt with deep despair" (1.125–26). God's superiority and Satan's own pain and exile are thus the subtext of the stated purpose for the meeting: "by what best way, / Whether of open War or covert guile, / We now debate; who can advise, may speak" (2.40–42). But the speeches that follow are not merely political speeches, as many have contended, and to characterize them only as such is too neat and neglects the fact that with remarkable consistency Milton does not think about politics without first thinking about theology. There is no secular realm for Milton, no space behind God's back, and no avenue of human making that his God does not have a prior claim upon. The limited political reading of the demonic orations dismisses the importance of Milton's theological imagination, ignores the metaphysical implications of the angels' severed language and proposed actions, and neglects the vision of justice and redemption that impels Milton as the poet-preacher.

As Joad Raymond pointedly argues, "Milton binds together doctrine and narrative with an intensity that is unique, and to lose sight of the connection between his fictional imperatives and the divine truths he intended to impart through them is to diminish the force and ambition of his poetry."[67] The infernal speeches are indeed political in nature. But each political solution that is offered in the speeches is predicated upon, by necessity, some prior assessment of God's character and capabilities. Their orations, then, are speeches about God *first*, and they become political only secondarily. Their political solutions advocating open war, possible redemption, continued exile, or guile and diversion are responses to the new reality of their pain and fallen existence. The qualification and quality of that existence are thus determined by a prior attempt to comprehend and offer instruction on the nature of God. In short, they are like the thousands of sermons delivered in the early modern period whose fundamental questions are, "What is the nature of God?" and "How shall one live as a result?"

In the process of their speaking, these ministers attempt to redefine and reconstruct reality, and the key to their being able to accomplish this is in their fallen understanding of that which had previously grounded their reality and language: the Name of Names. Satanic semiotics—the loss of the Sacred Grammar—allows them to go on, "therapeutically" we might say, as they play language games that empty God's Name of its metaphysical ultimacy and remove the Logos from the logos. In the infernal sermons that ensue, they "say and straight unsay" the Name; they are intended to console their chthonian congregation through the "cure" of language alone (recall Augustine), to determine the nature of their existence and God's character, and to move them to action and application. Consequently, of all the sermon types, the devilish preachers are most given to the consolatory mode wherein language itself *is* the only consolation.

The infernal ministers are gathered together in a "Synod of Gods" (2.391), and though we cannot seamlessly equate preaching and prophesying with the many duties of a synod, there are significant overlaps. In Milton's time, synods had different judicial functions and administrative powers; elected members delivered sermons, composed confessions of faith, regulated policy, settled disputes, and discussed, debated, and voted on issues of doctrine.[68] A 1642 pamphlet by "G. T." refers to the synod as the most reasonable, egalitarian, and "hopefull Remedie of our distempers." To settle disputes, G. T. rejects the notion of "implicit faith," where ecclesial authority is blindly followed, the prohibition of disputation, the doctrine of universal salvation ("that every man may be sav'd in his owne Religione"), and reliance on the church fathers or previous councils. He advises that synods should stay out of political matters and concern themselves only with "the Doctrine of Faith and manners"; positions on doctrinal issues should be presented in ordered speeches, moderated by "some kind of President," for the general purpose of "the illustration of Truth, the conservation and propagation of it, extirpation of errors, the peace of the Church, whence exists the glory of God, and the eternall salvation of man." Synods are places of sacred trust, and G. T. would have every door to such places emblazoned with gold letters that read, "*Let no man enter here, but he that is studious of Truth and peace; may God himself place his Angel with a flaming sword at the entrance of this Paradise where divine Truth and the lovely Concord of the Church is consulted about, to keepe back all those who are otherwise minded. Amen.*"[69] But G. T.'s hope in synods is checked by Milton's distaste for them in *Eikonoklastes*, at least insofar as they are comprehended into a national church, for synods are "liable to the greatest fraud" with little chance of finding a "redress of evil, but an increase rather" (*CPW* 3:535). Thus, it is with great purpose that Milton calls this devilish congregation a synod.

These infernal ministers are certainly "*otherwise minded*" and not given to a "redress of evil," as they deliver a series of redargutive and consolatory sermons in quick succession. We might say that Beëlzebub, Satan's second-in-command, acts as a kind of moderator, or perhaps G. T.'s "President," for the ministerial panel. His penultimate sermon, "first devis'd / By *Satan*, and in part propos'd" (2.379–80), sets up hell's senior minister to deliver the keynote address. Intriguingly, the gathering of this synod and the delivery of sermons by a panel of ministers bear a striking resemblance to the highly controversial assemblies of nonconformist Puritan ministers during the prophesying movements of the late sixteenth and early seventeenth centuries, the dynamics of which persisted in some form among the dissenting sects well after the Restoration. Prophesying throughout the period caused a political and ecclesial uproar of which Milton would no doubt have been mindful as he represents the demonic council scene.

In their Elizabethan roots, the prophesying assemblies tore at the fabric of the queen's church, challenged the reasons of church government, and became a vital part of the radical Puritan underground in the reigns of James I and Charles I. They modeled what would become the ideological core of not only the Presbyterian contingent in the 1640s, against whom Milton leveled some of his polemical attacks, but also the private meetings of dissenting sects like the Baptists and Quakers during the Interregnum and immediately following the Restoration. With the return of the monarchy and the established national church, these private meetings and prophesyings were actively prosecuted under the Clarendon Code. We may consider the demons to be dissenters from heaven's realm; thus, we would do well to explore the nature of their dissent, as well as the political and ecclesial nuances of the demonic council scene within this charged historical framework.[70]

In the late summer and early fall of 1576, the Puritan Thomas Wood exchanged a series of letters with the Earls of Warwick and Leicester, both important and influential allies to the Puritans. The purpose of these letters was to dissuade the earls from following through with the queen's wishes to censure the "godly exercises" of ministers throughout England. To Wood, these exercises provided ministers with a "benefitt . . . the like whereof were never erected in England before." When Leicester responds (19 August 1576), the earl defends his many past actions in support of the Puritans, but expresses reserve that "there be and have bene some places of exercises used that I doe mislike, and some over curious ministers also that give cause of the breach of the unity of our Church." Leicester having expressed this reservation, and fearing that the earls would not give their full support of the continuance of the exercises, Wood threateningly responds (7 September 1576):

> When [the exercises] are stopd, perseqution is like to followe which some looked for long agoe and wilbe as ready to suffer for the truth as our young Popes wilbe to persecute, who charge those good men to be troublers of the peace of the Church, where indeed it is the byshopes their accusers whom the Prince of this world hath bewitched with such welth and pufte up with such pride as they will not be content to submitt themselves to God's word in all points, but will have it to give place to their traditions or rather to Antichrist's.[71]

Even before the fall of 1576, when Wood writes his letters, the exercises had stirred up controversy. In 1574, Archbishop Matthew Parker ordered Bishop John Parkhurst "to suppress those vain prophesyings," an alternate name for the exercises, in Norwich.[72] Translated to Canterbury in early 1576 and summoned before the royal presence at the end of that year, Archbishop Edmund Grindal was ordered by Elizabeth to convey to his bishops the "utter suppression" of all "learned exercises and conferences" and for the "abridging" of the number of preachers.[73] In early December 1576, Grindal wrote a lengthy letter to Elizabeth refusing to follow her order: "I am forced, with all humility, and yet plainly, to profess, that I cannot with safe conscience, and without the offense of the majesty of God, give assent to the suppressing of the said exercises."[74] Grindal, not surprisingly, was immediately suspended and fell from royal favor. By 1577, the queen herself stepped in and suppressed the exercises in the southern provinces. In a final letter (undated 1577) to Earls of Warwick and Leicester, Wood reacts with profound sadness and prophetic judgment. To him and many others the censures represent "not only a great rejoysing to all God's enemies but such a service to Sathan as unles the whole religion shold be overthrown a greater could not be done." He writes with indignation, "this is but the beginning of greater plagues, whereof the stopping of the course of Christ's Gosple is a most fearfull signe."[75]

What were these "godly exercises" that caused so much trouble, that led to the silencing of thousands of preachers and the altercation between the queen and her archbishop, and that threatened to split the Elizabethan church apart? What, finally, would Milton's interest be in them many decades removed from the controversy? Historian Patrick Collinson, the most noted authority on the exercises, admits that the ecclesiastical record on the proceedings of these exercises, or "prophesyings," is scant. The prophesyings were modeled on a method of biblical study that many English preachers, having returned from Marian exile, adopted from churches on the Continent; their purpose was to bring out the "true" sense of the text by inviting several clergy to comment on the same passage of scripture. In England they served the crucial functions of educating the laity in the Reformed religion and educating the clergy on doctrinal issues. Collinson cites the Leicester minister John Ireton who in a letter (May 1598) to Anthony Gilby called these meetings "the universities of the pore ministries," which testifies to the woeful state of formal ministerial education early in Elizabeth's reign.[76] Ministers derived scriptural authority for them from 1 Corinthians 14:29–30: "Let the prophets speak two or three, and let the other judge. . . . For ye may all prophesy one by one, that all may learn and all may be comforted." This is a strange proof-text, given that this section of Paul's epistle deals with the *restriction* of the speaking of *tongues* in the church. Nevertheless, the prophesyings were intended to edify all those present.

The proceedings, many times taking place in the market towns and open to large crowds of the laity, had assumed by Grindal's time a common pattern. A senior minister, sometimes with the consent of the bishop and often without it, would call together a session. He acted as moderator for a panel of three to four preachers who took turns preaching a sermon on the same text of scripture. If an audience was present, the moderator would ask if any learned man, who undoubtedly would have his own bible open in his lap, wished to agree or disagree with the exposition of the text. The senior minister would then deliver a sermon of his own, after which the ministers would disperse to eat a meal and to discuss privately issues of doctrine with each other, and lay audiences would hotly debate what they had heard. According to Collinson, the practice helped to promote "a unity of belief based on instruction and assent rather than on ecclesiastical authority."[77] The prophesying model thus reinforced nonconformity.

Herein lay the threat to the Elizabethan church. The prophesyings were often the sites of controversy and scandal as much as they were places of edification. Moreover, in Scotland the exercises were seen as presbyteries; thus, when the prophesyings began to flourish in England in the 1570s, there was already a common assumption that these exercises were presbyteries "in embryo."[78] From these Scottish exercises had matured full-blown classes and synods, which constituted a genuine threat to episcopacy. Collinson reminds us, however, that the English exercises still maintained a sense of hierarchy. They were frequently convened by the bishops, who in turn required parishioners to attend; furthermore, the exercises were often moderated by the same distinguished clergymen. The potential threat loomed too large, however, for Elizabeth to tolerate, and enemies of the more extreme Puritans colored the exercises with insinuations of enthusiasm, even though for the most part the prophesyings were strictly moderated.[79] Preaching licenses were revoked, preachers were silenced, and Elizabeth commanded that any who continued in the proceedings were to be imprisoned.

These actions did not, however, have the intended effect. By the 1580s, these prophesyings had gone underground, meeting in clandestine synods, and remained so well into the next century. There is evidence to suggest that this model of prophesying persisted in the County of Suffolk as late as 1636, when Laudian innovations against the centrality of preaching were in full rigor.[80] By the early 1640s, the exercises, in whatever form they had assumed, would have been associated with the various dissenting groups working outside sanctioned ecclesiastical authority.[81]

As Christopher Hill points out, preaching, followed by public discussion and debate, was a standard sectarian position: "worship was not a matter of passively hearing the Word preached by a learned minister, but participation by the congregation after a gifted member had opened up the subject for discussion."[82] Certainly by the time of the Restoration, after more than a decade of proliferation, the exegetical model would have been well established among dissenting congregational sects like the Baptists, Quakers, and Seekers generally, who scorned the return of ecclesiastical conformity. Milton's contemporary and New Model Army chaplain, William Dell, speaks for many who opposed the power of parish clergy and the uniformity of worship, reasoning that prophesying was "a notable means to keep error out of the church," for the substance of the sermon was up for debate or correction from the congregation, and anyone could confront error.[83] This ideal was to be found most radically in Quaker meetings, where anyone prompted by the Inner Light was entitled to preach, encourage, correct, or rebuke. The Inner Light and the divine authority it brings belong equally to all. At the beginning of his ministry, George Fox claims that "the Lord God hath opened to me by his invisible power how that every man was enlightened by the divine light of Christ; and I saw it shine through all."[84] The need for a professional clergy is no more, for God is equally accessible to the poor, the itinerant, and the uneducated. England could indeed become the nation "of Prophets, of Sages, and of Worthies" that Milton desired (*Areopagitica, CPW* 2:554). Milton's prose, however, appears to be silent regarding the historical prophesyings plaguing the Elizabethan church. But it seems improbable that Milton would *not* have been aware of them, given Elizabeth's suspension of an archbishop of Canterbury who championed Puritan preachers. Moreover, Milton had long envisioned and prepared to enter the ministry of the state-sanctioned church; he had been schooled in English church history and the Church of England's shifting theologies; and he was sympathetic to Presbyterianism in the early 1640s, as well as to many of the nonconformist sects during and after the Interregnum, many of which adopted the practice of prophesying in some form. At the Restoration, Milton's generation witnessed a similar royal squelching of nonconformist preaching. On 24 August 1662, thousands of nonconformist ministers in the realm were deprived of their licenses and ejected for failing to adhere publicly to the strictures outlined in the Act of Uniformity.[85] Sectarian preachers had no public place in Restoration England, nor officially did they have a private place after the institution of the Clarendon Code, though unofficially sects continued to meet in a burgeoning underground.

In *Eikonoklastes* (1649) Milton writes, "I never knew that time in *England,* when men of truest Religion were not counted Sectaries" (*CPW* 3:348). The fallen angels are sectaries and separatists of the most radical sort. But as we will see, we need to exercise caution about assigning Milton's latitudinous praise of the sectaries, as upholders of "truest Religion," to the infernal preachers. Significantly, Milton describes Lucifer's refusal to sleep, wherein "All but the unsleeping eyes of God" close at twilight in order to participate in divine rest, as "dissent" (*PL* 5.647, 679). This refusal to participate in rest and "communion sweet" marks the beginning of the rebels' violent breach and initiates their fall (637). The exaltation of the Son, the anointing and granting of the name and title Messiah by the Father, awakens the "envy" and "Deep malice" that prevent Lucifer from sleeping (662, 666). While this restless angel indicates to the unnamed Beëlzebub that he takes offense at the "new Laws thou see'st impos'd" (679), the true source of his dissent from sleep is his inability to accept that another has been granted a name and performative role that he desires: the Anointed One who represents and speaks for God. The War in Heaven begins with a dissent from the doctrine of participation by a radical preacher who does not embody and charitably "infuse" the "good things" of God's Good Speech to his hearers. Instead, he is a preacher who "infus'd / Bad influence into th' unwary breast[s]" of "the Congregation call'd" together in assembly (694–95, 766).

Like many dissenters in Milton's turbulent age, these sectaries declare their freedom to read and interpret God's Word without political interference and against the ecclesial monopoly, or, as the fallen angel puts it, the "Prison of his Tyranny who Reigns" (2.59). But their declaration of freedom is a hermeneutical assault on God's Word, as they question the meaning of the Anointed One and his semiotic relation to the divine Text of which he is a part and expression. In his *Gangraena* Thomas Edwards takes issue with the "anti-scripturist" sects who cast doubt on the infallibility of God's Word: "right Reason is the rule of Faith," they assert, "and we are to believe the Scriptures, and the Doctrine of the Trinity, Incarnation, and Resurrection, so far as we see them agreeable to reason, and no further."[86] This first dissenting angel, an "anti-scripturist" of the highest caliber, appeals directly to reason and liberty of conscience as he questions God's decree and the Son's status. The "Orders and Degrees" of God, he persuades, "Jar not with liberty. . . . / Who can in reason then or right assume / Monarchy over such as live by right / His equals, if in power and splendor less, / In freedom equal?" (5.792–97). Gary S. De Krey comments that "arguments for conscience," advocated by many sectarians in opposition to the binding of crown and ecclesial authority, "became a wedge that loosened or uncoupled the nexus between prince and priest, and between magistrate and minister, that had been fundamental to English Protestantism since the 1530s."[87]

Lucifer's subjecting the exaltation of the Anointed One to interpretation occurs in spite of the Father's eternal "Decree, which unrevok'd shall stand" (5.602). This decree, the scripture or text that Satan reads and "reasonably" questions, is the Father's proclamation that the

Son, who is the "Effulgence of my Glorie" and "in whose face invisible is beheld / Visibly, what by Deity I am," shall reign as "Vice-gerent" (6.680–83; 5.609). The Protestant preacher William Ames writes that any decree of God "is his determinate purpose of effecting all things by his almighty Power, and according to his counsel. . . . In the decree of God there appeareth his constancy, truth, and faithfulness. . . . Every *Decree* of God is eternall."[88] God's decree — his "speech" — is also an expression of his character and essence. In his dissent from participation in divine rest, Satan claims the hermeneutical authority to read the "texts" of God's essence: his Name, and the visible expression of it in the Son who is the "exegesis of God."

In John 17:6 Jesus prays to the Father and declares, "I have manifested thy name" to the disciples entrusted to him. As Michael Lieb observes, the Son occupies a paradoxical position as both the expression of an essence that cannot be known and the performative revelation and visible manifestation of that essence. The Son "embodies the mystery of an existence which he reveals in order to let us know that it may not be revealed," yet his performance in the world proclaims "the fact that the 'I AM' does indeed have a real identity."[89] That "real identity" was first revealed to Moses on Sinai in what F. S. Donns calls "the pinnacle of theistic insight": הוהי, or YHWH, "I AM THAT I AM," or "I WILL BE WHAT I WILL BE."[90] The declaration of God's Name signifies self-existence beyond all temporal limits, eternity itself. "God's self, his real person, is concentrated in his name," and "is a sign of his real presence in the midst of his people."[91] In his *Commentaries on the Last Four Books of Moses* John Calvin writes that in this Name "God attributes to himself alone divine glory, because he is self-existent and therefore eternal; and thus gives being and existence to every creature. Nor does he predicate of himself anything common, or shared by others; but he claims for himself eternity as peculiar to God alone."[92] As Lieb observes, the theological tradition affirms that God's Name is not only the perfect expression of his timeless existence and eternal essence, but also his future promises. This is a dual signification that early modern commentators on the Name of God, such as Henry Ainsworth, Matthew Poole, and Milton, pick up on.[93]

Consequently, Lucifer's questioning and rejection of God's de-cree and apodictic government through his Son limit God's freedom to choose and open up a critical metaphysical, theological, and linguistic fissure. A satanic hermeneutics of flux enters, one based on the liberty of a dissenting, secular conscience and the freedom to "create" a new poli-tics of reading and a metaphysics and theology of language that is sev-ered from the "constant," "true," and "faithful" essence of God that Ames describes.[94] Milton may be the champion of dissent, but not when its economy seeks to drain God of his authority and to strip him of his pre-eminence in order to purchase liberty. Thomas Edwards observes that "the first time we read of Sathans making use of this plea of Liberty, in his Instruments and his Ministers, is in *2 Pet.* 2.19. where the Apostle shewes the false Teachers that brought in the damnable heresies, did tell them of liberty, *while they promise them liberty.*"[95] This false teacher and minister, theatrically thundering in a "bold discourse without con-trol," promises liberty and "Had audience" (*PL* 5.803–4). In that audi-ence, however, is the faithful Abdiel, who, "with constant mind," de-nounces Satan's rantings as an "impious rage" (845, 902). In his banter with Satan at the start of the War in Heaven, Abdiel identifies him-self as a dissenter among the dissenting, declaring, "I alone / Seem'd in thy World erroneous to dissent / From all: my Sect thou seest." Abdiel recognizes the trap that this satanic fissure presents, hidden below the passionate discourses of liberty and private conscience. Satan's fervent plea for sectarian liberty is slavery in disguise: "This is servitude, / To serve th' unwise, or him who hath rebell'd / Against his worthier . . . / Thyself not Free, but to thyself enthrall'd" (6.178–81). Like Milton, Abdiel holds fast to the sect of "truest Religion" that affirms that one's highest liberty is in "Faith" and subjection to the "Piety to God" (143–47). In *Of True Religion* (1673) Milton perhaps has this episode in mind as he ponders further the nature of dissent. While error always creeps in, God will surely pardon those who exercise genuine faith in discerning the scriptures for themselves. Dissent is to be tolerated, Mil-ton argues, as long as those who "profess to set the Word of God only before them as the Rule of faith and obedience; and use all diligence and sincerity of heart, by reading, by learning, by study, by prayer for Illumination of the holy Spirit, to understand the Rule and obey it" (*CPW* 8:423–24). Any form of dissent that argues differently is to be dissented from, and this is the point that Abdiel makes in parlé with Satan before battle: "I alone / Seemd in thy World erroneous to dissent / From all," he recounts, but now "my Sect thou seest, now learn too late / How few sometimes may know, when thousands err" (6.145–48).

Satan reveals that he once thought this piety, divine rest, and heavenly service to be equal to "Liberty"; now, however, his sect of dissenting angels deems it "sloth" to be "train'd up in Feast and Song" (166–67). From his perspective the heavenly angels do not engage in the great deeds of active reading and interpreting. God's decrees and "new Laws"—the expressions of his essence and character—restrict that liberty, and this is especially jarring to the rebel, who sees himself "In freedom equal" to the Son. As "Vice-gerent," however, the Son has the ultimate freedom of the Father to make decrees on the Father's behalf because he is the "Bright effluence of bright essence increate" (3.6). Satan's questioning the Father's decree is both an attack on the Father's Name and Presence, and an attack on the exalted Son who is the Father's performance and the Logos in the logos. Moreover, Satan's attack is mounted against the Son who possesses the Father's infinite freedom to read without interruption. As the Father's Vice-gerent, his eyes, too, shall be "unsleeping" as they ceaselessly rove over the abundant text of creation. Anti-scripturists all, the demons of Satan's sect embrace the restless hermeneutical freedom of individual conscience, and their enactment of that freedom continues (chronologically) in Book 2 where God's Name becomes the "text" that all the infernal preachers exegete to similar ends. As we turn to their sermons, we find that they "say and straight unsay" the Name of God in an attempt to secure their dissenting freedom to read God's essence, question his Presence as the infallible and inscrutable ground of reality, assail the Son who is his Good Speech, and thereby "create" their own language of preaching and a culture of violence severed from Transcendence.

For Moloch, the first infernal preacher of this prophesying assembly of divines, the Name has been interpreted as both the "Torturer" and the "fierce Foe" (2.64, 78). The first name suggests that Moloch is actually exegeting two "texts": not only the Name of God, but also the pain of his own body. We must remember how novel and overwhelming the sensation of pain is for these fallen angels; it defines the reality they face and the culture they inhabit. "[W]hat can be worse," he asks, "[t]han to dwell here, driv'n out from bliss, condemn'd / In this abhorred deep to utter woe; / Where pain of unextinguishable fire / Must exercise us without hope of end [?]" (85–89). Hell's crucible of suffering drives Moloch to disregard some of the rhetorical rules; as a sermonist, he skips the introduction (*exordium*) to move directly to the announcement of his subject (*propositio*), the treatment of the subjects of war and the pain of hell (*confirmatio*), and the removal of objections (*confutatio*). To many sermon theorists the *confirmatio*, or treatment of the subject, is the most vital part of the sermon, but without properly preparing an audience in the *exordium*, the preacher runs the risk of losing his audience before he even begins.

As a malevolent "son of thunder," however, Moloch prefers verbal combat and relies more on the ferocity of his own figure and thunderous delivery. Consolation for their pain, Moloch asserts, is to be found in aggression and intimidation, and his language reflects his participation in a culture of violence; consequently, his exegesis of the Name is also his own performance, reflecting the unity of form and content of the *kerygma*. The narrator describes him as the "Scepter'd King" who "Stood up, the strongest and fiercest Spirit / That fought in Heav'n; now fiercer by despair," and he wastes no time in stating his thesis and admitting his lack of eloquence: "My sentence is for open War: Of Wiles, / More unexpert, I boast not: them let those / Contrive who need, or when they need, not now" (43–55, 51–53). The treatment (*confirmatio*) of Moloch's text is one of "negative consolation" whose purpose "shew[s] that either there is no evil at all, or that it is not so great, or so unavoidable," as William Chappell describes.[96] Thus Moloch, whose "trust was with th'Eternal to be deem'd / Equal in strength," minimizes the threat (46–47). Striving for too much eloquence is a waste of time for Moloch; it is a delay tactic and an exercise characterized by weakness; his *confutatio* thus begins immediately, blended with the *confirmatio*, and continues throughout his sermon. What if the way is difficult? Ascent to their "native seat" is their "proper motion" (75–76). What if we provoke more wrath? Nothing can be worse than our current pain (85–92). What if we are destroyed? "[W]hat doubt we to incense / His utmost ire? which to the highth enrag'd / Will either quite consume us, and reduce / To nothing this essential, happier far / Than miserable to have eternal being" (94–98). The Torturer is the Foe, and he advises that they can gain consolation only through attempting "Revenge" (105). Consolation is to be found in the application (war) of his exegesis of a name that lacks any sense of eternity or omnipotence. His sermon is delivered, and the *peroratio* (conclusion) is found in his questioning their divine substance, which, if it "cannot cease to be" then they "by proof . . . feel / Our power sufficient to disturb his Heav'n" (100–102). Despite the comfort he offers in this hope, Moloch concludes with a frowning face (106), an image that probably is mirrored in the faces of his assembly as well.

Moloch's lack of eloquence is juxtaposed against Belial's calm demeanor, and Belial delivers the lengthiest sermon. He is the sophistical preacher whose "Tongue / Dropt Manna" and who could "make the worse appear / The better reason" (112–14). Belial at least makes attempts to address his audience in his *exordium* "O Peers" (119), a strategy that singly displaces Moloch's impressive figure and bellicose delivery, but we get the feeling that underlying Belial's whole sermon strategy is an extended *exordium*. Belial makes it clear that unlike Moloch he will not use intimidation. Instead, he will appeal to fellowship and his fellow sufferers' reason. His *confirmatio* reveals that his speech begins as a redargutive sermon, employed to correct the "doctrine" that Moloch's sermon expounded. Moloch's exegesis of the Name promised revenge; Belial's exegesis is full of questions without answers.

Interestingly, Belial is the most agnostic and therefore the most "reverential" of the demons in his exegesis of the Name. God is the "Enemy," the "Almighty Victor," "angry Foe," "Conqueror," and "Supreme Foe" (137, 144, 152, 208, 216). The seeming deference he pays in "Almighty Victor" grows not out of respect or awe, but out of his dubious knowledge of the extent of God's power to inflict even more pain. God's Name is thus the seat of nothing more than potential pain, and the uncertainty of the degree of that pain is reflected throughout the sermon by questions: What revenge can we possibly extol on an "Impregnable" fortress (129–42)? Will God even grant our destruction if we fail (146–59)? Is this place the worst punishment God can deliver to us (162–74)? What if God has only partially bestowed his wrath (174–85)? Open war? Not for Belial. The weight of these questions is his strategy; his sermon is intended, paradoxically, to move his audience to inaction—a suffocating paralysis. He switches his redargutive tact to one of consolation. But where Moloch offers negative consolation, attempting to minimize the power of the Name, Belial offers positive consolation. As William Chappell comments, the "Positive good tends to that, that if it cannot remove the evill of punishment (as sometimes it cannot) yet it may . . . make it tolerable."[97] Clearly, Belial ends his sermon with Chappell's "positive" consolation: "This is now / Our doom; which if we can sustain and bear, / Our Supreme Foe in time may remit / His anger . . . / . . . / This horror will grow mild, this darkness light" (208–20). What is Belial's *peroratio* and application? A deflated gesture toward "ignoble ease, and peaceful sloth" (227). This sloth is the outcome of their liberty; far from the divine rest that Satan and his cronies deemed a servility born of sloth, this existence is characterized, ironically, by restlessness: "Not peace," as the narrator clarifies (228).

The third infernal preacher is Mammon and his sermon is the shortest—odd, given his penchant for luxurious excess. His exegesis of the Name emphasizes God as king: "Heav'n's Lord supreme," "envied Sovran," and "Heav'n's all-ruling Sire" (236, 244, 264). But God is a king not worthy of serving; he is a tyrant who commands subjection and imposes "Strict Laws" (241). Any service offered to a tyrant amounts to extortion and "servile Pomp" (257); if they return to heaven they are doomed to conformity, uttering "warbl'ed Hymns" and "Forc't Halleluiahs" (242–43)—drawing a picture of God beyond that of just a political king—against the dictates of conscience. For Mammon there is no place in heaven for them "unless Heav'n's Lord supreme / We overpower" (236–37). Rather than risk war and incur wrath, the application that Mammon suggests in his exegesis is that they appropriate the kingly names for themselves: fashion the kingdom of hell to rival heaven.

While God's throne in heaven is obscured with the darkness of thick clouds, hell's throne will be brilliant with the reflected light of precious gems and the gilded shimmer of gold. Mammon, the "least erected Spirit that fell," is in fact the one responsible for erecting their grandiose underworld whose temple-like description extends for more than twenty lines (1.703–30). But Milton undermines its lustrous exterior with a single phrase when he describes it as an "ascending pile" (722). This indicates not only that their temple is a confused heap, but that it is a scatological nightmare, for the *OED* cites hemorrhoids as one possible early modern connotation for "pile." The demons "Rifl'd the bowels of thir mother Earth" and "Op'n'd into the Hill a spacious wound" in order for the work to be accomplished (687, 689). Like Satan's "calumnious Art" that in the end is all breath and no substance, through their "wondrous Art" Mammon and his crew manage to raise "like an Exhalation" what can only be likened to a dung pile poised to fall (5.770; 1.703, 711). "What we see here," Stanley Fish correctly asserts, "is the piling up of signs—lighting effects, tall structures made of diamond and gold—that strive to pass themselves off as signifieds, that present themselves not as the theater of glory but as the real thing."[98] Mammon builds on this precarious foundation in a sermon that makes attempts at consolation as well. He uses positive consolation to encourage his listeners to "raise / Magnificence" from the "hidden lustre" of hell (2.271–73), and he uses negative consolation to minimize the pain: "Our torments also may in length of time / Become our Elements, these piercing Fires / As soft as now severe, our temper chang'd / Into their temper" (274–77). Mammon's double consolation wins the favor of all those present as his sermon is met with riotous applause.

Beëlzebub, who in rising "[d]rew audience and attention still as Night," steps in as moderator of the infernal prophesying (308). His *exordium* is formal as he reminds his audience of their due right: "Thrones and Imperial Powers, off-spring of Heav'n / Ethereal Virtues" (310–11). In his *confirmatio* he corrects (redargutive mode) the misguided "doctrine" of Moloch and approves the doctrine espoused by the exegesis of both Belial and Mammon: God is the "Conqueror" who will not be defeated, war is pointless, and the devils can build their own empire. But this senior minister appeals to another Name of God, even though he does not say it. Beëlzebub's strategy is to refocus, through a *digressio,* the attention from God as King, Foe, and Conqueror to God as Creator of "another World, the happy seat / Of some new Race call'd Man" (347–48). So sure is he that his plan to either "waste his whole Creation" or "[s]educe them to our Party" (365–68) will prove profitable, that he bypasses the *confutatio*—there are no objections to answer. His sermon, too, tends toward consolation and his *peroratio* moves his audience, as "joy / Sparkl'd in all thir eyes" (387–88). It also serves as a platform of praise for the one who will accept the hazardous quest; here Beëlzebub, in cahoots with Satan (378–80), sets up the senior preacher to deliver the final sermon and accept the challenge.

Satan's exegesis of God's Name never takes place; after four sermons on the Name, Satan sidesteps it completely. God has been successfully exegeted into virtual nonexistence. The senior minister's sermon is one long *digressio* as he describes the various dangers of the journey ahead of him, only to refocus the attention on his glory and translation to hell's "anointed one": "But I should ill become this Throne, O Peers, / And this Imperial Sov'ranty, adorn'd / With splendor . . . if aught propos'd / . . . / . . . could deter / Mee from attempting" (445–50). His *exordium,* like his predecessor's, is formal. But despite his appeal to parity in the "us" of line 432 and the appeal to "O Peers" in line 445, the narrator twice refers to him as a monarch (428, 467). This prophesying meeting is not as Presbyterian in nature as we might first construe, and Satan reveals himself to be not a minister among the many in this synod, but a kind of bullying bishop, a "*New Presbyter*" who is "but *Old Priest* writ Large" ("On the New Forcers of Conscience," 20). The dreaded speaker rises after his sermon "and prevented all reply" (*PL* 2.467), perhaps having learned his lesson from Abdiel's vociferous earlier dissent.[99] Relying on his prodigious figure and terrifying tongue to silence his fellows, he assumes an authority that actually prevents participation and manages to "unsay" not only God's Name, but also the sermons that have preceded his. His presence, his monstrous bulk, his heroic exploits are the new scriptures, the only legitimate texts that the demons are now permitted to read, a point that we will explore more thoroughly in chapter 4. For the moment, we should question what kind of "reading" this is. True, Satan allows the demons the freedom to read their new scriptures; however, when he menacingly arises and "prevented all reply," Satan paradoxically denies his assembly the freedom and privilege of interpreting them. But how it is that one could read without also interpreting?

As absurd as this notion of reading sounds, it is precisely this paradigm that may have prompted some of the prophesyings in the first place, as many nonconformist Puritans sought the freedom not just to read, but to interpret the scriptures apart from state control. Consequently, it is the very reading paradigm in which Milton finds himself at the outset of the turbulent 1640s that led subsequently to the rise of a radical readership claiming unfettered access to scripture, and that resulted in the influx of "mechanic" preachers who typically were not university trained like the professional clergy.[100] Satan's denying the demons participation, his bolstering his own authority, and his refusing to allow readers of his scriptures to be also interpreters of them are the very things for which Milton caustically upbraids the prelates in *The Reason of Church Government*. Milton champions the Apostle Peter's proclamation that all believers are a "royal priesthood" (1 Pet. 2:9). But in their "appropriating that name [clergy] to themselves and their Priests only," Milton declares, the prelates are guilty of "condemning the rest of Gods inheritance to an injurious and alienat condition of Laity," and "exclud[ing] the members of Christ from the property of being members, the bearing of orderly and fit offices in the ecclesiastical body" (*CPW* 1:838–39). Like these "*Old Priest*[s] writ Large," Satan deprives his assembly the liberty of the "Clergy-right" (*CPW* 1:844) that they once claimed by joining him in his dissent from sleep and in his hermeneutical revolt against God's decree. He is the *only* anointed prelate of hell; his thunderous voice is the only that will be heard; and his bullying church government is the only that shall rule: end of discussion. Unlike the exercises of the 1570s or the later forms and manifestations of them before and after the Interregnum, Satan does not conclude this exercise by asking if there are any

learned devils in the audience who would like the opportunity to confute his message. Intimidated by his aggressive bearing, the assembly
"Dreaded not more th'adventure than his voice / Forbidding; and at
once with him they rose" (*PL* 2.474–75). The prophesying over, the
fellowship dissembles to occupy themselves in entertainments, games,
exploring, singing, writing poetry, and philosophizing. But all this is a
gesture to find ease for their pain until their anointed son of thunder
returns.

The angels' fall from heaven, an act of religious and political separation and dissent, is a fall away from the perceived hegemony of heaven;
it is a fall into culture—a radically different culture with a radically
different conception of language as the infernal sermons reveal. As
Stanley Fish has argued, when "the fallen angels deny the centrality of
God, they are committed to a moral and linguistic anarchy. All goals
and objectives are equally arbitrary, and there is no justification at all
for preferring one position to another."[101] From an Augustinian point
of view, the demons in hell have removed the Logos from the logos.
In the culture of hell, language barely rises above the level of being a
tool for aggression, manipulation, or temporary consolation. The well-
turned phrase, the most eloquent of arrangements, and the thundering
dramatic performances can be little more than smoke and mirrors that
either promote self-interest or attempt to "charm / Pain for a while or
anguish, and excite / Fallacious hope" (566–68).

But, as Milton must have recognized, this is precisely the language in
which all the fallen dwell. In a rather Fishian way, Dustin Griffin argues
that while Milton may often be pointing the finger at the demons and
rendering judgment, he is just as often pointing the finger at the reader
"to see that the scene and the problem are ultimately his own. In part by
means of the fallen angels, Milton teaches a reader both to see and to
judge himself."[102] Given Griffin's insight, then, one might intuit Milton's
own criticism of certain individuals of those dissenting sects who are
interested in politics at the expense of holiness. Furthermore, as Joad
Raymond impressively demonstrates, the sixteenth- and seventeenth-
century mind inherited a medieval tradition of using the example of
angels as "a laboratory for exegesis," for

angels can be seen as conceptual and ontological mediators between God and mankind. God in his infinitude cannot be represented, but angels can, and as finite yet spiritual substances they
can be used to explain two things of the utmost importance in the
sixteenth and seventeenth centuries: first, the nature of the spiritual world and its relationship to the material world of Creation;
and secondly, the relationship between God and man. Accommo-
dation and angels . . . walk hand in hand as a means of understanding man's place in the universe.[103]

Moreover, the demons are eerily (post-?) modern; their condition becomes Milton's meditation on the consequences of a fallen language
divorced and in exile from the defining Presence of God. What follows? one might hear Milton asking.

Intriguingly, we might construe this council scene as Milton's brilliant anticipation of Ludwig Wittgenstein's notion of language games:
the simple but powerful thesis that the meaning and purpose of language is in its *use,* and "to imagine language is to imagine a form of
life." For Wittgenstein, language is not an abstract theory or system of
signs but a structure of practice. He begins his *Philosophical Investigations* (1945–49) with a critique of Augustine's belief, set forth in the
Confessions, that we learn the meaning of language through ostensive
definition: pointing to an object, learning its name, and naming it. Like
Augustine, Wittgenstein suggests, we assume that it is really an easy
process; we name, then we can talk about what we name. Yet Wittgenstein observes with some simple examples that the role the thing
named plays is different: the words "three," "table," "red," and "square"
do not provide stable ostensive definitions, for one name is used for
only one kind of object, or another is used to refer to many things that
share a particular characteristic or quality. "That is to say: an ostensive
definition can be variously interpreted in *every* case."[104] Wittgenstein
asserts that a word "hasn't got a meaning given to it, as it were, by a
power independent of us, so that there could be a kind of scientific
investigation into what the word *really* means," but "a word has the
meaning someone has given to it." Instead, one should think of words

"as instruments characterized by their use, and then think of the use of a hammer, the use of a chisel, the use of a square, of a glue pot, and of the glue."[105] This is the nature of the language game: words have meaning according to the "rules" or "grammars" of the game in which they are used. The stability of language games is not derived, notes Fergus Kerr, in "objective metaphysical realities . . . nor subjective states of consciousness . . . but *Lebensformen* that are 'the given.' What is given is the human world: neither meanings in the head, accessible by introspection, nor essences in the objects around us, yielding to analysis, but the order that human beings establish by their being together."[106]

Milton's devils play language games with the Name of God, a Name that is drained of metaphysical reality and eternal essence; those language games generate and are generated by the culture of hell, a "form of life," as Wittgenstein puts it.[107] The "use" to which the demons put the Name is to cast God in a limited role as the Foe. In his envy of the Son, unfallen Lucifer desires a name that secures meaning as God's Anointed One, the Logos in the logos. When he cannot have it, his fall secures another name that will constantly call the meaning of the Name into question, yet one that paradoxically defines himself within a constrictive narrative role with no freedom to escape it: the Enemy. Rather than dwelling in the gaze of God that grants "beatitude past utterance" (*PL* 3.62), a surplus and saturation of meaning, Satan the Enemy of God ironically casts himself and his demons within the narrowest scope of meaning. Lucifer does not recognize the freedom he already has in the surplus of meaning generated by the Name of Names because he sees the Name as a totality instead of as infinity.[108] His satanic language promises individual freedom to interpret the Signified according to one's own conscience; rather than resulting in a promising proliferation of meaning through this "new found" liberty, however, what emerges is vapid sameness, a kind of *kenosis* without an accompanying *pleroma*. This *kenotic* sameness is the culture and language game of hell, where language is cast against the void with a desperate faith that beauty alone, divorced from the Good and the True, will ease or divert the sameness of their painful, *kenotic* existence. The language of Milton's hell is the language of exile, "wand'ring [in] mazes lost" (2.561).

The Milton of *Paradise Lost* stands on the cusp of modernity: Francis Bacon's *Novum Organon* (1620) battles against metaphysics in science; René Descartes's *Meditations* (1641) begins the epistemological turn inward; and the Rationalist project is only decades away and probably already existed in embryo. As Milton looks forward, he prophetically envisions new language games of science, of mathematics, of economics, and of philosophy that will create and be created by new communities; as he looks back (nostalgically?), he sees that the Name that once dominated and defined the singular language game of science, mathematics, and philosophy will no longer hold sway.

If this is the case, then we might also construe Milton's investigating language games in heaven and unfallen paradise as well. Language there has *use* as well within a (now separate) community: praise, hymns, celebration, liturgy—all to the end of participating in and bringing glory to the infinite Name. In Milton's heaven the angels are engaged in reverently praising the Name that cannot be exhausted:

> Thee Father first they sung Omnipotent,
> Immutable, Immortal, Infinite,
> Eternal King; thee Author of all being,
> Fountain of Light, thyself invisible
> Amidst the glorious brightness where thou sit'st
> Thron'd inaccessible. (3.372–77)

The "scripture" of God's inaccessibility paradoxically permits hermeneutical abundance. Moreover, the glorious works generated in abundance by the decree of that holy Name are praised and celebrated by "Millions of spiritual Creatures" who "walk the Earth / Unseen, both when we wake, and when we sleep" and "[Sing] thir great Creator" (4.677–78, 684). What emerges in *Paradise Lost*, then, are two competing language games, two competing "cultures." Although he does not pose it in quite the same way, I think this is what Stanley Fish has in mind when he points to the competing "storytellers" of the narratives of heaven and hell.[109]

Milton himself is convinced of the superiority of the one language game and narrative over the other, and he demonstrates it in the heavenly council scene of Book 3. Having foreseen that humanity will be seduced by Satan's language game—Satan transfers the qualities of the Name to Eve as "sovran Mistress," "Celestial Beauty," "Queen of this Universe," until she and Adam become "Gods"—the Father recognizes that fallen man will no longer be a participant in the language game of heaven (9.532, 540, 684, 712). "So will fall / Hee and his faithless Progeny: whose fault? / Whose but his own? ingrate, he had of mee / All he could have" (3.95–98). The Father's use of "ingrate" reveals that fallen language will be characterized by ingratitude: self-praise, self-interest, and self-imprisonment as "free they must remain, / Till they enthrall themselves" (125–26). For Fish, this satanic freedom is the "false freedom of irresponsibility," one that is "initially exhilarating" but that gradually becomes a prison, for "the more fictions you proliferate, the greater distance between you and what is real and true."[110] Human beings will fall from participating in the culture and language game of heaven, in order to dwell in their own fictions. As Milton depicts, this is an unbridgeable gap—unbridgeable, that is, until the Son reestablishes the possibility for participation in it again, a theme to which we will return with greater focus in chapters 3 and 5.

When the Son declares, "Behold mee then, mee for him, life for life / I offer, on mee let thine anger fall; / Account mee man" (236–39), we might add "language for language" as well. Now the Logos will inhabit the logos at the Incarnation (282–85). Crucially, the Son reestablishes the heavenly language game by *out-narrating* the language game of hell through his exercise of virtue and obedience to the Father:

> So Heav'nly love shall outdo Hellish hate,
> Giving to death, and dying to redeem,
> So dearly to redeem what Hellish hate
> So easily destroy'd, and still destroys
> In those who, when they may, accept not grace. (3.298–302)

Satanic language and the form of life that it generates will continue, observes Milton, but it does not have to dominate fallen language games. Grace provides entrance once again into participation with the divine. Here we see that Milton embraces a kind of narrative theology in which witness, the incarnated narrative of one's own life, demonstrates the vitality of the vocabulary of one language game over another, even if that language game also inscribes a politics. To confirm the point, one need only turn to the several instances in the poems and prose in which Milton reverts to autobiography to defend his politics.

Stanley Hauerwas observes that the story embodied in any tradition "directs us to observe the lives of those who live it as a crucial indication of the truth of their convictions. . . . At least part of what it means to call a significant narrative true is how that narrative claims and shapes our lives."[111] The Name, said and unsaid by Satan and his demons in a single breath, is said, and said, and said, and said ad infinitum—proclaimed—through the obedience of the Son. It is also proclaimed through the (narrative) exercise of virtue and obedience on the part of a poet who is devoted to out-narrating and out-preaching his contemporaries in so many ways, armed with a powerful language and vocabulary that participates in a gaze that bestows "beatitude past utterance." He sees the narrative of his own life as a performance that, like the Jesus of *Paradise Regained,* causes his antagonists to stand in awe, "mute [and] confounded what to say, / What to reply, confuted and convinc't / Of [their] weak arguing and fallacious drift" (3.2–4). While Milton understands their lives as being characterized by the duplicity, false eloquence, and restless drifting of the Adversary, Milton sees his life as that of the anchored, incarnated preacher who is "suspended" over the One in whom, by whom, and through whom all things move and have their being (Acts 17:28). For Milton, doxology, and the doxological life of virtue, is the saying that cannot be unsaid.

The implications of this doxological life are far-ranging, influencing not only Milton's aesthetics, poetics, and preaching, but also his hermeneutics and politics. In the following chapter, we examine the doxological life in closer detail by placing greater pressure on the perfectionist strain that pulses in the heterodox Christology expounded in

De Doctrina Christiana. Within the context of Augustinian and Ricoeurrian hermeneutics, Milton's Jesus cooperates with the "text" of the divine Logos, harnessing its virtuous potential. When combined with aspects of Milton's monism, the trajectory of this potential is the sublimation of the human creature and, by extension, the potential sublimation of reading and politics. The practice of divine virtue is the *sermo* with God, as adopted sons and daughters of God become his Good Speech.

part ii

Milton's Incarnate Reader

chapter 3

The Greatest Metaphor of Our Religion

The Radical Hermeneutics of Incarnation in Milton's *De Doctrina Christiana*

> *But first I mean to exercise him in the Wilderness;*
> . . . .
> *That all the Angels and Ethereal Powers,*
> *They now, and men hereafter, may discern*
> *From what consummate virtue I have chose*
> *This perfect Man, by merit call'd my Son,*
> *To earn Salvation for the Sons of men.*
> —Milton, *Paradise Regained* (1.155–66)

In his *Life of Moses* the Cappadocian Gregory of Nyssa (d. 395) understands Moses's transforming encounter with the "text" of the burning bush as a figure for the Incarnate Word—the Lord descends into creation to inhabit and underwrite material reality without consuming it. For Gregory, the ontic and perceptual horizons of believers are transformed by their encounter with the Word just as Moses's horizon is transformed by the theophany in the burning bush; like Moses, the believer is called from his "luxuriating . . . manner of life that is peaceful

109

and devoid of conflict" to behold the light of the truth that "dazzl[es] the eyes of the soul." Believers are thus called to appropriate and perform the Word in their lives through the exercise of "that virtuous conduct" that leads one to behold the deeper mysteries of the Incarnate Christ.[1]

Gregory's insistence that the exercise of virtue—the participation, performance, or actualization of the Word in the world—is the key to beholding the deep mysteries of God is of seminal importance to Milton. Not only is the exercise of virtue central to the hermeneutic of the author of *De Doctrina Christiana,* but also to the heterodox doctrine of the Incarnation set forth in it and the revolutionary implications such a doctrine holds. But in order to grasp the significance of those implications that give flesh to the doctrinal bones of Milton's peculiar Christology, we must first grapple with the centuries of debate regarding the twin natures of Christ. To be sure, many Jews and Greeks living in the late first century C.E. would likely have been scandalized by the Johannine assertion that the Word was made flesh (1:14). What does it mean for John to claim that "the Word was made flesh and dwelt among us"? Is it unique or derivative? More important, what conceptions of the Word empower Milton's understanding of the doctrine of the Incarnation, and how might these formulations help us to understand more precisely the performance of the Word in the world?

In the first section of this chapter, I offer a very brief account of the intellectual milieu out of which John formulates his great metaphor and how the "Word made flesh" was variously understood in the theological crucible of the early church.[2] This is a theological history with which Milton would have been well acquainted and from which he would form his own core doctrinal beliefs regarding the Incarnation. In the second section, I argue that Milton's philosophical monism provides the linchpin for the perfectionist strains in his "low" Christology as it is delineated in *De Doctrina Christiana.* Moreover, I consider how Milton's doctrinal understanding of the "Word made flesh" implies narrative. The various Christologies that Milton inherits are not just the dessicated remains of theological debates long removed from the issues and concerns fermenting and fomenting in his own age. As

Milton recognizes in *De Doctrina Christiana* and renders in his "brief epic" of "This perfect Man, by merit call'd my Son," these formulations constitute, rather, the very bones of the central hero whose actions in the world are the lifeblood of the tradition Milton holds sacred. The weight of these doctrinal claims inevitably bears upon the capacities and capabilities of those like Milton and his contemporaries who chose to inscribe themselves within the scope of that sacred tradition's narrative trajectories: filaments that both stretch toward and advance the horizons of the very world they help (re)define. Stanley Hauerwas suggests that stories "are not told to explain as a theory explains, but to involve the agent in a way of life. A theory is meant to help you know the world without changing the world yourself; a story is to help you deal with the world by changing it through changing yourself."[3] Hauerwas seems here to be making a distinction between two modes of vision that ostensibly order reality in disparate ways. But I suggest that for Milton, the theory, or doctrinal bones, of the "Word made flesh" cannot be easily separated from the blood and tissue of the story it implies, one that finds its most articulate expression in the blossoming life of virtue as one participates in the divine Text in the "hermeneutics of testimony" that Paul Ricoeur describes.

Conceptions of the Word, Performance in the World: Christology as Narrative in the Theological Tradition

In the Hebrew Bible, the phrase "word of God" is used to indicate both a word that originates from YHWH and a word that reveals something about YHWH; in both senses, the word of God is the vehicle for divine disclosure.[4] While its etymology is unclear, the Hebrew word for "word," "thought," or more generally "thing," is *dabhar,* whose root *dbr* is found in the verb *dibber,* "to speak." In the Hebrew scriptures *dabhar* is used by the prophets of Israel to refer to the "word of Yahweh that came to me," as in Jeremiah's calling. The word of YHWH comes to Jeremiah and *makes* him a prophet: "Then Yahweh stretched out his hand and touched my mouth, and Yahweh said to me: 'There! I have put my words into your mouth. Look, today I set you over the nations and kingdoms, to uproot and knock down, to destroy and overthrow, to build and to plant" (Jer. 1:9–10). For this reason, the *dabhar* of YHWH is closely tied to deed and intricately linked to identity.

YHWH's prophet receives the *dabhar* and in turn discloses it to the people of Israel for the purposes of immediate individual change and national transformation that are occasioned by a particular historical circumstance. The *dabhar* of YHWH is thus a creative "event" in the life of Israel, restoring them to the covenant; the Word of God "is in itself not only sound and breath but a reality. Since the word is connected with its accomplishment, *dabhar* could be translated 'effective word.'"[5] It is, therefore, linked to the will of God, but theologians maintain a careful distinction between God's absolute will and absolute word, and God's circumstantial will and circumstantial word. The former carries the sense of an inevitable accomplishment, while the latter is contingent on its audience's response and participation. Misunderstanding or open rebellion is just as likely a response as revelation and obedience, and each has its consequences, alternately resulting in destruction and ruin or life and prosperity.[6]

On both counts, *dabhar* in ancient Hebrew thought is performance, a speech-act par excellence. Its creative potency is further illustrated in Isaiah 55:10–11: "For, as the rain and the snow come down from the sky and do not return before having watered the earth, fertilizing it and making it germinate to provide seed for the sower and food to eat, so it is with the [*dabhar*] that goes from my mouth: it will not return to me unfulfilled, or before having carried out my good pleasure and having achieved what it was sent to do." The word uttered by YHWH's prophet is apodictic; the *dabhar* wields the authority to judge and the power to create, to order, and to destroy with complete efficacy. As a result, the prophet is closely identified with YHWH himself. But even though the prophets receive the *dabhar* of YHWH, no prophet declares, "I am YHWH's *Dabhar*." Such a statement would have been considered blasphemous in the Jewish community. "Jesus did not say this either," observes Bernard J. Lee, at least not in this manner. Yet this sense is precisely what John has in mind in his prologue and in his recounting of Jesus's various "I Am" statements, and Jesus's "earliest followers called him God's announcement."[7]

Philo of Alexandria presents us with an intriguing synthesis of Greek and Judaic thought regarding the doctrine of the Logos. As a Jew living in the greatest of first-century Greek cities, Philo is as equally indebted to ancient Hebrew thought as he is to Platonic and Stoic thought, and his connection to John's Gospel continues to be a subject of debate among biblical scholars.[8] Overall, Philo conceives of a (single) God whose essence is wholly Other and transcendent, but it is through the Logos that this God is partially disclosed. Philo's conception of the Logos is multihued. On one level, derived from the Platonist and Stoic tradition, Philo's Logos refers to the archetypal Ideas in the Mind (*Nous*) of God—God's ordered and eternal thoughts that provide the "blueprint" for creation. In this way Philo says that it represents the "archetypal ideas from which the intelligible world was framed, and the visible objects which are copies and likenesses of those ideas."[9] Human reason, believes Philo, is the "copy" or "image" of the Logos, the paradigm of Ideal Reason—an assimilation of the "image of God" in Genesis 1:27.[10] On another level, the Logos is the instrument that "performs" creation, the means by which Philo's unapproachable God, who does not have direct contact with primordial matter, "turns" toward creation. In this way the term is aligned with the creative "Word of God" in the Hebrew scriptures—the utterance of God rendered in the Septuagint (LXX) as logos.[11] Lee thus distinguishes two "stages" of Philo's Logos: the *Logos endiathetos,* or unuttered and preexistent Word (that which contains the "blueprint" for creation), and the *Logos prophorikos,* or uttered Word (that which is immanent in creation). We may thus perceive Philo's Logos as a kind of mediating figure, for it is both "like" the transcendent God (*ho théos*—"the [truly] God") and "unlike" the transcendent God (*théos*—"[as] a God").[12] Similarly, while we may see intriguing parallels to the figure of Jesus in Christian tradition, the doctrine of the Incarnation of the Logos as John conceives it is completely foreign to Philo. Philo's Logos, while immanent in creation, is not bound by time and history and certainly is not personal. C. H. Dodd concludes that while the Johannine author probably was influenced by Philonic conceptions of the Word, "the Logos . . . in the Gospel [is] fully personal, standing in personal relations both with God and with men, and having a place in history."[13]

Thus it is quite clear that first-century Jews or Greeks, John's target audience, probably could conceive of no finer opposition than the disparate horizons of Logos and *sarx*, "flesh." Aloys Grillmeier, S.J., suggests that this opposition was so deeply ingrained in late Hellenistic culture that it fueled the "ever-repeated attempts of a Docetic kind to deny the reality of Christ's flesh or to loosen the unity of Logos and sarx."[14] For John, however, the Word of God, the divine Logos, is man: a particular man born into a particular family and a particular culture. He appears visibly, is bound by time and history, suffers, and dies. "Word is man"—for many centuries following, Christian theologians would be faced with the challenge of understanding just how the divine and the human horizons meet and function in the poetics of the Incarnation.

The terms in John's metaphoric construction created significant problems for early theologians who were separated by cultural and linguistic barriers, and who struggled to understand the performative, narrative dynamics between the divine and human "horizons" in Christ. Endemic to any metaphoric formulation is the tension between resemblance and disparity, a tension that the early church thought must be carefully accounted for when one is interpreting sacred texts, formulating doctrine, and disciplining heretics. On one level, therefore, we might construe the early Christological debates as often one-sided attempts to resolve this metaphoric tension, rather than embrace and reside within the paradox it seems to generate.

Consequently, I want to consider the orthodox "poetics" of the hypostatic union decided at Chalcedon in 451, in order to examine the implications of the heterodox "poetics" of the Incarnation in Milton's *De Doctrina Christiana*. Framing the Christological debates on the hypostatic union in terms of metaphor will accomplish two things. First, it simply helps us to see that the Incarnation deeply informs Milton's views regarding the power of metaphoric language and, hence, the potency of poetic expression over rhetorical constructions and flourishes in the pulpit or elsewhere. As William Shullenberger suggests, in Milton's own formulation of the doctrine of the Incarnation we might consider the following illuminating substitution: "There is then in *metaphor* a mutual hypostatic union of two natures, or in other words, of two essences, of two substances. . . . And there is nothing to stop the properties of each from remaining individually distinct" (*CPW* 6:424; emphasis added).[15] For Milton, the Incarnation structures figurative language itself and occupies the very heart of poetic expression. Second, metaphor will help us to see the theological significance of the fusion of two horizons, divine and human, that do not compete against each other, but mutually work to "redescribe" a reality for true believers—a reality informed, as we will see, by Milton's philosophical monism, the centrality of free will, and the exercise of virtue.

The centuries leading up to the orthodox, doctrinal formulation surrounding the poetics of the Incarnation at Chalcedon are marked by the theological movements of a great pendulum between extremes. Aloys Grillmeier and J. N. D. Kelly suggest that we might construe these extremes as competing "frameworks," but I propose that we construe them as rival "poetics" that attempt to resolve the metaphoric tension between the divine and human horizons in Christ. While by no means comprehensive, Chalcedon nevertheless negotiated a tensive balance between these two horizons and two Christo-poetic rivals: the Antiochene *Logos-anthropos* poetic and the Alexandrine *Logos-sarx* poetic. Each of these poetics tended to emphasize one horizon over the other, thus resulting in a qualitatively different kind of narrative performance of the Word in the world.

Briefly, at one extreme was the Antiochene Logos-man poetic in which the humanity of Christ tended to be emphasized over his divinity. The most radical example of the Word-man poetic is the adoptionist, or dynamic Monarchianist, theology of Paul of Samosata (fl. 260s), condemned by the Synod of Antioch in 268 and denounced by Augustine in *De Haeresibus*. Not much is known of Paul, and like so many other heretics in the early church age, his particular heresies are preserved through the writings of his opponents, notably Eusebius and Athanasius. The former preserves the contents of the official synodal letter from Antioch, which accuses Paul of refusing "to acknowledge that the Son of God came down from heaven" and asserting that "Jesus Christ was from below," as a normal man.[16]

Taking the position that Jesus was mere man within the Word-man Christo-poetic, Paul of Samosata asserts that Jesus merits divinity by the conduct of his blessed life, is adopted as God's Son through grace, and achieves a likeness to God, not by his nature or preexistent status, but by his extraordinary moral cooperation with or participation in the divine. J. N. D. Kelly quotes a sixth-century writer who claims that Paul understood the "Word" not as the "self-subsistent Word Who was in Christ, but applied the title 'Word' to God's commandment and ordinance." Paul "did not say that Father, Son and Holy Spirit are one and the same, but gave the name of God to the Father Who created all things, that of Son to the mere man, and that of Spirit to the grace which indwelt the apostles."[17] Jesus is the "Word of God," not because he is a member of the preexistent Trinity, but because he becomes the fulfillment of the Father's commands and ordinances through the performance of his virtuous life; thereby, he is adopted through the Spirit of grace. It is in this sense that Jesus is to be understood as the divine "Speech" or "Son of God."[18] Paul's adoptionist model of the Incarnation thus defies a tensive metaphoric relation, for the divine and human horizons in Christ remain radically distinct, only to become radically collapsed through his (human) virtuous life.

Paul's adoptionist paradigm is at the most extreme within the Word-man poetic, and as we will see a bit later, there are intriguing similarities between his heterodox understanding of the Incarnation and that discussed in *De Doctrina Christiana*. The Word-man poetic continued to be influential after Paul with variations. Theodore of Mopsuestia (d. 428) was another proponent before Chalcedon, centering his poetic on an *assumptus* theory: the Word assumes human flesh as a garment, temple, or shrine (see John 2:19; 1 Cor. 3:16−17; 6:19). Significantly, this imagery recalls Milton's depiction of the Incarnation in the early "Nativity" ode: "That glorious Form, that Light unsufferable, / And that far-beaming blaze of Majesty" left the "Courts of everlasting Day, / And chose with us a darksome House of mortal Clay" (8−9, 14). Similarly, in

"The Passion" Christ dwells in a "poor fleshly tabernacle" (17), and in *Paradise Regained* the Son is "enshrin'd / In fleshly Tabernacle, and human form" (4.598–99).[19] The human nature that Christ assumes in this Word-man poetic is complete and independent, therefore allowing Christ to genuinely develop, to grow in knowledge and virtue, and to struggle with temptation.[20] Theodore reasoned that if the Logos had taken the place of the human soul, then Christ's body would have wanted for nothing, contradicting the Gospels' depiction of Christ as suffering from hunger and thirst.

Theodore's habit of separating the two natures in his writings, his belief that their interaction should be counted as a "conjunction," "coalescence," or "juxtaposition" rather than a true harmonic union, and his emphasizing the distinct contrast between the Word and the garment of flesh he assumed led many after his death, notably Cyril, bishop of Alexandria, to consider him a predecessor to Nestorius.[21] Like Theodore, Nestorius preferred to use the term "conjunction" rather than "union," in order to maintain a strict separation between the two natures, but he also insisted on the idea that the two natures dwelled in one *prosopon*. Scholars remain divided, but both Grillmeier and Kelly argue that Nestorius is more orthodox than he has been given credit for, insisting that Cyril consistently misrepresented Nestorius's views with astonishing success. Thinking Cyril's "natural" or "hypostatic" union insufficient to account for the separateness of the two natures, Nestorius insisted that the two terms must be kept distinct in order to ensure both the impassibility of God and the passion and freedom of humanity. Because of his ardent emphasis on the separation between the two natures, Nestorius was successfully represented by Cyril as reviving the Samosatene adoptionist position that the conjunction between divine and human in Christ was merely a moral one, but Kelly demonstrates that Nestorius was no adoptionist and found Paul's doctrine to be in error.[22]

In contrast to Paul's extreme Christology "from below," the Alexandrine school emphasizes the mystical, transcendent, and particularly Greek concept of the Logos. Concurring with Plato's assumptions that human beings are bodies and souls, and that the soul occupies a privileged position over the body, the Alexandrine poetics of the Incarnation generally assumes the primacy of Christ's divinity over Christ's humanity. Christ does not possess a soul in the same sense that human beings possess a soul; rather, the Logos takes the place of the soul in Christ. This is significant because according to this Word-flesh Christology the Logos became flesh without becoming fully human. This position is espoused by the third-century priest Malchion, voicing opposition to the divisive Samosatene Christology, and was most clearly articulated by Bishop Eudoxius (fl. 357–369): "We believe in . . . the one Lord, the Son, . . . who became flesh, but not man. For he took no human soul, but became flesh so that God was revealed to us men through the flesh as through a curtain; not two natures, since he was no complete man, but God in the flesh instead of a soul; the whole is one nature by composition."[23] Eudoxius's formulation echoes that of Apollinarius of Laodicea (d. 390), whose extreme version of the Word-flesh Christology was condemned at Constantinople in 381. "The flesh is dependent for its motions on some other principle of movement and action," says Apollinarius; in Greek thought this "other principle" is the human rational soul that "enters into fusion" with the flesh, as Apollinarius compellingly puts it. In Christ, however, the flesh "united itself with the heavenly governing principle [i.e., the Logos] and was fused with it." Such a unity, the fusion of Logos and flesh, results for Apollinarius in the divinization of Christ's actual flesh because it participates fully in the properties of the Word.

If we frame Apollinarius's formulation within the tensive structure of metaphor, one of the terms loses its own value, so to speak, because the flesh is so closely united with the Word as to become nearly indistinguishable.[24] The loss of the vitality of the fleshly term draws a "curtain," to borrow Eudoxius's image, around the Godhead. Thus, rather than opening up new narrative possibilities for believers through divine participation—so crucial to Milton's understanding of the Incarnation, as we will see in a moment—the Word-flesh Christology seems to negate the possibility for an expansion of perceptual horizons. Believers remain "curtained off" from the fullness of God, for Christ cannot radically be *pro nobis* because Christ remains so truly unlike us.

Consequently, Apollinarius's collapse of the terms results in believers having a high priest who cannot sympathize with human beings in their weakness (Heb. 4:15) and a narrative of suffering that remains defective without a genuine witness to Christ's own sufferings (Phil. 3:10). Since the human will is not redeemed by Christ's taking a human rational soul, believers remain fixed as slaves in a narrowly construed narrative that is characterized by the performance of *nothing but* sin.

The council at Chalcedon negotiated a tensive balance between these two Christo-poetic rivals. Many of the Antiochenes, following Nestorius, vied for the "two nature" theory of the Incarnation, while many of the Alexandrines, following Apollinarius and Eutyches, tended to argue the "one nature" theory. While many of the key terms in the settlement, such as *hypostasis* and *prosopon,* still lacked precise metaphysical definitions, Grillmeier suggests that those bishops present at Chalcedon were more practically minded and wanted merely "to express the *full reality* of the Incarnation."[25] In other words, they wanted to capture the narratological scope of the actions and performance of Jesus the Word in the world, maintaining that while there is a distinction between the two natures, Christ is still "one person." Echoing previous formulations and lodging their definition squarely in the tradition and witness of the church, Chalcedon states that Christ is "the Same perfect in Godhead, the Same perfect in manhood, truly God and truly man . . . ; consubstantial [*homoousios*] with the Father as to his Godhead, and the Same substance with us as to his manhood." Further, Christ is revealed "in two natures [that exist] without confusion, without change, without division, without separation; the difference of the natures having been in no wise taken away by reason of the union, but rather the properties of each being preserved, and concurring into one Person and one hypostasis."[26]

In the Chalcedonian Definition we finally have a balanced metaphoric relation between the two horizons. In Ricoeur's own understanding of metaphor, the "new reality" generated by metaphor occurs, not because the meaning of one term is transferred to the meaning of the other, as Aristotle formulated, but because two (or more) unlikely or unrelated terms are suddenly brought into predication. Metaphor occurs, argues Ricoeur, at the level of the sentence, and in fact extends to the structure of language itself. In the Chalcedonian formulation, we might say that "Christ" occupies the position of the predicate "is" between the two independent terms "perfect in Godhead" and "perfect in manhood." Christ perfectly performs both horizons, even though he gives up the full majesty of the Godhead at the Incarnation, and does not take on the sin nature of humanity, for he is "in all things like unto us, sin only excepted" (Heb. 4:15). His perfect performance of the hypostatic union, the balanced metaphoric relation between the terms, generates a new narrative of human possibility to perform in the world. Ricoeur, too, finds an intriguing analogy between metaphor and narrative. In the grammar of any sentence, "the novel—the not-yet-said, the unheard-of—suddenly arises in language" through the "*living* metaphor, that is to say, a *new* relevance in predication"; similarly, in the structure of narrative this newness is "wholly *invented* plot, that is to say, a *new* congruence in emplotment."[27] With the perfect hypostasis performed in the Incarnation, human beings who ardently listen to the symbol of the Word are newly "emplotted" along a different narrative trajectory than that set by Adam—a trajectory that is at the heart of Milton's incarnational *poiēsis* and poetry of proclamation. But as we will find, Milton's own incarnational "emplotment" radically differs from the orthodoxy of Chalcedon.

From Form to Beauty: The Monist's Jesus and the Hermeneutical Dimensions of Milton's Heterodox Christology

As Milton explains, his theological treatise is divided between "FAITH, or KNOWLEDGE OF GOD, and LOVE, or THE WORSHIP OF GOD." Yet we should not see them as distinct parts; rather, Milton admits that "in practice they are inseparable," for "obedience and love are always the best guides to knowledge, and often cause it to increase and flourish, though very small at first" (*CPW* 6:128–29). Consequently, one may infer that Milton thinks himself Gregory of Nyssa's virtuous and, hence, knowledgeable man.

Such boldness is characteristic of the authorial persona we encounter in the treatise's introductory epistle. In his endeavor to "puzzle out a religious creed for myself," he has eschewed the "repulsive afflictions" of the "tyranny and superstition" that have corrupted the Christian religion for centuries (*CPW* 6:118). Milton embraces a hermeneutic throughout the treatise that at once encompasses the disciplined erudition of the early reformers and the authoritative pneumatology of the radicals. He contends that God rewards not those who are "thoughtless and credulous," but those who "labor constantly and seek tirelessly after truth" (120). Unambiguously, he belongs to the latter group. When it comes to the explication of Christian doctrine, Milton is eager to distance himself from the "dabblers in theology" who confuse matters and whose works we should "fling out of God's temple as filth and rubbish!" (421). Despite his confidence and the surety of this method, however, the author is stunned into comparative silence when faced with the task of addressing the "greatest mystery of our religion" (420).[28] And, despite Milton's numerous warnings in approaching this mystery, he offers a heterodox poetics of the hypostatic union anyway.[29]

John C. Ulreich provides the clearest articulation of the heterodoxy of the doctrine of the Incarnation in *De Doctrina Christiana*.[30] While he fails to point to Paul of Samosata as a possible source for the treatise's heterodox poetics, Ulreich does bring its radical adoptionist theology into relief, and there are striking similarities between Paul's idea of moral cooperation and Milton's idea of virtue. While Chalcedon rules that Christ has two natures, divine and human, that operate in a single person through the hypostatic union without confusion, conversion, severance, or division, the author of *De Doctrina Christiana* argues that Christ is of two *persons*, even though the two natures are distinct. There is in Christ "a mutual hypostatic union of two natures, or, in other words, of two essences, of two substances and consequently of two persons" (424). The author understands "nature" to be "essence," perhaps following Aristotle's claim that "every essence in general is called 'nature,' because the nature of anything is a kind of essence."[31] "Person" he understands as a single being, and "hypostasis" he defines as "substance" or "subsistence." But Milton proceeds to collapse "nature" and "person," arguing that it is an "absurd idea" that the Logos would assume human nature without also assuming manhood: "Obviously, the Logos became what it assumed, and if it assumed human nature, but not manhood, then it became an example of human nature, not a man. But, of course, the two things are really inseparable" (422–23). In this collapse, Ulreich perceives an odd inconsistency, in that the author has seemingly re-created a dynamic similar to the formulations of orthodox Trinitarianism that he had previously called "bizarre and senseless." While Father and Son share the same substance, the essences of the Father and the begotten Son are distinct; they are thus "like" in substance, but "unalike" in essence, reflecting for us the tensive relationship between the terms in a metaphor. He reasons that "two distinct things cannot be of the same essence. God is one being, not two" (212).

If the essences of Father and Son are distinct, it would seem to follow that the persons of Father and Son are also distinct, for "the essence of the Father cannot be communicated to another person" (225). Ulreich queries, "if two (or three) persons cannot subsist in one being, how can one being, Jesus of Nazareth, be simultaneously two persons, both God and man?" Ulreich's conclusion is that "Milton's underlying purpose in all this would seem to be to deny that 'the person who was made flesh must necessarily be the supreme God' (*CPW* 6:425). This intention gives rise . . . to an even more radical proposition, that the Incarnation is a twofold process: 'the Logos became what it assumed,' both God and man, first by uniting itself with the already human person of Jesus, and then by participating consciously and *voluntarily* in God's will (*CPW* 6:416, 417)."[32]

Milton's point of contention, that Jesus of Nazareth "must necessarily be the supreme God," is an important one, for it suggests that the man Jesus in whom the Logos chose to dwell could have been resistant to or uncooperative with the Logos. In other words, Jesus becomes the Christ not simply through the act of embodiment, but through his voluntary participation in fulfilling the will of the Father through his activity. In short, Jesus perfectly performs the Word. Paul's radical adoptionist model allows us to reframe the theology and poetics of the hypostatic union within the context of hermeneutics. Recall that for

Hans-Georg Gadamer and Paul Ricoeur the moment of fusion or understanding occurs when readers adopt a hermeneutic of "listening," a stance of cooperation with the text in a moment of hermeneutical faith or critical suspension. To echo Anselm, this moment requires that the person must "believe in order to understand." Within this framework, it is profitable to construe that the horizon of the human Jesus, himself a listening "reader," "fuses" with the horizon of the "text" of the Logos.[33] For Milton there seems to exist an ontic creative interplay between the divine Logos and the flesh of the adopted believer. Ulreich suggests that Milton's doctrine of the Logos has much in common with Origen's, who states that the "Son of God . . . took not only a human body, as some suppose, but also a soul, and one like our souls in nature, but like Himself in purpose and power, and such as could fulfill . . . all the wishes and dispensations of the Word."[34] For Origen, and Milton it would seem, the divine Logos dwells in every human being in the same capacity that it existed in Jesus himself, leading to a metaphysics and soteriology characterized by abundance rather than scarcity. Potentially, everyone is Christ—a conclusion entrenched within the theology of Milton's radical contemporaries, as we will find in the following chapters.

The upshot of this heterodox poetics is that while the tensive relationship between the Father and Son remains because they cannot share the same essence, the substantial distinction between the Son and other believers is minimized to the degree that the believer actively participates by being obedient to the will of the Father through the infusion of grace mediated by the Son. Importantly, Christ "declares [John 10:38; 14:10, 20–21; 17:21–22] that he and the Father are one in the same way as we are one with him: that is, not in essence but in love, in communion, in agreement, in charity, in spirit, and finally in glory" (*CPW* 6:220). The denial of Christ's sharing the essence of the Father is one heresy that was surfacing in the 1640s, chronicled by Thomas Edwards: "That Jesus Christ is not very God, not God essentially, but nominally, not the eternall Son of God, by eternall generation, no otherwise may he be called the Son of God but as he was a man."[35] For Milton, who partially conforms to this heresy, "the ultimate object of faith is not Christ, the Mediator, but God the Father" (475).

In this way, as Ulreich observes, the Incarnation is "actual in one Man, potential in all men," for believers become the adopted "sons of God."[36]

Milton appears sympathetic to some of Paul of Samosata's theological positions. Paul declares that we can only properly refer to the Father as God; Milton argues that the Father alone contains the divine essence, points to the Son's testimony (Mark 12:28–29, 32; John 8:41–54; 17:3; 20:17) that the Father is the "one true God from whom are all things," and concludes that the "Father alone is a self-existent God" (214, 218). Paul states that Jesus was adopted as the Son of God through the Spirit of grace; Milton states that human beings are adopted as God's sons through justification, whereby "we become sons by a new generation and a new nature" (497), this new nature participating in the divine through the essential union with the Logos and purified through the exercise of moral virtue. There are, however, important differences, and Milton has a much fuller sense of the dynamics of the hypostatic union.[37] While Paul asserts that the Word is not the preexistent entity and that Jesus is mere man, Milton is careful to assert that Christ is not one-sidedly human because the Son is preexistent as the firstborn of all creatures, and is the instrument of creation (206, 301). For Milton, unlike Paul, Jesus is more than a virtuous man inspired by the Spirit because the preexistent Logos really dwells within him. Christ's imputed righteousness is essential for human salvation, and his unique position as the firstborn of creation is the avenue through which salvation takes place. Russell Hillier is thus right to point us to the poet's "forensic model of salvation" that shares its major tenets with Paul, Anselm, and Luther. "Milton's theory of the atonement holds that an objective atonement successfully counteracts sin's devastating effects. God's gracious incursion into human affairs becomes necessary because humankind is incapable of saving itself."[38] After salvation, however, Milton indicates that the Logos becomes more manifest in the regenerated lives of believers as they yield in obedience and cooperate with its creative potential throughout the life-long process of sanctification.[39]

The same Logos that abides in Jesus is available to every believer, but it remains only the "dead letter" until believers voluntarily listen to and cooperate with the spirit of the "text" of the Logos. The mystic Jakob Böhme uses the analogue of Marian cooperation as the *Theotókos* for understanding one's participation in the "familiar intimate and native innate work" of "entering into that Becoming Man or Incarnation of Christ."[40] Böhme's works became available in England in the 1640s and gained popularity among the English Böhmenists in the 1660s under the leadership of John Pordage and Jane Leade, and shaped early Quaker thought on yielding to the mysterious motions of the Inner Light.[41] In the first part of his lengthy treatise on the Incarnation, Böhme explains that "in *Adam* we are dead as to Paradise, and must Sprout and Grow again through Death and the *Corruption* of the body, into Paradise, as into another world, in the life of God, into the Heavenly Substantiality and Corporeity."[42] At his creation, Adam was a "looking glass" of God, partaking in the divine substance and perfectly reflecting the "Three Principles" of his creation: the First Principle of the Father, "fierce, wrathful, stearn, astringent . . . and fiery"; the Second Principle of the Son, the "meek light [that] maketh the stearn nature of the Father, meek lovely and merciful"; and the Third Principle, the Wisdom or Spirit of God that manifests itself in "this world's Nature and property." Desiring a looking glass of his own, Satan tempts Adam and causes man to become "a Beastial being or substance" whose knowledge of the blessed mystery of his creation is now made hidden. While Adam retains the eternal "Noble soul," it is "*covered* with an Earthly Garment, and darkned, and infected with the earthly source or quality, and poysoned by the false or Evil Imagination; so that *it* was no more known to be Gods Child."[43] Adam, along with all fallen human beings, "lost the Heavenly *Eyes*," as "his will with its *Imagination* took the Earthly Kingdom in the Souls fire for a lodging" and "went away from the Spirit of God into the Spirit of the *Starres* and the Elements." With his "pure eyes," however, Christ entered into this bestial state, but his "will-spirit" was fully intact and cooperating with the "Power of the Majesty" to put Adam to death so that human beings could regain their former knowledge as children of God and return to the state of paradise.[44] For Böhme, subsequent believers must follow the meek example of the Virgin Mary, whose flesh yielded to the Christ growing within, so that "even while we are yet in this world, covered with the Earthly Tent or Tabernacle, and are fallen home to the Earthly life, viz: meerely, in the *Imagination*" we "with our will enter into Gods will, and wholly unite and give ourselves into Him, which is called *Faith*, or, *Beleeving*." In doing so, we become the "Virgin of Christ," the "Virgin of Modesty and Chastity and purity . . . a Looking-Glass of the Holy Trinity wherein God beholdeth himself." Human self-knowledge and God's self-knowledge are at stake in this return; strangely, in our return God beholds an aspect of himself that otherwise remains hidden. Thus, Mary's resolution, "Behold the handmaid of the Lord; be it unto me according to thy word," and her prayer of exalting the Lord (Luke 1:38, 46–55) is for Böhme the believer's choice to "Cast away your Evil or wickedness, and enter into the Meekness, press into the Truth, into Love, and *yeeld* thyself up to God, and so thou shalt be saved or helped; for therefore is JESUS born."[45] For Böhme and the early Quakers, Jesus is born through a *kenosis* of the earthly self and a *pleroma* of the heavenly self.

This Incarnational dynamic finds its analogue in Milton's theology, where the exercise of moral virtue, the cooperation or "textual fusion" of the human horizon with the divine horizon of the indwelling Logos, becomes of paramount importance to the Christian life: it is through this free, moral cooperation that human "substance" is purified. Consequently, while Ulreich's explication of the doctrine of the Incarnation in *De Doctrina Christiana* is very lucid, it does not sufficiently link the doctrine to Milton's philosophical monism, described in the chapter "On Creation" in the treatise and resonating in several key passages in the poetry. Many scholars have written on the subject of Milton's monism, but as far as I can determine, no one has asserted that the doctrine of the Incarnation is its capstone.[46] This link would in turn account for the tendency of this heterodox poetics toward a kind of soteriological "perfectionism" or human divinization available in the present rather than at the consummation of history.[47] Chapters 6 and 7 will explore more fully the political implications of this perfectionist strain among radical groups in 1640s and 1650s England, but Milton makes the startling claim that believers can possess a "paradise within" that is "happier far" than the external paradise possessed by Adam and Eve. In his *Journal* George Fox writes in 1648 that through his "subjection to the spirit of God" he was "come up to the state of Adam which he was in before he fell," for "the Lord showed me that such as were faithful to him in the power and light of Christ, should come up into that state in which Adam was before he fell, in which the admirable works of the creation, and the virtues thereof, may be known, through the openings of that divine Word of wisdom and power by which they were made." In 1660, Fox preached in Bristol, a stronghold of the Quakers, explaining that "Christ was come to redeem, translate, convert, and regenerate man . . . up into the light, and life, and image, and likeness of God again as man and woman were in before they fell."[48] Fox was no monist, but the connection he makes between Christ's offer of redemption and humanity's "translation" or "conversion" resonates with Milton's monist perfectionism when Raphael explains,

> O *Adam*, one Almighty is, from whom
> All things proceed, and up to him return
>
> . . . .
> . . . one first matter all,
> Indu'd with various forms, various degrees
> Of substance, and in things that live, of life;
> But more refin'd, more spirituous, and pure,
> As nearer to him plac't or nearer tending
> Each in thir several active Spheres assign'd,
> Till body up to spirit work. (*PL* 5.469–78)

While angels, being pure spirit, understand divine things by intuition, humans understand them discursively (488–89). Throughout his spiritual autobiography, Fox asserts that Christ's birth or Second Coming (the two events seem interchangeable) occurs in a person who is subjected to the Inner Light, and it renders an analogous immediacy of divine knowledge. "Great things did the Lord lead me into, and wonderful depths were opened unto me, beyond what can by words be declared," Fox remarks, for those who yield to the Christ within are implicitly those whom Milton describes as being "nearer to him plac't or nearer tending" (*PL* 5.476) who "may receive the Word of wisdom, that opens all things, and come to know the hidden unity in the Eternal Being."[49]

In Raphael's speech, we see that Milton's conception of creation as *ex Deo* departs from the Hebraic *ex nihilo,* long recognized by Milton scholars. Matter is not infinite, but proceeds out of the eternal "one Almighty" with whom all creation shares its substance. The act of creation, declares Milton in his treatise, is a "demonstration of God's supreme power and goodness that he should not shut up this heterogeneous and substantial virtue within himself, but should disperse, propagate and extend it as far as, and in whatever way, he wills." Creation is pure gift, and all original matter is good and perfect because God, out of whom all matter proceeds, is Goodness and Perfection. Moreover, against objectors who would argue that bodies could not emanate from spirit, Milton uncharacteristically echoes the Scholastics, arguing that "spirit, being the more excellent substance, virtually, as they say, and eminently contains within itself what is clearly the inferior substance" (*CPW* 6:309). Christopher Kendrick observes that Milton's monism allows creation to be free and "open-ended" in the process toward purification. "Creation does not strive through its gradual scale toward something that it *lacks,* but rather toward what it truly *is:* a profound (because divine) identity runs through the whole plane of creation." Raphael's body, argues Kendrick, signifies to Adam and Eve the perfected spiritual body, functioning as a kind of "gloss" on creation, a "concrete teaching about the substance of creation."[50] Kendrick may well be right regarding this particular episode, but the angelic "gloss" does not sufficiently clarify the *means* by which humanity ascends. Nor is the model of the angelic being, of a disparate ontological species, to be taken as the most proper ontic *telos* for the human creature. The gloss therefore ceases to be useful, especially after the Fall, because unlike human beings the fallen angels have no hope for redemption.

To be sure, it is the paradigm of the Son's "obedience / Imputed" (*PL* 12.408–9), but also the obedience appropriated, imitated, and persisted in by the faithful in cooperation with the Logos, that displaces the angelic gloss after the Fall and provides the example of ascent. As Hillier shows, Milton's monist ontology allows for a sacramental view of creation; the Incarnation is the fulfillment of Raphael's cosmic picture of the "bright consummate flow'r" whose roots are firmly lodged in the soil of humanity and whose "Spirits odorous" yield the sweet invisible fragrances of salvation and good works (481–82).[51] For Milton the exercise of virtue, the conscious, voluntary cooperation or participation in the will of God modeled after the example of the Son—which is to say, the performance of the hypostatic union of a Logos available to all believers—is the means of ascent, but this ascent happens only after regeneration has occurred. Thus, while the original unformed matter from which human beings and all of creation were fashioned was perfect in itself, Milton asserts that the granting of "form" to that matter renders it "beautiful": "matter was not, by nature, imperfect" and the "addition of forms . . . did not make it more perfect but only more beautiful" (*CPW* 6:308).[52] Form here implies design and *telos,* and the beauty of the human form more precisely finds its most eloquent articulation in the virtuous figure of the Son, not the angels.

In the chapter "On Regeneration," Milton explains that the process of regeneration and sanctification "restores man's natural faculties of faultless understanding and of free will more completely than before." This radical statement is the prose analogue to Milton's poetic utterance that Adam and Eve shall inherit a "paradise within thee, happier far" than unfallen paradise. The process of regeneration "makes the inner man like new and infuses by divine means new and supernatural faculties into the minds of those who are made new" (*CPW* 6:461). Regeneration thus initiates this process of human ascent, the sublimation of the flesh toward spirit. Milton thus avoids the Pelagian heresy, for one's works do not merit salvation in any way, and salvation proceeds from the grace of God through Christ. While Milton seems here to downplay the sense of cooperation, he still emphasizes that regeneration is a *process,* begun by God the Father, through the Spirit, but implicitly continued by habits of virtue cultivated on the part of the believer to become more like the Son. Good works in and of themselves do not save a person, but they are crucial to maintaining salvation, quite apart from John Calvin's notion of the perseverance of the saints.[53] For the author of the treatise, predestination is a general election of those "who believe in their hearts and persist in their belief." Salvation is offered "to all equally, on condition of obedience to the Old Testament and faith in the New" (*CPW* 6:176–77)—a strident Arminian position. Consequently, the process of regeneration and sanctification initiated by the Father, the "one Almighty" who gifts his own substance to all of creation, can actually be reversed if one does not persist in his or her faith. This seems to indicate that repeated acts of disobedience, one's failures to perform the Word in the world, result in a diminishment of one's ontic status or spiritual perfection.

This point becomes clearer in the chapters on faith and virtue, for faith is primarily a verb for Milton—a performance in the world: "if to believe is to act then faith is an action, or rather a habit acquired by frequent actions, not merely infused" (489). But, following Aristotle in the *Nichomachean Ethics,* this doing is preceded by a notion of being.[54] The question for Milton, as it is with Aristotle, is not primarily, "What should I do?" Given Milton's monism, the central query is, "What should I be?" Addressing the recent work of Stanley Hauerwas, Emmanuel Katongole has addressed this ontology of ethical action, arguing for more of a hermeneutical circularity in the shaping of moral character: "in forming action, the agent forms himself. The agent develops a lasting disposition" and "makes it impossible both to separate the self from his or her agency and to understand action without reference to the agent."[55] As Milton sees it, faith is more than the interior intellectual assent, as moderns often characterize it; for Milton it is directed outward in one's performance in the world, and one's actions cannot be separated from the flesh in which humans dwell. There is a sense, then, that one cannot understand the inner workings of the hypostatic union without also understanding how Jesus the Christ engages the world and dwells in the sacred narrative. As Hauerwas puts it, one's moral character "is the category which marks the fact that our lives are not constituted by decision, but rather the moral quality of our lives is shaped by the ongoing orientation formed in and through our beliefs, stories, and intentions."[56] For Milton, the actions of the body thus become crucial to understanding redemption.

So, not only is faith an object, a gift that is given or "infused" into those who respond to the general call to election, but faith is also an action that requires one's active participation. In the chapter on justification, we see that faith involves both of these dimensions, whereas Calvinism tends to emphasize the former over the latter. Milton sees no contradiction between Romans 3:28 and James 2:24, stating that works of faith may be different from works of the law. Believers are "justified, then, by faith, but a living faith, not a dead one, and the only living faith is a faith which acts, James ii. 17, 20, 26. So we are justified by faith without the works of the law, but not without the works of faith; for a true and living faith cannot exist without works, though these may be different from the works of the written law" (490). It is therefore significant that the discussion of virtue and good works occupies the hub of Book Two of *De Doctrina Christiana*, "Of the Worship of God," for it is by one's living faith that he or she properly worships and participates in the "substance" of God.

As we saw in the previous section of this chapter, in Hebrew thought God is by his very nature a God who acts, and one who acts in and through historical circumstances; human substance is "purified" for Milton to the degree that humans act properly, that is, incarnationally, in the world. Milton's philosophical monism is thus importantly tied to the issue of worship and the hermeneutics of testimony. For Milton, the human person is "by gradual scale sublim'd" (*PL* 5.483). That sublimation becomes a function of how well believers appropriate, perform, or incarnate the Logos's potential as a transforming text.[57] In the chapter that follows, I hope to place some pressure on how Milton's heterodox Christology and the strains of his perfectionist theology of virtue shape a general hermeneutic for "sublimated" readers given to the task of discerning the multihued texts that are registered along one's horizon of understanding. Perhaps anticipating a version of poststructuralism's notion of the text, Milton states in *Areopagitica* that "what ever thing we hear or see, sitting, walking, travelling, or conversing, may be fitly call'd our book" (*CPW* 2:528). The activity of reading, whether it involves the leaves of a book or the facets of "this pendant world" (*PL* 2.1052), is ontologically inflected. Even though Milton confesses that he was "Church-outed by the Prelats," he continued to see his writing as emanating from his "Church-outed" pulpit, for in the early modern era the activities of reading and speech were not radically disjoined.[58] Writer is speaker; reader is hearer. Writing is a form of preaching for Milton, and reading is a form of pilgrimage; practicing divine virtue is the ontic crucible for both.

chapter 4

Milton's Parable of Misreading

Discernment, Self-Government, and the Hermeneutics of
the "night-founder'd Skiff" in *Paradise Lost*, 1.192–209

Fecisti nos ad Te, et inquietum est cor nostrum, donec requiescat in Te.
—Augustine, *Confessions*

We first meet Satan and his cohort of rebel angels in *Paradise Lost* as
they are engulfed in "livid flames" (1.182) and are ceaselessly tossing
upon the furious waves of hell's lake, newly vanquished and desirous of
relief. Trying to rouse his fallen troops Satan suggests they raise themselves from the flood and fly toward a "dreary Plain, forlorn and wild,"
and "there rest, if any rest can harbor there" (180, 185), so that they
may hold council about how to proceed. What immediately follows is
a lengthy and lavish description of Satan's magnificent body, which is
nothing less than a visual feast for the reader's hungry eyes as we find
ourselves attracted to this monstrous bulk. In an epic simile, Milton
compares him to both the Titans and Leviathan.

Curiously appended to this latter allusion, however, is a short narrative describing an inexperienced sailor who, mistaking the great sea-
beast for land, moors his small ship upon its back:

Thus Satan talking to his nearest Mate
With Head up-lift above the wave, and Eyes
That sparkling blaz'd, his other Parts besides
Prone on the Flood, extended long and large
Lay floating many a rood, in bulk as huge

· · · · · · · · · · · · · ·
              [as] that Sea-beast
Leviathan, which God of all his works
Created hugest that swim th' Ocean stream:
Him haply slumb'ring on the *Norway* foam
The Pilot of some small night-founder'd Skiff,
Deeming some Island, oft, as Seamen tell,
With fixed Anchor in his scaly rind
Moors by his side under the Lee, while Night
Invests the Sea, and wished Morn delays:
So stretcht out huge in length the Arch-fiend lay. (1.192–209)

Some readers are tempted perhaps to make little of Milton's "night-founder'd Skiff," relegating it to a mere commonplace. But Milton displays an especial fondness for nautical metaphors, scattered throughout his poetry and prose, and such consistent use by a very conscientious man of letters merits that we gauge the image with more import.[1] Alternately, readers may not delve into the implications of the short narrative because the skiff is overshadowed by Satan's sublime body. But I suggest that this is precisely the point. The idol that Milton carves for our gaze's consumption distracts us from the hermeneutical task at hand: how to read Satan and the physical and spiritual landscape of hell that follows.

    In the previous chapter we examined the prominent place of virtue in Milton's heterodox Christology and monist philosophy. In this chapter I want to illuminate how those doctrinal threads intertwine with Milton's hermeneutical assumptions and poetic imagination. The short narrative of the "night-founder'd Skiff" invites a novel consideration of Milton's use of the epic simile: as parable.[2] Milton draws upon a theological trope richly explored by Origen, Basil the Great, and Augustine, wherein the individual soul is likened to a ship navigating the perilous waters of spiritual existence.[3] In doing so, Milton as preacher and parable-maker accomplishes two things. First, through a negative example the parable teaches his congregation of readers that the individual soul moored upon Leviathan, understood by some expositors in the early modern period to be a figure of Satan, is characterized by spiritual restlessness. Second, Milton's parable of the "night-founder'd Skiff" becomes an object lesson in exegesis whereby divine virtue (the Latin *virtus* means, among other things, "power" or "skill") — radically reconsidered toward a view of human perfection in the previous chapter — becomes the crucial hermeneutical lens for readers of texts.[4] Just as the undisciplined sailor of the skiff incorrectly reads the "text" of the physical landscape before him, Milton's fallen angels and the undisciplined person will be unable to read correctly the ecclesial and political "texts" before them, as we find that the image of the vulnerable skiff becomes conflated with the ships of church and state.

In order to flesh out these spiritual implications for Milton's parable, this chapter focuses on three related contexts: the theological, the contemplative, and the homiletic traditions. The first section traces Milton's rich theological inheritance of the nautical trope with some observations on how Origen, Basil, and Augustine appropriate the image to comment on the necessity of cultivating virtue and spiritual discernment when the believer is confronted with various "texts." Milton co-opts the trope for his parable, and in the second section I draw out its spiritual implications. Like the fallen angels, these restless misreaders become indistinguishable from Satan himself as Milton draws upon a notion of virtue that is intimately related to early Christian philosophical contemplation and conversion. Further, I examine Satan's own restless wandering in the poem, for his restlessness and its causes and consequences are the archetypal template for Milton of all restless souls and misreaders: those moored upon the false stability of Leviathan by either choice or lack of vigilance and virtue. The third section gathers these issues together by exploring more closely Milton's role as preacher and parable-maker speaking truth to institutions of power — the ships of church and state — as we find that Milton borrows from the tradition of the medieval exemplum to construct his parable of the "night-founder'd Skiff." Exploring these hermeneutical contexts and interrogating the epic simile in this manner will prepare us for our examination of two of Milton's spiritual readers that we will examine in the following chapter. As "pilots" of their own "skiffs," Samson and Jesus are faced with the task of discerning the various "texts" placed before them in their trials and temptations as they encounter the "Leviathans" of false transcendence. Milton's "night-founder'd Skiff" thus offers us a narrative picture of the soul in reading, one that has far-reaching implications beyond Book 2 of his great epic.

A few words need to be said regarding the parable form. For the purposes of this chapter, Madeleine Boucher's definition suffices: "The *parable*, then . . . is a structure consisting of *a tropical narrative, or a narrative having two levels of meaning;* this structure functions as *religious or ethical rhetorical speech.*" Further, "the interpretation of a parable is always ethical or theological discourse."[5] The parable, as Frank Kermode explains in his classic study of the Markan parables, is inextricably bound with the issue of the audience that the parable creates. He argues that the parable is a kind of riddle and that "to divine the true, the latent sense, you need to be of the elect, of the institution. Outsiders must content themselves with the manifest, and pay a supreme penalty for doing so."[6] This is not to say that every parable must be obscure, however, as Boucher reminds us, but because the parable form is an "implied comparison" it requires "some insight on the part of the hearer if it is to be apprehended."[7] In his landmark *The Parables of the Kingdom* (1935), C. H. Dodd insightfully comments, "the parable has the character of an argument, in that it entices the hearer to a judgment upon the situation depicted, and then challenges him, directly or by implication, to apply that judgment to the matter in hand."[8]

For all of these critics, discernment is required of the parable's audience, and there is no guarantee that the parable will find its audience. Moreover, one might argue that the parable is an incarnational genre. Not only does it demand its hearers to bear testimony by giving flesh to the dynamic words of the narrative, but it also reflects the theological aesthetics of the Incarnation itself. The parable displays a kind of *kenotic* immediacy in its "meanly wrapt" narrative simplicity, but that immediacy is complicated by its *pleromic* potential as it attempts to communicate the profound spiritual truths of that "far-beaming blaze of Majesty" ("On the Morning of Christ's Nativity," 9). In the end, we are left with powerful disclosive metaphors that awaken hearers from their spiritual slumber and summon them into hermeneutical and enfleshed performance: "The kingdom of heaven is like . . . , therefore, he who has ears, let him hear."

As a discourse of preaching, therefore, the parable form is an exegetical crucible and a *mimesis* of the Incarnation as the w/Word dwells in the narrative of one's fleshly actions, and as the self is confronted with a possible *kenosis* (Paul Ricoeur's sense of alienation) and *pleroma* (Ricoeur's sense of appropriation). Given the dynamics that the parable imposes upon its audience, we would be remiss if we did not remind ourselves of Milton's own desire, expressed in the invocation to Urania, that his song "fit audience find, though few" (*PL* 7.31). Sharon Achinstein and David Loewenstein have both addressed how Milton and other revolutionary writers construct a "fit" audience. Milton's "aim became not simply to pass on his revolutionary messages in code," Achinstein writes, "but to mold a readership that was increasingly required to know how to decipher conflicting interpretations." Loewenstein similarly asserts that *Paradise Lost* "constantly challenges its engaged readers by showing them how to discern the treacherous ambiguities and contradictions of political rhetoric and behavior."[9] In using the parable form, Milton implicitly assumes the pulpit and acts as a kind of preacher exhorting his congregation to become more discerning readers, not just of books, but of the world-text, for "what ever thing we hear or see, sitting, walking, travelling, or conversing may be fitly call'd our book" (*Areopagitica, CPW* 2:528). Presently, we need to immerse ourselves with Milton in the perilous waters of the theological tradition in order to see how the nautical trope of Milton's parable was variously developed in the patristic tradition. Such a voyage will allow us to see how Milton appropriates the nautical trope and how the image helps us to comprehend the spiritual and exegetical implications of the parable.

Soul as Ship: Virtue as a Hermeneutical Lens in the Theological Tradition

As key patristic figures concerned with properly interpreting the Bible, Origen, Basil, and Augustine maintained particular assumptions about texts and readers of texts—whether those texts are pagan epics or entire philosophical systems, and whether those readers are initiates or wizened churchmen. These are assumptions that Milton, as one of the Bible's central interpreters in the seventeenth century, inherited and to which he gave assent. The first section of this chapter delineates one assumption in particular, that virtue is a general hermeneutical lens through which readers should read. Why? For these churchmen it is primarily the *soul* that reads in an act of *lectio divina* ("sacred reading"). Brian Stock explains that for "medieval thinkers reading was rarely an end in itself; most often it was conceived as a means to an end, which was the creation of a contemplative state of mind." This contemplative state allows the reader to reflect spiritually on the "soul's progress or education."[10] Milton's program of education intriguingly shares the assumptions of this medieval paradigm of reading, for the soul's progress can be partially measured in the narrative movements of the flesh, and Milton's heterodox Christology and theology of virtue are the foundation upon which his hermeneutic rests. Without the lens of virtue the soul is in a precarious position, at risk of being deceived or swept away by textual forces more powerful than the reader. Potentially, reading is a perilous journey; in this sense, reading is pilgrimage.[11] Consequently, for Origen, Basil, Augustine, and Milton, there is no better picture of the soul in reading than the ship upon the seas.

The image of the ship navigating the seas belongs to the category of tropes that view the Christian life as pilgrimage. Barbara Lewalski explains that "such metaphors were understood to be grounded upon true analogies between natural and spiritual things. . . . Also, though they were used in the service of doctrinal exposition, such tropes were not transformed into simple doctrinal statements, but rather provide an imaginative rendering of the experience of living the Christian life."[12] Although Lewalski does not mention the nautical metaphor, it is an enormously popular image in poems, sermons, and emblems of the early modern period. Milton makes extensive use of the image in both his poetry and prose. In *Paradise Regained,* for instance, Satan laments his loss of hope for redemption, saying, "worst is my Port, / My harbor and my ultimate repose, / The end I would attain, my final good" (*PR* 3.209–10). In *Samson Agonistes,* upon which we will place extended pressure in the following chapter, the protagonist reflects on his blindness, loneliness, and spiritual folly: "How could I once look up, or heave the head, / Who like a foolish Pilot have shipwreck't / My Vessel trusted to me from above, / Gloriously rigg'd" (*SA* 197–200). Edmund Spenser capitalizes on the metaphor in Book 2, Canto 12 of *The Faerie Queene.* The temperate Sir Guyon and the wise Palmer navigate their hazardous way to the island where lies Acrasia's erotic "bowre of blis." The two successfully steer through the "*Gulfe of Greedinesse,*" the "*Rocke of Reproch,*" the "*wandring Islands,*" the "*Whirlpoole of decay,*" and sundry other monsters and "fearefull shapes" whose purpose is to detract them from their task (2.xii.3, 9, 11, 20).[13] The seal that John Donne adopts for his family crest alludes to the trope, for as he explains "The Crosse (my seal at Baptism) spred below / Does, by that form, into an Anchor grow. / . . . / But he that makes our Crosses Anchors thus, / Is Christ, who there is crucifi'd for us."[14] In 1607, the preacher Robert Wilkinson delivered a sermon on Proverbs 31:14 in honor of his wife, likening the virtuous wife to a ship that "wafts him home."[15]

Such a lucid image easily lends itself to early modern emblems, and Francis Quarles, the collector and author of *Emblemes* (1635), provocatively suggests that an "Embleme is but a silent parable."[16] In Diego de Saavedra Fajardo's *The Royal Politician Represented in One Hundred Emblems* (English translation, 1700), the trope is extended to the ship of state with the emblem displaying a ship in full sail on turbulent waves, and the prince figured as the ship's pilot: "with no less Care and Diligence the Prince ought to Steer the Vessel of his State in the tempestuous Sea of his Reign. . . . He is a Pilot, to whose Conduct the Life and Safety of all is committed."[17] As we will see, Milton uses this popular image in his short narrative of the small skiff moored upon

Leviathan as an imaginative picture of the individual "ark of the soul" reading and navigating the waters of spiritual life, as well as a figure for the ships of state and church. The latter recalls for us Milton's caustic rejection of the Wordless clergy that we examined in his pastoral elegy, as the English church is likened to "that fatal and perfidious Bark / Built in th'eclipse, and rigg'd with curses dark, / That sunk so low that sacred head of thine" ("Lycidas," 100–102).

The distinctly scriptural locus for this nautical-metaphysical trope occurs in 1 Peter 3:18–22, in which the Apostle allegorizes the Genesis account of Noah's ark. Here Peter indicates that Noah's trial and salvation through water are similar to the ceremony of baptism for believers; by participating in baptism, the believer shares in and identifies with Christ, the new Noah.[18] What seems to be important to Peter, and to many early expositors, is that water is linked to the salvation of God's people through a kind of ceremonial cleansing.

The image of the ark lurching upon the furious waters of salvation/baptism is treated, characteristically, with some measure of hermeneutical "violence" in Origen's second *Homily on Genesis*. Origen analyzes the construction of the ark, adopts the language of individual virtue, and assigns spiritual meanings to the mundane. Broadly speaking, he likens the ark to the church and the animals and humans within as its people. The various decks and compartments in the ark represent different levels of spiritual progress within the church, even though all are saved by one faith through one baptism. Those who progress and live "by rational knowledge and are capable not only of ruling themselves but also of teaching others, since very few are found, represent the few who are saved with Noah himself and are united with him in the closest relationship, just as also our Lord, the true Noah, Christ Jesus, has few intimates." Those believers in the upper decks of the ark who are trained in the practice of virtue, capable of managing and subduing their passions, are to be distinguished from the "multitude" of those of the lower decks "whose fierce raging the charm of faith has not tamed."[19] Implicitly, the virtuous are less affected by the terrors of the storm outside, "anchored" as they are in their relational proximity to the mind of Christ; conversely, the spiritually slothful, whose passions still rule instead of Christ's presence in their hearts, are at the mercy of constant flux and undulation.

In yet another exposition, Origen develops this notion of individual virtue and vice. If a person, seeing that "evils are increasing and vices are overflowing, can turn from the things which are in flux and passing away and fallen, and can hear the word of God and the heavenly precepts, this man is building an ark of salvation within his own heart and is dedicating a library, so to speak, of the divine word within himself." He comments further that the virtuous man's ark, or his "library," is constructed from planks that are straight and squared, "that is, not from the volumes of secular authors, but from the prophetic and apostolic volumes."[20] The image of the ark upon the waters, then, is an appropriate metaphor for the spiritual life of the believer—the individual soul navigating the spiritual realities of existence where his virtue is tested. Additionally, as Origen makes clear, as much as the nautical metaphor befits an image of the individual soul, it is also a picture of the collective "soul" of the church, the one body with many members that functions in union and harmony with Christ (Rom. 12:4–5). Thus the individual person and/or church that heeds the divine commands and cultivates and exercises virtue will land securely upon Mt. Ararat, rather than being moored upon a sea-beast that might soon be plunging below the waves. Milton's little "skiff" is a far cry from Noah's huge ark, but he chose it precisely for its vulnerability and precarious position.

In his treatise *To Young Men on Reading Greek Literature,* no doubt familiar to Milton, who sought to accommodate pagan literature to Christian understanding, Basil the Great develops Origen's image of the "library" of the soul. He argues that pagan literature may help prepare the young man to receive the mysteries of the church, using the metaphor of a cloth being made ready through various treatments to receive the dye; "so we also in the same manner must first, if the glory of the good is to abide with us indelible for all time, be instructed by these outside means, and then shall understand the sacred and mystical teachings."[21] Like Origen, Basil is careful to articulate that the individual exercise of virtue is always with a vision for the ecclesial community; the individual young man learns to practice virtue so that he might be prepared to receive the sacraments of the church, and in this way join its mystical community. In reading the ancient poets and orators, the young man must develop the spiritual virtue of discernment, which is implicitly connected to reading, as he gleans that which is helpful in cultivating virtue and jettisons that which promotes vice.[22]

"[W]henever they [the poets] recount for you the deeds or words of good men," Basil urges, "you ought to cherish and emulate these and try to be as far as possible like them; but when they treat of wicked men, you ought to avoid such imitation, stopping your ears no less than Odysseus did."[23] We can fault Basil for not recollecting the episode of the Sirens correctly from Book 12 of *The Odyssey*. Odysseus did not stop up his ears; warned by Circe of the treacherous song of the Sirens, he was bound to the mast in order to hear the alluring Siren-song. Provocatively, however, we might imagine that Basil's mistake may be purposeful, thereby demonstrating to his audience that they were already hyperconscious of such details and thus prone to the very dangers he is describing. But Basil's intent seems clear: one is prepared to receive the sacred mysteries of the church through careful and constant spiritual exercise, in this case, a kind of virtuous mimesis. Again, we return to the nautical metaphor: the Sirens lured unwary, unprepared, undisciplined sailors to their deaths upon the rocks by the beauty of their tempting song, promising safe refuge. Odysseus is nearly driven mad with desire, and had it not been for his crew stopping *their* ears, his ship surely would have been lost much earlier than it was.

Virtue can be learned through literary example, argues Basil, but, predictably, so can vice. To Basil "the soul must be watched over with all vigilance," and pagan poetry has the power to seduce reason, will, and desire. Pagan poetry often depicts men "engaged in amours or drunken" or "define[s] happiness in terms of an over-abundant table or dissolute songs." For Basil such distorted images make a mockery of humanity's *telos* in conforming to the divine image. Further, they are blasphemous in their depictions of the divine itself when gods are represented in multiplicity, in adulteries, and in brutish actions. So, although Basil sees a value in pagan literature, he sternly admonishes "that you should not surrender to these men once for all the rudders of your mind, as if of a ship, and follow them whithersoever they lead."[24] With vigilant care, the ship of one's soul will navigate successfully the raging waters and find its proper moorings in the church and in divine love. The question, for Basil, is one of control: Who or what is at the rudder of one's "skiff" as a person navigates the waters of spiritual existence?

It is a question with which Augustine deals in his own spiritual autobiography. He perhaps makes the most extensive use of the nautical metaphor (and pagan poetry) to describe his own spiritual wanderings, his "sacrilegious quest for knowledge."[25] Augustine describes his restless soul, wandering the churning spiritual waters of Ciceronian rhetoric, Manicheism, Skepticism, and Platonic philosophy, until finally finding rest through his conversion to Christianity under the tutelage of Ambrose. Augustine relies heavily on the greatest Latin epic to describe this journey toward conversion, the story of one tossed upon the menacing waves of the Mediterranean, only to arrive finally at his destination in Rome. The influence of *The Aeneid* on Augustine's *Confessions* cannot be overestimated; in many instances, Augustine directly echoes passages from Virgil, only to reinscribe them within the context of his spiritual journey toward God.[26] Throughout the narrative, Augustine sees himself as the spiritual Aeneas, and by implication the epic hero, who cannot rest until he is truly "home." For Aeneas that home is on the seven hills of Palatine along the River Tiber, where Rome will one day flourish. For Augustine that home is in the city of God, a place to which the ravaged soul can always return because it is in eternity.[27] As with Aeneas's journey, Augustine's "skiff of the soul" was not to find the shore for many years, and he would experience much grief and restlessness while on the voyage.

Yet for Augustine the church on earth is the embodiment of this eschatological realization, constituted of individual souls engaged in practicing virtue and navigating their individual way, but paradoxically united in their voyage as a collective body under Christ, who is at the helm. It is for the edification of the church, the communion of the saints, that Augustine has written his *Confessions*: "Stir up the heart when people read and hear the confessions of my past wickedness. . . . Prevent their heart from sinking into the sleep of despair. . . . I am making this confession not only before you . . . , but also in the ears of believing sons of men, sharers in my joy, conjoined with me in mortality, my fellow citizens and pilgrims."[28] Augustine hopes that the experiences of one man's continued "misreading" of God will teach the community of saints how to properly read his text and respond to its exhortations.

As with Origen and Basil, Augustine collapses the part-whole dynamic, but without diminishing the crucial role of either. The individual soul must be responsible in its own care through personal discipline so that the ecclesial "ship" can properly function; the properly functioning church continues to offer vision and guidance so that all individuals might be delivered unto a safe harbor. If the "skiffs" of individual souls are "restless" because they are not properly anchored in the discipline and virtue of Christ, then the ecclesial ship will have little hope than to churn restlessly upon the waves as well, or (worse yet) end up "night-founder'd." Clearly then, in the theological tradition the nautical trope is a figure for both the individual soul and the united body of Christ navigating the waters of the world—a kind of sacred hermeneutical circle.

We find this part-whole dynamic at work in Milton's parable as well. If we understand Milton's skiff as a figure of the individual in a hermeneutical relation to a church, then we must pay closer attention to the spiritual aspects of reading and the virtue of discernment. For Origen, Basil, and Augustine, individual readers of texts, whether sacred or pagan texts, or entire philosophical systems, must exercise care in discerning how these texts impact the spiritual course of one's life, for those texts will influence, in turn, the course and direction of the church. In particular, Milton's parable of the "night-founder'd Skiff" is a picture, then, of both the individual and the corporate soul—Satan and the demonic counterpart of the church—who are engaged in misreading.

Milton's Restless Readers: Infernal Reading and Diminished Ontology

Milton inherits this rich theological tradition and works it throughout the fabric of *Paradise Lost*. If we read the passage concerning the "night-founder'd Skiff" as a parable of misreading with this exegetical tradition in mind, what is unfolded? In this section I address the spiritual implications of Milton's parable through the early Christian philosophical and contemplative tradition, so influential upon figures such as Basil and Augustine. I want to suggest that we understand early Christian contemplative practice as one species of *lectio divina,* the soul in reading, whereby a person *becomes* that which his mind gazes upon. Reading, then, was conceived as an incarnational practice as the flesh gave form and expression to the concerns of the soul. Within this context the undisciplined pilot in Milton's parable becomes indistinguishable from Leviathan, and the careless soul who has attached himself to Satan will potentially share in his spiritual restlessness and in his destruction.

Satan understands God's sleepless reading as power. In Satan's restless dissent from sleep, he becomes a restless oppositional reader of God's essence and God's speech. Ross Chambers argues that reading mediates shifts in desire. He suggests that "oppositionality taps the strength of power in ways that produce deflections in desire, and hence a certain mode of change." Chambers understands this oppositional or "seductive" reading as irony, "that is, as the production through reading of a meaning that is not said, a (mis-)reading that thereby appropriates the discourse of power."[29] In Satan's readerly seduction of the angelic host, he creates his own culture and *ecclesia* of restless readers that co-opt the divine power to read in order to produce a meaning "not said": God can become a subject, a text they can master rather than the Text in whom they participate as signs. We understand at the outset of Milton's parable that Satan is a reader of texts and is in charge of his own ecclesial vessel, as he is engaged in "talking to his nearest Mate" (*PL* 1.192). As we will find, however, the irony that the demonic readers produce diminishes not only their own ontology, but also the ontology of those human readers who unwittingly attach themselves to Leviathan. It behooves us to ask: How have the fallen angels fared in their own navigation, in their own sacred reading? What have their minds gazed upon that defines their course and destination? Perhaps more important, what are they becoming in the process?

To address these questions we must begin with the practice of philosophy in the ancient world, for in their desperate attempt to "charm / Pain for a while and anguish," the fallen angels practice "false Philosophie," a "discourse more sweet" than epic song (2.566–67, 565, 555). In *Philosophy as a Way of Life,* Pierre Hadot examines the attitude of many ancients toward the interpretation of philosophical texts. Hadot argues that many Greco-Roman philosophers had a much different conception of the practice of philosophy from moderns. For the ancients, the "philosophical act is not situated merely on the cognitive level, but on that of the self and of being. It is a progress which causes us to *be* more fully, and makes us better." The focus of philosophy among many Stoics, Epicureans, and early Christians was centered on reshaping the self: "It is a conversion which turns our entire life upside down, changing the life of the person who goes through it. It raises the individual from an inauthentic condition of life, darkened by unconsciousness and harassed by worry, to an authentic state of life, in which he attains self-consciousness, an exact vision of the world, inner peace, and freedom."[30] The purpose of philosophy was the shaping and reshaping of the self in all its facets: spiritual, emotional, and intellectual. In this sense, the philosophical life was a true exercise in virtue manifested through self-dialogue and meditation in order to understand better one's position in the world, one's experience of it, and the true nature of reality as conceived in each conceptual system. The purpose of these practices is to bring the philosopher into greater self-awareness in order to foster spiritual vigilance; in short, they are meant to gain control over the will.

Meditation, or contemplation, seems especially germane to Milton, who must have spent hours each day in the occupation.[31] Hadot classically defines meditation as "an effort to assimilate an idea, notion, or principle, and make them come alive in the soul."[32] The notion of assimilation has its roots in Neo-Platonic contemplation. In both cases, pure contemplation of the Good, the One, the Beautiful results not only in knowing them and their essence, but also in becoming them. In his *Enneads* Plotinus describes the moment of transformation through meditation upon an object: "Then the seer no longer sees his object, for in that instant he no longer distinguishes himself from it; he no longer has the impression of two separate things, but *he has, in a sense, become another.*"[33]

The Christian philosopher was in constant communion with the active Presence of God, and the practice of Christian philosophy was in conforming to the model of Christ, the divine image, through the exercise of reason and will. Hadot quotes Basil: "We must keep watch over our heart with all vigilance . . . to avoid ever losing the thought of God."[34] Remembrance of God and meditation upon and obedience to his divine law are central in becoming "fused" with God, in will, mind, soul, spirit, and action; the object upon which his mind gazes is that which the Christian philosopher becomes. Removing God from one's thoughts was to remove (or, at the very least, limit) God's active Presence in one's life.

This contemplative tradition, therefore, understands that the spiritual life is governed in significant ways by the object of the mind's gaze. When we couple this tradition with the theological tradition, which understands the "skiff" to be a figure of both individual and corporate spiritual life, what is revealed in Milton's parable? We have seen in Origen, Basil, and Augustine that diligence and vigilance must characterize one's treatment of his or her soul, and that this vigilance (or lack thereof) spills over into the community of saints. The question is: to what or whom does the rudder of one's contemplative soul belong? Upon what is the soul gazing, and in the process *becoming:* the divine who promises rest, or Leviathan who promises restlessness?

In Milton's parable, the sailor appears to lack the necessary vigilance and discernment required of him to interpret the immediate situation and preserve his small skiff. We gather implicitly that the pilot is inexperienced, perhaps lost, for he is "night-founder'd" and wishes for morning to arrive with greater haste (1.208). By fixing his anchor upon the "slumb'ring" sea-beast, the pilot has unwittingly abandoned hope for returning home, finding rest, or perhaps simply surviving—a terrifying realization he will have all too soon if he finds himself lurching and plunging at the whims of the great creature and unable to sever his link. If we push beyond the literal level to the spiritual level of the parable, we find that the sailor of the skiff (the individual soul), in his mooring (in contemplation) on the sea-beast, has for the moment given over the control of his craft (mind and will) to Leviathan (Satan) so as to be indistinguishable from the whims (will and desire) of the creature. Such a joining has physical consequences for the sailor (among them a precarious fight for survival or a death by drowning) and spiritual consequences for the soul (restlessness and potential destruction).

Peter C. Herman fruitfully takes critics to task for assuming too resolutely conclusions such as these, delineating the ways in which this sea-creature is *not* like Satan. Unlike Satan, the whale intends no evil; the pilot's error is a matter of chance, as indicated by the whale's "haply slumbring on the *Norway* foam" (203), whereas the Fall of Adam and Eve is not. Also, the trajectory of the narrative is incomplete and "suspended" between night and morning, suggesting to Herman that the moral or spiritual implications of the incident are "inconclusive."[35] His first objection that the whale intends no evil must be conceded. Concerning his second objection, however, the whale's presence may be a matter of happenstance, but the pilot's error in discernment (like that of Adam and Eve) is most emphatically not. Herman's third objection rests on his principle of incertitude. The scene of the skiff anchored on Leviathan is certainly a liminal moment, as Herman points out, as are all moments of temptation whether they involve one's full, intentional cooperation or one's unwitting participation because of ignorance, deception, or a lack of spiritual vigilance. The ultimate fate of the pilot is left suspended because for Milton temptation can be a positive force for spiritual formation and instruction, as he argues in *Areopagitica.* But while forgiveness is available through grace, spiritual failure exacts a high price, as the poem demonstrates through Satan's example, and "it is indisputable that even the least sin renders a man liable to condemnation" (*De Doctrina Christiana, CPW* 6:392). Herman argues that the "cumulative effect" of "unresolved choices" in Milton's work "is not so much to enforce upon the reader the limitations of fallen cognition [*pace* Stanley Fish] . . . but to instill a pervasive sense of uncertainty."[36] Is it not the case, however, that for Milton uncertainty is precisely one illustration of the limitation of "fallen cognition"? Herman's incertitude principle can be simultaneously illuminating, liberating, and paralyzing, leaving readers to encounter a Milton who was riddled with profound doubt as a result of the catastrophe of the Restoration. Taken to an extreme, however, Herman's incertitude principle renders to us a Milton who rarely made up his mind or who deliberately obscured his own purposes.[37]

To be sure, Milton did change his mind on a number of issues as a result of the pressures exerted in the crucibles of history and experience. But Herman's argument that Milton's overarching goal is to nourish in readers a "pervasive" state of confusion and quandary is an overzealous claim. Surely Milton thought there is apprehendable, relatively stable, and demonstrative "truth"; otherwise, he would not have engaged in a polemical career as a political pamphleteer that extended beyond the Restoration, neither would he have cultivated a prophetic persona, nor have sought to clarify and explicate Christian doctrine for the express purpose of "restoring religion to something of its pure original state," as the opening epistle to the treatise delineates (*CPW* 6:117). On the other hand, however, is not this state of quandary precisely where Milton wants his reader? The ambiguity, uncertainty, or "inconclusive" hermeneutics places the reader in the position most lauded by Milton: as heretic, or "one who chooses." It seems to me more likely that *this* virtue is what Milton wants to instill in his readership: a "pervasive sense," not of "uncertainty," as Herman argues, but of reasoned liberty, whether in matters inconclusive or indifferent. We might liken the contending readers of this particular epic simile (and other similar points in the poem) to the various seventeenth-century sects arguing over inconclusive points of doctrine and practice that Milton addresses and supports in *Of True Religion* (1673).[38] There, he invokes the rule of charity and memorably declares that "no true Protestant can persecute, or not tolerate his fellow Protestant, though dissenting from him in som opinions" (*CPW* 8:421). Milton freely states that there are some in those sects who dwell "in a true Church as well as in a false," and for illustration he resolutely comments that Job's friends were surely "much mistaken . . . in some Points of Doctrin," but he is convinced that "God will assuredly pardon them" nonetheless (8:422, 424). In the paragraphs that follow, I can only hope that my "fellow Protestants" will recognize a reasoned interpretive choice, and thereby extend the rule of charity (if not pardon).

Significantly, "Leviathan" derives from the Hebrew *livyāthān* and means "to twine," "to abide with," "to cleave," and "to join." Milton's Leviathan in this passage is an allusion to Isaiah 27:1, in which the Lord "shall punish Leviathan, the piercing serpent, even Leviathan, that crooked serpent; and he shall slay the dragon that is in the sea."[39] The image of the Dragon recalls Revelation 12:9, in which John calls Satan the "great dragon . . . that old serpent . . . which deceiveth the whole world," as well as Revelation 13, in which the Beast "having seven heads and ten horns" (v. 1) rises out of the sea and is given authority by the Dragon.[40]

John Calvin offers some relevant insight into the figure of "Leviathan," for he, too, explicitly uses the nautical image to describe the perils of the Christian life: "It ought therefore to be observed, that we have continually to do with Satan as with some wild beast, and that the world is the sea in which we sail. We are beset by various wild beasts, which endeavor to upset our ship and sink us to the bottom; and we have no means of defending ourselves and resisting them, if the Lord do not aid us." Calvin emphasizes Satan's "cunning devices" to deceive the elect: "Wonderful are the stratagems with which he comes prepared for doing mischief, and dreadful the cruelty which he exercises against the children of God."[41] The Lord's "aid" is his great sword (Isa. 27:1), but one might also infer that the vigilant soul who cultivates a healthy habit of contemplating the divine and its workings in the world will be granted a certain kind of illumination to see through the various hermeneutical "stratagems" that Satan sets—the sundry illusions of stability, transcendence, and safety that threaten the security of the individual and the church.

Calvin's commentary on Isaiah 27 also widens the scope of Leviathan's realm to include secular and ecclesial governments. He posits that "Leviathan" refers immediately to the king of Egypt, but allegorically extends to Satan and the agents of his kingdom who are constantly at work against the elect. To be sure, the waters of spiritual existence are occupied not only by the solitary figure of Leviathan—he has minions, the "other enemies of the Church," encompassing the civil and ecclesial powers that may be conspiring against the elect.[42] In Ephesians 6:12 Paul emphasizes that the believer wrestles "not against flesh and blood, but against principalities, against powers, against the rulers of the darkness of this world, against spiritual wickedness in high places." Paul indicates that the believer's struggle is ultimately a spiritual one, but some early modern preachers and expositors comment that demonic forces may be at work in current political and ecclesial institutions.[43] This passage, preceded by Paul's exhortation that believers "put on the whole armour of God" (v. 11), and others focusing on Christian militancy were embraced by the "hotter-sort" of Protestants as legitimate grounds for civil disobedience and even holy warfare.[44]

In his 1637 rail against the prelates, John Bastwick encourages just this zealous warfare. In his introductory epistle "To the Courteous Reader," Bastwick offers the *Letany* as a kind of primer to oppositional reading. By their "serious contemplations" and "prayer," studious and meditative readers will ascend the "ladder of my devotions" in order to "mount into the empyrean Paradise." In doing so, the reader "mayst be guided in thy whole Christian warfare, rightly to march and orderly to fight & warre against all thy spiritiall enimyes." In large part, the prelates deserve the brunt of this attack. The *Letany* will allow the reader to climb to the top of Mt. Pisgah to view not only the paradise of Canaan, but also the "*seas and gulfes of all episcopall deformity and PRELATICAL wickednes and ungratitude.*" Moreover, attentive readers "shalt with as great facility descerne those Leuiathans that deuoure the soules, bodyes, and goods, of all those that by the tempest of the world are driven into their Ocians."[45] The prelates seduce others into trusting them and their understanding of scripture, a temptation that leads to the spiritual destruction of a nation.

Clearly for Calvin and Bastwick, "that Sea-beast *Leviathan*" alluded to in Milton's parable is a figure of Satan, who will eventually be toppled and brought under judgment. Because the image of Leviathan is associated with biblical prophecy, Milton's allusion to it in the parable becomes apocalyptic.[46] Sharon Achinstein reflects on how radical writers often had to "write between the lines" during times of suppression, but observes that this was not "the only reason for elliptical writing." The "radical obscurity" may also "point to an otherworldliness that is beyond representation."[47] Milton's parable, however, manages to conceal, to reveal, and to represent that "otherworldliness." The implicit warning within his parable is that the careless soul and ecclesial community—which lack discernment and discipline, which do not practice virtue, which "gaze" indiscriminately or haphazardly—are in danger of obliteration along with Leviathan, Dragon, and Beast when Judgment is rendered.

But while these eschatological consequences are clear, Milton's parable also points to an even more immediate consequence to cleaving to Leviathan: spiritual restlessness, of the sort that occupies the center of Augustine's narrative. In order to draw out this implication we must turn briefly to the figure of the Leviathan of Milton's poem. By examining Satan's own restlessness and peregrinations in *Paradise Lost,* that which occupy the gaze of his mind and the minds of his own infernal *ecclesia,* we gain greater insight into these spiritual dimensions of the parable as Milton further alerts his congregation of readers to the realities of spiritual life while one is moored upon Leviathan.

One of the recurring motifs in *Paradise Lost* is restlessness and rest: from the peregrinations of Satan across the "Illimitable Ocean" of the "wild Abyss" (2.892, 910), through the cosmos to the garden; to the demons' wanderings "O'er many a Frozen, many a Fiery Alp, / Rocks, Caves, Lakes, Fens, Bogs, Dens, and shades of death" (620–21); from the slumber of the angelic throng in heaven "Fann'd with cool Winds" (5.655), and the amorous embraces of the "Blest pair," lulled to sleep by the dulcet songs of nightingales (4.771–75) before the Fall; to the violent surges of biblical history eventuating from the "wand'ring steps and slow" of the solitary pair after their banishment; and finally to the "eternal Paradise of rest" effected by the Son's obedience (12.314). Throughout his epic Milton is preoccupied with divine rest and rebellious restlessness, and he confirms Augustine's assertion, "You have made us for yourself, and our heart is restless, until it rests in you."[48]

What occupies the gaze of Satan's mind and the minds of his infernal *ecclesia*—that which determines the course and *telos* of their individual skiffs and collective ship—is nothingness. Recall Augustine's realization that in his spiritual wanderings he became to himself "a region of destitution": "You [my soul] seek the happy life in the region of death; it is not there. How can there be a happy life where there is not even life?"[49] In the poem Satan echoes Augustine's grief when he admits, "which way I fly is Hell; myself am Hell" (*PL* 4.75). The desolation and pain within, marked by the absence of God's life-giving and life-sustaining Being, are mirrored by the desolation without, in the hellish landscape where the demons "view'd first thir lamentable lot, and found / No rest: through many a dark and dreary Vale / They pass'd, and many a Region dolorous" (2.617–19). Milton goes to great lengths to describe their infernal inheritance, simultaneously a "Dungeon horrible" and a "great Furnace," whose flames reveal "regions of sorrow" and "doleful shades," and "where peace / And rest can never dwell, hope never comes" (1.61–62, 65–66). Much like Milton's Chaos, hell is characterized by its boundlessness and mutability—the only constants are "torture without end," "utter darkness," and "tempestuous fire" (67, 72, 77).

This boundlessness and mutability suggest the demons' inability to contemplate anything of substance for any significant period of time except the pain of their own fallen spiritual bodies. But as Peter Fiore explains, within an Augustinian framework even this fixation on their body in pain is *no-thing-ness*. According to Augustine's ontology, wherein "that which exists is good and that which has fallen from existence is evil," the fallen angels now represent "nonentities": nonbeing.[50] Their alienation from God's Presence is irreversible. Because Augustinian ontology assumes that every created being has the *telos* of reaching its particular perfection by participating in God's Being, a "bending back" to God, the fallen angels are no longer able to achieve this perfection and no longer able to participate in Being. Being ("very being itself," as Augustine puts it) contains being, and to change in such a way so as to lose forever one's proper *telos* is to cease to exist. "I would have no being, I would not have any existence, unless you were in me," Augustine writes. "Or rather, I would have no being if I were not in you, 'of whom are all things, through whom are all things, in whom are all things' (Rom. 11:36)."[51]

No longer participants in the Being that gives being, even the contemplation of their pain—so closely tied to their new identity—is a contemplation of nothingness, and this nothingness gives rise to their restlessness. The demons wander hell's caverns endlessly in search of meaningful occupation and momentary escape from their pain, and the "philosophers" of hell in particular are characterized by their aimlessness, caught "in wand'ring mazes lost" (*PL* 2.561) as they try to think through the intricacies of a theology with a distorted conception of the *théos*. Like the undisciplined pilot of the skiff they, too, have "cleaved" and "joined" themselves to *livyāthān* in their rebellious misreading, thinking their "dread Emperor" (2.510) to be a secure alternative to the "tyrannous" God, and will hence suffer the same fate. In an odd slippage within the parable, Satan is both reader and text: he is a reader because as a spiritual creature with free will he has been entrusted with navigating spiritual reality; he is a text because he is the Leviathan whose promises of security, transcendence, and stability are illusory.

If we extend these insights into Milton's parable, we begin to see just how profound its message becomes. To be moored upon Leviathan means for Milton that spiritual life, individual and corporate, is characterized by chronic "misreading," here defined in terms of the shiftlessness of real hunger rather than the anchored discipline of "Real Presence."[52] One is exiled from the rest afforded by the regenerative and redeeming power of Christ as anchor and ultimate hope—a common and related meditative emblem in the early modern period.[53] The parable becomes one whose object lesson is centered on a negative exemplum as we conflate the wanderings of Leviathan/Satan and the wanderings of the small skiff anchored upon him.

Nothingness occupies the center of satanic contemplation and theology: the "debt immense of endless gratitude" that he cannot pay (4.52), which results in permanent *kenosis*. His spiritual wanderings stem from his skewed views of grace and obedience, a brand of debtor's theology that Paul addresses in Acts 17:24–25 and Romans 4:4–5. Paul's sentiment seems to be that God is not and should not be served by human hands as if he needed it, for he is complete in himself and has given everything out of grace as pure gift.[54] The consequence of debtor's theology is that every act of obedience or disobedience then pushes the debtor farther into debt, one that cannot be repaid, thereby nullifying the efficacies of grace.

Satan construes precisely this kind of debtor's theology, and it is this "debt"—this nothingness or *kenotic* metaphysics of Absence—which paradoxically occupies the center of Satan's contemplation. In his soliloquy at the beginning of Book 4, Satan's "bitter memory" of lost paradise is stirred by his first glimpses of the sun after his fall (4.24). He laments not the immediate relationship with the divine that he once had, the proper response to contemplating the visible symbol of God; rather, the beams only remind him of himself in his once glorious state: that "bright eminence" (44) now corrupted, dimming, and ultimately "nonexistent." He meditates on his fall, revealing his fallen theology as well:

> What could be less than to afford him praise,
> The easiest recompense, and pay him thanks,
> How due! yet all his good prov'd ill in me,
> And wrought but malice;
>
> .   .   .   .
>
> The debt immense of endless gratitude,
> So burdensome, still paying, still to owe;
> Forgetful what from him I still receiv'd,
> And understood not that a grateful mind
> By owing owes not, but still pays, at once
> Indebted and discharg'd: what burden then? (4.46–57)

The soul moored upon Leviathan is restless not only because it is not fastened on an object worthy of contemplation, but also because restlessness is driven by God's constant emanation of grace to complete his work of paradise within. Satan's dilemma stems from a misreading of God's grace. He privileges the contemplation of his work of "still paying," that is, continually paying a debt of gratitude over that which he "still receiv'd"; he is "[ƒ]orgetful" of the continual grace and divine love to shape the self in past, present, and future (54; emphasis added). Satan's theological error is centered on present and future grace, for he cannot envision anything but meaningless repetition that, as he sees it, will never repay the past debt. As Regina Schwartz comments, Satan "depicts an awesome obligation so impossible to fulfill that failure is inevitable: he can only flee such an exacting creditor, declaring moral bankruptcy, as it were."[55] The only wage he can earn for his work is spiritual desolation, a constant *kenosis,* or emptiness, without an accompanying *pleroma,* or filling. His debtor's theology assumes the debt *can* be repaid, thus exalting the contemplation of self (not-being) over the divine (very Being itself).

Satan as reader and gazer, as pilot of his own skiff navigating spiritual reality, has substituted a hollow text—himself—for the Text that promises a restless proliferation of meaning and an abundance of rest: the divine Name sung in heaven as the "Omnipotent, / Immutable, Immortal, Infinite, / Eternal King; thee Author of all being" (3.372–74), as we explored in chapter 2. Satan's misreading of the divine Text is infectious, as he offers his own magnificently carved body, his own "bright eminence," for his cohort of rebellious misreaders to gaze upon rather than upon the Son as Messiah (5.756–65). Moored upon this monstrous bulk Leviathan, these demons have little choice but to follow as his ecclesial ship, even as they slavishly and sluggishly rise from the flames of hell's tumultuous lake.

If we assume Milton's "night-founder'd Skiff" to be a parable of misreading, Leviathan appears to the undiscerning pilot of the skiff to be a secure text upon which to anchor. But given Augustine's ontology with regard to the fallen angels, Milton's Leviathan as a figure of Satan can finally be no more than a sign without Text, unless we understand that text "to be" *no-thing-ness.* In spiritual terms Milton's parable seems to be warning its audience that without conversion—appropriating the Son's obedience in order to cultivate "Virtue, Patience, Temperance, . . .

Love" so that one might possess the "paradise within thee, happier far"—human beings are readers without discernment as well as unanchored signs without Text (12.583, 587).

For Milton it appears that proper reading is closely associated with the fruits of divine virtue, carefully tended and maintained through the daily exercises of contemplation and practical obedience—points to which we will return in the following chapter when we examine the Jesus of *Paradise Regained*, whose extraordinary participation in the divine Text anchors him through the storm of Satan's temptations. Proper reading for Milton is the discipline of *becoming* in the flesh that which the soul gazes upon, the ship of one's soul anchoring on the divine through the reception of a constantly emanating grace and a focused, discerning vision.

"the only Son of light": Milton, Self-Government, and the Ships of Church and State

It is fair to say, however, that Milton is critical of most of us as readers. After all, he is seeking a narrowly construed "fit" audience to receive his poem. So far I have described this fit audience as including those who share Milton's views regarding the role of divine virtue in the act of reading, views that coincide with those of Origen, Basil, and Augustine, and views that converge with the heterodox perfectionist tendencies among some of the radicals. It will become clear in this concluding section that Milton's parable of misreaders, those readers who are not anchored as the Son in divine virtue, becomes both a lament and an unflinching censure of the powers that be. I hope to make clear that Milton's parable of misreading extends to the ships of church and state as a critique of the current historical situation after the Restoration; like the infernal church, they, too, have misread their text(s) for a lack of discernment and have moored upon Leviathan. The same hermeneutical circle between individual skiff and corporate ship is at work in the relation between the individual's exercise of virtue and the properly functioning state. Without Milton's virtuous and disciplined man governing his own skiff, the ships of church and state are in peril of sinking, like the "perfidious bark" that betrayed Lycidas/Edward King.

Mindele Ann Treip observes that Milton's epic has much in common with homiletics, whose purposes are to "enlighten and instruct fallible man, to comfort and offer hope, and, in the moral sphere, to lead him to the kind of self-understanding and acceptance of individual responsibility which alone can provide a foundation for restoration."[56] The influential Puritan divine John Preston sums up the office of the pulpit when he says that the "end of our preaching is not that you should know, but that you should do and practice. . . . Practice is all in all; so much as you practice, so much you know."[57] Given the didactic purpose of the parable form and the dynamics that it involves with the audience it creates, it is this role that seems most germane to these important passages in *Paradise Lost*.

As we saw in chapter 2, Milton adapts the tradition of language theory he has inherited and contemporary Puritan sermon theory in order to understand the metaphysical implications of the demonic speeches. He uses the historical phenomenon of prophesying among nonconformists as a framework to illuminate the political and ecclesial dynamics of the "Synod of Gods." Distrustful of sermonizers, Milton adopts the role as parable-maker, and I want to suggest further that we examine an area of homiletic theory and practice that has not been considered by scholars, and one that had been used by the medieval clergy to instruct and confront both lay and royal audiences: the tradition of the medieval exemplum.[58] John Burrow remarks that the "exemplary mode is not very attractive to modern readers"; stories that present themselves to modern readers as nothing more than examples are "something of an embarrassment."[59] But medieval and early modern audiences would have appreciated the exemplum's ethical scope and narratological flexibility. While the medieval exemplum had largely been eclipsed by plain, unadorned Reformation proclamations of the Word and the many sermons aimed at teaching or refuting doctrine, we find Milton creatively reworking that tradition in his parable.[60]

Larry Scanlon draws a distinction between sermon exempla and public exempla. The former were collected in volumes such as Gregory the Great's *Dialogues,* Jacques de Vitry's *Sermones Vulgares,* and Cesarius of Heisterbach's *Dialogus Miraculorum.* Sermon exempla were usually employed by the growing numbers of itinerant preachers in teaching and indoctrinating urban lay audiences, emphasized the miraculous, and blended folklore with hagiography. Because the medieval sermon exemplum incited the popular imagination it tended to be apolitical, only insofar as one can separate the magisterium of the medieval church from the court. Public exempla, on the other hand, were derived from classical exempla dealing with the *rei publicae* and were used to teach civic leaders about public duty and the centrality of moral order. Scanlon notes that with the public exemplum, there is the "presumption that social order must take an exemplary form, that communal values can have no force until they are concretized in or by a single authoritative figure."[61] In this way, suggests Scanlon, these public exempla are closely related to the Carolingian *Fürstenspiegel* ("Mirror of Princes") produced by clerics who advised the court on the moral education of princes.

In his parable of the "night-founder'd Skiff," we find Milton making use of both types of exempla. G. R. Owst explains that in the sermon exemplum "even the most familiar objects of the English countryside take on an atmosphere of mystery and of wonder, when viewed through the spectacles of the natural philosopher." In the beast exemplum in particular, snakes, turtles, birds, and whales become the loci for meditations on human nature. Intriguingly, one of these sermon exempla tells the story of sailors who, mistaking a "sea pig" for an island, disembark onto its back, light a fire, and are subsequently drowned when the creature plunges below the waves.[62] It also appears that Milton participates in the homiletic tradition of the politically charged public exemplum with some qualification. Interestingly, Scanlon notes that the public exemplum "had a propensity toward the evil example, toward narratives which demonstrate the efficacy of their *sententiae* by enacting violations of them." Consequently, the negative exemplum insists "on the inherent disorder of the historical world it addresses."[63] Thus it seems likely that these exempla are intended to communicate a sense of urgency for political and ecclesial leaders to consider soberly their civic and moral responsibilities.

The negative public exemplum is closely tied to the popular early modern homiletic style of correction and reproof that "called for the preacher to identify deviations from the standard of virtue and to dissuade his hearers from continuing in such deviations."[64] William Chappell, Milton's notorious first tutor at Christ's College, comments on this method: "[The presence of the evil] may be taken chiefly from the proper adjuncts, and opposites without a medium; because that from these we may always argue, both affirmatively and negatively."[65] As Jameela Lares observes, preachers employing this mode are operating on the rhetorical principle, expounded by Aquinas in the *Summa,* that "the straight is the measure both of the straight and of the crooked."[66]

Milton's parable of the skiff centers on just this kind of negative example, and it involves the archetypal figure of moral and spiritual failure. In this context, the long angelic narration of Satan's spiritual rebellion in Books 5 and 6 can be read as the dramatic subtext and extended negative exemplum story for the compressed parable of the "night-foundered Skiff" whose movements and destiny are soon to be indistinguishable from Leviathan's when the great sea-creature awakens. The boundlessness of hell and the restlessness characteristic of its new inhabitants insist on the inherent disorder of the *spiritual* world that it addresses.

The image of the ship upon the seas can be extended, I would suggest, to include the political and ecclesial worlds as well, such that the image reflects the restlessness and disorder of the historical situation in which Milton finds himself in the tumultuous wake of the Restoration. Consequently, we might consider *Paradise Lost* as its own species of *Fürstenspiegel,* offering incidental lessons of virtue and leadership to church and civil leaders. Governing magistrates, argues Milton, need to develop the virtue of discernment—right reading—as they scan the political and ecclesial situations before them.

But there are important differences between the medieval public exemplum and Milton's exemplum. Where the classical and medieval public exemplum was employed to confer and re-center power on the prince or monarch, Milton the preacher uses it to criticize and to deconstruct the monarch's power by associating the powers-that-be with the undisciplined pilot who lacks the skill, discernment, and necessary virtue to read the text before him and bring his ship into a safe harbor. As Milton argues in *The Tenure of Kings and Magistrates,* titles of authority and kingship are granted "in trust from the People, to the Common good of them all, in whom the power yet remains fundamentally, and cannot be tak'n from them, without a violation of thir natural birthright"; the tyrant is "he who regarding neither Law nor the common good, reigns onley for himself and his faction" (*CPW* 3:202, 212). Consequently, while the medieval public exemplum made nobility the exclusive ground for moral law and hence authority, Milton makes the exercise of right reason and virtue under the auspices of obedience to the divine will the bedrock to any governing authority, be it collectively embodied in a representative figure or dispersed in a commonwealth. Milton's tyrant cannot achieve the common good because he lacks personal virtue; the tyrant's version of kingly rule is the exercise of brute power without the virtue of discernment and the people and nation will suffer because of it.

The basis of freedom, argues Milton, is piety and *self*-government, an issue we will explore more fully in the following chapter when we turn our attention to Milton's depictions of Samson and Jesus, who are each poised in a battle for self-government. For Milton, "to be free is precisely the same as to be pious, wise, just, and temperate. . . . [H]e who cannot control himself . . . should not be his own master, but like a ward be given over to the power of another. Much less should he be put in charge of the affairs of other men, or of the state. . . . If to be a slave is hard, and you do not wish it, learn to obey right reason, to master yourselves" (*Second Defense, CPW* 4:684). Like Augustine, Milton thinks that governments are a necessary evil, put into place as a result of the Fall; the loss of self-governance necessitated the erection of exterior power structures that would provide, in the best of situations, a corrective to personal and collective sin and injustice.[67] "Yet sometimes Nations will decline so low / From virtue, which is reason" that these institutions demonstrate the dangerous capacity to "Depriv[e] them of their outward liberty" as well, "Thir inward [liberty] lost" (*PL* 12.97–101).

Sharon Achinstein usefully comments that Milton "was surprisingly committed to a single goal, that of making his audience fit to achieve self governance through training in virtue."[68] The Jesus of *Paradise Regained* points to these ideals of self-government and inward freedom; as Milton's virtuous reader, he turns away from Satan's temptation to worldly riches and external power, as he retorts:

> he who reigns in himself, and rules
> Passions, Desires, and Fears, is more a King;
> Which every wise and virtuous man attains:
> And who attains not, ill aspires to rule
> Cities of men, or headstrong Multitudes,
>
> . . . .
>
> But to guide Nations in the way of truth
> By saving Doctrine, and from error lead
> To know, and knowing worship God aright,
> Is yet more Kingly. (*PR* 2.466–76)

For Milton, incarnated virtue and the exercise of self-government—how one navigates his own skiff—is the basis of a free, just, and responsible ethics and politics in the governance of the ship of state.[69] Moreover, politics is, finally, ontological, as it is connected to Milton's perfectionist strain, prevailing views of meritorious adoption to sonship, and the exercise of divine virtue in the world.

Through his parable, Milton the man of virtue and the ideal reader distances himself from the unfortunate sailor of the small skiff, and in the process he distances himself from the current civil and ecclesial powers. Milton's pilot of the skiff has not taken greater care in the learning of his craft, and by his carelessness has anchored himself upon the seabeast. In *The Reason of Church Government* Milton writes, "there is not that thing in the world of more grave and urgent importance throughout the whole life of man, then is discipline" (*CPW* 1:751). "Discipline" is Milton's mantra throughout the tract. Personal discipline, the government of one's soul, extends for Milton beyond individual responsibility and bleeds into the political and ecclesial realms. While the Jesus of

Paradise Regained ardently argues for self-discipline while eschewing the primary importance of external governance, the Milton of 1642 advocates that the "disciplined" man, who is free of spiritual restlessness and anchored in his faith, is he that must be given responsibility for the government of the nation and church. Milton continues:

> how much lesse can we believe that God would leave his fraile and feeble, though not lesse beloved Church here below to the perpetuall stumble of conjecture and disturbance *in this our darke voyage* without the card and compasse of Discipline. . . . [B]ut if it [the happiness of the civil state] be at all the worke of man, it must be of such a one as is a true knower of himselfe, and himselfe in whom contemplation and practice, wit, prudence, fortitude, and eloquence must be rarely met. (*CPW* 1:752–53; emphasis added)

Here we see Milton making use of the nautical metaphor beyond the auspices of the poem. The "night-founder'd Skiff" is no less than the ships of church and state—a common conflation among the early church fathers as well, particularly in regard to the former, as the church negotiated its way upon the dark floodwaters of the world. The ship of state metaphor is an ancient one that appears in Book 6 of Plato's *Republic*. In his discussion with Adeimantus about a mutinous crew, Socrates explains that "the true pilot must give his attention to the time of the year, the seasons, the sky, the winds, the stars, and all that pertains to his art if he is to be a true ruler of a ship. . . . With such goings on aboard ship [i.e., mutiny] do you not think that the real pilot would in very deed be called a stargazer, an idle babbler, a useless fellow, by the sailors in ships managed after this fashion?"[70] Milton, who must have considered himself one of the true pilots of Oliver Cromwell's administration, must have been called these names and worse.

Robert Fallon asserts that immediately before the Restoration, Milton looked back to the early days of Cromwell's Protectorate Council for a model of disciplined government. Milton's ideal government, Fallon describes, is decentralized, counterpoised by healthy local governments, and checked by a military whose might ultimately belongs to the people.[71] For Milton, the state ought to be ruled by a Grand Council "of ablest men, chosen by the people to consult of public affairs from time to time for the common good," and which serves as "both foundation and main pillar of the whole State" (*CPW* 7:432–34). As long as these "ablest men" persist in the discipline of virtue, Milton advises, they deserve to hold their seats for life. On the eve of Restoration, he defends this position and their present course: "The ship of the Commonwealth is alwaies under sail; they [the General Council] sit at the stern; and if they stear well, what need is ther to change them; it being rather dangerous?" (*The Readie and Easie Way, CPW* 7:433–34). As is evident, for Milton the rigors of personal discipline can save a sinking church without direction, and can guide the citizenry of a nation very nearly into bliss itself.

Milton returns to the nautical exemplum at the end of the poem during Adam's hearing and viewing of biblical history as given by Michael. Similarly, the figure of the man in whom are "rarely met" the virtues that Milton esteems appears in Noah, with whom we can now safely intuit Milton identifies. Michael narrates:

> the floating Vessel swum
> Uplifted; and secure with beaked prow
> Rode tilting o'er the Waves, all dwellings else
> Flood overwhelm'd, and them with all thir pomp
> Deep under water roll'd; Sea cover'd Sea,
> Sea without shore; and in thir Palaces
> Where luxury late reign'd, Sea-monsters whelp'd
> And stabl'd. (*PL* 11.745–52)

As the saving remnant, itself a trope throughout scripture, the "true virtue" (790) of those in the ark is contrasted with the "pleasure, ease, and sloth, / Surfeit, and lust . . . wantonness and pride" (794–95) of those without—the same vices Milton, William Walwyn, John Lilburne, Richard Overton, Gerrard Winstanley, and others consistently use to characterize the current civil and ecclesial governments. For instance, in *Londons Liberty in Chains Discovered* (1646) Lilburne attacks the lawyers and the professional clergy who keep the common person "captivated to the Lawes, covetous Lusts, and the Arbitrarie unlimited power and dominion of your illegally imperious lording Magistrates." The "Arbitrarie" power and dominion that Lilburne tenaciously fought against was denounced by Winstanley, who understands that oppression in allegorical spiritual terms as belonging to the kingdom of Adam/Esau rather than the kingdom of Jacob/Christ. Those who rule according to Adam are full of "Covetousnesse, or self-love," that when coupled with Eve, the Imagination, "does beget fruit or children . . . as pride, and envy, hypocrisie, crueltie, and all unclean lusts pleasing the flesh."[72]

Thinking themselves safe in their "luxury" and without discernment, the civil and ecclesial governments, too, have moored upon Leviathan. And, as is likely to be the case of our sailor, these institutions have been corrupted and destroyed by their careless attachment, while the sea-monsters now mock their self-assured resting places, the "palaces" wherein once they "reign'd." Noah is hailed as "the only Son of light / In a dark Age" and the "one just Man alive" (808–9, 818). Despite the horrifying implications for the rest of humanity, Michael's exposition of Noah ends hopefully: "For one Man found so perfet and so just, / That God voutsafes to raise another World / From him, and all his anger to forget" (876–78). Noah's obedience and steadfastness culminate in the ark's resting on Mt. Ararat, "anchored," we might say, on God's promise to abate his wrath. That promise finds its most powerful manifestation ("O goodness infinite, goodness immense!" [12.469]) for Milton in the Incarnation of Christ, the obedient Son who becomes the new Noah. But it also finds expression in Milton's own disciplined life of virtue: the "paradise within" that he has so carefully cultivated, the hermeneutical lens that has helped him navigate the troubling political and ecclesial seas, and the Christic anchor that has preserved him from the pernicious and restless whims of Leviathan. One could perhaps argue that Milton's disillusionment with politics in the twilight of his years is, figuratively speaking, the unhooking of his own misplaced anchor. The poet-preacher finds comfort in the hope that perhaps God will raise another world out of him, a man broken, blind, and dejected in the wake of the Restoration, but a man no less sanctioned as God's own, and one of God's ideal readers.

Milton recognizes that interpretation and spiritual discernment is always a laborious and thorny exercise, as he states in *Areopagitica*:

> Good and evill we know in the field of this World grow up together almost inseparably; and the knowledge of good is so involv'd and interwoven with the knowledge of evill, and in so many cunning resemblances hardly to be discerned, that those confused seeds which were impos'd on *Psyche* as an incessant labor to cull out, and sort asunder, were not more intermixt. It was from out the rinde of one apple tasted, that the knowledge of Good and evill as two twins cleaving together leapt forth into the World. (*CPW* 2:514)

"Hardly to be discerned": the weight of the entire paragraph—if not the argument at large in *Areopagitica*, and Milton's entire hermeneutic endeavor—squarely rests on the dubious shoulders of this sobering phrase. From his perspective, Milton's habits of virtue, his own performance of the Word in the world as citizen, poet, and preacher, condition him to engage in that "incessant labor to cull out, and sort asunder" the Good, the True, and the Beautiful from their "cunning resemblances."

Discerning those "cunning resemblances" through the hermeneutical lens of virtue makes all the difference for Milton. In the following chapter, we will hone our examination of this general hermeneutic of virtue, adroitly delineated in *De Doctrina Christiana* and illustrated by Milton's poetic imagination in the "night-founder'd Skiff," by interrogating one particular virtue so integral to two of Milton's readers and "pilots" who are tempted by the narrative snares of illusory stability and transcendence. The exercise of temperance is essential to the situations facing Samson, as he moves toward the temple of the Philistines, and Jesus, as he wanders in the desert. Their way of being-in-the-world shapes their way of seeing-the-world, as hermeneutics is subject to ontology. Milton's understanding of temperance, principally defined by him as self-restraint rather than moderation, has implications for how we understand Samson's failure and catastrophic violence, as well as Jesus's success and quiet retreat.

chapter 5

Fashioning the True Pilot

Temperance and Political Transcendence in
Samson Agonistes and *Paradise Regained*

*The end then of learning is to repair the ruins of our first parents
by regaining to know God aright and out of knowledge to love him,
to imitate him, to be like him, as we may the neerest by possessing
our soules of true vertue.*

—Milton, *Of Education*

In the previous chapter we explored the poetic, parabolic, and theological trope of the ship upon the seas as a keen image of the soul in reading that is faced with the dangers of false stability and transcendence in the figure of the Leviathan. The emblem epitomizes Milton's argument that the practice of virtue, as delineated in his heterodox Christology, is a necessary prerequisite for readers of texts—whether those texts are the sacred scriptures, political orations, sermons, philosophical systems of thought, or theological claims and systems. For Milton and many other early modern readers, textual interpretation, especially biblical interpretation, is inseparable from the narrative of its lived performance in the world. Roger Chartier has commented that reading "is not only an abstract operation of the intellect: it puts the body into play and is inscribed within a particular space, in a relation to the self or to others."[1] In this chapter, I want to seize upon Chartier's understated phrase that the activity of reading "puts the body into play" as we seek to understand how Milton's incarnated reader and pilot repairs the ruins of reading.

In the 1671 joint publication of *Paradise Regained* and *Samson Agonistes,* Milton provides us with models of questing readers who are confronted with the precarious and onerous task of discerning the "cunning resemblances" between good and evil, and who demonstrate that the activities of reading and interpretation "put the body into play." Having established a theological framework for the importance of virtue in Milton's doctrinal Christology as well as in his brand of *lectio divina* in the previous two chapters, we now turn our attention to two readers who are shaped by one virtue in particular. Temperance is central to Milton's depictions of Samson and Jesus, who are linked as readers of the "texts" placed before them and of the narrative possibilities of the self that emerge.[2] John Calvin asserts that "no moderation can be seen in the depravity of our nature, in which all affections with turbulent impetuosity exceed their due bounds." He praises temperance above many other Christian virtues because it is the principle capable of ordering the disordered soul. His model is the temperate Christ, who "was upright, all his affections were under such restraint as prevented everything like excess."[3] Moreover, William Perkins explicitly links temperance and discernment: "That this Moderation of mind may be learned and practiced, we must remember that two especiall meanes are to be used. First, we must labour to discerne between things that differ, Phil. 1.10 . . . second . . . to consider that wee are in this world, as pilgrimes and strangers, 1. Pet. 2.11."[4] Here Perkins reverses the paradigm of the virtuous, incarnated reader that I explicated in the previous chapter. As he states, temperance or moderation is learned through the process of discernment, and not the other way around. But in Perkins's proof-text from Philippians, it is clear that Paul's prayer for the church members at Philippi is that they "abound in love" and the fruits of righteousness "so that" (v. 10) they may be able to discern and "approve things which are excellent." Although removed from the orthodox theological world of Calvin and Perkins, the Digger Gerrard Winstanley also argues that a mode of being-in-the-world is connected to a way of discerning the world. As we will explore more fully in chapter 6, temperance anchors his theological anthropology. The "spirituall man" who models himself after Christ's life of self-restraint is he "that judges all things according to the law of equity and reason, in moderation and love to all"; but the "man of the flesh . . . cannot judge any thing in righteousness; for all his judgement and justice is selfish."[5] For theologians as diverse as Calvin, Perkins, and Winstanley, the disordered soul requires discipline, and we might say that temperance is the apple of the "great task-Master's eye" ("Sonnet VII," 14).

In the first section of this chapter, I examine Milton's debt to Aristotelian *phronêsis*, the intellectual virtue of practical wisdom or discernment, and its relation to *sōphrosunē*, or temperance. The two become inextricably linked in many works of the Miltonic canon, most notably in *De Doctrina Christiana, Comus,* and *Areopagitica,* where temperance is often understood as self-restraint rather than mere moderation. In the second and third sections, I delineate how this paired understanding functions as a specific hermeneutical lens for both Samson and Jesus, two "pilots" tempted to moor upon the Leviathan of false transcendence and shaped by the movements between *kenosis* and *pleroma*. Bodily temperance is analogous to the theological concept of *kenosis*, a "pouring out" of the self and its own desires that leads both readers ironically to *pleromic* excess.

Aristotle's Conversion: Prudence and Temperance in *De Doctrina Christiana, Comus,* and *Areopagitica*

Aside from the Bible, Milton's ethics were shaped in part by Aristotle, whom he describes as "one of the best interpreters of nature and morality" (*CPW* 3:204); moreover, Aristotle's *Nichomachean Ethics* was the focal textbook on ethics in the university curriculum in early modern England.[6] Milton's insistence that reading and interpretation require discernment or practical judgment, in order to establish the right conditions for just and responsible action, is closely related to Aristotle's intellectual and moral virtue of *phronêsis,* often translated "practical wisdom" or "prudence." What follows is a brief discussion of Aristotelian *phronêsis* and Milton's response to it in his development of the Christian *phronimos,* who, in addition to exercising discernment, practices temperance, a virtue that has received marginal critical attention in Milton's works despite its pervasiveness. Yoking these two virtues together in this first section will permit us to gauge the hermeneutical challenges facing Milton's Samson and Jesus as readers who "put the body into play."

Aristotle posits that "the function [*ergon*] of a man [is] a certain kind of life, namely, activity or *actions* of the soul with reason, and of a virtuous man we posit these to be well and nobly done." Only Aristotle's man of virtue achieves that end, what he terms *eudaimonia,* which "both ordinary and cultivated people call . . . 'happiness', and both regard living well and *acting* well as being the same as being happy."[7] Many scholars debate what Aristotle means by "happiness," but most agree that Aristotle has something other than the psychological state of being content or seeking pleasure. William Prior suggests that *eudaimonia* certainly includes those dimensions of happiness, but the Greek word more likely embraces notions of "achievement, success and moral excellence."[8] Thus we might alternately state that for Aristotle the proper good of man is the "excellent life," and "the good for a man turns out to be an activity of the soul according to virtue, and if the virtues are many, then according to the best and most complete virtue."[9]

That highest virtue for Aristotle is *phronêsis*—judgment, practical wisdom, or discernment—and it is implicitly a virtue connected to the activity of reading, as I have broadly defined it. *Phronêsis* unifies the intellectual virtues (e.g., reason, understanding, wisdom) and the moral virtues (e.g., courage, temperance), and that is why it is also Aristotle's prime political and aristocratic virtue. Morally, Aristotle's *phronimos,* or man of practical wisdom or discernment, is courageous because he has habitually acted courageously, and he is temperate because he has habitually acted temperately. Intellectually, the *phronimos* is virtuous because he understands *kata ton orthon logon,* "according to right reason," or according to what is needed in particular cases, because he has had excellent systematic instruction in law, politics, and ethics by other *phronimoi*. As Alasdair MacIntyre explains, the *phronimos* transforms his "initial naturally given dispositions into virtues of character" by "gradually coming to exercise those dispositions *kata ton orthon logon.*" Moreover, the "exercise of practical intelligence requires the presence of the virtues of character; otherwise, it degenerates into or remains from the outset merely a certain cunning capacity for linking means to any end rather than to those ends which are genuine goods for man."[10] William Prior maintains that for Aristotle deliberation leads to correct perceptual knowledge, which in turn leads to a rational choice, and results in a specific action that brings about a desired end.[11]

It seems to me, however, that Prior is only partially correct, and that the process ultimately works as a hermeneutical circle. Proper perceptual knowledge for Aristotle *anticipates* the deliberative phase for the *phronimos,* and that perceptual knowledge stems in part from the habitual cultivation of moral virtue, organized finally by the moral and intellectual virtue of *phronêsis,* or discernment. Aristotle implies this conclusion: "One might say that all men aim at the apparent good but cannot control what appears to them to be good, and that the end appears to each man to be of such a kind as to correspond to the kind of man he is. Now if each man is in some way the [moving] cause of his own habit, *he is also in some way the cause of what appears to him"* — an important point to which we will return in our examination of Samson and Jesus.[12] Aristotle's *phronimos* is thus the man who is able to discern the correct course of action given any situation because he has attained the excellent character he describes; the *phronimos* is charged not just with choosing the good, but with the responsibility of how "the good" appears to him in the world.[13]

Briefly revisiting Milton's metaphor of the "night-founder'd Skiff," or Socrates's example in the *Republic* of the ship navigating the seas, one finds that the distinction between the "true pilot" and the mutineers becomes clearer. The true pilot or *phronimos* sees the course ahead, carefully considers his way, and acts accordingly because he has cultivated a life of habituated virtue; the mutineers, meanwhile, do not share their captain's virtue or disciplined vision. Each has a competing vision that inevitably will lead to collective ruin. Thus, from Aristotle's reasoning, one might argue that the parabolic pilot of Milton's "nightfounder'd Skiff" has made a critical mistake in perception—lodging his anchor upon the back of sleeping Leviathan—precisely because he has made habitual mistakes in defining, choosing, and acting upon the "good." Stephen Everson remarks, "what makes him [the *phronimos*] happy . . . is not that he has achieved excellence in respect of his *ergon*, but that, in possessing *phronêsis*, he is able to make correct judgments about what is valuable and what is not."[14] Yet as Aristotle observes, making those correct judgments and discerning what is ultimately "valuable" are not immediately intuited. The best "end is not apparent to a man who is not good, for his evil habit perverts him and causes him to be mistaken about the starting point of *action*. Hence it is evident that a man cannot be prudent if he is not good."[15] It is this process of deliberation—the rightly rational assessment of a situation accompanied by practical judgment and an excellent character, and the ensuing action that will best achieve an end defined by the good—which constitutes for Aristotle genuine *eudaimonia*, genuine virtue, and a genuinely free political state.

Temperance, or *sōphrosunē*, is one particular virtue that contributes to shaping the excellent life of the *phronimos*. Although the virtues that Aristotle describes in Books 3–5 of the *Nichomachean Ethics* are interrelated, Charles M. Young observes that he nowhere addresses their particular connections to practical wisdom.[16] In Book 3 Aristotle defines *sōphrosunē*, or temperance, as a virtue that regulates the pleasures of the body exclusively, and Young suggests that even when one errs toward gross profligacy or overindulgence, Aristotle does not necessarily treat the failure in all cases as a moral one—the offenders may be afflicted with *gastrimargoi*, or "mad-bellies."[17] Self-indulgence, however, is in most cases a voluntary state, more so than a vice such as cowardice because one cannot fault a coward for wanting to avoid pain, but one can reproach an intemperate man for inordinately pursuing appetitive pleasure above all things. "The intemperate man," Aristotle states, "*desires* all pleasurable things or the most pleasurable, and he is led by his *desire* to choose these instead of others."[18] Natural appetites arise and must be satisfied, but Young asks why a virtue is needed to regulate our appetites, once the need has been satisfied.[19] For Aristotle, the answer lies in how the temperate man and the intemperate man respond differently to those appetites and pleasures. The former "is not pleased by the things which please the intemperate most—but is rather displeased by them—nor pleased at all by those he should not." Thus, while the intemperate man "loves such pleasures more than they are worth," Aristotle's temperate man "loves such pleasures as right reason dictates" (3.14, 1119a). Note that Aristotle does not say the temperate man does not enjoy pleasure; that is not the issue. What distinguishes the temperate from the intemperate is the exercise of "right reason," and this is perhaps where we might profitably yoke *phronêsis* (discernment) and *sōphrosunē* (temperance). If reason is for Aristotle the attribute that separates the human animal from all other animals, then temperance is subject to reasoning rightly about bodily appetites and their fulfillment. Put another way, *phronêsis* determines the reasonable fulfillment of the appetite (i.e., *sōphrosunē*) in such a way that one fulfills both the genus as animal and the species as rational creature.

Milton converts Aristotle's temperate *phronimos;* moreover, he appears to have no trouble co-opting classical secular virtues within a Christian matrix of grace. Ernest Sirluck has argued that Milton disagrees with Aristotle's account of the virtues as deriving from habit. Regarding virtue generally, Sirluck explains that "Milton never makes it dependent upon habit," and "the moral significance of habit in its collective form—custom—receives from Milton a great deal of attention, virtually all of it hostile. Custom is for him the great seducer, inimical to reason and hence generally to truth, and the natural accomplice of error."[20] But individual virtue cannot be conflated seamlessly with collective custom, and Milton plainly uses the language of habit to describe the virtues in *De Doctrine Christiana*: "The IMMEDIATE CAUSES of good actions are, generally speaking, good habits. These are called VIRTUES, and in them is comprised the whole sum of our duty both towards God and towards man" (*CPW* 6:647). Virtue and habit are thus interchangeable, as Sirluck notes, but his conclusion that Milton did not intend to describe habit as the source of virtue is mistaken because that is precisely what Milton does in using the language of causality here.

Perhaps akin to Aristotle's notion of *phronêsis* is Milton's account of the intellectual virtue of prudence, "the virtue which allows us to see what we ought to do and when and where we ought to do it." This process of discernment is shaped by wisdom, the other intellectual virtue that comes about when we "EARNESTLY SEARCH OUT GOD'S WILL, CLING TO IT WITH ALL DILLIGENCE . . . AND GOVERN ALL OUR ACTIONS BY ITS RULE" (651, 647). Like Aristotle's notion of *phronêsis*, Milton's virtue of prudence appears to operate as a similar organizing principle, for prudence is "a seasoning to be added to every virtue, as salt once was to every sacrifice" (651). Milton indicates here that prudent choices, prudent actions, and prudent interpretations are sacrifices; they are acts of devotion properly directed to God, and they constitute a person's duty to neighbor and to oneself. The more attuned a believer becomes to hearing and participating in the "divine sounds" of "That undisturbed Song of pure concent" through the practice of virtue, the more "Jarr[ing]" and "disproportion'd" the false song will appear ("At a Solemn Music," 3, 6, 20). He thus transforms Aristotle's thorny process of deliberation and interpretation into an exercise in discerning and testing the spirits (1 John 4:1) that follows upon regeneration. Regeneration "restores man's natural faculties of faultless understanding and of free will more completely than before. But what is more, it also makes the inner man like new and infuses by divine means new and supernatural faculties into the minds of those who are made new" (*De Doctrina Christiana, CPW* 6:461). In this passage Milton does not elaborate on the degree to which the "natural faculties of faultless understanding" are restored through regeneration, beyond his stating that they are made so "more completely." One finds a similarly vague statement in the chapter "Of Ingrafting in Christ, and its Effects," where Milton states that in the "new spiritual life the intellect is *to a very large extent* restored to its former state of enlightenment and the will is restored, in Christ, to its former freedom" (478; emphasis added). The restoration of the faculties to deliberate and the will to act upon those prudent deliberations are the crucible out of which Milton's idea of the Christian *phronimos* emerges.

Further, this rational and prudent deliberation is for Milton an aspect of the Christian *phronimos*'s general righteousness, which is described in *De Doctrina Christiana* as "right reason in self-government and self-control." Righteousness thus regulates one's "inner affections," secures the "pursuit of external good and resistance to or endurance of external evil," and is "the fountain-head" of special virtues such as temperance (720). Milton finds an unlikely ally in Bishop Joseph Hall, who calls temperance the "silken string that runs through the pearl-chain of all vertues." In a sense, Hall is correct because even for Aristotle temperance is related to all the virtues as a person deliberates a course of virtuous action that is lodged in the middle way between the extremes of two vices that indicate a deficiency or an excess (e.g., courage is the virtue between cowardice on the one hand and foolhardy bravado on the other). Moreover, Hall asserts that temperance ought to occupy the center of one's passions. Without temperance the world is thrown into "meere vice and confusion": justice is reduced to "cruell rigor" and mercy to "remisnesse"; pleasure and love become "bruitish sensuality" and "frenzy," respectively; finally, anger erupts into "fury," and sorrow degenerates into "desperate mopishnesse." For Hall, temperance is the linchpin of order in the universe; remove it, and all becomes "universal ruine."[21]

Although at odds with Hall on prelacy and church government, Milton likely would agree with his opponent's zealous assessment of the value of temperance. Under the aegis of temperance itself Milton includes the practical virtues of sobriety, chastity, modesty, and decency. Unlike Aristotle, however, for whom temperance governed only the pleasures of the body, Milton's virtue is specifically associated with a spiritual disposition under the category of holiness or godliness. Albert W. Fields argues that the "ethical habits" delineated by Milton in *De Doctrina Christiana* are "Aristotelian and Spenserian in their emphasis on moderation, each virtue having 'opposites' and usually representing a mean between extremes." Additionally, James Holly Hanford asserts that "temperance, not asceticism, is his real principle of action" that operates in his ethics.[22] In the theological treatise, however, Milton aligns temperance with the *kenotic* principle of self-restraint rather than moderation. Sobriety, for instance, is "forbearance" from gluttony or, alternately, it is "abstention from mental sluggishness"; chastity is "forbearance" from "unlawful lusts" such as "voluptuousness, sodomy, [or] bestiality"; modesty is "abstinence" from vulgar language; and decency is the "avoidance" of "anything shameless or suggestive in one's dress and personal appearance" (6:728). This special virtue is prominently featured in such works as *Comus, Areopagitica, Paradise Lost, Samson Agonistes,* and *Paradise Regained,* all of which are concerned with the harmonic relations between appetites and modes of perception, ontic dispositions, prudent deliberations, and processes of interpretation.[23] Milton wavers between defining temperance principally as restraint or as moderation in these works, but pulsing in the cadences of his oeuvre is the steady thrum of this particular virtue; diminish or neglect its importance, and Milton's *phronimos* falls.

All of his early biographers mention that Milton led a spare and temperate life. Milton's large body of work reveals a remarkable consistency of valuing the virtue of temperance, despite how differently he may have conceived of the potential for human perfection or the theology of the Incarnation at various times.[24] In *Comus* the Lady initially falls by deception and accompanies the "Gentle villager" to a "low / But loyal cottage" nearby (304, 319–20). Thus the incident early on indicates that successful *lectio divina* is not a foregone conclusion, even for the virtuous reader. As Rosemond Tuve has pointed out, *Comus* in particular demonstrates that a virtuous disposition is not enough to "see through to the true nature of that which . . . simply says it is other than it is."[25] John Guillory echoes Tuve: "[t]he presence of higher powers in the masque (the Attendant Spirit) tells us from the very beginning that chastity is not enough." For Guillory, the relation between heaven's aid and virtuous self-reliance may be summed up in an ambiguous statement made by the Elder Brother to his younger: their sister's chastity is "yet a hidden strength / Which, if heaven gave it, may be term'd her own" (418–19).[26] Comus's attempts to seduce the Lady at his palace are thwarted by her tenacious rhetorical defense not just of chastity—the ostensible central virtue that the masque celebrates—but of temperance.

Echoing the poets of the carpe diem tradition, Comus argues that beauty ought not to be "like a neglected rose" that "withers on the stalk with languish'd head," for it is "nature's brag, and must be shown" and enjoyed "in mutual and partak'n bliss" (*A Maske*, 743–45, 741).[27] Her "dainty limbs" are meant for "gentle usage and soft delicacy," and her praise of a "lean and sallow Abstinence" betrays the generosity and *pleromic* abundance of "Th'all-giver" who would remain "unthank't" and "unprais'd" by her refusal (680–81, 709, 723). The virtuous Lady, however, discerns the specious claims of his argument, for Comus's emphasis on *pleromic* abundance turns the goodness of the earth's fruits into an excuse for consumption and evil self-indulgence. The Lady refutes the argument, stating that the abundance of "innocent nature" is to be enjoyed by "the good / That live according to her sober laws / And holy dictate of spare Temperance" (762, 765–67). The Lady confronts Comus's faulty theology of the "all-giver": heaven's goodness is not validated by gross consumption, she argues, but by "a moderate and beseeming share / Of that which lewdly-pamper'd Luxury / Now heaps upon some few with vast excess" (769–71). Temperance is thus closely allied to the "Sun-clad power of Chastity," or the "sage / And serious doctrine of Virginity" (782, 786–87)—the pun on sun/Son in the first is probably intended, as Merritt Hughes's footnote indicates.[28] In contrast to Comus's "dazzling fence" of "dear Wit and gay Rhetoric" (790–91), the Lady's parry through her temperate restraint leads ironically to sacred excess and a kind of iconoclasm:

> the uncontrolled worth
> Of this pure cause would kindle my rapt spirits
> To such a flame of sacred vehemence,
> That dumb things would be mov'd to sympathize,
> And the brute Earth would lend her nerves, and shake,
> Till all thy magic structures rear'd so high,
> Were shatter'd into heaps o'er thy false head. (793–99)

The very abundance of the "brute Earth" that Comus consumes without gratitude will thus rise up as his accuser and executioner. The Lady's parry of moderation has been transformed into a surfeit of fatal thrusts, and the sorcerer and prophet of profane abundance cringes: "I feel that I do fear / Her words set off by some superior power," for "a cold shudd'ring dew / Dips me all o'er, as when the wrath of *Jove* / Speaks thunder" (800–804). Despite his trembling, Comus renews his rhetorical attack and offers a sip from his enchanted cup, while entreating her to "Be wise, and taste—" (813). This moment in the text forces some hermeneutical suspension because as readers of the action rather than viewers, we do not know if Comus's lingering whispers and charmed cup have withered the Lady's defenses.[29] The brothers burst upon the scene to smash Comus's cup, perhaps at the very moment when its glass rim is upon the Lady's quivering lips. She thus occupies a liminal space, poised between the extremes of a puissant potential that results in aligning herself to temperance, and an impotent surrender that results in yielding to intemperance. When the Attendant Spirit appears to castigate the brothers for rashly smashing Comus's cup but neglecting his wand, the Lady has been petrified by the spell, sitting in "stony fetters fixt and motionless" (819)—suggesting, at least, her partial defeat again. Perhaps Comus has succeeded in splitting her (in)temperate body from her temperate mind; discerning rhetorical arguments is one thing, but navigating the conflicts of fallen desire is quite another. If the character of Comus serves as an early draft of Milton's Satan in *Paradise Lost,* one might argue similarly that the Lady is a thumbnail sketch of the Jesus who appears in *Paradise Regained.* The Lady of *Comus* is not the hero we find in the brief epic, whose integrity of mental and bodily temperance is tested without failure, but she is most certainly on his side.

A similar dynamic of *kenotic* restraint and *pleromic* excess is at work in *Areopagitica,* as Milton addresses Parliament on behalf of the discerning English reader. The Miltonic persona at the outset of *Areopagitica* is one that hearkens back to the classical orator Isocrates, whose political speeches dutifully addressed the "Parlament of *Athens*" in order to "advance the publick good" (*CPW* 2:489, 486).[30] William Haller comments that when Milton composed *Areopagitica,* he wrote "not a pamphlet but a poem."[31] Milton, however, more precisely envisions it as a sermon, and the virtue of temperance might well be one of his major points of proclamation. After Milton has sufficiently greased the wheels of his juggernaut in the *exordium* to Parliament, he explains that what follows is to be understood as "a Homily" that seeks to dismantle the assumptions about the efficacy of the Licensing Order of June 1643 (*CPW* 2:491). The word "homily" comes from the Greek word *homilia*, which means to share verbal intercourse with another person; in both the Catholic Church and the Church of England liturgies, the homily immediately precedes or follows the Eucharist. So, Milton delivers the homily as a meditation on the Word, a context that has been all but ignored by critics, as the republican readers he envisions prepare themselves to consume the w/ Word. But what might this entail, and what role do temperance and excess play in this meditation?

Milton's ministerial oration to Parliament argues that the activity of reading, which is so central to his vision of republican politics, is ultimately incarnational.[32] The thrust of his homily is not centered on the moral or immoral status of certain books, nor is it simply concerned with extending toleration. Rather, as Nigel Smith advances, Milton's pamphlet is principally concerned with the ethics of reading and discernment, "the exercise of choosing in a virtuous way" so that "the reformed 'truth' may be reconstituted."[33] Smith rightly links this virtuous choosing to republican politics, as do Blair Worden and Martin Dzelzainis.[34] Readerly temperance is central to the development of the republican virtues that Milton has in mind in the homily, for God "did . . . creat passions within us, pleasures round about us," but these very pleasures and the passions they arouse must be "rightly temper'd" in order to become the "very ingredients of vertu" (527). An excess of books is thus needed in order to aid the *phronimos* in the quest to temper or restrain the passions.[35]

Moreover, the Licensing Order has disastrous effects on the republican search for truth, which seeks to avoid a "second tyranny over learning," and where truth and understanding are not commodified as "wares . . . to be monopoliz'd" (539, 535). Instead, truth and understanding are gathered, dispersed, and consumed by the faithful *phronimoi* as sacred parts of the body of Christ. This is so because Milton's central locus for truth in the homily is the Incarnation of the Word, for "Truth indeed came once into the world with her divine Master, and was a perfect shape most glorious to look on." When Christ ascended, however, a "wicked race of deceivers . . . took the virgin Truth, hewd her lovely form into a thousand peeces, and scatter'd them to the four winds." Milton's republican readers, the "sad friends of Truth," are thus called to imitate Isis's promiscuous gathering of the "mangl'd body of *Osiris,*" a spiritual and hermeneutical task that continues "till her Masters second coming" (549).[36] The Licensing Order thus prevents the ontological sublimation of the human creature in this republican "politics of virtue," to borrow Blair Worden's phrase, which has as its center the Incarnation of the w/Word.[37] Truth is reassembled and disclosed through the open and intemperate activity of passionate and reasoned discovery, and then distributed, excessively devoured, and incarnated by the faithful *phronimoi* in the republic.

Consequently, one might argue that temperance is one of the precise virtues that Milton identifies with this republican process of reconstituting and incarnating truth; the intemperate consumption of books is permissible to the one who exercises temperance.[38] This is illustrated in one of Milton's biblical proof-texts against the Licensing Order in his homily, which derives from Acts 10:9–16. In a vision, Peter is commanded by God to rise, kill, and eat from a table filled with ceremonially unclean animals. From this example, Milton reasons that even those books considered forbidden or noisome will "serve in many respects to discover, to confute, to forwarn, and to illustrate" the masquerades of evil in the world, but only to the truly "discreet and judicious Reader" (*CPW* 2:512).[39] Milton's incarnated *phronimos,* however, has not only the spiritual disposition to remain unaffected, but also the alchemical capacity to convert bad books into a holy repast for the soul. This process is similar to the angels' ability to "transubstantiate" the inferior and corporal to the superior and incorporal, as Raphael explains to Adam (*PL,* 5.404–43).[40] Milton then concludes that in expanding "the universall diet of mans body" God also "left arbitrary the dyeting and repasting of our minds"—but only insofar as this judicious reader observes the "rules of temperance" that run "through the whole life of man" (*Areopagitica, CPW* 2:513).

Milton's idea of temperance, however, is further linked with excess as he develops this point by alluding to God's providing manna in the desert following the Exodus. Recall that YHWH commands the people to gather only what they will need for the coming day except the day before the Sabbath, when they are instructed to gather twice as much (Exod. 16:16, 18). YHWH presents a perfectly balanced economy, but Milton understands God's charge toward moderation not as balance, but as over-satiety and *pleromic* abundance: "that Omer which was every mans daily portion of Manna, is computed to have bin more then might have well suffic'd the heartiest feeder thrice as many meals" (*CPW* 2:513). Further in the homily, Milton ironically agrees with Comus's argument about enjoying the *copia* of "Th'all-giver." He states that God "powrs out before us ev'n to a profuseness all desirable things, and gives us minds that can wander beyond all limit and satiety." Therefore, we should not "affect a rigor contrary to the manner of God and of nature, by abridging or scanting those means, which books freely permitted are, both to the triall of virtue, and the exercise of truth." But upon closer inspection, Comus's argument of indulgence is only partially endorsed, and Milton echoes the Lady's virtuous position just as vehemently. Presumably, the *phronimos* can enjoy and indulge, or wander away from and transgress, those limits as long as those activities are accompanied by one's putting into practice God's command to exercise "temperance, justice, [and] continence" (2:528). This homily has at its center the i/Incarnation of the w/Word, and for Milton temperance is the *sine qua non* of the republican ideal of promiscuous reading.

The activities of reading and deliberation, assessing the starting point of actions and following them to their good ends, are grounded in the temperate example of the Incarnate Son—Milton's ideal *phronimos,* to which we will turn our attention in a moment. For Milton, the excellent life led by Aristotle's *phronimos* and his successful attempt to "cull out" and "sort asunder" good from evil entails his conforming to the image of the Son through the obedience that follows from regeneration. All the moral and intellectual virtues are united in the Son, and it is a unity toward which regenerate believers like Milton must strive, and a unity that he is called to reflect in the world. The limbs of sacred truth may be scattered, but the *phronimoi* are divinely permitted to wander far and wide to gather and devour them, as these readers are sustained in the desert by the manna of the virtue of temperance.

"foolish Pilot" and Fifth Monarchists: Temperance, Transcendence, and the External Kingdom in *Samson Agonistes*

In Milton's letter to Richard Jones, a former student of Milton's (at Oxford in September 1656 studying under Henry Oldenburg) and the son of his friend, Katherine Jones, Viscountess Ranelagh, he cautions the young man's admiration of men wielding power. "Victories of Princes, which you extol with praises, and matters of that sort in which force is of most avail, I would not have you admire too much, now that you are listening to Philosophers," Milton warns. "For what should be the great wonder if in the native land of *wethers* there are born strong horns, able to *ram* down most powerfully cities and towns? Learn you already from your early age, to weigh and discern great characters not by force and animal strength, but by justice and temperance."[41] The passing admonition, a kind of amiable shot across the bow of Jones's nascent and vulnerable "skiff," transforms into a broadside against the ships of church and state fifteen years later when Milton publishes the joint volume of *Paradise Regained* and *Samson Agonistes*.

As we have seen, the rule of temperance governs Milton's idea of the *phronimos*. In the sections that follow, I turn my attention to the poet's final dyptich of *kenosis* and *pleroma* in his portrayal of two *phronimoi;* one might argue that Samson's downfall can be attributed to his failure to practice the virtue of temperance wholeheartedly, while Jesus's "glorious work / . . . to save mankind" (*PR* 4.634–35) begins and fruitfully ends as a result of his tenacious commitment to it. Temperance, principally rendered in these works as self-denial, plays a keen role in keeping the two reader-protagonists connected to the *methexis* of each poem's transcendent causes: patriotism and national liberation in the case of Israel's judge, and devotion to the will of the Father and humanity's redemption in the case of God's Son.

The fulfillment of Samson's cause in particular has been hampered by his passionate desire for Dalila, such that we cannot speak of the one without addressing the other. His threatening to tear Dalila "joint by joint" (*SA* 953) finds its bloody fulfillment at the conclusion of the drama—a violence that is required to secure the vision of transcendent politics associated with the exaltation of God's Name above that of the idol Dagon. Samson remarks to Manoa that YHWH "Will not connive, or linger, thus provok'd, / But will arise and his great name assert: / *Dagon* must stoop" (466–68). The necessity of this violence and the ambiguities of agency that surround it have energized critics for decades, made even more germane in a post-9/11 America. Assessing the upshot of the play's moral difficulties results in a wide array of conclusions: that the dramatic poem endorses Samson as regenerated hero; that the drama offers a critique of violence; that Milton figures forth just one of many radical responses to the Restoration; or that Milton's adaptation of the Judges narrative is shrouded in uncertainty or indeterminacy.[42] We might gain some perspective by thinking through Milton's Samson as reader, whose horizon of perception ought to be shaped by his temperance and dedication to the Mosaic Law and the Nazarite vows, but who instead participates in and appropriates the proliferating erotic "text" of Dalila's "lascivious lap" (536), which I will argue constitutes the Leviathan of false transcendence. Further, by examining the poet's changing perceptions of Samson, I hope to link the bloody fruits of the Nazarite's "rousing motions" with the ambitions of the Fifth Monarchy Men, whom Milton expressly criticized. The Fifth Monarchists' militant members shared both Samson's recovered zeal for the Mosaic Law as well as his desire to establish a transcendent politics through violent action that was believed to be legitimated by the Spirit.

Like the parabolic pilot of the "night-founder'd Skiff" Samson is an erring reader, one who rereads the texts of his election and reckons that his failure to discern has caused the present catastrophe. We see Milton making use of the nautical metaphor we examined in the previous chapter to describe the Nazarite's failure. Samson:

> How many evils have enclos'd me round;
> Yet that which was the worst now least afflicts me,
> Blindness, for had I sight, confus'd with shame,
> How could I once look up, or heave the head,
> Who like a foolish Pilot have shipwreck't
> My Vessel trusted to me from above,
> Gloriously rigg'd. (*SA*, 194–200)

Though this failed *phronimos* and "foolish Pilot" laments the loss of sight, his physical blindness is a suitable analogue for his darkened spiritual disposition. He confesses that even if he had sight, it would serve to increase his sense of shame and isolation. He tells the Chorus that the glorious rigging of his "Immeasurable strength," granted when the Spirit of the Lord rushed upon him, was ill-matched with a "wisdom nothing more than mean" (206–7). Anchored in the pride of his *pleromic* strength, but without "a double share / Of wisdom," Samson learns belatedly that such strength becomes "vast, unwieldy, burdensome, / Proudly secure, yet liable to fall / By weakest subtleties" (53–56).

As we have already seen in *Comus, Areopagitica,* and *De Doctrina Christiana,* the wisdom, or *phronêsis,* necessary to discern those subtleties, weak or strong, might gainfully be tied to the exercise of temperance. The Nazarite claims his successful abstinence from the "turbulent liquor" that "cheers the heart of Gods and men" (552, 545), a resistance that will demarcate him from the Philistines' merry drinking during their "Idolatrous Rites" (1378). But he marks his failure to exercise temperance in other arenas:

> But what avail'd this temperance, not complete
> Against another object more enticing?
> What boots it at one gate to make defense,
> And at another to let in the foe,
> Effeminately vanquish't? by which means,
> Now blind, disheart'n'd, sham'd, dishonor'd, quell'd,
> To what can I be useful, wherein serve
> My Nation, and the work from Heav'n impos'd. (558–65)

The failure of this virtue has far-reaching consequences, short-circuiting Samson's notion of election, his service to Israel, and the "work from Heav'n impos'd."

Samson has been "Effeminately vanquish't" by Dalila, but it is not as a result of his utter lack of *phronêsis*. Dalila's erotic efforts to wrest the holy secret from him are not elaborately veiled; he is not Redcrosse Knight faced with the illusions and trickery of Duessa or Archimago. Each time Dalila came to him, Samson recognized "How openly, and with what impudence / She purpos'd to betray me" (398–99). His defeat is tied to his failure to exercise temperance over his sexual passions. But what does this failure of temperance entail? Michael Schoenfeldt surmises that in the early modern period "temperance comes to mean the work of self-control, the daily, even hourly, effort to govern a series of forces from within and without that threaten the integrity of the subject."[43] Dalila's constant nagging and her "importunity and tears" (51) certainly play a role in destroying the integrity of Samson, but the sea-change comes as a result of his being intemperately roused by the pleasures of her Comus-like "fair enchanted cup, and warbling charms" (934–35). Unlike the Lady of *Comus*, however, Samson drinks from the abundant cup and falls prey to the tempting charms: "into the snare I fell / Of fair fallacious looks, venereal trains, / Soft'n'd with pleasure and voluptuous life" (532–34). Recall that Aristotle's temperate *phronimos* responds differently than the intemperate man to the body's appetites and pleasures, as the excellent man loves pleasure only as right reason dictates. The temperate man is charged not just with self-control, but also with correct perception, for "he is also in some way the cause of what appears to him" (*Ethics*, 3.7, 1114b) as a potential good in the world to pursue. As already explored, this task of perception becomes a spiritual exercise for Milton's *phronimos*. Therefore, the question I want to pose immediately is this: Is Samson's failure to exercise temperance fundamentally due to his inner weakness against Dalila's charms, a momentary but costly lapse in the hourly battle for temperance that Schoenfeldt describes, or is it due to the way those charms and her beauty appear in the world to Samson? Is his failure personal or phenomenological?

Given Samson's attraction to Dalila's exotic beauty, we might turn briefly to *Paradise Regained* to begin to address these questions. During the infernal meeting of the angels, Belial suggests offering the same enchanted cup of physical pleasure to Jesus; those beautiful women "Expert in amorous Arts" have the magnetic power to "draw / Hearts after them tangl'd in Amorous Nets" (*PR* 2.158, 161–62). Belial champions the power of these "amorous Arts," which rely on artifice and deceit and work with such efficiency that they can dissolve hope, draw out desire, and "soft'n and tame / Severest temper" (163–64). Merritt Hughes glosses "temper" as "temperament" or "character"; these are accurate synonyms in one sense, but they can be misleading. The *OED*'s primary definitions refine Hughes's understanding by suggesting that the virtue of temperance governs that temperament or character: "The due or proportionate mixture or combination of elements or qualities" (I.1), or the "Proportionate arrangement of parts; regulation, adjustment; hence, mean or medium, a middle course" (I.2). Belial recognizes that the narrative webs of seduction confuse that due proportion and skew the perceptions of sailing the "middle course." Yet, paradoxically, seduction involves at base the most transparent—and literal—of texts: *pornographia*, which threatens to sever Samson from his patriotic and sacred cause.

Belial casts beauty and the "amorous Arts" in transcendent terms, and when Milton addresses beauty and desire, he repeatedly gestures toward transcendence. For Belial, "daughters of men" are "more like to Goddesses / Than Mortal Creatures" (*PR* 2.154, 156–57), and the *kenotic* approachableness of their "Virgin majesty with mild / And sweet allay'd" betrays the sense of dread that their *pleromic* beauty should inspire in their beholder, for these goddesses are "yet terrible to approach" (159–60). The best of men follow after them, Belial states, even as these goddesses are "Skill'd to retire, and in retiring draw" (161) their prey into their snares. Desire is spurred on by the rules of this seductive game, which playfully oscillates between *kenosis* and *pleroma*, between the accessible virgin and the saturated phenomenon of the goddess. In "Elegy I" Milton writes of the young women in London as "stars that breathe out soft flames," full of the "miraculous grace of a form which might make decrepit Jove young again" (51–54). Nearly overcome, the young poet reluctantly flees the *pleromic* "city of delight" and the "infamous halls of the deceiver Circe" for the *kenotic* "bare fields" surrounding Cambridge, the "reedy fens of the Cam," and the dull "hum" of school (13, 86–87, 89–90). In *Paradise Lost* Eve's beauty is similarly engaging and potentially dangerous. In his conversation with Raphael, Adam describes Eve's transcendent loveliness as "absolute" and "complete" (*PL* 8.547–48); Raphael delivers his warning, but unlike the speaker in "Elegy I," Adam fails to recognize the simulacrum of transcendence that is of his own making.

Samson is perhaps as guilty as Adam in this regard. Because of the gift of his *pleromic* strength, Milton's Samson once viewed himself in transcendent terms, "like a petty God" who seemed to live with few restraints and "walk'd about admir'd of all and dreaded / On hostile ground" (*SA* 529–31).[44] Samson takes his fleshly pleasures from Dalila while repeatedly denying her the pleasure of the truth behind God's "holy secret" (497). Joseph Wittreich assembles an impressive countertradition in the seventeenth century that turned away from Samson as a model of imitation, partly because of this lustfulness.[45] The proliferation of erotic pleasures from Dalila's "lascivious lap" (536) and the plenitudes of the "voluptuous life" (534) seem to present themselves to this "petty God" and intemperate *phronimos* as a kind of imitative transcendence, if only for the moment. The hermeneutical circle between a way of discerning, according to "right reason," and a way of being-in-the-world, through the habituated practice of temperance, has been interrupted. The exchange of the one type of transcendence (political liberation and the exaltation of God's Name) for the simulacrum of the other (personal satisfaction of desire) is encapsulated in the emblem of Samson's laying his head of hair, one of the external signifiers of Nazarite temperance and devotion to the mysterious "hallow'd pledge," in the lap "Of a deceitful Concubine who shore me / Like a tame Wether, all my precious fleece, / Then turn'd me out ridiculous, despoil'd" (535–39).[46]

Samson's failure to discern the false transcendence that Dalila's love represents is complicated by his earlier belief that marrying the woman of Timnah *was* divinely sanctioned, despite YHWH's general command to Israel forbidding exogamy. While Milton's Samson believes that his marriage is divinely sanctioned, the certainty of the matter is highly suspect in the Hebrew language of Judges 14:4. The verse reads, "But his father and his mother knew not that it was of the LORD, that he sought an occasion against the Philistines: for at that time the Philistines had dominion over Israel." In the phrase translated "he sought an occasion" the pronoun could refer either to the LORD or to Samson. If the LORD is the agent of "he sought" in verse 4, then Samson need not be explicitly aware of God's motives. Milton perhaps captures the ambiguity of agency in the Hebrew when Samson tells the Chorus that his parents "knew not / That what I motion'd was of God" (221–22). The Hebrew word that is translated as "occasion" is more interesting, meaning "occasion, time of sexual heat or copulation, and sexual drive," and carrying the dual connotations of an opportunity for a quarrel and the kind of copulation occurring between the beasts.[47] The sought-after vengeance against the Philistines, whether Samson knows about it or not, could be understood as a violent sexual tryst, and it is clear who will do the beast-like "penetrating." The prophets often figured Israel's disobedience as prostitution with foreign gods, and Manoa echoes the prohibitions against exogamy in his lament, "I cannot praise thy marriage-choices" (*SA*, 420). But in the prior conversation with the Chorus, Samson reveals that although his parents did not approve of marrying a non-Israelite, he knew from "intimate impulse" that by this marriage "I might begin Israel's deliverance, / The work to which I was divinely called" (223–25). Marriage to a non-Israelite is the means by which he will obtain political deliverance for Israel and simultaneously exalt the Name of God over the idols of the Philistines. In his mind, the two enterprises cannot be separated; Samson's violation of YHWH's general prohibition against exogamy participates in the transcendent cause of political liberation precisely because of this conflation.

Both the biblical narrative (Judges 16:4) and the dramatic poem (878) clearly identify love as Samson's motivation for the marriage to Dalila. In the rhetorical moment, Milton's Samson speaks about his love in terms that resonate with an act of charity, one that Dalila transgresses: "I before all the daughters of my Tribe / And of my Nation chose thee from among / My enemies, lov'd thee, as too well thou knew'st, / Too well, unbosom'd all my secrets to thee" (876–79). The second "Too well" possibly has a double referent, adding either a shameful double emphasis on Dalila's knowing and using it against him, or a self-reproachful assessment of the *pleromic* and immoderate love that causes the profane and *kenotic* emptying of the Lord's glorious secret. Samson's transgressive love for the exotic Philistine woman, however, finds an earlier analogue in the kinds of readers that Milton champions in *Areopagitica*. Like the faithful *phronimoi* of the republic, who are permitted to read promiscuously partly because Milton likens their endeavor to the divine command to Peter to consume ceremonially unclean animals, Samson assumes the freedom to marry outside of Israel because he perceived having God's sanction in the previous marriage to the woman of Timnah: "I thought it lawful from my former act, / And the same end; still watching to oppress / *Israel's* oppressers" (*SA* 231–33). Unlike the faithful *phronimoi*, however, Samson does not adhere with rigor to the "rules of temperance" that govern judicious reading and that ought to run "through the whole life of man" (*Areopagitica, CPW* 2:513)—the crucial caveat that Milton provides. Milton's temperate *phronimos* is able to "transubstantiate" any book to feed his soul, but try as he may, intemperate Samson cannot "purify" Dalila.[48]

Too late, Samson acknowledges, "I to myself was false ere thou to me" (824). As Barbara Lewalski remarks, Milton's Samson gains self-knowledge "partly by encountering and overcoming versions of his former self."[49] His marriage to Dalila ended, she is the shadow of his former self, which was subjected to his bodily passions and desires. But woman remains a riddle, the Chorus elaborates. Even to the wisest of men she appears "Seeming at first all heavenly under virgin veil, / Soft, modest, meek, demure" (1035–36). The Chorus confirms the danger of Belial's celebration of "Virgin majesty" that lures men to be "tangled in amorous nets" (*PR* 2.159, 162), and the image of the "veil" carries a host of connotations, including hiddenness, distance, or the terrible fullness of deity.[50] But "Once join'd" to that heavenly beauty, "the contrary she proves, a thorn / Intestine" and "cleaving mischief, in his way to virtue / Adverse and turbulent" (*SA,* 1037–40). The Chorus also employs the nautical metaphor, for woman is both the raging storm that threatens and the co-pilot of the ship steering toward destruction: "What Pilot so expert but needs must wreck / Embark'd with such a Steers-mate at the Helm?" (1044–45). Even the most wary and discerning of sailors fail, much more one "without a double share / Of wisdom" (53–54). Much like the angels who followed the beautiful Lucifer, who is rendered both as a fellow companion "talking to his nearest Mate" (*PL* 1.192) and the Leviathan upon which they moor their fates, this stripped vessel of Samson, once gloriously rigged, has realized that he has been "night-founder'd" upon the Leviathan of false transcendence.

We might suggest that the proliferating pleasures and digressions offered through Dalila amount to a version of Jean Baudrillard's simulacrum that "threatens the difference between 'true' and 'false,'" and that aims to unhinge Samson from the perceived *methexis* of national liberation via the "Spirit of the Lord" that habitually "came mightily upon him" (Judg. 14:6). The simulacrum harbors a destructive potential that, as Baudrillard comments, caused the iconoclasts centuries ago to fear it. Their "millennial quarrel" to tear down images, he argues, arose "precisely because they predicted the omnipotence of simulacra, this faculty simulacra have of effacing God from the conscience of man, and the destructive, annihilating truth that they allow to appear: that deep down God never existed, that only the simulacrum ever existed; even that God himself was never anything but his own simulacrum." For Baudrillard, the simulacrum defies the system of exchange between sign and referent, for it implies *"the radical negation of the sign as value,"* and the nothingness behind it.[51] The Nazarite's failure to exercise temperance has led to his seduction by an imitative transcendence, which in turn leads him, if only momentarily, to confront the haunting possibility of the nothingness behind the visible sign of his "redundant locks / Robustious to no purpose clust'ring down, / Vain monument of strength" (*SA* 568–70).

There are limits to which we can apply Baudrillard's theories to Milton's poetic drama. Samson is no atheist, even if he falls for a simulacrum of transcendence. His father interprets these growing locks with the anticipation that God has "caus'd a fountain at thy prayer / From the dry ground to spring" (581–82). But Samson's hopes for experiencing what he and his father perceive as a true transcendence remain "all flat" (595)—dangerously reducing him to a similar kind of *kenotic* finitude that no longer participates in the *methexis* of God's Spirit that we explored in chapter 2 through the language games and culture of hell. Samson's "Myself, my sepulchre, a moving grave" (102) resonates with Satan's "Which way I fly is Hell; myself am Hell" (*PL* 4.75). Samson is resigned to the probability of "Heav'n's desertion," for YHWH "now hath cast me off as never known" (*SA* 632, 641), which amounts to annihilation. It is not the case that Samson's failure has caused him to cease to believe that God exists. From his perspective, it is rather that God ceases to "believe" that Samson exists, as a result of his chosen deliverer's failure to discern between "true" and "false" transcendence and to choose his actions accordingly.

His fear of being forsaken by God leads to his belatedly eschewing the possibility of viewing his temperance even as a "middle course." Just as Milton defines the virtue in *De Doctrina Christiana*, Samson's revised notion of temperance with respect to sexual passion must be equated with abstinence and avoidance, a pouring out of selfish desire in order to be filled with God's desires; being "not complete" (*SA* 558) in one area compromises the integrity of the whole. Before her exit, Dalila lingers to touch Samson's hand. Her motives may be driven by her high-minded intention to offer "redoubled love and care / With nursing diligence" as well as an honest desire for forgiveness (923–24, 909). But her attempt to stroke his hand elicits from Samson abrupt resistance and the threat that her simple touch will awaken "My sudden rage to tear thee joint by joint" (953). Samson's power to resist her charms and to temper his sexual passions—in essence, YHWH becomes his lover, in imagery that is replete in the Hebrew Bible—gives way to his newly discovered zeal to cooperate with the text of the "rousing motions" of the Spirit (1382). Like the Lady of the *Maske,* Samson's inchoate devotion to restraint leads him, ironically, to sacred excess and a comparable act of iconoclasm, as Dagon falls before Samson, if not Samson's God.

The messenger tells Manoa that Samson was brought in when the "noon grew high and Sacrifice / Had fill'd thir hearts with mirth, high cheer, and wine" (1612–13). The Semichorus differently describes the scene by indicating that the Philistines were "Drunk with Idolatry, drunk with Wine, / And fat regorg'd of Bulls and Goats, / Chanting thir Idol, and preferring / Before our living Dread" (1670–73). Samson anticipates this latter scene in his previous conversation with the Officer, knowing that "the people on thir Holy-days" act intemperately, "Impetuous, insolent, unquenchable" (1421–22). His newly reclaimed sexual temperance stands in stark contrast to the Philistines' inebriated celebration. The two competing representations of the Philistines perhaps reveal Milton's own ambivalence on the "Blood, death, and deathful deeds" (1513) that follow, and contribute to the critical quagmire regarding how readers ought to understand Samson's violence.

In the dramatic poem this violence, even if it appears morally repugnant to twenty-first-century readers, is the ritual means to establish the ascendancy of Samson's new self aligned with the works and laws of the Mosaic covenant. On his exit Samson is able to affirm to the Chorus, "Yet this be sure, in nothing to comply / Scandalous or forbidden in our Law," and they ought to expect "Nothing dishonorable, impure, unworthy / Our God, our Law, my Nation, or myself" (*SA* 1408–9, 1424–25). The order of priority that Samson articulates in this latter verse is important. Samson's renewed temperance, an emptying of the self that leads to the reappropriation of the self through the "texts" of his trials and conversations, permits the susceptibility to the "rousing motions."

Milton's use of the word "motions" to describe the catalyst for Samson's renewed devotion is vague and complicated by both the reader's removal from their inner workings and the ambiguities of agency that arise when Samson previously uses the word to describe his marriage to the woman of Timnah (221–23). Thus, the source of origin for these motions has been a contentious topic. While Anthony Low acknowledges no ambiguity in their divine origin, Abraham Stoll charts the poetic drama's "descending scale of certainty" when assessing God's role in Samson's actions. Stanley Fish goes further, arguing that Milton refuses to deliver the clarity that readers familiar with the biblical story anticipate, such that "the only wisdom to be carried away from the play is that there is no wisdom to be carried away." William Kerrigan perhaps takes a middle position here, pointing out that Milton revises his old reliance on the clarity of choice that "right reason" provides by moving closer to "intellectual intuition"; reason instead becomes the "guardian of readiness" when the "rousing motions" come upon Samson and Jesus. I am inclined to agree with Richard J. DuRocher's assessment here, who persuasively situates the relationship between rationality and inner "motions" through Augustinian and Aristotelian theories of the passions. Their articulations on the place and scope of human emotions were adapted by prominent theorists of "faculty psychology" in the period, such as William Fenner and Philip Melanchthon, who influenced Milton's overall positive assessment of the passions, and who argued that the emotions cooperate most intimately with the movings of the divine Spirit. While scholars may continue to argue about the significance of what Samson accomplishes, DuRocher concludes, there would be little doubt in seventeenth-century minds about the origins of these "rousing motions." As DuRocher insists, they arise from Samson himself, but they are the intimate point of contact for the Spirit's enabling power: "The workings of Samson's 'rousing motions' exemplify Melanchthon's ecstatic description of the way in [which] the divine spirit itself can be mingled with an individual's animal spirits, with the threefold result that the human being may gain clearer knowledge of God, may more resolutely ascend to God, and may feel more ardent desire for God." These motions represent Samson's intention to perform God's will, and as Stanley Fish persuasively argues elsewhere, in agreement with the tenor of DuRocher's analysis, the inner disposition is everything: "[W]hat is asked of us is not a specific performance, but a specific intention, the intention to do God's will."[52]

The intentions of Milton's Samson are shaped by vacillating emotional and spiritual states that find a parallel in many spiritual autobiographies from the period, including those of John Bunyan, Charles Marshall, and George Fox.[53] There are variations, but the emotional and spiritual pattern often moves from the certainty of righteousness and election after an initial conversion experience, to despair, self-doubt, and paralysis, and finally to reassurance and the clarity of intention. Biblically, this spiritual evolution in Samson is analogous to the theological transitions between the worlds proposed and described by the persona of King Solomon in Proverbs, Ecclesiastes, and the Song of Songs. As one commentator suggests, these three wisdom books were likened by Jewish rabbis to the structure of the Temple and the deepening levels of divine encounter: outer courts (the surety of knowledge and righteousness in Proverbs), inner court (the confusion of existence leading to despair and fear in Ecclesiastes), and Holy of Holies (the pierced veil of intimate love in the Song of Songs).[54]

Samson is stripped of everything: his sight and his hair; his strength and the surety of his calling; the pleasures of Dalila and the praises of his people. All that remains is suffering in body and mind (*SA* 606–32), and he languishes in the desolation that arises from the meaninglessness resulting from "Heav'n's desertion" (*SA* 632). Like the speaker in Ecclesiastes, Samson discovers the vanity of "life under the sun," as all of his idols—once infused and suffused with meaning—are smashed, including his assumptions about the God who is his own iconoclast. The surety of the world of Proverbs, which preceded the action of the drama, has been shattered; the contradictions and confusions of "life under the sun" that is described in Ecclesiastes descend like a darkened veil. If we understand the "rousing motions" as Samson's reconnecting with the divine, then the exclusive love that characterizes the personas of King Solomon and his lowly beloved in the Song of Songs awaits Samson as that veil is pierced—and done so with terrifying results. This "love is strong as death; jealousy is cruel as the grave: The coals thereof are coals of fire, which hath a most vehement flame" (Song of Songs 8:6). In his intention to move toward the horizon of this jealous love, Samson burns like a coal and is himself consumed.

As Michael Lieb explains, the emotional life of Milton's God, the *theopatheia,* is "real and indeed holy"; "the *odium Dei* and the *amor Dei* are seen to be complementary expressions of the same idea."[55] Holiness is emotionally characterized by both God's hatred toward all false loves that challenge it and God's love toward those who dread it. Despite the contradictions of "life under the sun," the Solomonic persona of Ecclesiastes ends with a renewed affirmation of the Torah and a resolution to fear "our living dread": "Fear God, and keep his commandments: for this is the whole duty of man" (Eccl. 12:13).[56] When Samson exits declaring that the Chorus shall not hear of anything "dishonorable, impure, unworthy / Our God, our Law, my Nation, or myself" (*SA* 1424–25) that has transpired, he, too, is affirming that "whole duty of man." Samson's new devotion to the Law and to the law of temperance, now made "complete / Against" *any* "object more enticing" (258–59), allows him to reconnect with the vision of transcendent politics that the dramatic poem and the biblical narrative put in place, and that had been supplanted by both the false transcendences of Dalila's erotic pleasures and the pride of Samson's strutting about as a "petty God" (*SA* 529).

That jealous love held Milton's fascination for a long time, judging by his repeated sorties with the Samson narrative. As many have noted, Milton invokes the image or narrative of Samson frequently to suit his rhetorical purposes. In *Areopagitica* he famously compares the figure of Samson to the chosen English nation (*CPW* 2:557–58). Perhaps he has this earlier context of reformation in mind when he writes the *First Defense* (1651), where Milton positively uses the example of Samson to defend the killing of tyrants like Charles I. He justifies this point from the biblical example of the slaying of the Moabite King Eglon by Ehud (Judg. 3:12–30), even though Milton obscures the implications that follow from verse 12: "the LORD strengthened Eglon the king of Moab against Israel, because they had done evil in the sight of the LORD." Eglon is an enemy king used by God with great purpose, blurring the hermeneutical lines between what is sacred and what is profane.[57] The biblical text does not specify that the deliverance effected by Ehud must of necessity involve killing the Moabite king, but it is clear that God sanctions the action; God placed King Eglon in power, but because the people cry out to the Lord "the LORD raised them up a deliverer" (v. 15), and Eglon's death brings eighty years of peace. Milton comments that "Ehud . . . is held to have acted at God's command" (*CPW* 4:401), and the action is to be praised as just, as is Samson's actions against the

Philistines. He equivocates about the origin of Samson's violence, however, "whether [it was] prompted by God or by his own valor" (402). It seems to make little difference to Milton; again, what matters is intention. In spite of this ambivalence, the Milton of 1651 positively endorses Ehud and Samson as models to imitate in killing tyrants like Charles I, for Samson "thought it not impious but pious to kill those masters who were tyrants over his country" (402).[58] Samson's actions are praiseworthy, he argues, but Milton's position about the piety of this regicide is built upon an earlier passage that is crucial to framing his conclusions.

Milton attacks Salmasius's argument that Christians must submit to tyrants because Christ in humility chose to be born under tyranny. The ground of contention here for both Salmasius and Milton is the significance of the *kenosis,* when Christ "made himself of no reputation, and took upon him the form of a servant, and was made in the likeness of men" (Phil. 2:7). "You base your first argument on the person of Christ," Milton begins, "who took upon himself the form not only of a subject but even of a slave, so that we might be free." But the freedom Milton has in mind steps well beyond one's deliverance from the power of sin and death:

> I do not speak of inward freedom only and omit political freedom. The prophecy of his advent foretold by Mary his mother, "He hath scattered the proud in the imagination of their hearts; he hath put down the mighty from their seats, and exalted them of low degree," must indeed be but idle talk if his advent is instead to strengthen tyrants on their thrones and subject all Christians to their savage power. (374)

Against Salmasius, Milton argues that Christ was made to suffer under tyranny in order that Christians did not have to: "at the cost of his own slavery, he put our political freedom on a firm foundation" (374–75). Christ's *kenosis* enables both our *pleromic* strength to withstand under tyranny and persecution when it occurs, and underwrites our entitlement to enjoy full political freedom. Milton seamlessly links the freedom of the inward kingdom that is established through Christ's *kenosis* with outward political freedom. For the rhetorical moment, the Milton of 1651 appears to shrink the distance between Christ's humble *kenosis* and Samson's terrifying Spirit-filled *pleroma* since the end result of political freedom is the same (even if temporarily secured).

Milton's reasoning here may not be consistent, however, on the eve of the Restoration. In *The Readie and Easie Way* (February or March 1660) he appears to balk at aligning divine will with earthly politics, declaring that there should be "no medling with Church matters in State counsels" where "everie faction hath the plea of Gods cause" (*CPW* 7:380). As Barbara Lewalski comments, there is no perfect political allegory for understanding the issues that *Samson Agonistes* raises, but there are political elements in the work that invite comparisons. David Loewenstein, for instance, aptly demonstrates how Milton's tragedy echoes the wide-ranging radical invocations of the Spirit in response to the Restoration.[59] In Milton's radical milieu, Samson's apocalyptic violence to end the oppression of the Philistines and to destroy the unrighteous resembles that of the Fifth Monarchists and some millenarian Baptists during the 1650s and after. Although there is no evidence to suggest that Milton ever attended a Fifth Monarchist meeting, there seem to have been agitators in his immediate neighborhood and parish. According to Bernard Capp, there was an active assembly of Fifth Monarchists meeting in Beech Lane beginning in 1661, not far from Milton's house on Jewin Street off Aldersgate, which the poet occupied in late 1660. By 1663, this congregation was under the leadership of John Vernon, one of the more prominent leaders of the movement, Nathaniel Strange, and Thomas Glasse. Despite the deaths of all three of these by the middle of the decade, Capp notes that this gathering persisted until 1676, and when Milton took up lodging along Artillery Walk in Bunhill Fields in early 1663, its congregation would have been located just around the corner. A separate assembly of Fifth Monarchists met from 1662 to 1665 in the house of Mary Winch in St. Giles, Cripplegate, Milton's parish.[60]

The political and theological radicalism of the Fifth Monarchists stemmed from both "a desire for liberty in place of tyranny, and for godliness in place of idolatry."[61] Although they were a diverse lot, drawing their numbers mostly from various Congregationalists and Baptists, Capp identifies at least three common elements: a conviction that the saints will actively displace the idolatrous Fourth Monarchy of earthly politics, by force if required; a belief in a millennium where the saints would rule alongside or in place of Christ; and an investment in England as an elect nation that would be responsible for destroying the perceived idolatry of the Roman Church and ushering in the end of time.[62] The seeds of their millenarianism were sown by earlier commentators on Daniel and Revelation, whose influential and complex exegetical systems drew connections between contemporary politics and biblical prophecy.[63] Just as Samson brings down the "Sea-Idol" of Dagon along with the ruling "Lords, Ladies, Captains, Counsellors, or Priests, / Thir choice nobility and flower" of "each *Philistian* City round" (*SA* 13, 1653−55), the Fifth Monarchists aimed to bring down the idols and representatives of the earthly governments of Oliver Cromwell, and then Charles II, in order to establish the political theocracy of Christ the King—realized eschatology, ushered by the blade of a sword if necessary.

For William Aspinwall the Fifth Monarchy includes not just Christ's spiritual kingdom, but his earthly political one as well, a "Civil" kingdom whose universal dominion is "inconsistent with Church-power." Aspinwall does not assent to the notion that Christ himself will personally reign during the millennial period. In his place are Christ's elect, for the "Saints shall be his *Vicegerents* during the time of this Monarchy," those who "shall exercise and mannage this supremacy of power, in the first rise of this fifth Monarchy . . . [for these] are such as have been actors with Christ in warring against the whore, *who are called chosen and faithfull,* Rev. 17.14. I mean the Lambs Military Officers." The militant process of purging and purifying begins in the present, and Aspinwall avers with "much faith and confidence . . . that a tenth part of the City (which is spiritually called *Sodome,* and *Ægypt*) was fallen already." This purging will "undoubtedly caus the name of Christ, yea and their names also, that are fellow-workers with Christ, to be magnified, from the rising of the sun, to the going down thereof."[64]

Samson's failure has caused the opposite to occur: "I this pomp have brought / To *Dagon* . . . / . . . to God have brought / Dishonor, obloquy, and op't the mouths / Of Idolists and Atheists; have brought scandal / To *Israel,* diffidence to God" (*SA* 449–54). Aspinwall's England is purged and the saints exalted; Israel's political future under Samson, however, looks bleak indeed.

Part of the campaign to purge the nation involved social reform. Many Fifth Monarchists in the early 1650s proposed a return to elements of the Mosaic Law in order to impose by legislation godliness and righteousness on a lapsed nation.[65] This agenda had already gained a broad base in the Rump Parliament, whose godly inclinations were enshrined in the moral authority of the Decalogue, but whose civil and criminal elements were reminiscent of the Mosaic Law as both the Adultery Act (May 1650) and the Blasphemy Act (August 1650) indicate. When prominent Fifth Monarchists like Arthur Squibb, Hugh Courtney, and Captain John Williams gained seats as MPs in the Barebones Parliament and/or served on the Council of State in 1653, there was even further hope to bring the nation in line. Aspinwall indicates that while "Christ alone hath . . . Legislative power," the saints would rule by a new devotion to the precepts and morals of Mosaic Law. The vocal Fifth Monarchist and minister John Rogers urged the Barebones Parliament that it was "not enough to change some of these *Lawes,* and so to *reforme* them" for "that wil be to poor *purpose,* and it is not *your worke* now, which is to provide for the *Fifth* [Monarchy] . . . by bringing in the *Lawes* of *God* given by Moses."[66]

The ambitions of the Fifth Monarchy Men to legislate and to compel the "whole duty of man" to "fear God and keep his commandments" were cut short. When Cromwell dissolved Parliament and assumed the position of Lord Protector soon afterward (December 1653), Fifth Monarchist hopes for Mosaic reform and the peaceful initiation of Christ's government shriveled.[67] But the Restoration shattered and demoralized the Fifth Monarchists. Just as Samson found himself "a prisoner chained, scarce freely draw / The air imprisoned also, close and damp" (7–8), leading Fifth Monarchist leaders, including Thomas Venner, Robert Overton, Hugh Courtney, John Vernon, and Vavasor Powell, were arrested and imprisoned in the years immediately before and after the Restoration. When he was released from prison in 1659 after a failed uprising two years before, Thomas Venner took up arms to establish the vision of transcendent politics. His zeal renewed, in 1661 Venner led an uprising that left about forty people dead, with thirteen Fifth Monarchists including Venner upon the gallows. Unapologetically, Venner said to his confessor, "There must be conviction before there can be confession, which I cannot find in my own conscience."[68] The violence was perfectly justified against the idols of church and state. Planned uprisings, in imitation of Venner's, were spoiled in Yorkshire in 1663; that same year the Baptist Derwentdale plot to "rise in rebellion against the government, and to destroy Parliament, and murder all Bishops, Deans, and Chapters, and all other ministers of the Church" was foiled, and the plot by Colonel Henry Danvers to kill the king and reestablish the republic was discovered in 1665.[69] Despite conflicting assessments about the dating of the composition of *Samson Agonistes,* the protagonist's "revenge, yet glorious" (the phrase provocatively placed at line 1660) against the Philistine nobility, priests, and their idols, in order that Samson might exalt the Lord's Name, deliver Israel, and usher in the kingdom of God, certainly resonates with elements of the Fifth Monarchist agenda.[70] So, too, does their failure—Israel is not finally delivered by Samson's violence, nor is the *parousia* initiated by the likes of Venner.

David Loewenstein notes that Milton was often silent in his prose works regarding individual sects.[71] When he does mention them by name, however, we ought to pay attention. *The Readie and Easie Way* castigates the Fifth Monarchists, and any others like them, for their "hypocritical pretenses" toward securing political transcendence through their "Ambitious leaders of armies":

> If ther were no medling with Church matters in State counsels, ther would not be such faction in chusing members of Parlament, while every one strives to chuse him whom he takes to be of his religion; and everie faction hath the plea of Gods cause. Ambitious leaders of armies would then have no hypocritical pretenses

so ready at hand to contest with Parlaments, yea to dissolve them and make way to thir own tyrannical designs: in sum, I verily suppose ther would be then no more pretending to a fifth monarchie of the saints: but much peace and tranquilitie would follow.[72] (*CPW* 7:380–81)

As we saw earlier in the *First Defense*, Milton had no problem invoking "the plea of Gods cause" through the models of Samson and Ehud when it suited him and the political moment. When he writes *A Treatise of Civil Power* (1659) on the eve of the Restoration, however, something has shifted. Previously, Milton had argued that Christ's *kenosis* freed humans from both the burden of sin and the necessity of suffering under tyranny; nearly a decade later, Milton does not seamlessly link Christ's *kenosis* under a tyrant with the justified militancy of a Samson, for "Christ hath a government of his own" that "governs not by outward force" but "deals only with the inward man and his actions." To use outward force to accomplish Christ's kingdom is "a disparagement, and degrades it from a divine and spiritual kingdom to a kingdom of this world" (*CPW* 7:255–56). Like the general tenor of the *Treatise*, the immediate thrust of the passage above from *The Readie and Easie Way* argues for the necessary separation of church and state in order to avoid just the kind of specious claims that might lead potential "Samsons" among the Fifth Monarchists to sectarian violence.

His assessment in *The Readie and Easie Way* of the Fifth Monarchist agenda is partly in line with a passage in *De Doctrina Christiana*, when Milton addresses Christ's mediatorial office. The internal law of Christ's kingdom, granted through the gift of the Spirit, "was given at Jerusalem on the fiftieth day after Christ's passion, just as the Mosaic law was given on Mount Sinai on the fiftieth day after Passover, Acts ii.1." The distant synchronicity of these events leads Milton to conclude that Pentecost trumps the authority of the Decalogue. Christ's superiority dictates that "the weapons of those who fight under Christ, the King, are only spiritual weapons." Moreover, Christ rules over all kingdoms, "not by force or by physical weapons, but by those things which, in the opinion of the world, are the weakest of all. Therefore external force should never be used in Christ's kingdom, the Church" (*CPW* 6:436). The immediate contexts differ: in *The Readie and Easie Way* Milton is addressing the state and the necessity of the liberty of conscience; in the passage from *De Doctrina Christiana* Milton is addressing the church, where Christ "rules not only the body, as a civil magistrate does, but above all he rules the mind and the conscience" (436). But are we to understand, then, that Christ has authority only over the minds and consciences of those inscribed within the church, but not over those in the political realm? The difficulty, as Milton observes in *The Readie and Easie Way,* is that despite the differing contexts, the two realms are not separate. If Christ's kingdom is superior to all other kingdoms, and by implication all other kingdoms are subservient to its rule; and if Christ has authority over the minds and consciences of all humans and not just some, because all will be judged according to their "individual conscience" (6:623); then it appears that human violence to bring about a vision of transcendent politics is not to be endorsed.

But what might this mean for the world of Samson? I do not think it means that Samson is not a hero; it is just a question of what sort of hero Samson is. Here, the relationship between *Samson Agonistes* and *Paradise Regained* has some bearing. Joseph Wittreich claims that "the Samson story functions as a warning prophecy, an oracular threat that would avert the disaster it announces." Milton, Wittreich asserts, presents readers not with a regenerate Samson, but one who undergoes a "second fall."[73] Consequently, the dramatic poem "is a symbolic inversion, a counter-commentary," of *Paradise Regained.* David Loewenstein, however, is more measured in his assessment of Samson, demonstrating that many radical Puritans welcomed the unpredictable and secretive movements of God precisely because they keep the saints available for his own purposes, overturn worldly expectations, and infuse a sense of dread. Moreover, Loewenstein remarks that the juxtaposition of *Samson Agonistes* and *Paradise Regained* registers "alternative eschatological responses" among radical groups reacting to the Restoration that are not necessarily at odds. He evenly surmises that "there is no need . . . to see one response as negating the other," by which I infer that readers ought not to feel the pressure to choose between the two works.[74]

By publishing the two works together in the 1671 volume, we might argue that Milton in effect gets the separation of state and church that his historical context did not allow. The Samson of *Samson Agonistes* dies for a vision of the state, and his new devotion to temperance or self-restraint allows him to "see" the difference between the false transcendence of Dalila's erotic delights and the true transcendence of nationhood that the dramatic poem and the biblical narrative set up as God's cause. The Jesus of *Paradise Regained* lives for a vision of the church; as we will see in a moment, his temperance allows him to see the difference between the false transcendences that Satan offers and the true transcendence of his own kingdom within. By the time he writes the brief epic, Milton no longer appears to link easily the freedom of the inward kingdom that is established through Christ's *kenosis* with outward political freedom. The *kenosis* of Christ transcends a vision of the state. Loewenstein is right to say that the two works do not negate one another. But this does not mean necessarily that Milton did not encourage his readers to make a choice between them or their visions of transcendence.

Samson's repentance and renewed devotion to the Law indicates that there is room for a regenerist understanding of his condition under the Law. One critic registers dissatisfaction with the idea that Samson could contribute to his own deliverance because the "notion that Samson's works could possibly merit the reward of divine grace would have been anathema not only to Milton but to the overwhelming majority of his readers."[75] But who exactly are the "overwhelming majority of his readers"? Is there a Calvinist consensus in post-Reformation England? As we have seen, Milton is not against the theology of merit. In *De Doctrina Christiana,* Christ himself was "RAISED TO IMMORTALITY AND TO THE HIGHEST GLORY . . . BY VIRTUE PARTLY OF HIS OWN MERIT AND PARTLY OF THE FATHER'S GIFT" (*CPW* 6:440–41). This statement should not cause a crisis about the status of human merit in salvation, he later assures, for "the fact that we shape ourselves to Christ's image does not add anything at all to Christ's full and perfect satisfaction, any more than our good works add anything to our faith. It is faith that justifies, but a faith not without works" (451). Samson's faith is a faith with works. John Shawcross demonstrates that even though Milton's drama presents the reader with a bevy of uncertain choices, the work also affirms that "a keeping of covenant, or a faithful adherence to God's teaching and law, regardless of seemingly insurmountable barriers, will lead to God's sustenance and deliverance," an important pattern he detects in "Sonnet IX," *Comus,* the example of Abdiel, and the binding of the poem and drama in the 1671 edition.[76] Samson's new zeal to fulfill the transcendent principles of the Mosaic Law and the nationalist politics associated with them, begun by his inchoate devotion to temperance, renders him heroic and regenerated. But the heroic and regenerated self that emerges, as well as the transcendent vision of politics secured in part through catastrophic violence, is only appropriate under the Law.

Milton's chapter in *De Doctrina Christiana* on the theological and hermeneutical relationship between the covenants of Law and grace, as well as the chapter on Christian liberty that follows, may provide some clarity on this point.[77] Milton makes it clear that the written code of the Mosaic Law was "INTENDED FOR THE ISRAELITES ALONE" as a pattern that offers the "RECOURSE TO THE RIGHTEOUSNESS OF THE PROMISED CHRIST." While Moses, as the giver of the Law, was unable to lead his people into the Promised Land, "an entrance was granted to them under Joshua, that is, Jesus" (*CPW* 6:517, 519). Moses's general conquered the land of Canaan by the sword, and Samson is certainly a part of that world. "Jesus" is the Greek form of "Joshua," but his methods of delivering his people into the holy land do not accord with his namesake who was living under the Law. As Milton elaborates in the chapter following, when the gospel of Christ appeared, "then all the old covenant, in other words the entire Mosaic law, is abolished," and since Christ has "annulled the whole law, then obviously we cannot be bound by any part of it" (525–26, 529). Samson's heroism is inscribed by the Law; the Law's righteousness and the instrumental human violence enlisted to preserve it were "INTENDED FOR THE

ISRAELITES ALONE." If the gospel abolishes the Law, then it raises the possibility that Samson's apocalyptic violence, like that intended by the Fifth Monarchists, is not to be imitated by those under the authority of the gospel. It is only for Christ to bring in his kingdom, not the saints who want to carve it by the sword into their own image. Milton's Jesus does not move as far as the Quakers did on this point; citizens ruling the kingdom within vitally instruct nations and churches to steer the better course (*PR* 2.466–80). It is unfair to characterize the post-Reformation Milton as a quietist or pacifist. John Coffey usefully distinguishes between violence and force in Milton's work, the former always exercised by illegitimate power (e.g., the fallen angels or tyrants) and the latter by legitimate agents of God. Violence is not an "eternal principle" in Milton's cosmology, Coffey illustrates, but an "intruder in God's creation" that is brought about by Satan and imitated by fallen humanity.[78] Jesus's repeated refusals to use the vast armies, cities, and thrones that are offered to him suggest that, under the gospel, the state of the state has shifted. Jesus redefines the kingdom and the means to attain it. In Samson's vision under the Law, the state cannot be separated from soteriology. In Jesus's vision under the gospel, the state is a simulacrum—a necessary construct of human making that, under the best of circumstances, is subject to charity, striving for justice, and providing freedom. But it is a rival, nonetheless, that will be crushed by a jealous God.

Milton's assessment that the gospel abolishes the Law sounds final and complete, but it actually is not. He concedes that "in reality the law, that is, the substance of the law, is not broken by this abolition. On the contrary its purpose is attained in that love of God and of our neighbor which is born of faith, through the spirit" (*CPW* 6:531). Admittedly, charity does not lend itself easily to a characterization of Milton's Samson; as Derek N. C. Wood notes, the word never occurs in the drama despite its prevalent use in Milton's other work.[79] But his Nazarite does get the "substance of the law" right, or partially so, in two regards. First, although Dalila's betrayal did "raise in me inexpiable hate" (*SA* 839), Samson does manage to forgive "[a]t distance" (954) his most personal and most hurtful enemy; the fact that she is not satisfied with accepting it indicates she has other motives. Second, Samson dies on behalf of those who in his estimation do not deserve deliverance and are thus as much an enemy as the Philistines: "*Israel's* Governors, and Heads of Tribes, / Who seeing those great acts which God had done / Singly by me against their Conquerors / Acknowledg'd not, or not at all consider'd / Deliverance offer'd" (242–46). Loving their "Bondage with ease" more than their "strenuous liberty" the Israelites instead despised, envied, and handed over their own deliverer (271–74). Against perceived idolatry, whether from the Israelites' love of "Bondage with ease" or the Philistines' devotion to Dagon, charity has its limits, and the hatred of God's enemies becomes one's "religious duty," for as Milton declares, "some hatred" toward the enemies of God "is a religious duty" (*CPW* 6:743)—this in a chapter devoted to expounding upon charity owed toward one's neighbors.[80] The newly temperate Samson could be viewed as being on the Son's side, but as a "type" of Christ he remains shadowy indeed.

"true pilot": Temperance, Transcendence, and the Kingdom Within in *Paradise Regained*

Like Samson, the Jesus of *Paradise Regained* finds his temperance tested, as he wanders in the landscape of narrative possibilities and faces Satan's presentations of false transcendence. But the goalposts, so to speak, have been moved. In Milton's brief epic, Jesus's resistance to external power implies that the state itself, whether empire, monarchy, or republic, is a version of Baudrillard's simulacrum. Politics, while important, necessary, and subject to ethical action, dangerously offers itself—even to the "godly" involved in the state-making process—as a false soteriology and parody of the kingdom within. Jesus's temperance and *kenosis* provide the lens necessary to recognize the simulacrum.

Jesus will not be seduced by the likes of Dalila. Satan realizes the potential, but ultimate failure, of seductive beauty as he immediately rebukes the method of Belial's temptation for Jesus. A *pleromic* "Beauty stands / In th'admiration only of weak minds / Led captive"; when met with strong minds that "cease to admire," however, there is a deflating *kenotic* effect wherein "all her Plumes / Fall flat and shrink into a trivial toy" (*PR* 2.220–23). Satan understands that this kind of beauty presents itself as a false *pleroma* that is too easily discerned by readers such as Jesus. Better, he avers, to appeal to "manlier objects" that "have more show / Of worth, of honor, glory, and popular praise; / Rocks whereon greatest men have oftest wreck'd" (225–26) the ship of their souls. But Jesus the true pilot recognizes all the temptations as versions of Belial's gesture toward false transcendence. As Michael Bryson correctly observes, "each temptation has been a call to focus on things in themselves, on last things, on a world of objects that may have its origin in the divine, but looks resolutely away from that origin."[81] What is missing in Bryson's assessment, however, is the means by which that connection is restored or maintained. Jesus's temperance is the earthly analogue to his heavenly *kenosis;* his mode of being-in-the-world contributes to his mode of perception.

Milton's brief epic presents us with two readers, Satan and Jesus, who are engaged in the hermeneutical struggle of discerning the same texts of scripture, a point that has not gone unnoticed by critics. Ken Simpson points out that the hermeneutical contest "prefigures the apocalyptic battle at the end of history," and Anne K. Krook argues that the outcome of the contest shifts the grounds of victory from the politics of a "single historical moment" to correct interpretation.[82] What is lacking, however, is a coherent account of how the ontological dispositions of these two readers shape their interpretive strategies. Jesus's interpretations of the scriptures are anchored to transcendence through Milton's ideal of temperance as self-denial, which we will find is virtually synonymous with charity in *Paradise Regained* and which is the soul of the hermeneutical *canon caritatis.* But what precisely is this rule, and how does it impinge on Miltonic temperance as Jesus "figures foorth" the Father through his virtuous performance?

Rhetorically, Milton appeals to the hermeneutical rule of charity in the title of one of his most notorious pamphlets, *The Doctrine and Discipline of Divorce . . . guided by the Rule of Charity* (1643; the latter phrase is omitted in the title of the 1644 version), as well as at the outset of his argument. "[C]haritie," he argues, ought to be "the interpreter and guide of our faith," rather than a slavish devotion to the "mere element of the Text" (*CPW* 2:236). The hermeneutical feats that Milton accomplishes in the divorce pamphlet turn not just on the proper tools of biblical exegesis, but also on the spiritual dispositions of both the interpreter and those who engage his commentary.[83] Regina Schwartz pierces to the core of Milton's rule of biblical exegesis when she states that for him "*what* the Bible means is bound to *how* it means."[84] *Theoria* is ineluctably shaped by *praxis;* or, to put it another way, interpretation is incarnational. The "how it means" is thus ideally determined by the rule of charity, or the *canon caritatis,* even though at times Milton is certainly guilty of a self-serving hermeneutic in *The Doctrine and Discipline of Divorce.* Milton so tenaciously defends the rule of charity that he concludes, "we cannot safely assent to any precept writt'n in the Bible, but as charity commends it to us" (2:340).

Generally speaking, the *canon caritatis* advocates that in instances of questionable evidence or ambiguous meaning or intent, the exegete ought to interpret a text with a view to the most favorable outcome toward his neighbors in order to prevent a selfish manipulation of the text. Moreover, interpretations guided by this rule must be accompanied by the *canon fidei,* or the rule of faith, as derived from the creed.[85] Augustine comments that whoever "thinks that he understands the divine Scriptures or any part of them so that it does not build the double love of God and of our neighbor does not understand it at all." The interpreter may err in discerning the intention of the author or fail to consider fully the passage in its proper context, which for Augustine amounts to a kind of deception. But as long as the interpreter "finds a lesson there useful to the building of charity," and so long as the interpretation does not violate the creed, then the exegesis is sound, for "if he is deceived in an interpretation which builds up charity . . . he is deceived in the same way as a man who leaves a road by mistake but passes through a field to the same place toward which the road itself leads."[86] The detour is certainly not preferable, and can in fact be quite dangerous, as Augustine warns, but the end result of the interpretation is the same: to lead oneself and one's neighbor to a deeper understanding of the self and an enjoyment of God.

Many of those associated with the Leveller movement in the 1640s invoked the necessity of the rule of charity in interpretations of scripture, the Law, and in the formation of political policy. Without its guiding through-line everyone suffers, and the glory of God's image in all human beings—powerful or powerless—is compromised. A theological anthropology, and its resulting politics, is at stake; while the state may attempt to reduce human beings to individuals with or without property rights, many Levellers fought against that definition by reclaiming the prior definition of human beings as created in the image of God and bound primarily by charity rather than merely the social contract. John Wildman, one of the Army spokesmen during the Putney Debates, understands that the divine commands to love God and one's neighbor have implications for political and social action, for "every man should seek the good of his neighbour, and consequently much more the good of the Nation." He continues, "No man showes forth any luster of the image of God in him unless by doing good," for the man "approved by God" is he that "serveth God in his generation," a position seconded by John Lilburne, for whom doing "good in his generation" was "the great end wherefore God sent man into the world."[87]

Even the wealthy saints are indicted for a self-serving hermeneutic; instead of being full of the positive *pleroma* of charity, the professing Christians are satiated in a negative *pleroma* of the world. In a pamphlet attributed to William Walwyn, the author scorns the "proud boasting Churches," whose members are approved of by their pastors, elders, and deacons, and are "mere worldlings indeed" who "spend the greatest part of their time, either in making, buying, and selling of baubles and toyes, such as serve only to furnish out the pride, luxury, and fantasticallnesse of the world."[88] Walwyn's pamphlet criticizes an uncharitable hermeneutic among those who have "a hankering after persecution" and who desire to punish any who disagree with them by "making whom they please Atheists, Anti-scripturists, Antinomians, Antimagistrats, Polligamists, Seekers, or what they will." Perhaps more dangerous from Walwyn's perspective are those who are "Goded with God, and Christed with Christ" to such a degree that they claim that the scriptures matter not at all; zeal and personal experience of the "fals presence of the Spirit" lead them to "Idolize their own fancies" when interpreting the Spirit's directives. If they are challenged in their teaching, they turn their heads away and condemn the challenger for being unenlightened. The result of this self-serving hermeneutic is a negative *kenosis,* a fleshly church and congregation that are "empty shels without kernels, empty clouds that hold no water," rather than the fleshly tabernacles filled with the Spirit and shaped through the hermeneutical rule of charity.[89]

Milton's appeal to the rules of faith and charity in the divorce pamphlet is echoed in the theological treatise as well, and certainly informs the way that his Jesus interprets the scriptures in *Paradise Regained.* While Milton argues extensively that the scriptures are "both in themselves and through God's illumination absolutely clear," and that every believer is equipped to comprehend them, he advocates that if there is disagreement between believers about the proper sense of scripture then "they should tolerate each other until God reveals the truth to all." Accordingly, each party ought to be supplied with the guidance "from that same Spirit operating in us through faith and charity" (*CPW* 6:578, 584, 586). Unlike Augustine, however, Milton does not derive his rule of faith from the creed lest it be used by a magistrate to compel the conscience of the individual and make the "house of God" into a "rule to itself." Instead, Milton derives the rule of faith from scripture alone, for in all "controversies there is no arbitrator except scripture, or rather, each man is his own arbitrator, so long as he follows scripture and the Spirit of God" (585). Milton's subtle shifts here are twofold. First, Milton subverts the external authority of scripture to the internal authority of the Spirit. While the scriptures are of "very considerable importance" regarding the rule of faith, the testimony of the Spirit is the "pre-eminent and supreme authority" (587), a position that places Milton's theology on this point firmly among antinomian sects such as the Ranters and Quakers.[90] For Milton, one's hermeneutical cooperation with the text of the divine Logos exceeds the authority of the scriptures. Second, Milton argues that controversy is at least in part to be adjudicated by how well the interpreter "follows the scripture and the Spirit of God," as displayed in the narrative of his or her own life of virtue and sanctification. The purpose of scripture is to make its readers and interpreters holy, and the principal seat of the holy virtues is "Charity," which is called by Michael "the soul / Of all the rest" (*PL* 12.584–85). As Milton argues in *Areopagitica,* the *parousia* will bring the final adjudication of all questions of meaning; for the time being, however, Milton's *phronimos* interprets through the lens of realized eschatology, the "now-ness" of the divine future ushered in through the *canon fidei* and guided by the Spirit. In this realized eschatology, meaning is presently lived and principally ordered by the *canon caritatis.*

These exegetical principles are the crucible of Milton's brief epic in which the interpretations of scripture offered by Jesus and Satan are placed under pressure. One finds that the former is able to yield the most fecund interpretation of the scriptures because of the crucial link between his theological *kenosis,* bodily temperance, and the *canon caritatis.* The solitary Jesus is led by the "strong motion" of the Spirit into the "bordering desert wild" (*PR* 1.290, 193) where he descends into himself—only to discover that his neighbor is continually present. There, in "holy meditations" and "far from the track of men" or angels, Jesus reflects that the rule of charity has been his steady guide since childhood, both in learning and in deeds (202–4). His charitable mission of "public good" (202) featured in the agon of the brief epic, however, is defined largely by his tenaciously private self-restraint during the temptations toward seizing upon the false transcendence of earthly power. Milton's earlier meditations on and definition of temperance as self-restraint, rather than the more common understanding of the virtue as moderation, thus converge in the scenes in the desert to such a degree that one might be permitted to understand the *kenosis* as conceptually related to the conflation of temperance (self-restraint) and charity (love of neighbor) in the brief epic.

The tightly wound relations between Jesus's temperance and charity compel Satan, exasperated in his tempting, finally to cry, "What dost thou in this world?" (4.372). This response is perhaps the central query that occupies Milton's epic. The intemperate angel constructs "well couch't fraud, well woven snares" (1.97) to seduce Jesus into pursuing other narrative possibilities for the self by demonstrating his power and divine Sonship apart from the Father's will, or according to the proper time.[91] Satan's goal is to sever Jesus from the *methexis* of the Father's divine plan for human salvation. Their encounter is a hermeneutical agon: both are aware of the scriptural prophecies concerning the coming Messiah, and both are in the process of determining the nature of Jesus's person and mission. In the demonic council, Satan relates to his cohort how he thinks Jesus is the preacher and reader who will deliver "that fatal wound / . . . / Upon my head" (1.53–55):

> For this ill news I bring, the Woman's seed
> Destin'd to this, is late of woman born:
>
> .   .   .   .
>
> Who this is we must learn, for man he seems
> In all his lineaments, though in his face
> The glimpses of his Father's glory shine. (1.64–65, 91–93)

Satan is puzzled by the play of *kenosis* and *pleroma,* as Jesus's temperate body, made gaunt from his fasting, shines with the excess of the Father's glory residing within.

At times, however, Jesus seems more uncertain than Satan regarding his own person. Although he has had heroic thoughts since a boy (1.201–20), has been instructed by Mary about his birth (1.227–60), and hears the testimony from heaven and from John at his baptism (1.270–80), he is unaware why the Spirit has led him into the wilderness (1.290–93). Like Samson, he appears to have had some "rousing motions in me which dispose / To something extraordinary my thoughts" (*SA* 1382–83), but his submission to these motions leads to a radically different outcome. The Father testifies in heaven that he has led Jesus into the desert so that "all the Angels and Ethereal Powers, / . . . and men hereafter, may discern / From what consummate virtue I have chose / This perfect Man, by merit call'd my Son, / To earn salvation for the Sons of men" (*PR* 1.163–67). Barbara Lewalski comments that Milton's Jesus "has no consciousness of himself as 'first-begot' or of any pre-existent state in heaven"; she is thus inclined to favor a Jesus who has limited self-knowledge, the only possibility one can entertain if there is to be "a genuine dramatic action and a real conflict" in the brief epic.[92] The hermeneutical agon centered about the scriptures is the arena where the integrity of Jesus's self is challenged and shaped.

So, how well does Jesus hermeneutically cooperate with the text of the scriptures? How well does Jesus appropriate or incarnate its narrative possibilities in a Ricoeurrian fashion? Jesus's reading the prophecies about the Messiah in the scriptures constitutes a genuine search for self-knowledge and how that self "would function within the practices of a community."[93] Paul Ricoeur proposes that the self can only be known in and through the mediation of texts: "it must be said," he writes, "that we understand ourselves only by the long detour of the signs of humanity deposited in cultural works. What would we know of love and hate, of moral feelings and, in general, of all that we call the *self*, if these had not been brought to language and articulated by literature?"[94] The self is constituted in and by a text that gives us the semblance, or to use Aristotle's terminology, *mimesis,* of a possible world, one that a reader can choose to reject or one in which the reader can choose to dwell. The contest between Satan and Jesus in the dramatic poem is a contest for defining selfhood as potential versions of Jesus's *ego* emerge and recede, and Samson's narrative in Judges, with its cataclysmic outcome, is certainly one of the potential texts that he could hermeneutically appropriate and indwell. For Ricoeur a reader's self does not remain in alienation; subjectivity is, rather, enlarged: "As a reader, I find myself only by losing myself. Reading introduces me into the imaginative variations of the *ego*. The metamorphosis of the world in play is also the playful metamorphosis of the *ego*."[95] In this way, a text fashions its audience and potentially sets them free from their illusions. Milton's brief epic demonstrates Jesus's process of understanding himself and the world's illusions through the principal texts of the scriptures, the thrust of which is guided by the two greatest commands to love God and to love one's neighbor (Deut. 6:4–6; Lev. 19:18; Mark 12:29–31), the core or "substance" of the Mosaic Law that Milton identifies in *De Doctrina Christiana* as the only part of the Law that Christians must obey (*CPW* 6:531). Milton's Jesus reads with this *mimesis,* this performance in mind: a *pleromic* performance that proclaims the Father's love for creation, and a *kenotic* performance of temperance or self-denial that is embedded in the life of the community, as his interpretations are directed toward loving his neighbor. In Jesus's limited self-knowledge, his temperance is truly tested and each successful performance of obedience both enhances his temperance and expands the horizons of his self-knowledge.

Satan recognizes this mode of performative reading, and his attack is directed against the Son's fully attaining that vision of selfhood. Like Andrew and Simon (*PR* 2.30–48), Satan is the most literal of readers and interprets the prophecies about the Messiah in terms of fleshly power, pleasure, and prestige. But in the first temptation Satan, disguised like Comus's rustic appearing to the Lady, appeals to the miraculous as he couches his temptation in an act of charity: "But if thou be the Son of God, Command / That out of these hard stones be made thee bread; / So shalt thou save thyself and *us* relieve / With Food, whereof we wretched seldom taste" (1.342–45; emphasis added). Jesus does not hesitate, but deconstructs the pretenses of Satan's narrative snare by questioning whether God or bread has the greater power to relieve their hunger, and then points to other narratives in which the prophets Moses and Elijah were sustained by God himself. Satan immediately drops the veil of his disguise, and is rebuked by Jesus for his "craft" of "mixing somewhat true to vent more lies," and constructing narratives that are "dark / Ambiguous and with double sense deluding" (1.432–35), as Satan's initial appeal to the rule of charity rings hollow.

The first temptation continues a bit later when Satan appears again, this time not as a mock shepherd/pastor caring for his sheep, a parody of Lycidas and the virtuous Edward King, but as a richly clothed courtier (2.298–300). With "fair speech" he attempts to use Jesus's own narrative logic against him by pointing, "as story tells" (2.307), to instances when God provided for his people in the desert. Ishmael, Elijah, and Israel, he alludes, were well provided for in the desert, and Satan insinuates that Jesus must be physically and spiritually abandoned because he has received nothing from God. In order to prevent Jesus from appropriating the potential of the prophets and patriarchs, Satan suggests a different narrative in which to dwell. Echoing Comus's argument of abundance to the Lady, Satan asserts that Nature should present its best bounty for the King of Nature, and he presents a lush table before him whose copious description runs in excess of twenty-five lines. Unfazed, Jesus "temperately replied" to the rebel angel, yet his bodily self-restraint is measured against the dread power of which he is capable: "I can at will, doubt not . . . / Command a Table in this Wilderness / And call swift flights of Angels ministrant / Array'd in Glory on my cup to attend" (2.378, 382–86). As we find in the other temptations, Jesus's temperance cannot be defined apart from the power that he is capable of unleashing. His temperance is simply a feature of his *kenotic* Incarnation, the moment when the high "sovereign Priest, stooping his regal head / . . . / Poor fleshly tabernacle entered" ("The Passion," 15–17). Jesus's *kenosis* is precisely why this bodily temptation and the other temptations of wealth or power do not appeal to him, a *kenosis* that is driven by and figures forth an excessive, *pleromic,* and charitable love for fallen humanity.

Satan's more elaborate narrative snare occurs when he parades the armies and kingdoms of the world in front of Jesus, arguing that he could do the most good to free his people from the seat of Rome. He whisks Jesus to a mountain where he views "what numbers numberless / The City gates outpour'd, light armed Troops / In coats of Mail and military pride" (*PR* 3.310–12) at his command. Later, Satan advises that he should "Aim therefore at no less than all the world," rather than pursue the lowly throne of David, where Jesus will most certainly sit "not long / . . . be prophesied what will" (4.105, 107–8). Self-restrained Jesus, "unmov'd" (109) by the narrative, again deconstructs its empty pleasures: "what honor that, / But tedious waste of time to sit and hear / So many hollow compliments and lies, / Outlandish flatteries?" (122–25). Earlier, Milton's Jesus does not deny the necessity of earthly politics, for the governing of the inner man is a necessary key "to guide Nations in the way of truth / By saving Doctrine, and from error lead" (2.473–74). But he emphatically realigns the priority of the internal kingdom over the exigencies of the external kingdom. Samson's militancy and catastrophic violence is rejected.

Worldly fullness characterizes all of Satan's temptations in *Paradise Regained*, where the spiritually bankrupt Satan thinks that fixing external wealth also secures the arsenal needed to establish a politics according to one's will. "Great acts require great means of enterprise," he reasons. "Therefore, if at great things thou would'st arrive, / Get Riches first, get Wealth, and Treasure heap" (412, 426–27). George Fox criticized the Fifth Monarchists and some millenarian Baptists for a vision of worldly wealth and power. He writes that leaders of movements such as these mistakenly "looked upon this reign to be outward, whenas he was come inwardly in the hearts of his people to reign and rule there, these professors would not receive him there. . . . But Christ is come and doth dwell in the hearts of his people and reigns there."[96] The militancy of a Fifth Monarchist or Baptist millenarian, like the martial heroism of Satan at the beginning of *Paradise Lost* or the "Blood, death, and deathful deeds" (*SA* 1513) enacted by Samson, is challenged by the internal "deeds / Above Heroic" of the meritorious Jesus who rules himself.[97] For Milton and Fox, self-government through realized eschatology is true liberation from the world; without this liberation the state becomes the idol. Milton's "true pilot" Jesus recognizes that there can be no freedom, for either the ruler or the ruled, without the internal bounty of virtue that is produced through virtuous cooperation with the divine Logos.

Instead, the spiritual kingdom Jesus will establish on David's throne, according to prophecy, according to the Father's season, and according to the dictates of temperance and the rule of charity, "shall be like a tree / Spreading and overshadowing all the Earth, / Or as a stone that shall to pieces dash / All Monarchies besides throughout the world" (*PR* 4.147–50). While the organic image of the tree summons to mind the heavenly kingdom of those connected to the "true vine" (John 15:1–8), one might well question what is so charitable or temperately restrained about the apocalyptic image of the stone from Daniel 2. As one might imagine, the image was a favorite for Fifth Monarchists. William Aspinwall invokes this image to describe the coming kingdom of the ruling saints for it shall be the stone that "shall crush and break in pieces all the other four Monarchies, *Dan.* 2 34.45."⁹⁸ But Milton's Jesus is not interested in earthly, militant politics and his allusion to the stone in Daniel 2 does not evoke the same presentist meaning as Aspinwall's allusion. As we explored in the previous section, Samson's violence is defined according to the world of the Law, but under the gospel, Jesus will not allow a vision of politics to become an idol. "Much ostentation vain of fleshly arm / And fragile arms, much instruments of war / Long in preparing, soon to nothing brought, / Before mine eyes thou hast set," he counters; while these instruments are perhaps "Plausible to the world," Jesus flatly states that they are "to mee worth naught" (*PR* 3.387–90, 393). Met with Jesus's *phronêsis,* the "double share / Of wisdom" (*SA* 53–54) that Samson confesses he himself lacked, the false *pleroma* of earthly might that Satan presents is just as deflated and emptied as the beauty that Belial previously championed. The stone that crushes and forces the *kenosis* of the glorious kingdoms of the world is also the tree that sustains the faithful as it spreads the *pleroma* of its branches, for the Miltonic "Or" (*PR* 4.149) that connects the images of the tree and the stone is not one of opposition or choice, but one of identity and continuation.⁹⁹ Jesus's temperate self-restraint during the combined temptations to power, arms, and wealth leads to the unrestrained act of iconoclasm or "virtuous violence," to borrow Stephen Greenblatt's memorable phrase, that will come at the end of the age.¹⁰⁰ Jesus's cooperation with the prophetic texts in a charitable way connects him to the transcendence of the Father he serves, yielding a far richer, more fecund possibility for the community because of his own performance of abundant self-restraint.

Following closely on the heels of Satan's temptation to power and politics is the sinister temptation to knowledge and wisdom, a strategy he adopts when he sees that Jesus "seem'st otherwise inclin'd / Than to a worldly Crown, addicted more / To contemplation and profound dispute" (212–14). In both cases, Satan attempts to cloak his temptation in an act of charity. When Jesus refuses to cooperate hermeneutically with the "text" of earthly politics, Satan suggests that this "trial hath indamag'd thee no way, / Rather more honor left and more esteem" (206–7). Echoing Milton's argument in *Areopagitica* for the necessity of temptation, Satan implies that the temptation itself has contributed to his attaining more of the *pleromic* glory he is to "figure foorth." When he promises the knowledge and wisdom of the world, Satan argues that these will "extend thy mind o'er all the world," an expansion much needed if "with the *Gentiles* thou must converse, / Ruling them by persuasion as thou mean'st" (223, 229–30). Persuasion through discourse and reason, he argues, will be impossible if he does not speak their language. Jesus's response, the casting away of all classical learning, has puzzled critics for a long time: Why would Milton, Douglas Bush queries, deeply indebted to ancient learning, "turn and rend some main roots of his being"? E. M. W. Tillyard describes Jesus's denunciation of classical learning as if Milton were spurning a lover, one who "goes out of his way to hurt the dearest and oldest inhabitants of his mind."[101] Northrop Frye suggests that if a Christian were to read Plato and Aristotle, one might find them "profitable." But "if he were to exchange the direct tradition of revelation for their doctrines, which is what Christ is tempted to do, he would find in them only the fine flower of a great speculative tree, with its roots in the demonic metaphysics and theology described in the second book of *Paradise Lost*."[102] Satan has suggested that Jesus's mind ought to ingest the scope of human learning, but with that consumption comes the fallen language games of hell and the evisceration of God's Name as defining Presence that we examined in chapter 2. Understanding what is at stake in Satan's conflation of knowledge and wisdom will account for Jesus's scornful rejection of classical learning.

Satan's temptation to knowledge is cloaked with charity and filled with the abundance of an empire of converts whose "Idolisms, Traditions, Paradoxes" (234) will have been smashed or refuted. Part of Satan's strategy has been to link uncritically knowledge (*scientia*) and wisdom (*sapientia*).[103] Notice this easy slippage when he exhorts,

> Be famous then
> By wisdom; as thy Empire must extend,
> So let extend thy mind o'er all the world,
> In knowledge, all things in it comprehend. (221–24)

Initially, Satan suggests that classical learning will only function as a necessary supplement, but as the temptation unfolds over the next fifty lines of Satan's praise of ancient eloquence, the studious retreats of the Greek landscape, the inspired minds of Attic philosophy, and the charms of Doric poetry, it becomes clear that these are meant to eclipse and not supplement *"Moses'* Law" (225): "These rules will render thee a King complete / Within thyself, much more with Empire join'd" (284–85). As I previously suggested with Samson's attraction to the false transcendence of beauty and pleasure, perhaps Satan intends here to extend the shadow of Baudrillard's "omnipotent" simulacrum, such that it causes God to be effaced "from the conscience of man" while simultaneously allowing "the destructive, annihilating truth . . . to appear: that deep down God never existed, that only the simulacrum ever existed; even that God himself was never anything but his own simulacrum."[104] Secular knowledge is just as valuable as, if not identical to, scriptural wisdom for rendering Jesus a true king.

The separatist preacher Samuel How expresses disdain for those who blur the differences between carnal learning and biblical wisdom. The "knowledge of the Arts and Sciences, diverse Tongues, much reading, and persisting in these things, soe as there-by to be made able to understand the *mind* of *God* in his Word: this is it that I condemn from the word of Truth." For How, human learning is an idol that clouds one's perception of divine things. The Digger Gerrard Winstanley registers his agreement on this point: "your Divinity darkens knowledge; you talk of a body of Divinity, and of Anatomyzing Divinity: O fine language! But when it comes to trial, it is but a husk without a kernall; words without life."[105] In Book 12 of his treatise on the Trinity, Augustine reflects on the important distinction between knowledge and wisdom that Milton's Satan erases, but he is ardently not against human learning. For Augustine, *scientia* and *sapientia* are differing faculties of human rationality, with knowledge being analogous to the desire for temporal satisfaction and wisdom being analogous to the desire for eternal truth. The distinction, he elaborates, is illustrated in the Fall: "The Fall of man is the result of 'lower reason' throwing off the control of the 'higher,' and devoting itself to the pursuit of the material and temporal."[106] Human beings are permitted to pursue earthly knowledge, but only as preparation to behold divine wisdom. Knowledge, Augustine describes, dwells on human history and has a value in instructing human beings about moral truth. But knowledge is in the service of wisdom for the purposes of right worship; the growth of one's knowledge about the self and the world ideally leads to a better contemplation of the Lord's glory. The distinction is real and necessary for Augustine as temporal knowledge, properly viewed and pursued, must be connected to transcendence.

Not so for Satan. In his temptation of Eve, Satan promises that by eating the fruit earthly Eve will gain her audience with the gods (*PL* 9.708–18); inversely, Satan promises high-minded Jesus that by consuming earthly knowledge he will attain the lower common ground necessary to have access to the earthly gentiles in order to "hold conversation meet" and to "reason with them" and "refute / Thir Idolisms, Traditions, Paradoxes" (*PR* 4.232–34). Unlike Jesus, however, and despite her reasoning capacity, Eve intemperately falls, for "Greedily she ingorg'd without restraint" (*PL* 9.791)—another reminder that even though one is equipped and trained in virtue success in discernment is not guaranteed. Via Satan's conflation of the categories, Jesus identifies the temptation as an intemperate and unjust love: "Think not but that I know these things," replies Jesus, "or think / I know them not; not therefore am I short / Of knowing what I ought" (*PR* 4.286–88). Similarly, Augustine does not completely denounce the value of knowledge, for "the lower reason [i.e., knowledge] has its proper place in the right use of things temporal, as means to eternal life."[107] Knowledge has its "proper place" if this latter end is kept in sight.

Jesus's initial retort echoes Sir Guyon's response to Mammon in Book 2 of *The Faerie Queene*, when the Knight of Temperance is tempted toward possessing control of the miners and producers of wealth: "all thine ydle offers I refuse. / All that I need I haue" (*FQ* vii.39.2–3). But when Satan suggests indulgence beyond knowledge's proper scope, the Son of God's final scorning assessment of the idol of knowledge can only be characterized as an act of iconoclasm, one that is simultaneously coupled with an excessive love for divine wisdom.

"But these are false, or little else but dreams, / Conjectures, fancies, built on nothing firm" (*PR* 4.291–92), Jesus derides, for they are "found far unworthy to compare / With *Sion's* songs, to all true tastes excelling, / Where God is prais'd aright" (346–48). The reading soul that moors upon these dreams and fancies will find himself in the position of the parabolic pilot of the "night-founder'd Skiff," anchored to "nothing firm." Milton's ideal *phronimos* here understands what Augustine calls "ordinate love," or the holy act of discerning the "intrinsic value of things." Such a person "neither loves what should not be loved nor fails to love what should be loved; he neither loves more what should be loved less, loves equally what should be loved less or more, nor loves less or more what should be loved equally."[108]

Augustine's theological reflections echo Aristotle's secular summation of the temperate man as one who "loves such pleasures as right reason dictates."[109] As we have discovered already, right reason is for Milton an ontic disposition of the redeemed that has been cultivated by a habitual practice of obedience and godly virtue. Jesus's right reason dictates that his desires succumb to temperate self-restraint, in order that his excessive love for the Father and for his neighbor might prevail.[110] Satan's literal, immanentist interpretations of scripture clearly emphasize the Son's earthly glory, only to aspire to undo it; his reading is an act of spite against God, the Son, and humanity. Instead of the rule of charity, linked in the poem to temperance, satanic exegesis is guided by the rule of cupidity. Augustine describes this rule as "a motion of the soul toward the enjoyment of one's self, one's neighbor, or any corporal thing for the sake of something other than God."[111] What Augustine cautions against, and which Milton's Jesus seconds in spirit with regard to knowledge that is "found far unworthy" (346), is not love or enjoyment of knowledge per se, but an inordinate love that unjustly values knowledge over wisdom, does not participate in divine love, and does not consider one's neighbor. Satanic exegesis labors in death, as the reality that Satan promises to Jesus is suspended over the void instead of divine Presence.

When Jesus stands up on the pinnacle of the Temple in the final temptation and declares, "Tempt not the Lord thy God" (quoting Deut. 6:16), we may see him as declaring his confidence in his divinity, claiming all the authority that is due to the Son of man and the "True Image of the Father" (4.596).[112] The dramatic casting down of Satan, through all the Son's glory and power, is yet again checked by a temperate retreat, as "unobserv'd / Home to his Mother's house private [he] returned" (4.638–39). But while the poem seemingly ends anticlimactically, we are left with Jesus's *pleromic* readings of the prophecies and the scriptures. The image of his mother's house suggests the fertility of his coming ministry that will culminate in a different kind of excess, derived from his pleasure of charitable reading: the Son's love for humanity that will impel him toward the cross "because in thee [the Son] / Love hath abounded more than Glory abounds" (*PL* 3.311–12). Like the Lady of *Comus* or the newly devoted Samson, Christ's temperate reading is iconoclastic, and as Ricoeur states, "extreme iconoclasm belongs to the restoration of meaning."[113] In Ricoeurrian terms, Christ throws down the idols in order to listen to the power of the symbol. Jesus's iconoclastic reading is a labor of love as humanity harvests its blossoming fruits: the paradise within where virtue, and implicitly right reading, resides, flourishes, and repairs the ruins.

In this second part of our study, we have considered how textual interpretation is inseparable from the narrative of its lived performance and proclamation in the world. For Milton's *phronimos*, hermeneutics involves the transformation of the self in light of the holy and divine revelation, as exegetes are alienated from themselves in their encounter with the "otherness" of texts, an otherness that intrudes or disrupts, that requires discernment, and that invites its appropriation as a "projected world." As we turn to the final section of the book, we unite Milton's heterodox theology of the Incarnation, which accentuates human moral perfection through continued obedience to God, and his hermeneutics of reading, which emphasizes the reader's appropriation of a text through an early modern "action-model" of reading. Both axes—theological and hermeneutical—figure prominently in the works and legacies of Milton's radical contemporaries: the Independent preacher John Everard, the Digger Gerrard Winstanley, and the Quaker James Nayler. All are as committed as Milton to listening to the symbol of the Word, to appropriating its potential in their lives, to feeding their own flocks, to fetching the Age of Gold, and to becoming "True poems." As we will find, Milton shares with them not only their scorn for the Word-less clergy and the tyrannical powers that set them in place, but a revo-lutionary view of the Christic potential in all believers that Milton de-lineates in his theological treatise and imaginatively renders in his poem dedicated to "This perfect Man, by merit call'd my Son," whose cooperation with divine power earned "Salvation for the Sons of men" (*PR* 1.165–66). Believers who incarnate Christ are "adopted" as God's sons and daughters in the same way that Jesus is adopted as God's Son: because of his perfect obedience. If Christ and the Father are united and become one "not in essence but in love, in communion, in agree-ment, in charity, in spirit," then adopted believers who persist in their faith and obedience become one with the Father in the same way (*CPW* 6:220). Given this Christic potential, the realms of proclamation, her-meneutics, and politics are ineluctably shaped by ontology. A subli-mated mode of being-in-the-world purifies and perfects those realms. The particular incarnations and performances of Everard, Winstanley, and Nayler summon all the fury of the divine firestorm to scourge the ruins of English society, in order to liberate those dwelling among the ruins in want and oppression.

part iii

Revolutionary Incarnations and the Metaphysics of Abundance

The Perfect Seed of Christ

Allegory and Incarnation in the Works
of John Everard and Gerrard Winstanley

O thou immortall light and heat!
Whose hand so shines through all this frame,
That by the beauty of the seat,
We plainly see, who made the same.
　　Seeing thy seed abides in me,
　　Dwell thou in it, and I in thee.
　—Henry Vaughan, "Cock-Crowing"

For the Presbyterian minister Thomas Edwards, "publishing was . . . an entirely partisan affair." His massive compendium, *Gangraena* (1646), aroused more than twenty published responses in the year following its publication and significantly contributed not only "to Presbyterian petitioning campaigns and collective condemnations of error in 1646–8," as Ann Hughes cogently comments, but also to the negative ways in which radical individuals and dissenting sects were figured and represented in print.[1] Kristen Poole has demonstrated that anti-sectarian writers of the revolutionary period often depicted the sects with vivid images of pestilence or teeming insect life in order to communicate the urgency of their extermination.[2]

Champion of orthodoxy and the established clergy, Edwards insists that without the strong cooperation between the church and civil governments, these plagues of heresy will lay England to "wasting, and ruine." Mixing his metaphors, he writes that "a spark not quenched may burn down a whole house, and a little leaven leaveneth the whole lump: So small Errors at first . . . are grown now to many thousands." A church that does not exercise proper censure or slothfully neglects the defense of doctrine, he admonishes, is like a "Garden and Vineyard without a hedge and fences," a "City without walls and Bulwarks," or an "Army without Discipline"—images with particular resonance when the large-scale enclosure of land was on the rise and armies were gripped in bloody Civil War.[3] Listed among the many heresies of concern to Edwards are those that declare believers to be equal to Christ as God's adopted sons and daughters. Christ's Incarnation, reason these heretics, "does us no good, it must be a Christ formed in us, the deity united to our humanity." Radical believers are identified as an incarnation of the deity, declaring that "God is in our flesh as much as in Christs flesh; he is as much in the flesh of the members, as the Head." This particular doctrine is often coupled with the belief in the earthly perfection of the saints, and is celebrated in at least one Anabaptist hymn, which Edwards reprints: "All sinne we find is out of mind, / the Saints are made divine / . . . / None are so dear, nor yet so near, / with God they are made one, / Who now doth see them sure to be / as his only Sonne."[4]

The present chapter and the one that follows both consider how Milton's heterodox theology of the Incarnation resonates within the constellation of other radical adoptionist and perfectionist theologies unsystematically espoused in early modern England. The Independent preacher John Everard and the Digger Gerrard Winstanley are considered together in this chapter, for they both revive an allegorical understanding of scripture that is grounded in an incarnational epistemology. For Everard and Winstanley, the Incarnation is the site of convergence between the material and spiritual worlds, and it legitimates allegory by affirming the ambiguities of the w/Word and the world as both the letter and the spirit, a hermeneutical relation that we might align with the theological grammar of *kenosis* and *pleroma*, respectively.[5] The Quaker

James Nayler, whose scandalous pageant into Bristol in imitation of Christ's entry into Jerusalem is the subject of chapter 7, lays claim to the incarnated perfection of the divine seed within and dramatically enacts the Christic narrative. All these radical figures held the view that Jesus was adopted as God's Son because he perfectly participated in the divine through his obedience, or as the Father declares in *Paradise Regained*, "From what consummate virtue I have chose / This perfect Man, by merit call'd my Son" (*PR* 1.165–66). But as the Anabaptist hymn that Edwards reprints celebrates, Jesus's adopted status and perfect performance on earth are available to and achievable by other devout believers as well. What follows is how the particular Incarnational poetics of Everard, Winstanley, and Nayler have a bearing on the activities and economies of preaching, reading, and politics.

In my illuminating these performative theologies of the Incarnation, and by my aligning them with Milton's own theology, however, I want to avoid arguing for any strict "influence" by these sects on Milton's own peculiar thinking about the Incarnation. As David Loewenstein has effectively argued, Milton maintains in his prose a "certain aloofness with regard to contemporary radical groups and writers," and I am inclined to agree with his point that we ought to pay attention to Milton's silence.[6] My first purpose is simply to challenge, though not subvert, a well-established scholarship on the pivotal role of pneumatology in radical Protestant theology and politics. This is a role prioritized with good reason, for the Spirit was invoked time and again as the ultimate source of authority in matters of preaching, interpretation, and dissent; in some cases, as with the Ranters and Quakers, the authority of the Spirit exceeded even that of scripture itself. The Quaker Alexander Parker bears witness to this idea, for the scriptures are to be understood as merely "an outward declaration" of salvation, but "the Scriptures themselves, are not the Rule of Life, or the way to salvation, nor the will and mind of God. . . . There is but one Rule of life, and that is the Spirit of God."[7] In his classic work on Puritan pneumatology, Geoffrey F. Nuttal observes, "from 1650 onwards there is a perpetual controversy, whether the Word is to be tried by the Spirit, or the Spirit by the Word."[8] In these last two chapters, however, I want to refocus our attention and argue that Christology ought to occupy a more central place in our construal of these sects during the Interregnum, for these theologies generated and inflected particular brands of anticlericalism, theories of reading and language, and political agendas. My second purpose is to continue our discussion on the relation between the Incarnation and its performance in the world. For Everard, Winstanley, and Nayler, incarnating Christ results in a radical divine economy, one that is inscribed within a theology, narrative, and metaphysics of abundance, rather than a present reality that is characterized by exclusivity and crippled by scarcity.[9]

"This Rending of the Vail": The Incarnation of John Everard and the Abundant Economy of Allegorical Reading

Thomas Edwards, whom Milton debases as "shallow" in his 1646 poem (published in 1673) "On the New Forcers of Conscience Under the Long Parliament," along with the conservative Presbyterian contingent, desperately wanted to contain or eradicate heresy in England by erecting civil, ecclesial, and theological bulwarks and hedges against the encroaching sects that proclaimed them. Kristen Poole writes that Edwards's compendium imposes a "taxonomic system" that tries to quell the din of the sectarian swarm "as a means of re-establishing ecclesiastical and social harmony." While many of the radicals were holding strongly to the ideas of liberty of conscience and toleration, Presbyterian conservatives like Edwards viewed it as "a cry for a radical individualism, an anarchical substitute for ecclesiastical order."[10] The Independent Milton held the opinion that to suppress and to punish heresy with the "Civil Sword" is to "force our Consciences that Christ set free" (5–6). Milton laments that "Men whose Life, Learning, Faith and pure intent / Would have been held in high esteem with *Paul,* / Must now be nam'd and printed Heretics" (9–11). Milton's allusion to Paul is an embedded call for toleration, for the Apostle's own conversion serves as a reminder that believers of a different conscience, or even nonbelievers, can be persuaded and used by God.[11] The poet surely considered himself among those men of "Learning, Faith, and pure intent" who did his best to embody the Word in the world, even though he risked being deemed a heretic (or worse) by "shallow" men.[12]

It is doubtful, however, that the Apostle Paul would have held Milton or many of his radical contemporaries in "high esteem" on a number of theological issues. Chief among these that we will consider in this and the following sections is a theology of earthly perfection, derived not only from a radical pneumatology, but also from adoptionist paradigms. For the Apostle Paul and the Reformed theologians like John Calvin and Martin Luther who are indebted to him, perfection is not attainable in this life, for the reality of sin causes us only to see God "through a glass darkly" (1 Cor. 13:12). But as we will find, such a limitation has little currency among radical thinkers like John Everard, Gerrard Winstanley, and James Nayler. In particular, this section examines Everard's spiritual and incarnational hermeneutics of reading, derived from a Catholic medieval tradition that emphasizes the exegete's dialogical encounter with scripture. Resonating with many radicals, Everard's theology blurs the Trinitarian distinctions between Son and Spirit, and understands Christ as another "figure" or "type" for our example, rather than as *the* anti-type and final fulfillment of the Mosaic Law and the prophetic scriptures. This understanding generates a new economy of reading, one that challenges the hermeneutic monopoly held in trust by the professional clergy. Everard's model of reading revitalizes the hermeneutic abundance of allegory and is explicitly centered on the body of Christ.

The status of Christ's Sonship is often eclipsed by scholarly preoccupations with pneumatology in the seventeenth century. The historian J. G. A. Pocock argues that "the claim to personal inspiration by an indwelling spirit" is "the essential characteristic of Puritanism." This doctrine, showing forth in all its antinomian splendor, has the dangerous potential "to turn the social as well as the metaphysical world upside down."[13] But the historian Geoffrey Nuttal usefully comments that the indwelling of the Holy Spirit is seen differently by theological conservatives and radicals: while both parties agree that the Spirit indwelled the original biblical writers and apostles, the former tend to characterize that indwelling as "extraordinary," while the latter define it as "ordinary"—prescriptive for contemporary believers rather than restrictive or dispensational.[14] As Richard Baxter puts it, "There are two sorts of the Spirit's motions; the one is by extraordinary inspiration or impulse, as he moved the prophets and apostles. . . . This Christians are not now to expect, because experience telleth us that it is ceased; . . . The other sort is of the Spirit's working . . . to guide and quicken us."[15] Richard Hollingworth would agree. Concerned with the dangers of enthusiasm, and warning his readers to beware of false and demonic spirits, Hollingworth makes it clear that scripture ought to be the rule by which we test and try every spirit. He clarifies the doctrine of the Holy Spirit's indwelling: "When I speak of the *Spirit's being*, or *dwelling in a Saint*: I mean not an essential or personal in-being or in-dwelling of the Spirit, as he is God or the third Person of the Holy Trinity." Instead, "this Scriptural phrase of *in-being* and *in-dwelling*, doth import only inwardness, meer relation and close union."[16] Yet the weight of one's "experience" is precisely the point of departure, so that what Baxter or Hollingworth might see as the now defunct "extraordinary inspiration" of the Spirit among the prophets and apostles may appear to others such as Winstanley, Everard, or Fox as quite ordinary, if not prescriptive, for everyday Christian living.

For the mystical preacher John Everard, the Spirit's indwelling remains unbroken from apostolic times and fully present in the "experimental" life of the saints. In the dedicatory epistle to *The Gospel-Treasury Opened* (1657), a posthumous collection of several sermons by Everard (d. 1640/41?), Rapha Harford laments, "Oh how *rare*, how *precious*, how excellent and sweet is this *spiritual, practical, experimental* life? but where to be found? . . . How *few* do discern the true way to that *High, Rich, Supereminent life*?"[17] Among those few is Everard, whom Harford commends "would often say, that he desired to be acquainted with men who had *experience* of Christ, rather than men of notions or speculations . . . ; and he did in his *publick* preaching averr it, that though they were never so *mean, poor,* and *despised* by the world, yet if they were but acquainted *with such experimentall truths* as these, they were *more welcome to him* then so many *Princes* and *Potentates*."[18]

The breach between the orthodox-minded and the radically inclined, reflects Nuttal, is widened to the degree to which the priority of the Spirit and personal experience is exalted over the authority of scripture to test those inclinations.

For Everard one must experience the spirit of the living scriptures. Harford comments that Everard insisted we must "know Jesus Christ, & the Scriptures more then Grammatically, literally or Academically, viz. experimentally."[19] But what does Harford mean by this cryptic statement describing Everard's hermeneutics? Does it imply that Everard holds to a fundamental opposition between the letter and the "experiential" spirit? In this section I want to turn our attention to Everard's own "idiosyncratic system of divinity" that "challenged almost all the assumptions of early Stuart Christian piety."[20] David Como has admirably reflected on Everard's system of divinity and his allegorical method. But he does not sufficiently account for the integrity of the Incarnation, the perfect fusion of the *kenotic* material and *pleromic* spirit, as its epistemological and hermeneutical core. Like Winstanley, Everard frequently emphasizes the ascendancy of the fullness of the spirit over the barren letter of the text: "*The flesh profiteth nothing, it is the Spirit* (the mystery) the marrow *that giveth life.*" But this emphasis often leads us mistakenly into a binary trap. For all his jettisoning of the letter or flesh for the spirit within, we find that Everard, like Winstanley, cannot finally escape the letter, leading him to an incarnational epistemology. "We are not able to conceive of the *spiritual meaning,* and Gods minde," Everard claims, "without *something* represented and proposed sutable to our *Element,* to our *language,* to our *sphear,* to our *condition:* something bodily must be presented. . . . *Be sure still, To maintain* the letter of the word *Undefiled, Untouched, Uncorrupted* . . . for without the letter you cannot have the Spirit."[21] That "something represented" for Everard is the Incarnation, the fusion of letter and spirit. In fact, allegory actually "recovers," "redeems," or enlivens the letter and the flesh—spirit working *through* the letter or the flesh—rendering new possibilities for both, as Christ's Incarnation and Resurrection demonstrate. Thus, rather than consigning the letter of scripture or the flesh of the believer to the flames as something that must be consumed or transcended, the spirit of allegory paradoxically infuses, saturates, or reinstantiates a now sublimed letter. Reading and interpretation are a sacramental participation in the Incarnation, and Everard's allegorical reader is a reflection of this wedded integrity of the material and the spiritual in the hypostatic union. His incarnated reader recognizes the life in and through the letter, because he himself has been incarnated and resurrected to its possibilities, and awakened to its saturated potential as a word participating in the great Word.

In four inventive sermons on the mundane text of Joshua 15:16–17, in which Caleb gives his daughter, Acsah, to Othniel because he successfully captured the Canaanite city of Kiriath Sepher, Everard pronounces that without the Spirit the scriptures are covered as with a veil. Those who read the letter of the Word remain in "the *Outward Court of the Tabernacle*"—readers who do not penetrate into the marrow and life of the Word, and readers who do not cooperate with and appropriate the spirit of the text. In order to rend the veil, step into the "*Sanctum Sanctorum,*" and taste the "hidden *Manna,*" Everard resorts to allegory. While allegory is an interpretive lens spurned by many biblicists who advocated the "plain sense" of the scriptures, Everard justifies its use from Galatians 4:24–31, where Paul argues the difference between slavery under the Law and freedom under Christ. Here the Apostle allegorically renders the Jewish Christians, who desire to revive the authority of the Mosaic Law, to Abraham's son, Ishmael; true Christians are likened to Isaac as the son of the promise, and the one who represents Christians as heirs of freedom. Moreover, we find that Everard revives the medieval Catholic, and radical Anabaptist, practice of spiritual reading, a practice that we will find is also Incarnationally inflected.[22]

As Scott G. Huelin explains, the practice of spiritual reading was the dominant mode of encountering the scriptures in the premodern era; it "refers to ways of reading texts other than for their grammatical/historical meaning," and takes its cue from Paul's exhortation in 2 Corinthians 3:6 that the "letter kills, but the spirit gives life."[23] In this mode, the scriptures contain a level of meaning not immediately accessible, for as Henri de Lubac recounts, in this tradition scripture is profoundly allegorical: a deep forest with innumerable branches (Jonah of

Orleans), "an infinite forest of meanings" and a true labyrinth (Jerome), an unfathomable abyss (Autpertus), a vast sea (Ambrose) and ocean of mystery (Origen), or a raging torrent (Gilbert of Stanford).[24] In order to navigate its mazes and plumb its spiritual depths, the exegete resorted to the "four-fold method": the literal, allegorical, tropological, and anagogical levels of meaning. A verse in circulation as late as the sixteenth century encapsulates the four-fold method of medieval exegesis: "The letter shows us what God and our fathers did; / The allegory shows us where our faith is hid; / The moral meaning gives us rules of daily life; / The anagogy shows us where we end in strife."[25] Put another way by Adam of Perseigne (ca. 1221), "the first has to do with history, which is a narrative of deeds that have been done. The second concerns . . . the spiritual significance of these deeds. . . . The third pertains to moral reasoning. The fourth . . . leads the soul upwards."[26] The scriptures are thus prayerfully experienced in a mystical sense, as they are radically internalized and then enfleshed in the life of the believer. Through the encounter the reader is also transformed, for in the process of interpretation the reader is exercising the theological virtues: the allegorical sense relates to faith, or the doctrines one should believe; the tropological relates to charity, or how one is to treat his neighbor; and the anagogical relates to hope, or one's realized potential in Christ. De Lubac lucidly comments on the nature of this dialectical encounter between reader and text. The spiritual meaning "is the meaning which, objectively, leads us to the realities of the spiritual life and which, subjectively, can only be the fruit of a spiritual life"; it is "the meaning we discover—or rather, in which we penetrate—by living that mystery."[27] As Huelin observes, spiritual reading is as much a process of the reader discovering herself or himself within the light and virtue of Christ, as much as it is an unfolding of the nature and character of God.[28]

We see Milton affirming this assumption, as we are reminded of the poet's first invocation to the Spirit in Book 1 of *Paradise Lost*. As he himself is engaged in reading and discerning the scriptures during his time of composition, the poet compares the abundant chaos of his own heart to the "vast Abyss" over which the Spirit "Dove-like satst brooding" at creation and "mad'st pregnant," as Milton prayerfully pleads,

"What in me is dark / Illumine" (1.21–23). Milton appropriates the text of creation for the purposes of describing poetic composition, but as Huelin elucidates, just as the practice of spiritual reading implies the face of the reader in the text, it also implies that the text appropriates the reader. It is Milton's hope that the Spirit, who "dost prefer / Before all Temples th'upright heart and pure," appropriate his virtuous heart to accomplish the task set before his servant: no less than the defense of God (1.17–18, 24–26). Jean Leclerq observes that scripture is "not primarily a source of knowledge, of scientific information; it is a means for salvation, its gift is the 'science of salvation': *salutaris scientia.* . . . Each word it contains is thought of as a word addressed by God to each reader for his salvation. Everything then has a personal, immediate value for present life and for the obtaining of eternal life."[29] In Milton's spiritual reading and poetic interpretation, his singing of the Son's virtue, his own salvation lies, as well as that of the world to which the poet is speaking.

Everard's hermeneutic operates according to the same principles. It is in Everard's spiritual reading, wherein the believer "strive[s] *To take off the Vail*" by coming "to see *His own face* in the Scriptures, as a man seeth *His natural face in a glass,*" paired with his "living" interpretation of the scriptures, that the Incarnation figures forth. For Everard, the "Hebrew," or literal understanding, of Joshua 15:16–17 yields "nothing to us," but an "English" translation, or spiritual understanding, of the passage yields a hermeneutical abundance reflective of the Promised Land itself, "so fruitful, so good, so replenished with milk and honey, so fruitful in every way, so delightful, so commodious, so desireable." What are the "English" spiritual (allegorical) meanings to be discerned in this city in Canaan, in the giving of Caleb's daughter, Acsah, to Othniel? In "translation," offers Everard, the passage reads thus: "And my heart said, or a good heart [Caleb] said, That whosoever [Othniel] smiteth and taketh the City of the Letter [Kiriath Sepher], to him will I give the Tearing or Rending of the vail [Acsah]." Everard's spiritual reader is Othniel, to whom "shall be given the mysteries of the Kingdom of God; he possesses *full content,* heaven and all happiness, and whatever *his heart can wish for* . . . if God permit." Through the arts of war, the Othniel of Joshua 15 conquers and unlocks the gates of a key city for the Israelites as they move into Canaan; through the "*skill and Art*" of spiritual (allegorical) reading, Othniel the reader unlocks the abundant potential of even the most mundane of biblical texts.[30]

But for Everard this "skill and Art" is not given to the learned or to the professional clergy, which contradicts the implicit assumption in Catholic allegorical exegesis; on the contrary, spurred by self-love instead of charity, lured by the promises of worldly reward, and driven by selfish ambition, these ministers conspire to keep their congregations in the Outer Courts rather than welcoming them into the *pleroma* of the Holy of Holies, for "no body *must know more then they,* and they *must have* the honour and praise *of all:* they must and will be sure to keep men within *their compass* and knowledge, always *holding them* in the letter . . . in the *shadows* of Religion." These modern-day Pharisees read the scriptures, but remain distant from the "Christ [that] *dwells* in every creature" because they are precisely not spiritual readers. "Is it not a strange thing," he asks, "that He should be *in* Us, be *so near us,* and be *our light, and our life, our sun and our shield,* and yet *we not* know him, *we* not be acquainted with him?" Mired in self-love and ossified by their sin, the "kernal" of the *pleromic* Christ within is overburdened by a hardened shell impossible to crack. Where university learning and earthly wisdom fail, however, God succeeds in and through the "*despised, . . .* the poor Fishermen and the like; that *the Creature* might be convinced, that *the power* is of God."[31] Everard echoes the Protestant notion that scripture ought to be available to all, and demonstrates the radical bias against the professional clergy. Yet his impulse to "democratize" Christ and the unfettered access to the Word is problematized by the very tradition of allegory upon which he draws. The "skill and Art" required to discern the "*Mystery*" and "*Secret Woof* [i.e., woven threads] *in the Web of the Letter*" still remain fairly elusive to all but the most "fit" of readers; de Lubac makes it clear that in the tradition of spiritual reading exegetes submitted to strenuous years of training and discipline to ensure that the freedom and abundance that allegorical interpretation afforded did not betray a pious and "authentic" reading.[32] "Allegory," remarks Anthony Thiselton, "presupposes the possession of an interpretive key

which can be used by *insiders* to unlock the code by a series of transpo-
sitional exercises on the individual components of the narrative."[33] For
Everard, the interpretive keys that open up the hermeneutical abundance of the Promised Land are twofold: human perfection and the
body of Christ.

The first hermeneutical key entails the reader's gradual climb toward moral perfection, and it is not surprising that the frequency of the
practice of spiritual reading proportionally increases within a charged
theological climate where mysticism flourishes and the doctrine of
earthly moral perfection is preached and published. James Nayler's
pamphlet *Weakness Above Wickedness* (1656) states that no one could
come to an intimate knowledge of God or Christ except through the
doctrine of perfection. In a formal response to Nayler, the anti-Quaker
Jeremiah Ives voices a common objection that "it is one thing for men
to come to perfection, and another thing for them to come before a
God that is perfect: for *Paul* was not come to perfection, when he himself saith, *Not as though I had ALREADY ATTAINED.*"[34] True, Jesus had
exhorted his followers, "Be ye perfect, as your father in heaven is perfect" (Matt. 5:48), and the Apostle Paul had stressed that believers be
"imitators of God" (Eph. 5:1), but the Quakers had taken Jesus's exhortation too far, according to Ives. God in Christ is perfect, Ives acknowledges, but human perfection will only occur at the consummation of history. And yet, perhaps more than ever, the doctrine of human
moral perfection on earth flourished. Radical preachers such as George
Fox, James Nayler, and the prominent Army chaplain John Saltmarsh
consistently preached human perfection; among the favorite metaphors
they used to describe the progress and gradual perfection of believers
was that of the divine "seed." Leo Damrosch explains that the "seed"
metaphor had great appeal because of "its promise of continued organic development" toward perfection.[35] Like Winstanley, whose work
we will discuss in the following section, Saltmarsh juxtaposes the "eternal seed" of Christ, whose "fullness is already in the saints, or all true
Christians," against the "seed of the serpent" in those who live inde-
pendently of God—two seeds whose harvest results in radically different incarnations in the world.[36]

Everard's own metaphor is that of the kernel in a shell, used not only as an image that distinguishes the "*Sap, the Life, the Sword,* [and] *the Light*" of *pleromic* spiritual reading from the "*Bark, the Outside, the Sheath,* [and] *the Lanthorn*" of *kenotic* grammatical reading, but also as an image that describes the perfected life of the individual believer. For the preacher Everard, "*this word* and *Christ* and the *Spirit All dwell Among us,* dwell *In us.*" The human creature is thus a reflection of scripture, a little book we might say; the essence, or to use Everard's vocabulary, "substance," of scripture and the substance of humanity are the same: "And this is, Onely Christ *Co-Essential* with the Father: This is *that word which* the Scripture speaks of, which is able to *make the man of God perfect.*" All the individual letters of scripture are included in that "One *Great* and mighty word," just as all the individual creatures "*are but* as so many Letters of the GREAT Word." Reading by the Spirit, piercing the veil, and entering the Holy of Holies is thus Incarnationally realized in the narrative of one's life. Though none can see God and live, Everard preaches that it is through the believer's appropriation of God's "*well-beloved in us*" that one is able to see as much of him as possible in "the Effects and Fruits of truth."[37] Consequently, the believer's incarnation and gradual progress toward perfection are crucial to his or her reading, as the reader becomes a living scripture for others to read, and perhaps causing others to neglect the reading of scripture itself.

The publication of Continental works in England contributed to the prevalence of perfectionist doctrine. As Nigel Smith recounts, Counter-Reformation mystical works, such as Benet of Canfield's *The Rule of Perfection* (ca. 1593) and the *Theologia Germanica* (1516), both of which advocated the "supereminent" life, gained greater currency in England when they were translated, respectively, by Everard and the prolific radical publisher Giles Randall.[38] The popularity of the doctrine of perfection was also assisted by the rise of anti-Trinitarianism in the 1640s and 1650s and resurgences in debates about the dual nature of Christ. In order to confirm this assertion, we might turn briefly to the Socinian *Racovian Catechism,* a document that had circulated on the Continent for decades and had great currency in Poland and the Low Countries especially. In England, a Latin version was apparently licensed by Milton against government policy and published in August 1650, and an English translation of the catechism followed in 1652.[39] Its anti-Trinitarianism and rigorous application of logic to exegesis, its denial of original sin, God's Incarnation, and the eternity of Christ, and its rejection of the "satisfaction theory" of atonement—all of these fueled such a controversy that Parliament ordered the seizure of all copies in London for public incineration, and the vice-chancellor of Oxford at the time, John Owen, was enlisted to compose a vigorous attack against it.[40] In Milton's last pamphlet before his death, he offers support for the sects, among them the Socinians (*Of True Religion*, *CPW* 8:437), and we might understand his licensing of the catechism as an act of toleration, if not an outright endorsement of its strict biblicism and rational method in exegesis. It is by no means a necessary conclusion, however, that Milton was theologically invested or sympathetic to some of its tenets, and one might just as tenably argue that he was simply being faithful to his own convictions, outlined earlier in *Areopagitica*.[41]

On the doctrine of the Holy Spirit, the catechism is relatively taciturn, but the issue that energizes and dominates its pages is the author's preoccupation with the nature, person, and offices of Christ. Unequivocally, the author denies that Jesus had a divine nature because it poses a logical problem: "two substances indued with opposite properties, cannot combine into one Person, and such properties are mortality and immortality." While Jesus is not to be understood as simply "meer man" because of the circumstances of his birth, divinity is only to be ascribed to God the Father: "whatever divine excellency Christ hath, the Scripture testifieth that he hath it by gift of the Father. . . . Jesus Christ doth perpetually ascribe all his Divine acts not to himself, or any Divine nature of his own, but to the Father."[42] The author repeatedly emphasizes the humanity of Jesus Christ and his extraordinary participation in the divine will, evoking for us the heretical Samosatene Christology we examined earlier. He is "one with the Father" (John 10:29–30) because between Father and Son there is "onenesse in will or power, as to the businesse of mans Salvation," and not as a result of the Son's sharing in the Father's divine nature—conclusions reminiscent of Milton's own. For Milton, Christ "declares [John 10:38; 14:10, 20–21; 17:21–22] that he and the Father are one in the same way as we are one with him: that is, not in essence but in love, in communion, in agreement, in charity, in spirit, and finally in glory" (*CPW* 6:220). Because Jesus perfectly revealed the will of God through his actions, Christ is thus to be understood as the "Son of God" in the catechism because "amongst all the Sons of God, he is both the chiefest, and most deare to God, as *Isaac* . . . was most deare to *Abraham.*" Works performed in faith and obedience are thus a necessary part of human salvation, recalling Milton's primary understanding of faith as a verb and his insistence on cultivating habits of virtue: "Q. *What is that obedience?* A. That . . . according to our ability, we perform the Will of God. . . . In short, that we contract the habit of no sin, but gain to our selves the habits of all Christian Vertues." The author makes it clear that, like Jesus, human beings require the gift of God's power to persist in "habits" of obedience; thus, while the author of the catechism does not place the burden of salvation squarely on human shoulders, he does insist that human beings as "sons of God" must persevere as "co-authors" of it. Christ is our example, and the imitation of Christ consists "in the exercise of those vertues which the Lord Jesus proposed to us in himself, as in a living pattern."[43]

This "living pattern" brings us to Everard's second hermeneutical key to unlocking the abundance of the scriptures, the body of Christ, for it is one's appropriation of the text of Christ's torn body that prompts "*this rending of the vail.*"[44] While the *Racovian Catechism* understands Christ primarily as a figure for our emulation, many radicals, including Winstanley and Nayler, understand Christ as something more than mere example: as yet another "type" or "figure." Their belief that Christ was a type or figure is still compatible with the orthodox doctrine of Christ as a sufficient sacrifice. While it does not necessarily deprive Christ of his unique status as God's "chiefest, and most deare" son, such an understanding does aid in establishing new economies of abundance by elevating the potential for human perfection, jettisoning the need for a professional clergy, and reinvigorating the allegorical reading of scripture. The Ranter John Saltmarsh, for example, explains that Christ's appearance in the flesh "was a *figure* of *God* whose design is to make his *Saints* his *Temple,* his *Tabernacle,* his *Body,* his *new Creation,* his *new creatures,* his *habitation* or *house.* And God thus *manifested in flesh* was a *figure* of that mystery of *godlinesse* in us, or God becoming an *Immanuel,* or *God with us.*" It is through a believer's perseverance in cultivating a "true and lively faith" through the exercise of "*faith, repentence, love, new obedience*" that the believer is purified and reenacts the performances of the Christic figure. Like Jesus, God's incarnating the believer as his "*habitation* or *house*" is a function of the believer's own "habits of grace."[45] Such habits, as Saltmarsh indicates by his title, brighten the "sparkles" of divine glory that reside within believers.

The crucial lesson we are to learn, exhorts Everard, is that "*Christs body and his actions* were symbolical." Echoing the Thomist view of transubstantiation in the Eucharist, Everard asserts that the miracles of healing that Jesus performed were the "accidents," not "*the Substance,* nor the End of his coming; for he by them *shadowed* out to us what he doth internally in our souls. . . . He is for a sign *in the flesh, and in his Humane nature,* of what he did from the beginning, and what *he is* still in doing: He himself, *in the body,* in his humanity, *and All his actions,* were typical." At issue here appears to be an understanding of Christ's relation to the Mosaic Law: Is Christ to be seen as the only fulfillment of the Law, as orthodox ministers such as Richard Baxter and John Owen state, in which case Christ is uniquely the Son of God? Or is Christ to be seen as another *figura,* as Saltmarsh and Everard observe, in which case the perfection of the "sons and daughters of God" could be possible, depending on their level of participation in the divine? If Christ, whose adoption as God's Son is a condition of his obedience rather than his being the preexistent second person of the Trinity, is understood as scripture's perfect reader, then becoming a perfect son or daughter means also that one's adoption and continued cultivation of the divine seed within render the believer a perfect reader as well—one who cooperates with and appropriates the spirit of the scriptural text. The Quaker James Nayler certainly sees himself as having fulfilled that law. In his divine participation he "came to see that I through the law must be redeemed from the law, and that my redemption from it must not be by making it void, but by fulfilling it . . . and the words of Christ [Matt. 5:17] I found true."[46] Everard would concur, for Nayler's bold claim is the bedrock assumption of Everard's spiritual reader. For Everard, we must read scripture in such a way as to be able to affirm, Incarnationally with Christ, "*This day is the Scripture fulfilled in thee* [i.e., in me]," for "there is no part of holy Writ but is fulfilled *alwaies* in all times . . . in every member of the Church."[47]

While Everard does emphasize the priority of the kernel and the spirit of scripture and the Word residing within the human person, the outer shell, letter, or flesh remains important to the process of reading and perfection. Just as "you cannot have the Oyster without a shell: so neither can you have these *mysteries,* these Allegories, without the flesh, [and] without the shell . . . something bodily must be presented, that we may conceive *of that* which is in the same proportion, done *in us* spiritually."[48] So, while scholars like Nigel Smith and Geoffrey Nuttal are generally correct in asserting that many of Milton's contemporaries thought that Joachim of Fiore's "Age of the Spirit" had finally arrived, superseding the "Age of the Son," or that many were debating whether the Spirit or the Word ought to have primacy, I would invite us to see a much tighter, more organic, connection between the Incarnation and the Spirit.[49] Theologically speaking, without the Incarnation there would be no promise of the Spirit, even though, paradoxically, a radical theology of Incarnation gains this prominence by denying the orthodox formulation of the Trinity. For Everard, it is precisely in and through the Incarnation that the promise of the Spirit of truth is realized. The letter of the scriptures is none other than the body of Jesus Christ that must be broken and torn asunder for the hermeneutic abundance of the Spirit to be unleashed, so that God may "Glutt you with happiness." Everard's Othniel must "Take it, *Strike* it, *Smite* it, *Tear* it all to pieces" in order to feast upon the Word "as men do by meat, they tear it, *champ* it, *chew* it between their *teeth* . . . because they would get *all the nourishment out* they possibly can."[50] Proper spiritual reading is figured as consumption, but not just any consumption—it is, rather, the consumption of God's Real Presence as Everard evokes a Catholic understanding of the Eucharist. Everard would have his audience believe that this readerly consumption of the Word is the essence of Christ's declaration at the Last Supper, "This is my body which is broken for you."

Consequently, Everard's spiritual reading is ultimately an act of thanksgiving, a eucharististic hermeneutic as readers receive their nourishment from the gift of Christ's Incarnated body. It is a body that is fragmented and broken, but in that very brokenness it is also "distended"—distributed in and shared by the church as the body of Christ. Hence, the result is a metaphysics of abundance, a communal participation in a body that continually perpetuates itself, as opposed to an "aporetics of lack."[51] The abundance secured in the piercing, breaking, sharing, and digesting of Christ's body is realized and reflected in the holy violence committed against the spiritual reader's body, against the "giants," "mutiners," "Philistims," and "*Golia's*" within that prevent the reader from thankfully inheriting such an abundant gift. "There is," Everard remarks, "[*I*] *my Self,* to be overcome." This self that reads without understanding, that is overburdened by external worship, that mistakes earthly learning for heavenly wisdom, and that is motivated by "*Self-Love* and *self-interest,* by *Fears, Hopes* and *Rewards,*" is the idol of our own creation, "*another God* [created] *to your selves*" that must be shattered and abandoned. Until then, readers are self-consumed, self-devouring, and never renewed, pictured like one "in a mist, *Groping* in darkness, and . . . *feeding himself* with his own *devices.*" To Everard, these "devices" upon which we feed are nothing more than "*dung and excrements,*" leading to our lack rather than our abundance and our death rather than our life.[52]

Contrarily, when Christ's Incarnation is made complete within, through the reader's appropriation of his broken body, the reader draws upon the depths of Christ's flowing blood as an eternal spring or fountain. As if demonstrating the wealth of that fountain within himself, the pages of Everard's last sermon move at a dizzying pace as image is piled upon image, superlative upon superlative, and scripture upon scripture. His spiritual reader is likened to Job, who found favor with God when he was convinced of his own "Vileness." Alternately, Everard is the Ark of the Covenant surging with YHWH's Power and

Glory as it is carried before the Israelites into Canaan (Joshua 3–4). For Everard, form and content cannot be separated, for external glory and internal glory are perfectly fused: "there is *the Ark of the Covenant overlaid all over round about with pure gold; to shew, that from this spring and fountain* cannot but *proceed* all purity and holiness *in our external actions:* then they cannot *but must* shew forth." Like the Ark he contains within himself the life of the Mosaic Law, as well as the other objects placed about the Ark in remembrance of God's provision. Everard the incarnated reader and preacher is the Israelite in the wilderness who is sustained by the manna from heaven, or he is like Aaron's rod that buds anew, "*alwayes flourishing and green;* . . . ever after bring[ing] forth *fruit* like a tree *planted by the rivers of waters*"; ultimately, he is among the crowd of saintly witnesses in the heavenly city, lavishing in the presence of God, where "we shall be *Ravished* with *Seeing; Satisfied* with *Enjoying; And Secured* for *Retaining.*"[53] The veil before Everard's eyes is torn asunder.

It is in that ravishing divine gaze that we find Milton also dwelling, a gaze fundamentally fixed upon the seminal act of God's entering the world. For Everard, the believer must not be content to know the letter of the scriptures "Grammatically, literally or Academically"; rather, the reader must transcend the letter "experientially" by embodying the spirit to which it points.[54] But as I have been arguing, the letter is not discarded, but suffused and saturated with meaning by means of Everard's hermeneutical sacramentalism; analogously, the body is saturated with meaning when the Holy Spirit dwells within, transforming the individual into a fleshly tabernacle. In Milton's scriptural hermeneutics, he generally favors a literal sense for determining meaning, arguing that "when God wants us to understand and thus believe in a particular doctrine as a primary point of faith, he teaches it to us not obscurely or confusedly, but simply and clearly, in plain words" (*CPW* 6:287). But as Russell Hillier demonstrates, "Miltonic literalism can become surprisingly mobile and elastic, demonstrating complex figurative meanings, obliquely expressed, that are variously metaphoric, metonymic, allegorical, and anagogical." Flesh and spirit, or literal and allegorical, are thus not opposed to one another but constitute a continuum; the letter is the nexus that constitutes the vital point of access to revelation. This hermeneutical continuum finds its analogy in Milton's doctrine of *creatio ex Deo,* which ensures a material creation that is infused with the capacity for revelation. Milton's cosmos and his poetry are deeply informed by what Hillier elegantly terms "an allegorical-sacramental form where the Son irradiates Creation as its creative Logos and divine-human intercessor," an incandescent universe effecting an "*explication filii Dei.*"[55]

In the prologue before the description of the heavenly council in Book 3 of *Paradise Lost,* the narrator is melancholy about his blindness, unable to see the "sweet approach of Ev'n or Morn, / Or sight of vernal bloom, or Summer's Rose," and yet the poet willingly trades his earthly, veiled eyes for a piercing vision of the "Celestial Light" that purges the mists of his understanding (*PL* 3.42–43, 51). The spiritual eyes of God can see even if Milton's fleshly ones cannot. As the "Almighty Father from above" surveys "His own works and their works at once to view," Milton, like John Everard, is among those readers who receive from God's sight "Beatitude past utterance" (3.56, 59, 62). In that divine gaze, and in the believer's appropriation of its blessing, Milton and Everard hope to become the living scriptures themselves, the adopted sons, and the "True poem . . . and patterne of the best and honorablest things."

Sacred Flesh or Serpent Flesh: Gerrard Winstanley and the Narrative Economy of Silence

In describing the abundant yield of allegorical-incarnational reading, Everard resorts to metaphors of earthly and heavenly plenty and prosperity. For Gerrard Winstanley, leader of the short-lived Digger movement, this allegorical-incarnational paradigm of reading must transform these metaphors into powerful realities of material abundance and just political action. In the introductory epistle to his *Watch-Word to the City of London and the Armie* (August 1649), Winstanley justifies his actions on St. George's Hill, Surrey, on 1 April 1649 by negating his words. Prompted by a voice within, he had published *The New Law of Righteousnes Budding Forth* in January of that year, wherein he relates his conversion experience, describes the internal combat between the Beast and the Lamb in every human creature, and declares that the "whole earth shall be a common treasury for every man, for the earth is the Lords."[56] Despite these earlier proclamations, magnificent in their social boldness and theological creativity, Winstanley declares that his "mind was not at rest" following the publication of *The New Law* "because nothing was acted." By late March of that year, he had come to realize that "words and writings were all nothing, and must die, for action is the life of all, and if thou dost not act, thou dost nothing."[57]

Act he did. On a spring morning, Winstanley and a small group of men climbed upon the heath and unenclosed commons at St. George's Hill and began the small, but politically charged, labor of digging and sowing not only on their own behalf, but on that of the starving and landless poor. Historian David Underdown concludes that in the first years of the Commonwealth the Rump Parliament "was more protective of the rich and the powerful than of the poor and oppressed."[58] Winstanley's was an act of desperation, and he was responding to a present crisis that he felt was being neglected by the powers that be. We must wonder if Milton had this episode and other small acts of resistance to oppressive powers in mind when Adam states that those who "love with fear the only God," though they seem insignificant, can bring about God's kingdom "with good / Still overcoming evil, / and by small / Accomplishing great things, by things deem'd weak / Subverting worldly strong, and worldly wise / By simply meek" (*PL* 12.562, 565–69). In the next few days the meek number of Diggers swelled to twenty or thirty, calling upon the many who were devastated by the harvest failures of the previous two years to join them in cultivating the common and waste lands.[59] From the Diggers' point of view, the "Norman Yoke" had finally been cast off with the defeat of the monarchy, an idea that gained currency with the Levellers; with it came the end of the exclusive rights of lords of manors, and the land was rightly restored to all.[60] Christopher Hill remarks that Winstanley's digging was "no mere symbol: it was a political act." Nigel Smith comments that Winstanley's digging "reminds us that to dig the land is also to dig up the ideological infrastructure of social and state tyrannies."[61] In other words, the digging begun at George's Hill was an act of cultural conversion involving alienation and retrieval, and resulting in new economies. Commons and waste lands are alienated from their *kenotic* barrenness and transformed into *pleromic* places of shared abundance. Political and social narratives are alienated from the voluble Serpent and out-narrated by the silent performances of God's adopted sons and daughters, who act as preachers and embodiments of the Word, one to another.

It is appropriate that we begin with Winstanley's own narrative of conversion as described in *The New Law of Righteousnes*. He testifies that while in a trance he heard a voice saying, "*Worke together. Eat bread together;... Whosoever it is that labours in the earth, for any person or persons, that lifts up themselves as Lords & Rulers over others, and that doth not look upon themselves equal to others in Creation, The hand of the Lord shall be upon that labourer.*"[62] We are perhaps tempted to think that Winstanley's trance accords with the *OED*'s primary definition as "absorption, exaltation, rapture, [or] ecstasy." But Winstanley differs from medieval mystics such as Meister Eckhart, Christina of Markyate, or Margery Kempe. In contrast to the ascetics, the Digger is much more practical, much more engaged and invested in how his exegetical practices and his theology play out in the larger workings of the world around him. We ought perhaps to be satisfied with the *OED*'s alternate definitions of a trance as "an unconscious or insensible condition" or an "intermediate state between sleeping and waking." This is perhaps a more fitting characterization of Winstanley's trance.

But we should not minimize the fact that he viewed himself in the visionary mode and as having the authority of a prophet. He is, after all, proclaiming a distinctly *New Law of Righteousnes*.[63] Consequently, with the exception of his last pamphlet, *The Law of Freedom in a Platform, or True Magistracy Restored* (London, 1651–52), in which he seems to reverse his position that inner reform should precede outer reform, he is not concerned with the intricacies of laying out the practical "blueprint" for how to restructure society. As a prophet he is more concerned with confronting the hearts of his audience through the vision he receives. While Winstanley himself does not elaborate on the circumstances of his trance-like vision, Michael Lieb may help us to clarify its significance. Lieb has reflected on the "spirituality of vision" to great profit, particularly with regard to Ezekiel, and he delineates two axes of the divine vision: the "mystical or phenomenological dimensions" and the "interpretive or hermeneutical dimensions." While the former are engaged in describing and prescribing behavioral and experiential norms that lead to communion with the Godhead, the latter are concerned with exegetical frameworks, the elucidation of a particular text by establishing "interpretive structures through which that text can be better understood." Specifically, within Judaic and Christian hermeneutics, these frameworks might include the novel juxtaposition of one biblical text with another or the allusion to extra-biblical texts. Despite their distinguishing features, however, both the mystical/phenomenological and interpretive/hermeneutical axes operate in harmony and often overlap to render an experiential/representational model. As Lieb comments, the "idea of seeing God" is directly related to how texts depict the *visio Dei*.[64]

Winstanley, however, has a "vision of God" characteristically different from that of the prophet Ezekiel; there is no windstorm from the north, no flashing, winged creatures with four bestial faces who move like lightning, no throne of sapphire from which the voice and glory of God radiate. He does claim to have had "diverse matters" presented to his sight, but avoids their description because "here" they "must not be related." In fact, Winstanley nowhere elaborates on his visual perception of God. Instead, he focuses on its aural reception, the "annunciation" in the hollow of his ear, so to speak. The heavenly message bears the blessed fruit within: "I was filled with abundance of quiet peace and secret joy. And since that time those words have been like very fruitfull seed, that have brought forth increase in my heart, which I am prest in spirit to declare all abroad."[65] Perhaps like Mary, he sees himself as a willing vessel full of the "secret joy," the good news proclaimed to those who have been disenfranchised and excluded. Arguably, Winstanley's vision of God culminates in the image he uses in the title of his impassioned but unfinished prose work, *Fire in the Bush. The Spirit burning,* *not consuming, but purging Mankind.*[66] We have already seen how Gregory of Nyssa interprets the burning bush of Exodus 3 as a figure for the Incarnation, as an image of God dwelling in and affirming the flesh of the creature without consuming it. At creation, God takes on the "flesh" of the earth, what Winstanley calls the garment or "cloathing" of God. This language is very similar to the language used in a "*habitus* theory*" of the Incarnation, wherein God "dressed himself in the human nature as in a mantle," as Heiko Oberman relates.[67] The young Milton perhaps echoes this theory in his poem "The Passion," where the "sovereign Priest, stooping his regal head / . . . / Poor fleshly Tabernacle entered, / His starry front low-rooft beneath the skies; / O what a Mask was there, what a disguise!" (15, 17–19). For Winstanley, human beings in particular are the chief garments of God's creation; in human beings God "manifests himselfe . . . in life, strength, and wisdome more then in any other creature."[68] Winstanley thus forgoes describing the visual components of his trance because his *visio Dei* is bound so tightly to "seeing" God incarnated in the flesh of fellow believers, "manifest" in the "life, strength, and wisdome" of their actions in the world.

Despite the differences in Ezekiel's and Winstanley's visions of God, Lieb's two dimensions certainly complement each other in the Digger's trance, for the new righteousness he proclaims is both an issue of how we interpret the "text" of creation and how we respond to it. For Winstanley, that mystical/phenomenological experience of God culminates in the just distribution of God's creation. Moreover, we might suggest that the *ur*-texts that serve as Winstanley's exegetical lenses, what Lieb calls the "interpretive structures" that provide the basis for his particular hermeneutical framework, are the priestly writer's repeated stresses on the goodness of creation in Genesis 1 and the narrative of Edenic abundance in Genesis 2. Like his radical contemporary, the Army chaplain Joseph Salmon, Winstanley redescribes human beings themselves as the Garden of Eden: they are the "living Earth . . . wherein that spirit of Love, did walk, and delight himselfe principally, as being the Head and Lord of all the rest." More will be said in a moment about Winstanley's notion of the self, but when true believers "eat" of the Tree of Life, their internal gardens yield the "sweet flowers and hearbs" of truth. For Winstanley, to say that God walks in the garden in the cool of the day (Gen. 3:8) is as much as to say that the human creature walks in the shadow of the Tree of Life, in the burgeoning power of the "Seed Christ" that is "now rising up to fill the Earth, Mankinde with himselfe." Conversely, when believers "eat" of the Tree of Knowledge their internal gardens yield the "stinking weeds" of selfishness.[69] To eat of this Tree results in inner exile, a kind of polluted "enclosure" of the self: "And while Mankinde eates of this Tree . . . he is driven out of the Garden, that is, out of himselfe, he enjoyes not himself, he knows not himself."[70] One's true identity for Winstanley is to be found in the believer's participation in the community of universal brotherhood, and there is a direct connection between this enclosed self and the enclosure of the land.[71] To dig up and free the land is to dig up and free the self.

Consequently, we find that the land itself is charged with theological import; as James Holstun points out, for Winstanley "Christ descended into the earth and stayed there — as a chthonic deity, a divine manure."[72] I would add that for Winstanley the activity of digging and dividing of the land are equivalent to digging and dividing the body of God. Like Milton, Winstanley appears to adhere to the doctrine of *creatio ex Deo*. "*What is God?*" he asks in his catechism, *Truth Lifting Up Its Head* (1648–49). God, he answers, is the "incomprehensible spirit" who "willed that the Creation should flow out of him: . . . And he is called, the Father, because as the whole creation came out of him, so he is the life of the whole creation, by whom every creature doth subsist."[73] Winstanley wants to press the idea that we have a common creation story: "all things, that is A substantial being, looked upon in the lump, is the fulnesse of him, that fills all with himselfe, he is in all things, and by him all things consist."[74] Winstanley conceives of God as the "spirit" of material reality: "I have declared what I know, That Almighty power & ever living Spirit is, which rules and preserves the whole Creation; fire, water, earth and air, and of every creature in these elements; or that is made up of all these in compound matter as all flesh is."[75] Though we ought to be careful to maintain the differences of their contexts, we find that Winstanley's contemporaries Joseph Salmon and the Ranter

Jacob Bauthumley agree with this notion of spiritual materialism. As Salmon puts it, "God is that pure and perfect being in whom we all are, move and live; that secret blood, breath, & life, that silently courseth through the hidden veins and close arteries of the whole creation." For Salmon, as with Winstanley, "everything . . . is fraught with his presence, & brim'd up with the plentiful distils of a divine life."[76] That plentiful divine life infuses all creatures for Bauthumley as well. Echoing the language of the Eucharist, Bauthumley declares, "I see that God is in all Creatures, Man and Beast, Fish and Fowle, and every green thing . . . ; and that God is the life and being of them all, and that God doth really dwell, and if you will personally."[77] For Winstanley, Salmon, and Bauthumley, God infuses and enlivens creation because it is in some way a vital extension of his body; the material earth contains the Real Presence.

Strictly speaking, however, Winstanley does not adhere to a version of the common creation story that emphasizes our commonality at the expense of the hierarchical distinction made in Genesis 1:28–29.[78] For Winstanley, human creatures operate according to the mandate to rule over creation.[79] But what he does object to is a distorted creation story in which that hierarchical distinction is applied to relationships between *human* creatures. As *humans* we share a common creation story; thus, to lord over another person and to subdue and divide the body of God selfishly is not only to betray the economy of the "primal narrative," the God who gives abundantly of himself, but also to revolt against our "creatureliness." To Winstanley's mind, this looks suspiciously like the sin of Adam and Eve, and this is precisely the context in which Winstanley interprets the Fall: not as an event that happened on a distant theological horizon, but one that occurs in the here and now and that is reified in the narratives of oppression and disenfranchisement. The first Adam may have lived and died thousands of years ago, but he continues to live and thrive in the hearts of men and women who cooperate with his exiled narrative. This first Adam is alive in "every one that gets an authority into his hands, tyrannizes over others; as many husbands, parents, masters, magistrates . . . doe carry themselves like oppressing Lords over such as are under them."[80] The very bodies of these corrupted men infect the earth when they are buried. But with the Resurrection of Christ's perfect body, one that was buried in the earth and did not corrupt it, comes the redemption of the earth's "body." In his burial and Resurrection, Christ's material body perfects the four elements, the substance of all created things: his breath rises above the "corruption of the Ayre"; his "moysture" purifies the waters; his heat and warmth cleanse the fires; and his flesh and bones refine the earth and stones.[81] Humanity's redemption, intuits Winstanley, thus lies in the lawful use of the land; it lies in rewriting the present story, and in bearing testimony to the economy of the primal narrative.

David Loewenstein observes that the *New Law*'s charged revision of the doctrines of creation and redemption reflects the revolutionary zeal and hope for radical reform crackling in the winter air of early 1649. Winstanley writes his preface a day after Charles I is sentenced on 25 January, and a mere four days before the king's execution is carried out. "This was a historical moment," regards Loewenstein, "when the saints, inspired with millenarian fervor, could expect great things, now that Parliament had recently been purged [by Colonel Thomas Pride in December 1648] and kingly power seemed cast out of the realm for once and for all."[82] For Winstanley, this revolution without must first begin with the revolution within; or, to put it another way, digging up the soil of the self precedes, and then necessarily requires, digging up the soil of the world that is made barren by oppressive kingly powers: greedy lawyers, selfish landlords, learned clergy, and corrupt magistrates. Rather than the microcosm reflecting the macrocosm, a dominant model in the early modern period, Winstanley conceives that the condition of the cosmos reflects the condition of the self. This is made explicit in *The Saints Paradice* when he asserts that the "*world* is mankinde, and every particular man and woman is . . . a perfect created world; . . . so that I say, man is the *world*."[83] If man is the world, then the inner conflict has much at stake, for Winstanley sees the soul of the human creature as the primary battleground between the binaries of heaven and hell, sorrow and comfort, light and darkness, faithful angels and fallen angels. The fate of all creation hangs in the balance as a result of this intense inner battle.

These binaries, however, have caused some insightful scholars to sever too dramatically the relationship between the flesh and the spirit in Winstanley's revolutionary theology, perhaps leading us to neglect the place of an Incarnational theology that engages matters of the flesh working in (hypostatic) union with the spirit. One critic argues that Winstanley "envisions a kingdom of righteousness reigning within the self—ruled by the authority of the Spirit and subverting the kingdom of the flesh."[84] It is true that Winstanley often makes such a distinction between spirit and flesh throughout his oeuvre.[85] But he by no means consistently maintains the sharp contrast; I find many instances in which Winstanley—far from being Milton's Jesus, who turns away from the world's offerings—appears to be heavily invested in a kingdom of the flesh, though one that is qualitatively different. For instance, in *Truth Lifting Up Its Head,* Winstanley asks, *"When can a man call the Father his God?"* He answers, "When he feels and sees, by experience, that spirit which made the flesh, doth governe and rule King in his flesh." Question: *"But may not a man call him God, till hee have this experience?"* Answer: "No: For if he doe, he lyes, & there is no truth in him; for whatsoever rules as King in his flesh, that is his God." The crucial issue for Winstanley is not simply whether the spirit rules over the flesh, but which flesh is made king through its union with which spirit: that of the Serpent infused by the "spirit of venom," or that of the Anointed Christ, *"that glorious body"* made "subject to the Spirit."[86] The result is a kind of near-Manichean struggle between the flesh of the Serpent and the flesh of Christ.

This point is brought into greater relief in Winstanley's letter "To the Lord Fairfax," delivered on 9 June 1649 and occasioned by Fairfax's visit to St. George's Hill on 26 May. Fairfax's own response to visiting Winstanley that day is less than dramatic; as Brian Manning relates, the general thought the band of Diggers rather harmless and assured them they would come to no harm at the hands of his soldiers.[87] He had in fact little to fear, for in Winstanley's appeal for protection he pledges that the Diggers "shall not strive with sword and speare, but with spade and plow and such like instruments to make the barren and common Lands fruitful."[88] Despite Fairfax's yawning assessment of the import of their actions, the fiery Winstanley depicts the activity of their digging as a "pitched battaile" between the fleshly forces of Christ and the Serpent, "between the Lamb and the Dragon, between the Spirit of love, humility and righteousness, which is the Lamb appearing in flesh; and the power of envy, pride, and unrighteousness, which is the Dragon appearing in flesh."[89] It is imagery that would no doubt resonate with the combative Fairfax, who had recently returned from putting down the mutinous Leveller forces at Burford.[90] Whether Fairfax recognizes it or not, it is clear from Winstanley that much is at stake; divine or demonic, an incarnation erupts into the world. Joseph Salmon describes these differing incarnations in his *Antichrist in Man* (1648). Salmon interprets the Whore of Babylon, figured in Revelation 17–18, as the subtle "spiritual serpent" within that denies "Jesus to be come in thy flesh." She is the spirit that "is willing to let thee understand that Christ hath been made *flesh for thee*, but not *that the word is made flesh* in thee." Salmon's God has "begotten himself, and brought forth himself in his own likenes in *thee; that thou art this virgin that is over-shadowed with power from on high;* and hast *the immortall seed of God* in thee."[91] Like Salmon, Winstanley believes in the narrative manifestation of both a sacred flesh and a Serpent flesh, their incarnations hinging on one's listening to the whisperings of the particular spirit within.

Consequently, I would more strongly argue that it is the narrative of the Incarnation, and the peculiar dynamics of the hypostatic union, that allows Winstanley to figure the battle this way. The temptations of Christ in the desert (Matt. 4:1–11) demonstrate the Son's reliance on and cooperation with the leadings of the Holy Spirit rather than the venomous murmurings of his adversary, the "well woven snares" of the "Spiritual Foe" that we examined in the previous chapter (*PR* 1.97, 10). For Winstanley, the world has been seduced by these same temptations toward pride, power, and possession. Just as Jesus confronts the prideful and exclusivist ideology of the Pharisees, those who would deny others the life more abundant, Winstanley challenges those who are deluded by the same spirit, the landlords who would deny others the right to cultivate the wastes and wilds. Through the obedience of Milton's Jesus, the "perfect Man, by merit call'd . . . Son," an "*Eden* [is] rais'd in the waste Wilderness" (1.166, 7). This Eden is largely defined as the abundant kingdom within for Milton, but for Winstanley the Digger it is also the vision of an outward reality toward which all God's sons and daughters strive: an Eden cultivated in the wastes and wilderness for the starving and landless poor, a garden liberated from bondage, and a sublimated self turned inside-out.

T. Wilson Hayes cogently remarks that Winstanley "transforms what were believed to be static qualities of human nature (envy, covetousness, and pride) into changeable external properties of the state."[92] Winstanley teaches that the single body's being-in-the-world is inseparable from the power structures that its performance defies or reifies and in which it dwells. For him, the narrative of the self-in-the-world bleeds into the narrative of the state, and both are in need of redemption through the return of Christ. But as Christopher Hill accurately asserts, unlike the Fifth Monarchy Men, Winstanley did not give credence to a literal Second Coming of an external Christ; the Second Coming is in the heart of the individual believer when the hold of the Beast is broken by the power of the Lamb within the individual.[93] In Everard's sermon, "The Starre in the East, Leading unto the True Messiah," we find the preacher in agreement. To experience the nativity of Christ in the soul means that the believer "doth *the deeds of Christ,* in that *we shew the vertues of him that hath called us from darkness to light,*" and that to increase toward perfection is to be able to say, "*This day is the Scripture fulfilled in me.*"[94] The result for Everard and Winstanley is not a millennial kingdom ultimately accomplished by the external return of Christ, a belief central to groups such as the Fifth Monarchists, whose members were increasingly dissatisfied with Oliver Cromwell's regime. It is, rather, the establishment of a just commonwealth by the saints in the here and now, beginning with the just distribution of the land.[95]

Winstanley is able to proclaim the nature of the battle between Beast and Lamb, and Christ's Second Coming in the heart of believers, to his fellow creatures because he himself has embodied them. In his surveying the extent of the tyrannical powers, we might suggest, he stares his old self, grown to monstrous proportions, in the face. His conversion narrative, *The New Law,* delineates this continual striving between the two rival "governments" of Lamb and Serpent, or the two "Adams" of Jacob and Esau. According to Winstanley, each kingdom generates its own particular narrative, reflects an economy, and performs that narrative economy in the world. Thus, the real question for Winstanley remains one of narrative embodiment: To which kingdom is one allied? To which narrative text does one faithfully "listen"? With which narrative does a person cooperate and subsequently "shine forth" into the world?

From the narrative of the Lamb or Jacob, of Christ or the second Adam, springs the fruits of humility, meekness, abundance, liberty, generosity, and sincerity; these make "but one body Christ, or one Almighty power of Mercie and Justice, the holy breathing, or *Emmanuel, God in us*."[96] This latter phrase is a telling substitution, for "Emmanuel" is more properly translated "God *with* us," and Winstanley's (purposive?) mistranslation suggests a number of trenchant ideas. First, it communicates something about the human creature's essential or primal narrative: "In the beginning of time the whole Creation lived in man, and man lived in his Maker . . . for every creature walked evenly with man, and delighted in man, and was ruled by him. . . . [T]here was an evennes between man and all creatures, and an evennesse between man and his Maker the Lord, the Spirit." This "evennesse" occurs because unfallen humanity perfectly embodies and cooperates with the Spirit of the divine Text; those who have fallen away from this primal narrative, declares Winstanley, are "but the shadows of men and women." Second, the preposition switch from "with" to "in" suggests something about Winstanley's thoughts on Emmanuel himself and his relation to the Law. While the Apostle Paul, Luther, and Calvin hold that Christ was the *only* fulfillment of the Law (Matt. 5:17), Winstanley describes Christ as a "type" that can and must be emulated; the Law is thus repeatedly fulfilled through the actions of the faithful believer. Just as the "man Christ Jesus swallowed up *Moses;* and so the Spirit dwelt bodily in that Lamb, which was spread abroad in the types; And man-kind is to behold the Law of Righteousness, in none, but in that his wel-beloved Son. *Eph.* 4.6. *Rom.* 8.22, 23. Even so that single body is a type. . . . [A]nd man-kind shall be made onely subject to this one Spirit, which shall dwell bodily in every one, as he dwelt bodily in the man Christ Jesus, who was the Son of man." Thus the Law continues to be fulfilled by those who incarnate Christ by submitting to the narrative of the sacred flesh; the Law is consummated in the "man living in the light of the Father," or the one who is dubbed "*The wel-beloved Sonne,* because that one power of Righteousnesse dwells bodily in him, and the whole Creation is drawn up into that one centre, man."[97] The importance of Christ the Beloved Son is not that he was born, lived, and died long ago to offer a final redemption to be consummated at the end of history. Rather, the importance of Christ for Winstanley lies in the fact that he continues to be incarnated in the flesh of believers. As T. Wilson Hayes lucidly comments, the "Jesus of orthodox religion is merely a historical abstraction, a spirit-filled man who lived long ago. Christ is contemporary and empirical, a living creature of flesh and blood."[98]

Moreover, this living Christ empirically acting in the world and "breaking forth" as a manifestation of the "light of the Father" tends like all creatures toward perfection:

> For the wisdome and power of truth, that was poured upon the head of the Son of man, grows upwards towards perfection in sons and daughters: Even as wee see any tree, corn or cattell, grows up in the eye of man by degrees; for as these creatures doe not attaine to perfection on a sudden; neither doth the spirit of Righteousnesse rise up on a sudden perfection, but by degrees.[99]

Winstanley's monism is not as meticulously worked out as is Milton's, and he seems to take it for granted while Milton demonstrates a burden to prove its viability. Even so, like Milton we see him delineating a doctrine of participation based on it and issuing from a belief in *creatio ex Deo.* All creatures of God participate in the Being that gifts being, and there is a strong sense of *telos* in Winstanley's thought for particular manifestations of being; trees, corn, and cattle attain their perfections by degrees insofar as they fulfill their particular tree-ness, corn-ness, and cattle-ness. Such a view is reminiscent, though certainly unacknowledged on Winstanley's part, of Thomas Aquinas's anti-nominalist and teleological understanding of creation. In the *Summa Theologica* he states that "[n]atural things are said to be true in so far as they express the likeness of the species that are in the divine mind. For a stone is called true, which possesses the nature proper to a stone, according to the preconception in the divine intellect."[100] The Good, the True, the Beautiful are equated with being insofar as the object in question is fulfilling its essential nature. For Aquinas, being, beauty, goodness, and truth are convertible transcendental verities and all of creation has a *telos* in the Mind of God. John Milbank and Catherine Pickstock comment that in Aquinas's ontology and theology of participation a "thing is fulfilling its telos when it is *copying God in its own manner*, and tending to existence as knowledge in the divine Mind: so a tree copies God by being true to its treeness, rain by being rainy, and so on."[101] Thus for Aquinas, as with Winstanley and Milton, the issue is ultimately one of worship; all creatures glorify their Creator because the Hebrew scriptures testify to creation's goodness (Genesis 1; Ps. 19:1).

Many Puritans believed that one of the consequences of the Fall of man was that nature itself degenerated as well. But for Winstanley, the creation is inherently good; human beings withhold that abundant and essential goodness from others. As Daniel L. Migliore reminds us, "[w]hile the stars, the trees, and the animals do not speak or sing of the glory of God in the same way that humans do, in their own way they too lift up their praises to God, and for all we know, they do this with a spontaneity and consistency far greater than our own."[102] Winstanley would agree, for he sees the creation as adhering to the primal narrative. Human creatures arrive at their particular *telos* insofar as Christ is incarnated in their lives and they embody and perform the Word in the world, and insofar as they remain faithful hearers who cooperate with the Spirit of the primal text of creation. Unlike the rest of creation, however, Winstanley laments, human creatures can remain faithful hearers of another text, and their cooperation with it directly impinges upon their ascent to perfection "by degrees."

From the narrative of the Serpent or Esau, of the Beast or first Adam, issues domination, selfishness, barrenness, bondage, covetousness, and hypocrisy; these "powers make up but one perfect body of sin and death, one Devil, or one compleat power of darkness." Included in this kingdom are power structures that operate according to the "rule of tyranny" and an economy of scarcity: large-scale private land enclosures at the expense of starving thousands; justices who line their pockets instead of meting out peace and equity; magistrates who oppress their fellow creatures rather than liberating them. But Winstanley directs his fiercest and most sustained attack throughout his writings toward an ordained and prattling clergy with a monopoly on interpretation—false ministers full of words, but empty of the Word who promises to bring the life more abundant (John 10:10). A monopoly of any kind is akin to the economic practice of enclosure; the interpretive monopoly of the clergy "encloses" their own sheep, the members of their congregation. While the prelates see this enclosure as one that protects and ensures the welfare of all, however, Winstanley excoriates this enclosure as one that suffocates and excludes.

The oppressive kingly powers set up the ministers, and Winstanley laments that the clergy fill the mouths of their sheep with "Sermons medled with little but State matters . . . so that there is a confederacie between the Clergy and the great red Dragon: the Sheep of Christ shall never fare well so long as the wolf or red Dragon payes the Shepherd their wages."[103] Instead of preaching the Word, ministers proclaim that their congregants should embody the idolatrous and impoverished narrative of the state. Nevertheless, Winstanley confesses that before his conversion he was a "strict goer to Church" and a "hearer of Sermons, and never questioned what they spake." The seductive words they spoke "were like a pleasant song to me, while I was hearing," yet "still I forgot what I heard."[104] Like Augustine, who wandered from song to song and from narrative to narrative because he found them to be ultimately without substance, Winstanley finds his soul without nourishment, and he accuses these kingly divines of delivering "words without life" and a "husk without the kernall." This is why he refers to these "Adams" as both "Ah-dams," connoting an expression of lamentation, and as "A-dam," the "head of corrupted waters, of covetous, proud and imaginary flesh" that "stops the streams of the waters of life and libertie."[105] Their *pleromic* deluge of words paradoxically causes spiritual drought because their preaching is unsaturated by the Spirit and uninformed by the Word who dwells in the word. Their endless prattling leads Winstanley to develop a realized eschatology that is effected by the saints and characterized by a discourse of silence:

> This is the work of the Lord, that wil stop the mouths of all hearsay and imaginary Preachers; *All mouths shall be silent, and not dare to speak, till the power of the Lord within gives words to the mouth to utter.* . . . For now lip service is to be judged to death . . . ; for mens words shal grow fewer and fewer, their actions of Righteousness one to another more and more.[106]

> The manifestation of a righteous heart shall be known, not by his words, but by his actions; for this multitude of talk, and heaping up of words amongst professours shall die and cease, this way of preaching shall cease, and verbal worship shall cease.[107]

"Verbal worship shall cease": this is an astonishing proclamation, for it suggests that language, even the language of praise, no longer has potency because any need for mediation has been eclipsed. All that remains is the Word indwelling the narrative of the saints' lives, as the saints see God no longer through a "glass darkly" but "face to face" (1 Cor. 13:12) in their fellow believers. In this discourse of silence the saints become preachers one to another through the "language of testimony," in and through their actions as they bring heaven with them and effect heaven about them. In short, believers become living embodiments of the scriptures themselves. *"What use is to be made of the Scriptures?"* he asks. They are a "record of experimental testimony" whereby "every man and woman may declare what they have received, and so become preachers one to another."[108] But these are preachers who are not just proclaiming the gospel, but embodying and incarnating the *kerygma*, as form and content and sign and signifier become indistinguishable.[109] In Winstanley's mind, every saint is a "true heaven, or place of glory," as he puts it in *The Saints Paradice,* an idea that resonates with Michael's reassurance to Adam, "surmise not then / His presence to these narrow bounds confin'd / Of Paradise or *Eden*" (*PL* 11.340–42); God's Presence, instead, resides in the believer. This is so for Winstanley because just as the Father dwells in him, he dwells in the Father, "so that here is a mutual fellowship of joy, and oneness of love between them"—a dynamic relationship between Father and adopted son, reflective of the mutual poetics and hermeneutics of the hypostatic union in the Incarnate Christ who demonstrated the perfect fusion of horizons.[110]

For Winstanley, the saints incite the revolution of paradise about them by fulfilling the Law within (Deut. 6:6; Matt. 22:37–40), a fulfillment whose inward pulse is directed outward in shockwaves toward the lawful use of the land as a "common treasury." To put it another way, Winstanley proposes that believers "out-narrate" the text of the Serpent flesh operating within and through the kingly powers of oppression without via the silent actions performed in the saints' sacred flesh. Interestingly, this narrative one-upmanship is precisely how Milton depicts the work of the Son in Book 3 of *Paradise Lost*. Foreseeing the impending Fall, the Father declares that through the narrative of the Son's voluntary incarnation, through the performance of his righteous actions, and through his sacrifice "Heav'nly love shall *outdo* Hellish hate" (3.298; emphasis added). For Milton, like Winstanley, to dwell in this particular narrative is to outdo hell's hateful economy that is manifested in tyrannical power structures. Winstanley argues that "by degrees" the human creature is perfected and made into a "*fit temple*" or a "garden wherein [the Father] himself will take delight." Subsequently, "by degrees" the earth is perfected and transformed from "*Babylon the great City*," with its lavish kings, its enclosing walls rising thick from the sands, and its babel of discordant voices within, to a "*Land flowing with milke and honey*"— a common wealth that is boundless, abundant, and abundantly silent.[111]

Bronze Snake upon a Pole

In his *Life of Moses*, Gregory of Nyssa understands Moses's theophany in Exodus 3 as a lesson in reading and contemplation. For him, the letter and the spirit of a text are as the bush and the Presence: the material and the spiritual perfectly coinciding. Like Moses, by our "virtuous conduct" fellow believers can stand in that divine light, but only as they learn that they "cannot . . . run with bound feet up to that height where the true light has appeared without removing the dead and earthly covering of skins from our soul's feet." But notice that the letter of the flesh is not completely jettisoned, despite the implication of Gregory's statement; on the contrary, flesh and spirit work together. He that "removes his earthly covering . . . also looks at the light of the bush, namely the ray enlightening us through this thorny flesh." Moses's theophany is thus understood by Gregory as a figure for the Incarnation, as letter reveals spirit and as spirit shines through flesh. Virtuous readers, Gregory insists, are best equipped "to assist others to salvation, delivering into freedom all who are oppressed by wicked servitude." Moses is transformed in his encounter with the bush and the Presence, one that leads to the liberation of the Hebrews who are oppressed by Pharaoh. Similarly, reflects Gregory, readers of allegory who are transformed by the narrative of the Incarnation bring about "the overthrow of the tyrant and the liberation of those oppressed by him."[112]

In *Eikonoklastes* Milton observes that although they appear as "two sever'd Branches" springing from the soil, "Tyranny and fals Religion" share the same "dark roots" that "twine and interweave one another in the Earth" (*CPW* 3:509). Attack the one, he implies, and a person inevitably inflicts damage on the other. In Everard's and Winstanley's day, the Pharaohs and tyrants, under whose yoke they stumbled and against whose exclusive economies they struggled, were many and seemingly omnipresent: monopolizing merchants, dissembling lawyers, sophistical Parliamentarians, self-indulgent magistrates, rapacious landlords, and university-trained clergy. Bearing under the strain, with marginalized voices and broken wills, the people groan and cry for their Moses. How shall they be freed? What shall be the path of their exodus?

Like Gregory, Everard and Winstanley believe that "delivering into freedom all who are oppressed" begins with the incarnated person's abundant allegorical interpretation of scripture. Christopher Hill explains that in the seventeenth century scripture was the universal text used to comprehend and unlock all other spheres of learning and activity, including those of ethics, politics, economics, and the academy.[113] Consequently, for Everard and Winstanley the very texts that are used to enslave the oppressed under the tyrannizing powers will be the very texts that liberate them. Such a dynamic recalls for us another incident from the life of Moses in Numbers 21:4–9. As the Hebrews wander in the wilderness complaining of their lack of sustenance, the Lord punishes them with broods of poisonous vipers. When the people repent of their sin, Moses intercedes for them; the Lord instructs him to erect a bronze snake upon a pole so that all who are bitten by the snakes may be healed by gazing upon it. For Everard and Winstanley, the reader who has repented and harvested the inner seed of Christ will be healed by that which strikes him; the folds of allegory, entwined about the letter, are as the bronze snake entwined about the pole.

In the final chapter, we gaze upon one such incarnated reader, one who poses himself as a snake upon a pole and who, "like the Son of man," is "lifted up" in the streets of Bristol and the pillory of London, "that whosoever believeth in him should not perish, but have eternal life" (John 3:15). A deliverer has come, and his name shall be James, "the supplanter."

chapter 7

Pageant and Anti-Pageant

James Nayler and the Divine Economy of
Incarnation in the Quaker Theodrama

And all the trees of the field shall know that I the LORD *have brought
down the high tree, and have exalted the low tree, have dried up
the green tree, and have made the dry tree to flourish. I the* LORD
have spoken it and have done it.

—Ezekiel 17:24

*The only righteous in a World perverse,
And therefore hated, therefore so beset
With Foes for daring single to be just,
And utter odious Truth, that God would come
To judge them with his Saints.*

—Milton, *Paradise Lost* (11.701–5)

George Witherley was apparently among the first to see them in silent
procession that autumn afternoon late in October 1656. While the
townsfolk of Bedminster in western England were scurrying indoors to
avoid being soaked by the deluge that poured from the heavens, Witherley remarked a small group of men and women, drenched but seemingly oblivious to the rain, trudging through the deep mud on the cart

path. Two men, both on foot and struggling in muck up to their knees, led the procession: the first man, clearing the way, was wearing a common broad hat; the second man, bareheaded, marshaled the procession by leading the horse of a third, mounted man who was bearded and plain in appearance, gaunt, but with an unmistakable aura of strength and authority; following in tandem were two men and two women each on horseback, with yet a third woman walking on the causeway beside the group. Witherley called out, gesturing for them to come onto the causeway. "God required no such thing at their hands," he announced above the muttering rain, at which the members of the procession returned no answer.

Curious, Witherley followed the small parade in the near-mile stretching between the village of Bedminster and the environs without the large coastal city of Bristol. The group halted abruptly at the almshouse just outside Redcliff Gate, the main entrance from the south that led into the bustling heart of the city; as if taking their cue, the two women dismounted, placed themselves on either side of the haggard mounted figure, and began singing. At the time, Witherley could not understand the words of their song, perhaps because of the rising din of the onlookers gathering to gaze at the spectacle, but he noted that it sounded like a "buzzing melodious noyse." Throngs of citizens, ignoring the downpour, were presently crowding the sides of the road as the troupe entered the gates. Witherley, jockeying for position in the human wall and straining to hear, finally caught the words of their melodious song: "Holy, holy, holy, Lord God of Israel." Amid these songs and hosannas, the procession continued as the women doffed their soaked cloaks and placed them on the ground before the mounted figure. Unmolested by the captive audience, the procession wended its way through the busy market streets of Bristol, past the High Cross standing at the junction of Broad and Wine Streets, until finally coming to rest at an inn called the White Hart. The magistrates having been summoned, the company was upstaged and arrested. The small chorus of women continued to sing, and because the "great concourse of people" hindered it, immediate questioning was held in abeyance until the next day. A messiah debuted in Bristol, and the performance occurred in a year in which many were anticipating the Second Coming of Christ.[1]

If my rendition of this infamous entry into Bristol evokes the language and spectacle of the stage, it is with great purpose. With the exception perhaps of George Fox, no one among the early Quakers performed the role of Christ in the world with as much dramatic flair as James Nayler, the farmer and ex-soldier under Lord Fairfax and General John Lambert who turned itinerant preacher. The previous chapter examined how the Incarnation, as the site of material and spiritual convergence, functions as the epistemological and hermeneutical core of Everard's and Winstanley's work. The allegorical reader for them is the incarnated reader who has harvested the seed of the inner Christ, resulting in new hermeneutical and political economies of abundance, and deliverance from the oppression of the various tyrannical powers at work in the world around them. This chapter considers how the "letter" of Nayler's own incarnated body, saturated by the spiritual abundance of the Inner Light, disrupts the economies and metaphysics of lack in the market district, of marginalization in the almshouse, and of exclusive royal power in his triumphal entry.

I aim to discuss Nayler's imitation of Christ's entry into Jerusalem within the contexts of the Quakers' discourse of the Inner Light and the sect's radical adoptionist theology. But I want also to be sensitive to its nuances as a staged performance during a time when there was no king and when the theaters were still operating under the 1642 cessation order by Parliament. This is an aspect of the episode that has previously been undeveloped by both historians of the period and Nayler's biographers. Seventy years ago, Emilia Fogelklou referred to the Bristol episode in passing as a passion or miracle play, but she does not explore the larger political implications the dramatic context suggests. Leo Damrosch's excellent work illuminates these implications by looking at the conservative Puritan "crackdown" on the Spirit, and admirably addresses Nayler's symbolic performance as a misunderstood "sign" and dramatic *imitatio Christi*.[2] But how misunderstood was it? What if Nayler's dramatic entry was intended as a display of the fusion of human and divine horizons, such that there appears no aesthetic gap between sign and signified?

Here I urge us to understand Nayler's entry in terms of civic pageantry—the elaborately staged royal processions into towns and cities that functioned as both a public entertainment and, more significantly, a visual and psychological reification of sovereign authority.[3] Such a context is suggested by Nayler's antagonist, Ralph Farmer, who significantly refers to the Bristol march as a pageant, as does the MP Mr. Bodura when Nayler's case is deliberated in Parliament.[4] According to the *OED*, a pageant is a "tableau, [or] representation . . . erected on a fixed stage or carried on a moving car, as a public show; . . . exhibited as a feature of a public triumph." More generally, the word indicates the "part acted or played by any one in an affair, or in the drama of life," or "a scene acted on the stage," but with special reference to an act or scene in a medieval mystery play. Moreover, Stephen Orgel observes that "theatrical pageantry, the miming of greatness, is highly charged because it employs precisely the same methods the crown was using to assert and validate its authority."[5] Examining the episode at Bristol under this aegis thus enables us to understand better the various roles and power plays that emerge in the drama at Bristol, their radical and subversive narrative, political, and theological import, as well as allows us to discuss the limits of incarnation during a time of revolution.

"everyone is Jesus": Incarnation, Perfection, and the Quaker Theodrama

The God revealed in the Hebrew Bible and the New Testament is a lover of spectacle: he leads the Hebrew people as a pillar of fire and cloud, inspires a shepherd boy to slay a giant, whisks his prophet into the heavens in a chariot of fire, performs miracles of healing, judges the world in cataclysmic sublime. God is the playwright who descends into the drama of history, plays a role on the stage of the world, and gives himself over to the freedom of the audience to respond or reject, of its players to act and react. As Hans Urs von Balthasar comments, the "central issue in theo-drama is that God has made his own the tragic situation of human existence, right down to its ultimate abysses." God appropriates the human narrative and enters these abysses through his descent into flesh. The Incarnation is the culmination of the word preached and the event of transformation upon its hearing; it is the central act about which this tragicomic theodrama turns: "Here, in the 'now' of the kerygma, the event flashes like lightning between the hidden cloud where God is and the hidden heart of man. . . . Jesus Christ . . . is God's act."

For von Balthasar, there is no aesthetic "distance" between actor and role at the Incarnation because the Son gives himself completely over to the Father's script of his mission — so completely that in Christ's action the Son is able to exchange places with the other cast members, who also happen to be the audience in witness. Von Balthasar explains that for any play to be successful there must be a "communion" between actor and audience. Christ's perfect performance, in his utter embrace of the role of the other, makes such communion possible in the theo-drama. With the possibility of that communion established, the other actors/spectators in the theodrama are "invited to fashion [their lives] along the lines indicated by the play's solution; at the same time [they are] free to distance [themselves] from it critically."[6] Those who opt for the first become, as von Balthasar echoes the words of Paul, "a spectacle (*theatron*) to the world, to angels and to men" (1 Cor. 4:9). Those who are among the latter effectively "unmask" the players on the stage of the theodrama; to illuminate his point, von Balthasar quotes Erasmus's *Praise of Folly*: "If a man were to go up to actors on the stage and tear off the masks . . . would he not spoil the whole play and deserve to be thrown out of the theatre and be pelted with stones as a lunatic?" Yet even as they are cast out of the theater, von Balthasar asserts they remain players who still embody and perform other dramatic roles on the stage of the world, perhaps enacting the struggle for power, the desire to administer justice, or the incessant drive for self-preservation.[7] For von Balthasar, Christ's Second Coming initiates the final act of the theodrama, one that is marked by joyful comedy and marred by deepest tragedy.

Von Balthasar's insights may help to illuminate the dynamics and significance of the episode at Bristol. It is fair to say that James Nayler counted himself among those chief actors/spectators in the tragicomic theodrama, for his is a performance that bears witness to the incarnation of Christ within, implies the rest of the Christic narrative, and casts all parties involved into very specific dramatic roles. Reflecting on Nayler's charismatic but dangerous figure, the Bristol minister and Quaker adversary Ralph Farmer accurately articulates the significance of incarnating "the pure image of Christ" in Quaker theology. As Farmer relates, the Quakers believe that this pure image "must be brought forth" in order that the justified might strive "to be perfect and free from *all sinn*" and "have the greatest share of the *honor* of being their own *Jesus*." Moreover, he goes on, Quakers like James Nayler who claim to manifest or incarnate the image thereby also earn the name of the incarnate Son: "every one is *Jesus*," he contemptuously concludes.[8] We can identify some of the members of Nayler's supporting cast, who certainly thought he merited not only the role, but the honor and name of Jesus: Timothy Wedlock (Marshalling Man, walking bareheaded), Hannah Stranger and Martha Simmonds (Singing Woman #1 and Singing Woman #2, who jointly led his horse), and Dorcus Erbury (Woman #3, who walked on the causeway, but according to her testimony did not sing); we cannot determine exactly who played the remaining roles of the Lead Man, who cleared the way, and Mounted Man #2 and Mounted Man #3, who brought up the rear. One of them may have been John Stranger, the husband of Hannah; we might suspect that Thomas Simmonds, the husband of Martha and part of Nayler's core group, was one of the others, but according to Nayler's biographer William G. Bittle, Simmonds was in London at the time. George Bishop, who comments on the events of Bristol three days after the incident, claims that two of the other men present that day were Samuel Cater and Robert Crab, both former prisoners with Nayler at Exeter.[9]

In a search of their persons the magistrates discovered several letters written to Nayler by members of his entourage, variously addressing him as the "*everlasting Son of righteousnesse and Prince of Peace*," "*thou fairest of ten thousand, thou only begotten son of God*," "*Thou King of Israel,* and Son of the most high." John and Hannah Stranger close one letter declaring, "Thy name is no more to be called *James* but *Jesus*."[10] Bittle observes that such terms of address were not uncommon in Quaker correspondence, and letters written to George Fox, the other acknowledged "leader" of the Quaker movement, bear similar appellations. These titles were in fact justified, for according to Quaker theology these forms of address speak not directly to the person, but to the growing seed of Christ within each person or the dynamic Inner Light that directs and inspires one to act and speak. Fox, with whom Nayler had a very public falling out in the months preceding the Bristol episode, comments on this "democratization" of God in his *Journal*: "for . . . as many as should receive Him in His light, I saw that He would give power to become the sons of God. . . . I saw that Christ died for all men, and was a propitiation for all, and had enlightened all men and women with his divine and saving light." Moreover, he asserts that the saints are the "*Temples of God* and God doth *dwell in them,* that the Scriptures do witness; and if God dwell in them, then the Divinity dwels in them; and the Scripture saith, *Ye shall be partakers of the divine nature:* and this I witness."[11] Despite the justification for the divine titles of address that this adoptionist theology appears to allow, Bittle admits, "some of the group, caught up in the millenarian enthusiasm, had lost the ability to distinguish accurately between the indwelling Christ and His human vessel."[12] Alternately put, Nayler played the role of Christ so well on the stage of the world that his followers, operating both as playgoers sitting in witness of his role in the larger religious and political drama in England and as Nayler's fellow actors in the Bristol production, understood the shadow of the play as also the reality, the sign for the signified.

The testimonies of Wedlock, Stranger, Erbury, and Simmonds at their ministerial inquests bear this conclusion out, but we ought to proceed cautiously since their testimonies are recorded by those hostile to the Quaker movement. Captain George Bishop, in his ardent response to Farmer's pamphlet, warns readers against Farmer's deliberate misrepresentation of Nayler and the Quakers. Farmer's pamphlet is "covered with his loathsom Vomit and detestable Poyson," and is intended to turn the eye of the reader away "lest the serious consideration of those things when they should be presented, should work in luman effect."[13] We should thus be chary about how their testimonies are represented in these pages; while there is quite a lot of similarity between the different accounts of their trials, it is always possible that their answers to questions may have been edited in order to serve the purposes of Quaker detractors. But their "scandalous" responses to questions are typically what we might expect from these early Quakers. Moreover, in his testimony, Nayler shows himself a particularly shrewd interlocutor, not at all what we might expect from a hostile recorder.[14] Bearing this in mind, we can now direct our attention more fully to the significance of the elements of the pageant and the witness of its participants.

It is significant that Wedlock had doffed his hat before leading Nayler's horse in the parade, for Quakers notoriously did not adopt this social practice when in the presence of magistrates or other higher-ups since they were fellow creatures.[15] Many anti-Quakers saw their refusal as a sign of their general lack of respect for authority. Nayler and his followers were taken to task for this in a pamphlet entitled *The Perfect Pharisee* (1653), authored collectively by the ministers Thomas Weld, Richard Prideaux, Samuel Hamond, William Cole, and William Durant against the doctrines of the Quakers. Citing biblical examples of outward deference paid from one person to another (Joseph's brothers before him as vice-regent of Egypt; Abraham before the Hittites; Abigail before David; Jacob before Esau; Joseph before Jacob; Nathan before David), they take issue with the Quaker insistence that they honor the authority but not the particular person: "To which we say. What is the power, without the person? Government without Governors, but a mere fancy?"[16] Nayler, on the other hand, sees in these flattering outward shows of respect a dangerous display of worship that is reserved for God alone: "they that are guided by the spirit of the world, pleads for the worlds worships and customs; and where the serpent is, he would be worshipped; but the Spirit of Christ where it is, keeps the creature upright to God, and not to bow in pride."[17] God may institute authority, but as long as those authorities do not truly honor and fear God, the Christian is commanded not to pay respect. In light of this point, Wedlock's doffing his hat before Nayler communicates that the young man viewed Nayler as God made manifest. His questioner certainly recognizes the significance and brings attention to it, at which Wedlock responds that he was "moved by the *Spirit*" to do so.[18]

When asked if Nayler is the only Son of God, Wedlock and Erbury both confess it so, seemingly without making a distinction between the inner seed of Jesus and the outer James, Erbury declaring that she "knows (no other Saviour) but him." Her questioner objects: "Jesus Christ was crucified upon the Crosse, and how is this he?" Erbury responds that Jesus Christ is "manifested in him." By this, Erbury implies that the divine seed of Christ, implanted in all regenerate believers, has come to full earthly perfection in Nayler, a kind of hypostatic union so complete that there is no longer a division of identities between divine Christ and human Nayler. Nayler's body has been displaced and is now to her eyes the channel of unmediated revelation. The questioner again emphasizes the death of Jesus, but Erbury responds that Nayler "hath laid down his natural body. . . . Doth not the Scripture say, I will change thy natural body, and it shall be a spiritual body?" Questioner: "He [Nayler] hath flesh and bones, which a Spirit hath not." Erbury: "He hath new flesh and new bones."[19] In this latter response, it is not clear whether the "he" to whom Erbury is referring is James Nayler or Jesus Christ, but it does not matter: to speak of the one is to speak of the other because form and content in her mind are perfectly fused and perfectly manifested in Nayler. Throughout her examination, the questioner attempts to maintain the essential and narrative differences between Jesus Christ and James Nayler, commenting that Jesus gave life to the dead, had disciples and apostles, and sits at the right hand of the Father to judge the world. But Erbury's responses consistently blur these essential and narrative differences. Remarkably, she claims that she had been "dead two dayes, and he laid hands upon my head and said, *Dorcus* arise, and from that day to this, I am alive." We can only imagine the gasps and mutterings of the ministerial assembly present. The details of the incident at Exeter are not preserved or expounded upon, and we do not know if Erbury is commenting on a spiritual death and resurrection or a physical one. Further, Erbury considers herself and many abroad as Nayler's disciples, and claims that the Quaker Jesus "shall sit *at the right hand of the Father,* and shall judge the world."[20] Erbury grants Nayler a present authority that is projected to the eschaton, insisting upon Nayler's perfect performance as the embodiment of the Word.

Martha Simmonds, who took upon herself the persona of Nayler's surrogate "mother," perhaps because she so vehemently pushed for his leadership in the movement, confirms as much. When asked why she sang hosannas before Nayler, she responds, "I know not *James Nailer.*" Questioner: "*Do you know there was such a one?*" Simmonds: "He was but now is past to a more pure estate."[21] In other words, the person of James Nayler has been "sublimed" to a purer substance because of his extraordinary cultivation of the seed of Christ within, one that hinges on his moral participation in and cooperation with the Spirit. This is a state of perfection, however, that not every saint is able to attain. In *A Discovery of The Man of Sin,* Nayler witnesses that perfection is "the end for which God sent his Son manifest in the flesh," but maintains that it is only for those "that by him [Christ] . . . *walk not after the flesh, but after the Spirit,* Rom. 8.3, 4."[22] When discussing the issue of earthly perfection, time and again Nayler is careful to say that the seed of Christ is brought to fruition "in measure," indicating that it requires the cooperation and obedience of the individual. Quakers like Nayler could thus claim to have achieved what Jesus only encouraged in his followers: "Be ye therefore perfect, even as your Father which is in heaven is perfect" (Matt. 5:48). As Nayler puts it, "It is true, the light is but manifest in the creature by degrees, but the least degree is perfect in its measure, and being obeyed, will lead to the perfect day, and is perfect in itself, and leads up to perfection all that perfectly follow it."[23]

When, in 1652, Fox is arrested in Lancaster and charged with being "*as upright as Christ,*" the itinerant preacher responds, "Those words were not spoken by me," but he takes the occasion to bear witness anyway, declaring that as Christ is perfect, "so are we in this present world, and that the saints are made the righteousness of God; that the saints are one in the Father and the Son; that we shall be like him; that all teaching which is given forth by Christ is to bring the saints to perfection, even to the measure, stature, and fullness of Christ." In fact, Fox scorns those sects that fail to preach the doctrine of perfection. In contrast, says Fox, "I told them Christ was come freely, who hath perfected for ever by one offering all them that are sanctified, and renews them up in the image of God, as man and woman were in before they fell; and makes man and woman's house as perfect again as God had made them at the first."[24] Perhaps no other radical group in England was as engaged in "repairing the ruins of our first parents" as the Quakers. Leo Damrosch explains that for the Quaker entrusted with the immortal seed, sin was a distinct reality, but perfection was an obligation. A "Calvinist might sin and, with suitable self-condemnation, vow to try to sin no more. But a Quaker was supposed to be perfect; repeated sins simply showed that he or she was an unregenerate sinner and therefore not a Quaker."[25] But this exclusion from the Quaker community also implies the playing of a different narrative role: that of the Antichrist who suppresses perfection. Ministers who do not preach the reality of perfection, Nayler argues, "opposeth the end of Christs coming, which was to take away sin and to set free from it, and to present perfect unto the Father without spot or blemish, such are Antichrists." Answering his critics, George Fox comments, "If thou know'st what a Saint is, thou would'st know a Saints life; . . . Thou hypocrite, dissemble not with him: he that is perfectly holy, is perfectly just: where this is revealed, there needs no addition; for *the man of God is perfect.*"[26] In her examination, Simmonds reveals that Nayler ought to be worshipped, for "He is a perfect man; and he that is a perfect man, is the Prince of Peace." Yet a few lines later she demurs, "He is the Son of Righteousness; and the new Man within him, is the Everlasting Son of Righteousness; and *James Nayler* will be *Jesus* when the new life is born in him."[27] If Nayler was not yet identical to Jesus in his role upon the stage of the world, there is no doubt in her mind that he soon would be, and his glory would be manifest to all.

A Fleshly Tabernacle: Parading Nayler's Revolutionary Body

Perhaps the march into Bristol that soggy autumn day was intended to be the visual display of Nayler's final coming into that role. His entry may have evoked in the minds of his older audience the staginess of other processions into cities. These include not only the many plays that depict such progressions, scenes that we might describe as the early modern version of the big-budget, blockbuster action sequence intended to show the heroes at their apex of accomplishment and public honor, but also those elaborately crafted entrances of monarchs into cities in recent memory: Elizabeth I and Queen Anne (whose own pageants into Bristol occurred in 1574 and 1613, respectively), James I (who made official entries at London in 1604 for his coronation and Edinburgh in 1617), and Charles I (who made one royal entry into Edinburgh in 1633), as well as the Lord Mayor's Shows in London that were ritually enacted every year on 29 October, already gearing up even as Nayler and his group were being examined.[28]

In her valuable study on early modern pageantry, Alice S. Vernezky observes that pageants were much more than spectacle and popular entertainment; much like the mystery plays, they were infused with symbolic meaning and embedded with messages for the audience. Sovereigns monopolized the collective gaze of the audience while allegorical figures such as Virtue, Justice, or Prudence, or positive heroic exempla from the Bible, joyfully pranced about or escorted the monarch.[29] Moreover, she points out that the trains of many pageants were often preceded by two figures, one person acting as the "Whiffler," who cleared the way, and one person acting as the parade marshal, who actually led the procession.[30] We might thus construe the unidentified Lead Man as the Whiffler, and it is likely, though it remains unproved, that he carried a staff—a prop that no doubt helped him navigate through the thick mud on the cart path, which according to George Witherley was up to their knees, but which also may have doubled as the instrument used to clear traffic and to herald the pageant's approach. Vernezky also speculates that the use of actors employed in such pageants may have had its origins in the Palm Sunday celebration—the reenactment of Christ's entry into Jerusalem; as the procession entered the city gates, a choir of boys would sing the "Gloria." Many royal processions depicted on stage or traveling into cities were thus often preceded by singing, or they were greeted by prophetic orations of future prosperity.[31]

The *gloriae* sung by Simmonds and Stranger, therefore, function both as hymns of praise and as prophetic utterances. As evidenced in their testimony, they perceived Nayler as a person worthy of their reverence, if not their worship, and thus received him in the same adoring and awestruck spirit that characterized how early modern citizens received their entering sovereign. Unlike the latter, however, Nayler's entrance carries with it the deeply embedded but radical message that the spectators themselves can achieve a similar stature, if they are willing to embrace the Quaker message of sin and perfection; consequently, we might view the episode as a form of theatrical evangelism. Many revisionist scholars productively argue that public spectacles that include the sovereign and monopolize the gaze of onlookers can also be the site of subversion, wherein the sovereign is transformed into the "subject." "Representation," David Scott Kastan comments, "thus undermines rather than confirms authority, denying it its presumptive dignity by subjecting it to common view. . . . However much it insists upon its audience's admiration and respect, sovereignty's visible presence demands and authorizes an audience of commoners as a condition of its authority." The "privileged visibility" of the sovereign, as Stephen Greenblatt calls it, is thus a two-edged sword.[32] Representation need not be an either/or endeavor, a dynamic that sometimes occurs with revisionism of any kind. Representations of the sovereign on the stage are certainly full of ambiguity, made especially so because the sovereign is *not* mystically and personally present in his or her resplendent glory, but only imitated by an actor. But I am inclined to believe, against the revisionists, that in royal processions in particular the authority of the sovereign is instantiated and reified as a kind of "saturated phenomenon," a *"pleromic gifting"* to make an explicit theological connection, and that this effect happens far more often than does the opposite in the early modern mind. Nayler's radicalized royal procession, however, surely functions in the same dual capacity that the Incarnation does, as both a powerful enactment of authority and a demystification of it: Behold, the *pleroma* of the deity marching into Bristol with the authority of heaven to judge the world; behold, its *kenosis* in a thin, haggard man soaked by the rain and trudging in the mud like any other. His appearance, then, balances on the blade of that two-edged sword of representation; it is intended as both a confirmation of authority and a scathing critique of it, as Nayler's body becomes the site of revolution and revelation.

Moreover, Nayler's body converts the features of the urban landscape itself into sites of revolution and revelation. Steven Mullaney has written on the connection between the route of the monarch or lord mayor and the civic space in which it occurs, observing that the urban landscape functions as a "memory-theatre" for its denizens. Unlike modern cities, which arise from the intricate codes of urban planning, Mullaney points out that medieval and early modern cities are significantly shaped by the performances of "varied rites of initiation, celebration, and exclusion through which a ceremonial social order is defined, maintained, and manifested." Consequently, particular spaces, buildings, or landmarks along the plotted course are infused as sites of ritual meaning and cultural remembrance: "When the ceremony ceased, the city remained: a trace, a record, a living memory of the cultural performances it both witnessed and served to embody." In this way the ceremony of power never really ceases, but is in some way acted out before the eyes of the citizens even in their everyday activities. "The premodern or ceremonial city," writes Mullaney, "was a dramatic and symbolic work in its own right, a social production of space . . . composed and rehearsed over the years by artisanal classes and sovereign powers, for whom meaning was always a public event . . . and power a manifest thing, to be conspicuously bodied forth in the urban landscape."[33] This last phrase by Mullaney is revealing, though he himself does not call attention to its theological significance, for it echoes the language of incarnation. It is almost as if in its passing, vestiges of the saturated phenomenon of power seemingly seep into the walls and ground themselves, only to be transferred to passersby and evoked or incarnated in their own subsequent passing.

We ought therefore to examine the significance of the places along Nayler's route through Bristol, and how the "memory-theatres" of these pageant "stations" were transformed in his passing, an undertaking previously neglected by scholars of the incident. We should also note in passing that Bristol was not the site of the first pageant, nor was it to be the last. In ritual fashion and in play-like rehearsal, the troupe had previously marched in similar manner through the narrow streets of Wells and Glastonbury, and after Bristol they had apparently intended to march into London where there was a growing Quaker community that supported Nayler's leadership.[34] Whiffler and Marshalling Man (Wedlock) lead the procession through the village of Bedminster to their first "station," the almshouse outside Redcliff Gate.[35] It is at this point that Martha Simmonds and Hannah Stranger dismount and assume their positions, "lovingly," as John Deacon describes it, on either side of Nayler's horse and begin to sing.[36] Historically, almshouses are places of marginalization. They were catchalls occupied not only by the indigent, the outcast, the vagabond, and all sorts of other "masterless men" that troubled England and threatened to destabilize the social hierarchy, but also by the infirm, the mad, and the aged without family. Because many of them were also attached to parish churches or had chapels of their own, these were also sites of devotion because of their ministry to the poor. The fact of this almshouse's marginalization is made physically apparent at Bristol by its exclusivity from the city limits, outside its protective walls but ironically situated in the liberties of Bristol. This suggests that the almshouse occupies a liminal position: its threat to the social and civic order is far too great to be incorporated, and it is thus a place of "liberty" where one is released from the bondage or slavery of the law; yet, the almshouse is also a place of disenfranchisement and subject to municipal authority.

Consequently, the almshouse is the dwelling place of the "poor in spirit" whom Jesus named among the blessed in his Sermon on the Mount, for such as these would inherit the kingdom of God (Matt. 5:3). The poor in spirit are "blessed" not because they are happy, but because they are the ones who are absolutely dependent on God. In his sermon, Jesus transforms the value of their condition, instituting a new economy; rather than being outcasts, exiles, and mendicants, they are in the enviable position to receive the brunt of God's pleasure and abundance. In his approach into Bristol, Nayler takes his authority and "liberty" from this liminal space, and also "redeems" this place of poverty as the "holy Lord God of Israel." We ought to bear in mind that the Quakers themselves were often marginalized, always on the defensive, frequently seen as a menacing fringe, and particularly dangerous as embodiments of the most radical liberty and masterlessness, for the Inner Light, rather than social custom or obligation, prompts every movement and action. The Vagrancy Act of 1656 was inspired in part by JPs who desired to exercise some measure of control over the scores of itinerant Quaker and Baptist preachers and self-proclaimed messiahs.[37] Nayler's passing converts the marginalized almshouse and its inhabitants into the very center of inclusion, the locus of power, and the storehouse of wealth—all with a view toward liberating the new "outsiders," those in the gathering crowd, from their own captive illusions and crumbling ideological walls. From a Quaker point of view, these illusions and barriers keep them from harvesting the fruits of the abundance of the Inner Light and inheriting the riches of the kingdom within. For Nayler, this liberation is, and can be for others who gaze upon his sublimed and Christic body, a present reality and not an eschatological possibility; their poverty of spirit results in their being set upon the path to inward perfection apart from the law. I would suggest that the pageant thus functions as a drama of cultural alienation, one whose aim is to retrieve the newly alienated and to reinscribe them, charitably from a Quaker perspective, within the abundant divine economy in which the Quaker faithful participate.

This point comes into greater relief when we consider station number two: the pageant wends its way through High and Broad Streets, forming one of the main market avenues in Bristol that was likely packed with stalls and busybodies producing and consuming. No doubt many of them paused, and perhaps a few even stopped their activity altogether as they jostled for position to remark the passing crew. In those many multiplied pauses, we might find a disruption and critique of this burgeoning capitalist economy, as a Quaker theology and metaphysics of abundance that is directed toward the pursuit of the inner good is juxtaposed against an economics and metaphysics of scarcity that is directed toward the pursuit of external goods. This propinquity radically calls into question the fact-value, or is-ought, distinction in this proto-capitalist context, and thereby attempts to establish a new fact-value relation.

D. Stephen Long explains that the fact-value relation in capitalism operates within a metaphysics that is governed by scarcity. The *fact* that these people in the market have material needs, and that the sellers can in *fact* meet them with their products is a given; the goods thus have external *value*, but so does the time it takes for the sellers to produce and display their wares, and for consumers to leave their residences and families, the alehouse or their church, places of work or leisure in order to purchase them. But, as Long relates, "opportunity costs" arise: in the choices buyers and sellers make, other choices, values, and investments are sacrificed. What does it "cost" a seller to maintain his hours of operation when he could be spending time in devotion or worship? What does it "cost" a buyer to browse the wares, whether for individual consumption or on behalf of an employer, when he could be drumming it up with friends at the pub? As Long comments, this economy "contains a complex metaphysics that assumes all human action and language takes place in a tragic world of scarcity. . . . Any action that I take will be inscribed in a world of lack wherein my choice is made possible only by the other options I choose against."[38] This metaphysics oftentimes manifests a brutal face in the cases of the poor, propertyless, and disenfranchised wherein these peoples, whether modern or early modern, lack even the luxury of choice itself.

Moreover, the metaphysics of lack bears out in the relationship between buyer and seller. Aristotle and Thomas Aquinas, the forerunners of early modern economic theory, both posit that in theory a just price for the exchange of goods exists, and that this just price coincides with the inherent or "natural" value of the good in question. For both Aristotle and Aquinas, determining that inherent value and the just price requires the exercise of the virtues by both parties involved in the exchange. Long explains, however, that unlike Aristotle, Aquinas subsumes the entire exchange under the virtue of charity toward one's neighbor. For Aquinas, "any injustice . . . is unjust precisely because it does not allow our will its proper movement, which is to be turned *toward* a neighbor."[39] Money facilitates the exchange, and as long as both parties reach a common agreement and there is no duplicity involved in the exchange, a "just" price can be reached—even though this price may not accurately reflect the "natural" value if the parties involved fail to exercise the virtues. But this is only theory; with the rise in monopolies in the early modern era, the notion of an inherent value and just price rarely comes to fruition. The point that Nayler makes is that our wills are precisely *not* turned toward our neighbors or toward God; the result is the exclusion of justice and a violation of the eighth commandment not to steal.

While sometimes mutually edifying, the relationship between buyer and seller is antagonistic at base because each party is motivated by self-interest. Citing a famous passage from Adam Smith, wherein the economist explains that in the exchange buyers do not appeal to the "benevolence" or "humanity" of the seller, but to their self-love, Long observes that this appeal to self-interest implicitly sets up an either/or distinction grounded in and driven by our fears of scarcity. Either the seller's interests and self-love will be satisfied, or the buyer's; it is rarely the case that both are gratified, and the exchange is frequently a contest in the "manipulation of each other's will."[40]

But this is precisely the context in which the divine economy intercedes, and it is one that is incarnated in Nayler's march. As those in the market district momentarily pause in their gazing, or drop altogether what they are doing and follow the parade, they participate, however briefly (but exponentially determined in the collective), in the disruption and eruption of the divine economy. To echo Paul Ricoeur, such an intrusion "projects" a different and "possible world," resituating the human *telos* toward its proper end, defined by the Quakers as a participation in the abundance of God through the openings of the Inner Light, rather than as consumers busy with getting and spending. This participation manifests itself in one's tapping into the source and ordering principle of a divine economy: the theological virtue of charity toward one's neighbor, toward those who have all or those who have nothing, as the case may be.[41] Instead of buying and selling at the exclusion of others, Nayler's divine economy establishes a new fact-value relation and a new metaphysics of abundance.

When asked a series of questions about how he provided for and sustained himself as an itinerant, questions derived from and situated within the metaphysics of self-interest, self-preservation, and scarcity, Nayler responds as Jesus responds by revealing his complete dependence upon the abundance of the Father.

Q. How dost thou provide for a lively hood?
A. As the Lillies without care, being maintained by my father. [Matt. 6:28–34]
Q. *What estate has thou?*
A. I take no care for that.
Q. *Doth God in any extraordinary manner sustain thee, without any corporal food?*
A. Man doth not live by bread alone, but by every word that proceedeth out of the mouth of the Father.
Q. *How art thou cloathed?*
A. I know not.
Q. *How long hast thou lived without any corporal sustenance, having perfect health?*
A. Some fifteen or sixteen days, sustained without any other food except the Word of God.[42]

Emilia Fogelklou suggests that Nayler's prolonged fasting is reminiscent of Jesus's fasting; this, together with the nature of the questions and his responses, certainly evokes Christ's temptation in the wilderness.[43] The Jesus of *Paradise Regained* echoes Nayler's trust in God's abundance to provide for his prophets and his people. Confronted by Satan in the first temptation to change stones into bread, Milton's Jesus replies,

> is it not written
>
> . . . .
>
> Man lives not by Bread only, but each Word
> Proceeding from the mouth of God, who fed

> Our Fathers here with Manna? In the Mount
> *Moses* was forty days, nor eat nor drank,
> And forty days *Eliah* without food
> Wander'd this barren waste; the same I now. (*PR* 1.347–54)

In asking the question, the interrogator reveals that he does not participate in Nayler's divine economy, and the result is that in the exchange the minister interestingly, if unknowingly, casts himself into the role of the Adversary in the wilderness.

Like Jesus, Nayler's radical dependence on the divine economy to supply his needs leaves him completely free for the service of God. If they are supplied supernaturally by God, as was the case with God's prophets and his people, then from Nayler's perspective there is gain, for his personal devotion and the scope of his message only increase. If his needs are met through the charity of other Friends, who themselves must labor, there is also gain; their labor increases their reserve of the inner good and works to build the Quaker community.[44] Serving God may cause Nayler to neglect other values in the process (he certainly neglected his family in his incessant wandering, though he defends it by saying that God provides for them as well), but such service can only be defined within the context of the ultimate value and investment in God's kingdom, one that always returns more than one individual pays into it.[45] Thus, in Nayler's divine economy the "is-ness" of the facts of survival is not in conflict with the "ought-ness" of what one values; the way the world is or functions (the fact of an economic existence) is also the way the world ought to be (a Quaker community of charity). Nayler's sublimated and Christic body is a sign guaranteeing that unity as he travels through the streets of the haves and have-nots, the buyers and the sellers, the employers and those employed.

Continuing through the market district, the pageant arrives at its third crucial station en route: the High Cross, a short tower erected in 1373 that stood at the intersection of Broad, Wine, High, and Corn Streets in the very heart of the old city; from here, proclamations were often read and vagrants publicly whipped. Additionally, as if lending the blessing of their ecclesial stamp upon the monument, the medieval churches of All Saints, Christ Church, and St. Ewen stood on three of the four corners of the bustling intersection. Despite the recent execution of Charles I, and Colonel Nathaniel Fiennes's 1643 purge of royal ministers who served in these and other churches, the High Cross stood as an anomaly, a ghostly reminder of kingly and ecclesial power and authority.[46] Within its niches resided carved images of England's past monarchs who had granted significant city charters, including John, Henry III, Edward III, and Edward IV; the Cross was elevated to nearly forty feet in 1633 in order to accommodate the figures of Henry VI, Elizabeth, James I, and Charles I. The High Cross perhaps had become a standard station in other royal pageants, for it marked the geographical, economic, and spiritual center of the city.[47] Subsequently, I would urge us to understand this third station in Nayler's pageant as the pivotal place of convergence, where sovereigns, magistrates, ministers, buyers, and sellers all traffic together and merge.

Like Milton's Jesus, who responds to Satan's temptation to kingly power by declaring that "he who reigns within himself, and rules / Passions, Desires, and Fears, is more a King" (*PR* 2.466–67), the Quakers strove to be masters of themselves far more than they were tempted to seek offices of public magistracy. In *A Treatise of Civil Power* (1659) Milton the poet-statesman writes that "Christ hath a government of his own" that "governs not by outward force," but "deals only with the inward man and his actions." For Milton, as for the Quakers, this inward discipline manifests "the divine excellence of his spiritual kingdom, [which is] able without worldly force to subdue all the powers and kingdoms of this world" (*CPW* 7:255).[48] I have already commented on Nayler's response to magistracy, with particular attention drawn to the issue of doffing one's hat before one's superiors. Magistracy, acknowledges Nayler, is an ordinance of God, but it is only to be respected "Where Justice and Righteousnes is the head, and ruleth without partiality." Where this is explicitly not the case, God sends his prophets to speak against injustice and to use "all means to perswade them to *love mercy, do justice, & walk humbly with God,* that they might be established and the wrath of God turned from them."[49] Nayler's passing by this monument to kingly power is an act of judgment; however, from his point of view this act of judgment is also an act of mercy, for by his dramatic reenactment, he hopes by "all means" to turn unjust magistracy from the coming wrath of God. Moreover, the new proclamation and incarnation signifies this inner kingdom's eruption into the world, perhaps underscoring Milton's own subtitle to his *Treatise*: "Shewing that it is not lawfull for any power on earth to compell in matters of Religion." This suggestion is particularly striking when we consider that the image of Charles I, who vehemently sought to strengthen the royal grip on matters of religion, had been removed from the High Cross in January 1651.[50]

Included in those "powers" that "compel in matters of religion" are the established clergy like his opponent, Ralph Farmer. These are ministers who to Nayler appear as no more than pretenders, hypocrites, or mercenaries for hire, rather than as embodiments of the Word. The anti-Quaker Francis Higginson collects an impressive catalogue of Quaker denunciations against the clergy. According to the Quakers, the present ministers are "the Priests of the World, Conjurers, Theeves, Robbers, Antichrists, Witches, Divils, Lyars, and a Viperous and a Serpentine Generation, Blasphemers, Scarlet coloured Beasts, Babylons Merchants selling beastly Ware, whited Walls, ravening Wolves, greedy Dogs, *Baals* priests, Tithemongers, Deceivers, Hirelings, &c. . . . They affirm . . . that they do all for filthy Lucre."[51] Particularly relevant for our discussion is the image of ministers as "Babylon's merchants selling beastly ware," for one of Fox's and Nayler's principal objections to the clergy is that they treat the office of the pulpit as a "trade" rather than as a sacred calling. True ministers, like the original apostles sent by Christ, "counted it their gain to *make the Gospel without charge;* neither ever had they any set means, but went about, having no certain dwelling place; never were masters, but *servants to all for Christs sake.*" In other words, their objection rests on the fact that these hirelings do not participate in the divine economy based upon the charity of God and neighbor; instead, they participate in the economy and metaphysics of lack, securing their gain from the exchange of money for their preaching. In doing so, they "*make merchandise* of people; and . . . they have hearts exercised with covetous practices."[52] Their participation in this economy is made symbolically explicit at the station of the High Cross, for the bustling intersection must have been clogged and encumbered by the trafficking and exchange of merchandise. Bristol historian John Latimer observes that in March 1657 the Common Council ordered that the multitude of stocking-maker stalls, which were lined against the walls of Christ Church, be removed, and sellers were subsequently prohibited from gathering and displaying their wares there in order to make more space for meetings of the Common Council, which had been held for nearly a century in the cramped Council House located adjacent to St. Ewen's.[53] We might thus see in Nayler's passing by the High Cross, the constellation of market stalls, and the ministers of these churches an implicit and symbolic connection to Jesus's clearing the dishonest moneychangers from the Temple, cleansing and redeeming the sacred space for prayer and devotion (Matt. 21:12–13; John 2:13–17).

Before the troupe's conveyance to Newgate, the last station in this pageant route to be mentioned by the historical accounts is the White Hart (or Heart, as William Grigge spells it) in Broad Street, an inn owned by the prominent Bristol Quaker and member of the Barebones Parliament Dennis Hollister.[54] By now the crowd of onlookers must have been considerable, for when the arresting magistrates finally arrived, they were unable to question the company because of the "great concourse of people." Both Fogelklou and Bittle note, however, that the support of other Friends was conspicuously absent from this crowd.[55] Previous to that day in October, fellow Friends had surrounded Nayler's person and championed his leadership of the movement in London. They had followed him, anxiously waiting to hear him preach or shrewdly to engage a Quaker detractor, oftentimes in inns or taverns such as the Bull and Mouth, purchased by the Quakers in London. Nayler was apparently a mesmerizing speaker. A secondhand account in the diary of James Gough survives, in which Gough records that an ex-officer in the Army heard Nayler preach "with such power and reaching energy as I had not till then been witness of. I could not help staying a little though I was afraid to stay, for I was made a quaker, being forced to tremble at the sight of myself. I was struck with more terror before the preaching of James Nayler than I was before the Battle of Dunbar [in 1650]."[56] Friends in Bristol, however, were either struck with more terror from the magistrates, were too scandalized by the extremity of Nayler's performance, or were discouraged from supporting Nayler and his cast by George Fox himself, who met with Nayler the month before at Exeter and had publicly reproached him for, in essence, challenging Fox's prominence and authority in the Quaker movement.[57] If this latter is the case, the glaring lack of local Quaker support suggests the divisive struggle between charismatic leaders of an inchoate dissenting movement attempting to define its direction and what constitutes legitimate expressions of the seed of Christ.[58] Whatever the reason for the absence of Friends that afternoon, we might say that in their collective abandonment of Nayler they fulfill the role of the disciples who abandon Jesus after his arrest. The White Hart was probably chosen out of the prominence of its owner and because it was a central meeting place for Bristol Quakers. I think it safe to assume that Nayler's troupe enters the city knowing full well that they would be arrested, and, as if to perpetuate the theodrama, Nayler's "white heart" is offered for public sacrifice.

But Ralph Farmer and his cronies, those who ascend the stage of the theodrama and unmask its players, draw particular attention to the artificiality of the whole incident. In their response, we see them engaging in the traditional rhetoric used by many Puritans to denounce the stage, including injunctions against idleness and hypocrisy.[59] Interestingly, we find that Nayler himself is also an opponent of the stage on similar grounds, even though his entrance into Bristol is carefully crafted and highly theatrical. In an undated pamphlet addressed *To the Parliament of the Commonwealth of England* (probably written in the early 1650s), Nayler remarks that he witnessed what can only be described as impromptu street performances while he was traveling through the former theater district of Southwark. Having erected a scaffold in the open street, the small group of men were "transformed into several shapes, lifting wickedness up on high, and acting such abominable folly in words and actions, in the sight of the sun, as might make any tender heart, fearing God, to tremble at the sight of." Nayler upbraids Parliament, for he was "wounded to the heart to see, that ever such things should be tolerated under your government, for whom God hath so wrought that you might reform these evils." We do not know the extent of these street performances, but their existence ought to be further considered by theatrical revisionists. Apparently there were also private performances in houses as well, for Nayler comments that there were "several trumpets . . . sounding to gather vain minded people thereto."[60] Nayler draws attention to their "transformation" into that which they are not, resulting in what must be understood as an abomination and affront to God as their Creator.

Confronting Nayler's cast's own transformation and abomination, Farmer calls the troupe "*Impostors* and Deceivers" whose diligence in crafting their stage presence "facilitate[s] their delusions" in order "to gain upon simple people, who are taken with any *foppery* that comes in a way new, unusuall, and extraordinary." His language reflects another early modern understanding of "pageant": "A part acted to deceive or impose upon any one; a trick; something which is a mere empty or specious show without substance or reality." He laments those audience members who have been "deluded and deceived, by a *pack* of quaking lying *Mountebanks*, who pretended to *talk* to you from the *immediate* Spirit." Mountebanks are the classic snake-oil salesmen, charlatans who draw attention to themselves in order to attract a crowd of potential buyers. For Farmer, the ultimate snake-oil salesman and pretender is Satan himself, who according to the Apostle Paul can masquerade as an angel of light (2 Cor. 11:14–15), and the Bristol minister rails against this false impersonator of the Son, commanding, "Come down thou Lucifer, thou Son of the morning."[61] Interestingly, David Scott Kastan notes that in 1576 the Court of High Commission forbade the representation of God the Father, Son, or Holy Spirit on stage, fearing that it would compromise God's glory and majesty.[62] Essentially, the order was intended to curb the potential for blasphemy and idolatry, and significantly, Nayler was officially charged with "horrid blasphemy," while his retinue were guilty of committing idolatry. Summarizing his thoughts on the incident, Farmer concludes, "You have here (*de facto*) plain and horrid *Blasphemie*, in attributing those things and titles to a poor mortal wretch, which belong only to the blessed God, and our dear Redeemer: And also pure *Idolatry,* in giving religious worship . . . and *adoration* to the same."[63]

In the same spirit, John Deacon labels Nayler the "chief actor" in the incident. This not only brings to light Deacon's placing responsibility squarely on the shoulders of Nayler as its author, but it also speaks to its dramatic context, one that is only heightened when we consider that among the letters found upon their persons, Hannah Stranger and Martha Simmonds also had copies of a letter supposedly sent by Publius Lentulus of Judea to Caesar describing the physical appearance of Christ. Lentulus cannot but comment on Jesus's comely features, and speaks of his long brown hair split in the middle, his bushy forked beard, quick gray eyes, and fair speech. Deacon, however, describes Nayler as having a "ruddy complexion, brown hair . . . hanging a little below his jaw-bones; of an indifferent height; not very long visaged, nor very round; close shaven; a sad down-look, and melancholy countenance." Nayler must also have struck a pallid and gaunt figure because according to his own testimony he had been fasting for nearly two weeks. Despite the differences between Lentulus's praising description of Jesus and Nayler's actual appearance, Farmer finds enough common ground between them and objects to Nayler's conscious effort to look the part: "This wretch *James Nayler* . . . endeavours *artificially* to compose and dispose himself, asmuch (as he may) to this discription *parting* the hair of his head, cutting his beard *forked,* assuming an *affected gravity,* and other the like, as is there [in Lentulus's letter] expressed."[64] Farmer and his Bristol cronies intend to dispel the illusion of the theater by unmasking the drama's principal actor.

As Leo Damrosch notes, Major General William Goffe, who participated in the Putney Debates of 1647 against the radical contingent in the Army, found in Nayler not a fulfillment of Christ, but a sign of Christ's impending return because Nayler "has fulfilled a scripture, that false Christs should arise, 'to deceive, if it were possible, the very elect.' It ought to be a warning to us, to know how we stand."[65] To many eyes, perhaps even to many Quaker eyes, Nayler was playing a role that he himself had not intended to play and fulfilled a prophetic scripture he had not considered. Even though Farmer and Deacon engage in the standard Puritan rhetoric against the theatricality of Nayler's entry, the punishment secured for Nayler is highly staged as well. He narrowly escaped the death sentence in a vote by Parliament; instead, on 27 December the first part of his punishment was carried out in London where he was pilloried, a hole bored through his tongue with a hot iron, and branded on the forehead with a "B" for blasphemer. John Deacon was an eyewitness to the event. Remarkably, Martha Simmonds, Hannah Stranger, and Dorcus Erbury were audacious enough to continue the illusion of the theodrama, for Deacon observes that the three of them placed themselves at his feet "in imitation of *Mary Magdalen* and *Mary* the Mother of Jesus, and *Mary* the Mother of *Cleophas, John 19.25.* thereby to witness their still blasphemous and presumptious and heretical adoration of him, as Jesus the Christ." Moreover, another Quaker named Robert Rich placed "a paper over his head, in which it is said was writ, *This is the King of the Jews*."[66] What is perhaps even more remarkable is that apparently no one, not even his bitterest detractors, stopped Nayler's followers from reenacting the rest of the Christic theodrama.

From London Nayler was transferred to Bristol for the remainder of his punishment to be carried out: he was to be paraded through the streets, sitting backwards on a horse. If we understand Nayler's march through Bristol as a conversion of the "memory-theatre" of the urban landscape, the punishment doled out to Nayler in Bristol is a kind of anti-pageant, an attempt to reclaim those places and out-narrate his disruptive presence. Via Michel Foucault, this brutal narrative of the state disciplining and punishing the flesh of individual rebels is all too familiar. Damrosch observes that Nayler's anti-route was published in the newspaper *Mercurius Politicus,* and claims that this latter route retraced the original in reverse in an attempt to "undo" his crime. But Damrosch is not entirely accurate. If one consults Jacob Millerd's 1673 Great Map of Bristol, and compares it with the route published in the newspaper, one finds that in fact the route of the anti-pageant is much longer than the original parade route in Bristol.[67] According to the newspaper account, Nayler entered from the far northeast entrance to Bristol at Lawford's Gate, wound his way through several more streets, passed through at least one more gate inside the city walls (either Castle Gate or New Gate), emerged onto Wine Street, and passed the High Cross; he then proceeded down High Street and over Bristol Bridge where he dismounted, was stripped, and tied behind the horse to follow on foot; next, he was paraded southeast down St. Thomas Street (not Redcliff Street, which is the immediate street leading into the city after Redcliff Gate), where he was whipped in the marketplace, then back across Bristol Bridge (whipped), up High Street (whipped), passed the High Cross again (whipped), until the anti-pageant ended in Broad Street (whipped). While one of Nayler's fellow Friends was permitted to hold the arm of the executioner, thereby partially staying the full brunt and sting of the whip, it was an (out-)performance from which Nayler never fully recovered.[68] He died a short four years later, ironically after being mugged by one from among those marginalized men that his Christic performance sought to empower. The "supplanter" had himself been supplanted.

Milton and the Limits of Incarnation in the Seventeenth Century

Limits, in Milton's great epic, cannot be conceived without their transgression. The preceding chapters have tried to demonstrate, however, that Milton's vibrant and sustained thinking, reading, and writing about the Incarnation drive the threshold of those limits nearly to the edge of perfection. Some of his radical contemporaries strode across it in order to be translated by their encounter with the divine, and to translate that vision to others through creative interplay between the *kenosis* and the *pleroma* at work in their own fleshly tabernacles. In *Real Presences,* George Steiner remarks that interpretation approaches performance: "interpretation is understanding in action; it is the immediacy of translation." Or, to put it another way, "interpretation is, to the largest possible degree, lived."[1] *Gnosis* and *mimesis,* according to Steiner, are intimately related, and for Milton they find their crucial consummation in the Incarnation as the exegesis of God and the narrative picture of the "ruins of our first parents" in repair. John Everard, Gerrard Winstanley, and James Nayler confirm the accuracy of Steiner's assertion, for by their blurring of the Son and Spirit, they are able to figure themselves as the immediate "translation" of the Godhead.

Their detractors, operating from within their own communities and theological grammars, were unable or unwilling to participate. This is most graphically illustrated in Nayler's case, for his "translation" miserably failed, even within his own community. In a letter written to Margaret Fell just days before the pageant at Bristol, the recent Quaker convert Francis Howgill expresses his approbations, felt more widely among the Friends in the ensuing weeks: "Truly my dear J. N. is bad, . . . and there is such filthy things acted there in such havoc and spoil and such madness among them. . . . They have made truth stink in those parts."[2] As we have seen, few came to Nayler's defense despite his desire to share, what appeared to him, the blessings of the sacred language of Incarnation. Whether any appreciated or appropriated it or not, the "form of life" within the radical communities of Everard, Winstanley, and Nayler traces its varied expressions and performances from the goodness of creation and the abundant goodness of the Creator whose gaze bestows "Beatitude past utterance."

George Lindbeck identifies why religious traditions are so often "lost in translation": the status of doctrine. He asserts that in cognitivist models, perhaps the predominant paradigm among conservatives like Thomas Edwards or John Deacon, doctrines "function as informative propositions of truth claims about objective realities," leading to a philosophical or scientific understanding of religion. In expressivist models, on the other hand, typically the paradigm of many in the radical camps, doctrines are "noninformative and nondiscursive symbols of inner feelings, attitudes, or existential orientations," leading to an aesthetic understanding of religion. Both models, argues Lindbeck, appear incapable of leading to doctrinal reconciliation or cooperation between differing religious traditions; the one presents truth claims that cannot be refuted, the other exults in the "rousing motions" that stirred Milton's Samson and ignores or waters down doctrine so as to make it irrelevant.[3]

Lindbeck's insight can be quite instructive. For many conservatives in a seventeenth-century context, the science of correct doctrine leads to stability in the ecclesiastical and social order. Richard Hooker, defender of the doctrinally astute and university-trained clergy, worries about the whims of one's private reading of scripture: "When they and their Bibles were alone together, what strange fantastical opinion soever at any time entered into their heads, their use was to think the Spirit taught it them."[4] And as Jean-François Gilmont recounts, Martin Luther and John Calvin reveal their anxieties about the unrestricted publication of theological works and the unfettered access to scripture despite their commitment to a vernacular Bible. Calvin argued that in order for the people to be properly nourished, God desires "that the bread be sliced for us, that the pieces be put in our mouths, and that they be chewed for us."[5] The result, as Edwards writes in the closing lines of his dedicatory epistle to *Gangraena*, is a "*settle*[d]" church and government "*whereby we may be brought into one, and become terrible as an Army with banners, and like a strong and fenced City, both against schisms that may arise from within, and the assaults of enemies without.*" In his eyes, a weakened doctrinal identity yields a crippled national defense. Correct doctrine for Edwards is the "mighty fortress" and "bulwark never failing," to echo the words from Luther's hymn.

The incident at Bristol was just one that revealed a weakened bulwark. What Milton thought concerning the Christic theodrama at Bristol is unknown to us. He was otherwise occupied in state matters since the convening of Parliament on 17 September, and on 21 September he sent correspondence to Richard Jones at Oxford warning against the young man's admiration of men who held the traditional means of power. Additionally, he may have been spending time drafting the *De Doctrina Christiana*, but more impending was the widower's anticipation of his marriage to Katherine Woodcock on 12 November, having published the wedding announcement first on 22 October and the next two Sundays following.[6] Milton was silent regarding the incident, but Parliament was emphatically not in the coming months. Parliamentary debate on the nature of the Bristol event is recorded in the diary of Thomas Burton, Esq. (MP, 1656–59) and continued every day in Parliament for three weeks (5–26 December), and sporadically thereafter until 3 January 1657. The diary accounts bear out these domestic fears associated with a doctrinal levity. At the outset, Major-General Philip Skippon opines that "the growth of these things is more dangerous than the most intestine or foreign enemies," a position seconded by Major-General Edward Boteler, who comments, "My ears did tingle, and my heart tremble, to hear the report" and he identifies the pernicious civil threat posed by the Quakers, who "are generally despisers of your government, contemn your magistracy and ministry, and trample it under their feet."[7] The debate itself revolves around a few interrelated issues: whether or not the official report by the original fifty-five-member committee was accurate and ought to be considered authoritative; whether Nayler should be brought to bar yet again (he was) or if he ought to be charged based on his previous testimony; whether there was legal precedent for proceeding against Nayler; and, finally, whether the nature of his crime was the misdemeanor of disturbing the civil peace, or committing idolatry and either blasphemy or horrid blasphemy, the latter of which could possibly send the offender to the gallows.

Not all are agreed, however, as to what precisely Nayler intended by the pageant's staging of divinity, how it is to be interpreted, and in what way Parliament should rule in the case, even as the irked Oliver Cromwell was demanding an explanation. But the arguments become progressively more biblically savvy as the week progresses. The Nayler case thus functions as a window not only into the multivalent understandings and applications of scriptural passages, but also the already unsettled state of "correct" doctrine under the new regime. When Nayler is summoned to the bar for a fourth time, his hat being forcefully removed by the sergeant, Burton records that Nayler understood his entrance as "a sign to this nation, to bear witness of his coming." Sir Gilbert Pickerling recognizes the distinction Nayler at this point seems to be making between sign and signified, for the Quaker "gives himself not out, plainly, to be the son of God, but that he is a prophet, a type, a sign, to warn men of the second coming of Christ"; he may be guilty of idolatry, but Pickerling, who interestingly appeals to the liberty of conscience, confesses he will demur in passing down a death sentence. Lord William Strickland agrees, for he does not think Nayler blasphemes God because the Quaker obviously "has no evil spirit or malice in him against God," but he is under the devilish delusion that "more of Christ is in him than in any other creature." George Downing retorts that the "Jews and Rabbins" interpreted blasphemy not as cursing God, but "the making himself equal to God," and that this incident is "treason against Heaven." Perhaps playing on the meaning of the name "James," Downing comments, "Our God is here supplanted"; the collective-possessive pronoun serves to underscore Lindbeck's insight.[8] While some see Nayler as a viper among other vipers that have "crept into the bowels of your Commonwealth" and "swarm all the nation over," others see Nayler as simply deluded or bewitched, a martyr whose death must be avoided at all costs, the Antichrist come in the flesh, or a potential penitent and "instrument of the Church" like Paul.[9]

Despite these competing perceptions, nearly all the speakers recorded by Burton seem to display a great sense of the weight of the moment, for Nayler's case brings with it the critical and contentious issue of religious toleration and liberty of conscience, which persisted throughout the Cromwellian period and post-Reformation England. Colonel Alban Cox testifies that "the world abroad says it is liberty of conscience [that] has brought this fellow before you. I am of this same opinion." Under the Thirty-Eighth and Thirty-Ninth Articles of the *Instrument of Government,* issued by the new regime 16 December 1653, dissenters, exclusive of Catholics and those Protestants who favored prelacy, who "profess faith in God by Jesus Christ, (though differing in judgment from the doctrine, worship or discipline publicly held forth)" were extended toleration insofar as their actions did not cause civil injury or disturb the peace.[10] Yet Cox and other members view Nayler's act as clearly violating those bounds. "If this be liberty," Skippon pronounces, "God deliver me from such liberty," to which Sir William Strickland adds, "and let not the enemies of God have the upper hand, to have liberty to blaspheme his hand."[11] One could argue that they are perhaps inflating the stakes of the Nayler case more than it is due. But in their zeal, they voice concern that national and international eyes are watching, and that the defending of God's honor is at stake; fail in that, some warn, and his wrathful judgment will redouble on all of England. "All the eyes of the nation are upon you for it," Samuel Bedford admonishes, "to see what you will do for God in this business," a sentiment echoed by several, including Major-General Skippon, who revealingly discloses his own fears that "Nayler's sin will prove a national sin, and consequently a national judgement."[12]

Historians have ably demonstrated that local concerns in Tudor-Stuart England are enmeshed within the matrix of regional and national issues.[13] The "English city . . . was primarily a legal and political unit," describes David Harris Sacks, that "stood ready to fly apart as regional, national and even international developments affected its inhabitants." Given Bristol's crucial maritime economy, Sacks concludes that in "no place in England was this truer than Bristol."[14] As Sacks points out, Ralph Farmer is far from being just a local clergyman outraged at an isolated Quaker incident. He had in fact economic ties to the Earl of Berkshire, a member of Charles I's privy council and Farmer's associate in the monopoly of the malt kilns. Moreover, in 1639, when Bristol's chamberlain died, Farmer was among the candidates who failed to get any votes for the position, but who was subsequently endorsed by Charles himself.[15] The scandal of Nayler's march into Bristol is thus not locally confined, but reflects larger political and theological debates on toleration and the exercise of liberty of conscience when it comes to issues of worship, religious expression, and doctrine.

For groups like the Quakers, however, prescribed worship, formatted prayers, and settled doctrine petrify the "liquidity" of the Inner Light. Nevertheless, the absence of Friends supporting Nayler in Bristol suggests some early disagreement in the sect about the life of the Inner Light. Yet it is clear that to the early Quakers, rigidly defined doctrine and controlled religious expression are ultimately affronts to God's own freedom to act as he chooses. Far from being the sinister "individualists" that their conservative contemporaries thought they were, many radicals held to the belief that the Spirit operated most fully in those who demonstrated a marked absence of personal desire and will. The protagonists in *Samson Agonistes* and *Paradise Regained* certainly bear this out, but in categorically different degrees. Directly invoking the mysticism of Pseudo-Dionysius, John Everard refers to this openness and negation as the "way of poverty," the gradual removal or stripping of the self in order to experience, ironically, the fullness of union with the

Godhead. In "Christ the true Salt of the Earth," the opening sermon of *The Gospel-Treasury Opened,* Everard exhorts, "Silence then your selves, deny your own life, hear no longer your selves, nor your own lusts, what honour saith, what profit saith, what self . . . saith."[16] Everard's "non-self" becomes the ultimate vessel of the Most High and the instrument of his freedom. Such is the argument of the Quakers, and presumably Milton's tendency toward the prophetic vocation of the poet may align Milton's ideal poet with Everard's ideal preacher. Recall, for instance, his vatic proclamation in "Elegy V": "I am driven on by the madness and the divine sounds within me," for now "Apollo himself comes."

In Nayler's fourth appearance at the bar, he argues, "I am one that daily prays that magistracy may be established in this nation. I do not, nor dare affront authority."[17] The authority in question, however, is not primarily civil, but divine: "I do it not to set up idolatry, but to obey the will of my Father, which I dare not deny. I was set up as a sign to summon this nation, and to convince them of Christ's coming," for the English "have been a long time under dark forms, neglecting the power of godliness, as bishops." Incarnating Christ is an act of cultural alienation and iconoclasm that offers a critique of ideology in order to enable its own retrieval, and to lead to its own Exodus. Milton could certainly have written an anticlerical statement similar to Nayler's in any of the anti-prelatical pamphlets of the 1640s. Defending the bizarre behavior of other Friends who "walk naked as a sign," Nayler elsewhere vehemently attacks those "ignorant of the power of God," for "any wise man may know that these do it not in obedience to their own wills, but in obedience unto God."[18] Nayler, too, recognized that the significance of his own pageant went beyond the confines of Bristol, but intended it as a judgment against the nation. Additionally, Sharon Achinstein prudently observes that while the established clergy busily appeal to the reasonableness of doctrine and civil order, dissenters and enthusiasts consistently deny that the claims of reason were even valid or necessarily comprehensive for understanding the phenomenology of religious experience.[19]

The impasse results in a competition between two different "language games" of Incarnation. Each is vying for dominance, and each is

attempting to demonstrate the poverty of the vocabulary of its opponent, while simultaneously performing the richness of its own sacred
grammar. In their strife to out-narrate, out-perform, out-publish, and
out-legislate, members of each community and faction try to render
their opponents' form of life a dead language. In the Incarnational poetics of revolutionary England, Milton and his radical contemporaries
demonstrate their conviction that the "far-beaming blaze of Majesty,"
radiating through the cracks of their own fleshly vessels, is a superior
language game that seeks to "hold all Heav'n and Earth in happier
union" ("Nativity" ode, 9, 108).

Introduction. Repairing the Ruins

1. All quotations of Milton's prose are from *The Complete Prose Works of John Milton,* ed. Don M. Wolfe et al., 8 vols. (New Haven: Yale University Press, 1953–82), cited parenthetically in the text by volume and page number as *CPW.* All quotations of Milton's poetry are from *John Milton: Complete Poems and Major Prose,* ed. Merritt Y. Hughes (New York: Macmillan, 1957). *Paradise Lost* will be abbreviated in the text as *PL, Paradise Regained* as *PR,* and *Samson Agonistes* as *SA,* followed by book and/or line numbers.

2. Jan Amos Comenius, *A Reformation of Schooles, designed in two excellent Treatises,* trans. Samuel Hartlib (London, 1642), 21–22. Originally published by Hartlib, without Comenius's consent, as *Conatuum Comenianorum Praeludia* (Oxford, 1637).

3. On Milton's relationship to Comenius and Samuel Hartlib, see Barbara K. Lewalski, "Milton and the Hartlib Circle: Educational Projects and the Epic Paedeia," in *Literary Milton: Text, Pretext, and Context,* ed. Diana Benet and Michael Lieb (Pittsburgh: Duquesne University Press, 1994), 202–19.

4. John Leonard, *Naming in Paradise: Milton and the Language of Adam and Eve* (Oxford: Clarendon, 1990), 104.

5. Scholarship on the Incarnation in Milton's thought and poetics has been largely piecemeal, and the overriding centrality of the Incarnation to Milton's canon has only begun to be assessed. The most recent and comprehensive of these books is Russell M. Hillier, *Milton's Messiah: The Son of God in Milton's Works* (Oxford: Oxford University Press, 2011). Hillier resituates the importance of Milton's high Christology as it informs his theories of atonement and redemption in *De Doctrina Christiana* and *Paradise Lost.* Michael Lieb devotes lengthy attention to the subject in his *Theological Milton: Deity, Discourse and Heresy in the Miltonic Canon* (Pittsburgh: Duquesne University Press, 2006). In part, Lieb explores Milton's eclectic doctrinal positions in *De*

Doctrina Christiana with particular focus on the heresy of Socinianism, and points to the tension displayed in *Paradise Lost* between the *theopatheia* and radical unavailability of Milton's God, whose fervent emotions, including divine hatred, are comprehended or illumined through the Son. See also David Loewenstein, *Representing Revolution in Milton and His Contemporaries: Religion, Politics, and Polemics in Radical Puritanism* (Cambridge: Cambridge University Press, 2001). Loewenstein juxtaposes Milton's major works alongside the polemics and poetry of the English Revolution produced by the radical "left" — Diggers, Levellers, and Quakers. Even though Loewenstein's work has always been cautious about asserting too vigorously Milton's endorsement of any radical group, his chapter on *Paradise Regained* nevertheless situates the poem's inwardness within the context of Quaker responses against external power. The collected volume of essays *Milton and Heresy,* ed. Stephen B. Dobranski and John P. Rumrich (Cambridge: Cambridge University Press, 1998) — where one would expect more extensive commentary on Milton's Godhead — contains only one essay, albeit a rich one. See John P. Rumrich, "Milton's Arianism: Why It Matters," in *Milton and Heresy,* ch. 4. Rumrich questions why early readers of Milton pointed to the Arianism of *Paradise Lost* when so many twentieth-century readers have occluded it. See also the essay contributed by David Loewenstein, "Treason Against God and State: Blasphemy in Milton's Culture and *Paradise Lost,*" in *Milton and Heresy,* ch. 9. Loewenstein partially addresses the relationship between Father and Son in *Paradise Lost* through a narrow examination of the Son's confrontation of Satan's blasphemy in Books 5 and 6, which resonates with the fallout accompanying the 1650 Blasphemy Act. Aside from these recent works, it appears that the only multi-chapter treatments of Milton's views regarding the Incarnation occur in the antithetically paired *Bright Essence: Studies in Milton's Theology,* ed. William B. Hunter, C. A. Patrides, and J. H. Adamson (Salt Lake City: University of Utah Press, 1973), and Michael E. Bauman, *Milton and Arianism* (New York: Peter Lang, 1987). The first argues for Milton's narrow escape of the Arian heresy in *Paradise Lost* and severs the poet from the manifold heresies in *De Doctrina Christiana,* a critical position that has become increasingly less tenable. Bauman attributes the Arian heresy to Milton's depiction of the Son in *Paradise Lost* as it accords with that explicated in *De Doctrina Christiana.*

6. The authorship of *De Doctrina Christiana* continues to be a subject of vigorous debate among Miltonists. At this stage in the scholarship the burden of proof seems to rest on the shoulders of the naysayers. I will use "author" and "Milton" interchangeably. Many argue that Milton's hand is evi-

dent; since the manuscript, however, was unpublished at his death, and since we know little or nothing about the theological agendas of his amanuenses, some scholarly caution is appropriate. In his introduction to the treatise, Maurice Kelley identifies at least seven different amanuenses, and possibly as many as eleven different hands (cf. *CPW* 6:11–40). Moreover, Barbara K. Lewalski, a supporter of the treatise's authenticity, observes in her recent biography of Milton that prior to the poet's death an acquaintance named Daniel Skinner, about whom we know very little, recopied the first 196 pages of the manuscript— those chapters that are the most heterodox. See Lewalski, *The Life of John Milton: A Critical Biography*, rev. ed. (Oxford: Blackwell, 2003), 415–41, for a succinct summary of the contents of the treatise.

It has become the general practice that any scholarly work that cites the treatise must of necessity also contain a footnote that is fast-approaching epic proportions. The most recent foray, convincing in its multi-hued argument that Milton is the properly cited author of the treatise, is *Milton and the Manuscript of De Doctrina Christiana*, ed. Gordon Campbell, Thomas N. Corns, John K. Hale, and Fiona J. Tweedie (Oxford: Oxford University Press, 2007). A useful summary of the authorship debate occurs in Stephen Dobranski's introduction in *Milton and Heresy*, 1–17. The debate was recently spurred by William B. Hunter Jr. in "The Provenance of the *Christian Doctrine*," *SEL* (1992): 129–42. The ensuing "Forum: Milton's *Christian Doctrine*" appeared in the same issue with counterarguments from Barbara Kiefer Lewalski and John T. Shawcross, followed by a response from Hunter. Hunter's most recent contribution is *Visitation Unimplor'd: Milton and the Authorship of De Doctrina Christiana* (Pittsburgh: Duquesne University Press, 1998), in which Hunter concludes that "so many of Milton's genuine ideas are at odds with those in *DDC*" (153). For further rebuttals, see Barbara K. Lewalski, "Milton and *De Doctrina Christiana*: Evidences of Authorship," in *Milton Studies* 36, ed. Albert C. Labriola (1998); and Dobranski and Rumrich, *Milton and Heresy*. Lewalski finds that Milton's authorship is "beyond a reasonable doubt" (223), and Dobranski and Rumrich agree that the treatise "expresses Milton's thought and convictions . . . more fully and centrally than any other single work in the accepted canon" (10). See also Michael Lieb, "*De Doctrina Christiana* and the Question of Authorship," in *Milton Studies* 41, ed. Albert C. Labriola (2002): 172–230. For stylometic analysis of the treatise and Milton's other works, see Gordon Campbell, Thomas N. Corns, John K. Hale, David I. Holmes, and Fiona J. Tweedie, "The Provenance of *De Doctrina Christiana*," *Milton Quarterly* 31 (1997): 67–121.

7. On the tradition of apophatic theology, with particular regard to Milton, see Michael Bryson, "The Mysterious Darkness of Unknowing: *Paradise Lost* and the God Beyond Names," in *Paradise Lost: A Poem Written in Ten Books: Essays on the 1667 First Edition,* ed. Michael Lieb and John Shawcross (Pittsburgh: Duquesne University Press, 2007), 183–212. See also Noam Reisner, *Milton and the Ineffable* (Oxford: Oxford University Press, 2010).

8. John Milbank and Catherine Pickstock, *Truth in Aquinas* (London: Routledge, 2001), 39, 60.

9. For more on the phenomenology of the Incarnation, God's condescension to the human creature, and a critique of the Transcendent God in Jean-Luc Marion's work and the Transcendent Other in Emmanuel Levinas's work, see James K. A. Smith, *Speech and Theology: Language and the Logic of Incarnation* (London: Routledge, 2002). Smith, I think, overemphasizes the "top-down" condescension of God and undervalues the "bottom-up" notion of participation. It appears to me that both have to be equally at work in the Incarnation.

10. George Steiner, *Real Presences* (Chicago: University of Chicago Press, 1989), 8, 11.

11. Paul Ricoeur, "The Hermeneutics of Testimony," in *Essays on Biblical Interpretation,* ed. Lewis S. Mudge (Philadelphia: Fortress Press, 1980), 119–54; quote from 137, emphasis original. Originally published as "The Hermeneutics of Testimony," *Anglican Theological Review* 61, no. 4 (1979).

12. On the tradition of the *deus absconditus,* and Milton's response to it in his theological treatise, see Lieb, *Theological Milton,* 69–86.

13. Hillier, *Milton's Messiah,* 16–17, 34.

14. John C. Ulreich, " 'Substantially Express'd': Milton's Doctrine of the Incarnation," in *Milton Studies* 39, ed. Albert C. Labriola (2000): 101–28; quote from 114. For Ulreich's application of this statement with regard to Milton's Jesus in *Paradise Regained,* see esp. 114–18.

15. See Alastair Fowler, *Paradise Lost,* 2nd ed. (New York: Longman, 1997).

16. See Thomas Aquinas, *Summa Contra Gentiles,* trans. Charles J. O'Neil (Notre Dame: University of Notre Dame Press, 1975), 4.28.2–5; 4.4.

17. Quoted in J. N. D. Kelly, *Early Christian Doctrines,* 5th ed. (London: Continuum, 1977), 140.

18. Stanley Hauerwas, *A Community of Character: Toward a Constructive Christian Social Ethic* (Notre Dame: University of Notre Dame Press, 1981), 113.

19. Mindele Ann Treip, *Allegorical Poetics and the Epic* (Lexington: University of Kentucky Press, 1994), 222.

20. For more on how Milton and other English revolutionary writers seek to transform a "fit" readership, see Sharon Achinstein, *Milton and the Revolutionary Reader* (Princeton: Princeton University Press, 1994).

21. Regarding Milton and early modern preaching, see Jameela Lares, *Milton and the Preaching Arts* (Pittsburgh: Duquesne University Press, 2001); Robert Entzminger, *Divine Word: Milton and the Redemption of Language* (Pittsburgh: Duquesne University Press, 1985); and Boyd M. Berry, *Process of Speech: Puritan Religious Writing and "Paradise Lost"* (Baltimore: Johns Hopkins University Press, 1976). None of these studies addresses the relationship of the Incarnation to preaching, despite the fact that Christ is the first preacher. Lares argues that Milton was heavily influenced by early modern sermon theory; Entzminger explores Milton's ambivalent attitude toward language as both a corruption and a vehicle of God's truth; and Berry's work situates Milton among controversial Puritan discourses, such as debates on the Sabbath, marriage, or genuflection.

22. Ralph A. Haug, editor of the text of *The Reason of Church Government* in the Yale prose series, glosses over Milton's pairing of the aims of pulpit with poetry, emphasizing in his notes only the latter (816n109). These "functions of the *vates*" are reflected in the poetic genres: epic (the call to virtue and nationhood), tragedy ("allay" is equated to Aristotle's notion of purgation), and hymns and odes (celebrating God and his martyrs).

23. Thanks to Ethan Shagan for pointing this out to me.

24. Jameela Lares, "Milton and the 'Office of the Pulpit,'" *Ben Jonson Journal* 3 (1996): 109–26; quote from 109.

25. Roger Chartier, "Labourers and Voyagers: From the Text to the Reader." Originally published in *Diacritics* 22, no. 2 (1992): 49–61, trans. J. A. González. Reprinted in *Readers and Reading*, ed. Andrew Bennett (London: Longman, 1995), 132–49; quote from 138.

26. Augustine, *Confessions*, trans. Henry Chadwick (Oxford: Oxford University Press, 1991), 11.29.39.

27. Michel de Certeau, *Practice of Everyday Life*, trans. Steven F. Rendall (Berkeley: University of California Press, 1984), 175–76. Cited in Chartier, "Labourers and Voyagers," in *Readers and Reading*, 143.

28. Augustine, *Confessions*, 1.17.27; emphasis added.

29. Gerald L. Bruns, *Hermeneutics: Ancient and Modern* (New Haven: Yale University Press, 1992), 11.

30. For a point of comparison, see Hans-Georg Gadamer, *Truth and Method*, 2nd ed., trans. Joel Weinsheimer and Donald G. Marshall (New York: Continuum, 1997), 428. Like Augustine, Gadamer draws explicitly on the Incarnation for hermeneutics: "Christology prepares the way for a new philosophy of man, which mediates in a new way between the mind of man in its finitude and the divine infinity. Here what we have called the hermeneutical experience finds its own, special ground."

31. Paul Ricoeur, "The Hermeneutical Function of Distanciation," in *Hermeneutics and the Human Sciences: Essays on Language, Action and Interpretation*, ed. and trans. John B. Thompson (Cambridge: Cambridge University Press, 1981), 143; emphasis original. Hereafter, this volume is abbreviated in the notes as *HHS*.

32. Ibid., 139.

33. By this, Ricoeur sets himself against the Romantic impulse to divine the author behind the text. See Friedrich Schleiermacher, *Hermeneutics: The Handwritten Manuscripts*, trans. James Duke and Jack Fortsman, American Academy of Religion Texts and Translation Series, ed. Heinz Kimmerle, vol. 1 (Atlanta: Scholars, 1986). The archaeology of authorial intention is a Romanticist agenda, and led Schleiermacher as an early theorist of hermeneutics to conclude that the purpose of hermeneutics is to recover the world "behind the text," to understand the author better than he understood himself.

34. Gadamer, *Truth and Method*, 302.

35. Ricoeur, "The Hermeneutical Function of Distanciation," in *HHS*, 144.

36. Nicholas Wolterstorff, *Works and Worlds of Art* (Oxford: Clarendon, 1980), x, 14–22.

37. See, for instance, Peter C. Herman, *Destabilizing Milton: Paradise Lost and the Poetics of Incertitude* (New York: Palgrave Macmillan, 2005). Herman's introduction also provides a useful "roadmap" to the recent scholarly communities embattled over a view of Milton's overall unity and consistency or his contradiction and vacillation in his work and thought. For the most recent contribution on the flux of Milton's ideas over time, consult John T. Shawcross, *The Development of Milton's Thought: Law, Government, and Religion*, Medieval and Renaissance Literary Studies (Pittsburgh: Duquesne University Press, 2008). Shawcross maintains that the one constant throughout Milton's life and thought is his unwavering faith, though one that is certainly shaped by his evolving doctrine.

38. See Janel Mueller's important essay, "Milton on Heresy," in *Milton and Heresy*, ch. 1.

39. My thanks to an anonymous reader who insightfully challenged me to think about Milton's aesthetics along these lines.

Chapter 1. "Such harmony alone"

1. See Augustine, *Sermon CXC*, 3.4, in *An Augustine Synthesis*, ed. Erich Pryzywara (New York: Harper & Brothers, 1958), 182.

2. J. Martin Evans, *The Miltonic Moment* (Lexington: University Press of Kentucky, 1998), 14–15; cf. ll. 32, 45, 63.

3. *A Maske* ought to be considered as part of the English collection, and one may object that "poetry" in the seventeenth century includes both drama and verse. But Milton himself seems to have made a distinction between the *ars dramatica* and the *ars poetica* in *The Reason of Church Government* (*CPW* 1:812–16), where he categorically distinguishes drama from epic and lyric. See Barbara K. Lewalski, "Genre," in *A Companion to Milton*, ed. Thomas N. Corns (Oxford: Oxford University Press, 2003), 3–21.

Milton was very meticulous about the ordering of the poems in the volume. See the following: Colin Burrow, "*Poems 1645*: The Future Poet," in *Cambridge Companion to Milton*, 2nd ed., ed. Dennis Danielson (Cambridge: Cambridge University Press, 1999), 54–69; Stella Revard, *Milton and the Tangles of Neaera's Hair: The Making of the 1645 Poems* (Columbia: University of Missouri Press, 1997); Leah Marcus, *Unediting the Renaissance: Shakespeare, Marlowe, Milton* (New York: Routledge University Press, 1996), ch. 6; C.W.R.D. Moseley, *The Poetic Birth: Milton's Poems of 1645* (Aldershot: Scolar, 1991); John K. Hale, "Milton's Self-Presentation in *Poems . . . 1645*," *Milton Quarterly* 25 (1991): 37–48.

4. Paul Ricoeur, *The Rule of Metaphor: Multi-disciplinary Studies of the Creation of Meaning in Language*, trans. Robert Czerny (Toronto: University of Toronto Press, 1975), 7.

5. Paul Ricoeur, *Freud and Philosophy*, trans. Denis Savage (New Haven: Yale University Press, 1970), 531.

6. Frederic B. Tromly, "Milton's 'Preposterous Exaction': The Significance of 'The Passion,'" *ELH* 47, no. 2 (Summer 1980): 276–86; quote from 276.

7. *A Milton Encyclopedia*, ed. William B. Hunter Jr., 9 vols. (Lewisburg: Bucknell University Press, 1978–83), 6:120.

8. E. M. W. Tillyard, *Milton* (London: Chatto & Windus, 1966), 39.

9. Michael Schoenfeldt, "'That spectacle of too much weight': The Poetics of Sacrifice in Donne, Herbert, and Milton," *Journal of Medieval and Early Modern Studies* 31, no. 3 (Fall 2001): 561–84; quotes from 579–80.

10. See Tromly, "Milton's 'Preposterous Exaction,'" 279.

11. Lewalski, *The Life of John Milton*, 38.

12. See, for instance, Louis L. Martz, "The Rising Poet," in *The Lyric and Dramatic Milton*, ed. Joseph H. Summers (New York: Columbia University Press, 1965), 3–33; William B. Hunter, "John Milton, Autobiographer," *Milton Quarterly* 8 (1974): 100–104.

13. John Calvin, *Institutes of the Christian Religion*, trans. Henry Beveridge, 2 vols. (Grand Rapids: Eerdmans, 1983), 2:17.

14. Martin Luther, *The Sermons of Martin Luther*, ed. John Nicholas Lenker, 8 vols. (Grand Rapids: Baker Book House, 1988), 7:165.

15. Joseph Hall, *The Works*, ed. Philip Wynter, 10 vols. (Oxford: Oxford University Press, 1863), 2:664; Henry Jacob, *A Treatise of the Sufferings and Victory of Christ, in the work of our redemption* (London, 1597), 80, 33. Quoted in Debora Kuller Shuger, *The Renaissance Bible: Scholarship, Sacrifice, and Subjectivity* (Berkeley: University of California Press, 1994), 108.

16. Shuger, *The Renaissance Bible*, 107, 7.

17. Ricoeur, "The Hermeneutical Function of Distanciation," in *HHS*, 143; emphasis original.

18. James Holly Hanford and James G. Taaffe, *A Milton Handbook*, 5th ed. (New York: Appleton-Century-Crofts, 1970), 115.

19. Richard Halpern, "The Great Instauration: Imaginary Narratives in Milton's 'Nativity Ode,'" in *Re-Membering Milton: Essays on the Texts and Traditions*, ed. Mary Nyquist and Margaret W. Ferguson (New York: Methuen, 1987), 3–24; quote from 6; Shullenberger, "Doctrine as Deep Structure," 189 (see full citation below, 324n15).

20. Louis L. Martz, "The Rising Poet," in *The Lyric and Dramatic Milton: Selected Papers from the English Institute*, ed. Joseph H. Summers (New York and London: Columbia University Press, 1965), 3–33; quotation from 4.

21. The testimonial poems and Diodati's epistle are reprinted and translated in Roy Flannagan, ed., *The Riverside Milton* (New York: Houghton Mifflin Company, 1998), 174–78.

22. For the best attempt to "destabilize" Milton's authorial presence in the 1645 *Poems,* consult Marcus, *Unediting the Renaissance,* 204–27. In part, she cites Milton's contempt for William Marshall's engraving on the frontispiece of the 1645 *Poems,* as well as the poet's Greek inscription below the frontispiece that insults the engraver, who himself apparently had little knowledge of Greek. But Marcus then proceeds to declare that through "this disclaimer, Milton denies the appearance of authorial control over the *volume* that is set in motion through the verses beneath the picture" (219; emphasis added). Marcus is absolutely right to point out that many books produced in the early modern period are "communal production[s]," and that Marshall proves himself a capable engraver with other frontispieces. Milton's aspersion cast upon the engraver, however, does not strike me as significant enough to merit the conclusion that Milton denies "authorial control over the volume" at large.

23. Revard, *Milton and the Tangles of Neaera's Hair,* 1–3.

24. Roger Chartier, "Reading Matter and 'Popular' Reading: From the Renaissance to the Seventeenth Century," in *A History of Reading in the West,* ed. Guglielmo Cavallo and Roger Chartier, trans. Lydia G. Cochran (Oxford: Polity, 1999), 269–83; quote from 275; "Labourers and Voyagers," in *Readers and Reading,* 138.

25. Marcus, *Unediting the Renaissance,* 216.

26. Ricoeur, *Freud and Philosophy,* 27.

27. Ricoeur, "Hermeneutics and the Critique of Ideology," in *HHS,* 63.

28. Ricoeur's philosophical hermeneutics thus functions as a mediatory "hinge" position in the well-known debate between Gadamer and Habermas. See Jürgen Habermas, *Erkenntnis und Interesse* (Frankfurt: Suhrkamp, 1968); English translation, *Knowledge and Human Interests,* trans. Jeremy J. Shapiro (London: Heinemann, 1972).

29. Ricoeur, "Hermeneutics and the Critique of Ideology," in *HHS,* 97.

30. Ibid., 99. Cf. Gadamer, *Truth and Method,* 250–51.

31. Evans, *The Miltonic Moment,* 15–16.

32. Halpern, "The Great Instauration," 6–7. See also Michael Lieb, "Milton and the Kenotic Christology: Its Literary Bearing," *ELH* 37 (1970): 342–60.

33. The *kenosis* described in Philippians 2:6–11 presents obvious theological problems if we do not keep the *pleroma* in mind. Augustine, *De Trinitate* (15.26–29), reminds readers that the members of the Trinity display mutual humility and charity within their relations. See Hans Urs von Balthasar, *Love Alone* (New York: Herder and Herder, 1969). Von Balthasar comments that the first *kenosis* is between the members of the Trinity, wherein each member

"empties" himself into the other, but it is a *kenosis* that does not constitute a loss of "self." See also Sara Coakley, *Power and Submissions: Spirituality, Philosophy and Gender* (Oxford: Blackwell, 2002).

34. The headnote does not appear in the 1673 *Poems.* On the teleological dangers of dating Milton's work generally, and with specific reference to "Sonnet 19," see Jonathan Goldberg, "Dating Milton," in *Soliciting Interpretation: Literary Theory and Seventeenth-Century English Poetry,* ed. Elizabeth D. Harvey and Katharine Eisaman Maus (Chicago: University of Chicago Press, 1990), 199–222. Goldberg argues that critics often assign dates to Milton's work under the assumption that the poet is always "'growing' into himself, never changed, or split, by historical experience" (201), thus presenting a Milton who is in the service of the narrative the critics are telling. But even if one argues that there is not a static or unified "Milton," does not Goldberg's conclusion also imply a critical narrative that he is telling?

35. For studies that argue for the headnote's politically radicalizing effect upon the ode, see Colin Burrow, "*Poems 1645*: The Future Poet," in *The Cambridge Companion to Milton,* ed. Dennis Danielson, 2nd ed. (Cambridge: Cambridge University Press, 1999), 54–69; Revard, *Milton and the Tangles of Neaera's Hair,* ch. 3; I. S. MacLaren, "Milton's Nativity Ode: The Function of Poetry and the Structures of Response in 1629," *Milton Studies* 15 (1981): 181–200.

36. See James Dougal Fleming, "Composing 1629," in *Milton's Legacy,* ed. Kristin A. Pruitt and Charles W. Durham (Selinsgrove, Pa.: Susquehanna University Press, 2005), 149–64. Fleming skillfully situates Milton's encomium within the genre of other Christmas poems written around 1629–30, nearly all of which assume a pro-Caroline stance, given Henrietta's miscarriage of the young prince in May 1629 and the birth of the future Charles II in May 1630. Fleming admits that the "Nativity" ode perhaps functions as Milton's reaction against the developing genre, but only problematically so, since the messianic imagery, the cessation of war, and the celestial music are ideologically consistent with pro-Caroline poetry.

On the ode as reactionary to the pro-Caroline Christmas genre, see Michael Wilding, *Dragon's Teeth: Literature in the English Revolution* (Oxford: Clarendon Press, 1987), 14; Barbara K. Lewalski, "How Radical Was the Young Milton?" in *Milton and Heresy,* 49–72.

37. *The Early Lives of Milton,* ed. Helen Darbishire (New York: Barnes and Noble, 1965), 61.

38. See William Ames, *The Marrow of Sacred Divinity* (London, 1642), originally published as *Medulla S. S. Theologicae, ex sacris literis, earumque, inter-*

pretibus, extracta, methodice disposita (Amsterdam, 1627; London, 1630). Ames is one of the two systematic theologians that Phillips mentions as having an influence on Milton. He begins with the essence of God, the attributes of God, the persons of the Trinity, and the meaning of the Father "begetting" the Son. The other theologian that Phillips mentions is Johannes Wollebius. See his *Compendium Theologiae Christianae* (1626), which similarly begins by explicating the essence of God, the persons of the Godhead, and the nature of God's decrees. Milton begins his Christology in Chapter Five of *De Doctrina Christiana*, but Wollebius does not address Christ's office or nature as the "God-man" until midway through the treatise. On the importance of Wollebius's systematic theology to Milton, see Maurice Kelley, "Milton's Debt to Wolleb's *Compendium Theologiae Christianae*," *PMLA* 50, no. 1 (March 1935): 156–65. Kelley notes that Wollebius's treatise is not mentioned in *De Doctrina Christiana*, so there is no corroborating external evidence, aside from Phillips's statement, that Milton looked to it as the best example. Nevertheless, Kelley convincingly argues that Milton's treatise is the heir of Wollebius's *Compendium*, based on a near-identical structure, sentences, the order of biblical citations, and theological arguments.

39. Revard, *Milton and the Tangles of Neaera's Hair*, ch. 3; Wilding, *Dragon's Teeth*, 14.

40. Evans, *The Miltonic Moment*, 17; emphasis original. Evans is, of course, not speaking of a literal conversion effected in the reader by encountering the poem, but this is precisely what I am suggesting is Milton's aim in his poetry of proclamation. Cf. Catherine Belsey, *John Milton: Language, Gender, Power* (Oxford: Blackwell, 1988). Belsey argues that the poem is a "redemptive text" (5), but does not elaborate what that redemption entails.

41. Thomas Edwards, *Gangraena, or A Catalogue and Discovery of many of the Errours, Heresies, Blasphemies and pernicious Practices of the Sectaries of this time* (London, 1646), 1:21.

42. Joseph Salmon, *Anti-christ in man, or, A discovery of the great whore that sits upon many waters wherein is declared what that whore or inward mystery is, together with the destruction thereof, by the powerfull appearing of Christ in us* (London, 1647), sig. A. 2v, 34, 47.

43. Belsey, *John Milton*, 3.

44. Wilding, *Dragon's Teeth*, 10–11. Wilding notes that while the first sentence of the superscription appears in the Trinity manuscript, the second sentence does not. On the biblical allusions, see David S. Berkeley, *Inwrought with Figures Dim: A Reading of Milton's "Lycidas"* (The Hague: Mouton, 1974),

33–34; Joseph A. Wittreich Jr., "'A Poet Amongst Poets': Milton and the Tradition of Prophecy," in *Milton and the Line of Vision*, ed. Joseph A. Wittreich Jr. (Madison: University of Wisconsin Press, 1975), 117–23; Lieb, *The Sinews of Ulysses*, ch. 5 (see full citation below, 324n19). In Haggai the LORD of Hosts promises, "Yet once, it is a little while and I will shake the heavens, and the earth, and the sea and the dry land." In this passage what passes away, as Lieb notes, is the "belief in and commitment to the old Temple as it is superseded by the new" (56). The writer of Hebrews, however, appropriates Haggai to reinscribe it within a New Testament framework, so that in Hebrews "what will pass away is the belief in and commitment to the old dispensation as it is superseded by the new, which in turn will provide a means of ultimate salvation." Lieb demonstrates that the writer of Hebrews embraces a "radical hermeneutic" by transforming Haggai's formulaic Hebrew phrase "*a'od achat m'at he*" into the reformulated "*to de eti hapax, deloi*," resulting in the shift in context toward the New Testament's eschatological vision of the Second Coming (58–59).

45. Cf. Milton, *An Apology Against a Pamphlet* (London, 1642). In his last anti-prelatical pamphlet, Milton responds to the anonymous writer, probably Bishop Joseph Hall, of *A Modest Confutation*. Milton counts himself among those who "nothing admire his Idol Bishoprick" (*CPW* 1:928–29).

46. John Bastwick, *The Letany of John Bastwick* (London, 1637), 3, 6–7.

47. Insightful scholarship by literary critics on the prolific pen of Lilburne include the following: David Loewenstein, *Representing Revolution in Milton and His Contemporaries: Religion, Politics, and Polemics in Radical Puritanism* (Cambridge: Cambridge University Press, 2001), ch. 1; Nigel Smith, *Literature and Revolution in England, 1640–1660* (New Haven: Yale University Press, 1994), ch. 4; Sharon Achinstein, *Milton and the Revolutionary Reader* (Princeton: Princeton University Press, 1994), ch. 1. The best biography is Pauline Gregg, *Free-born John: A Biography of John Lilburne* (London: Harrap, 1961).

48. John Lilburne, *A light for the ignorant* (London, 1638), 8, 15–16.

49. Bastwick, *Letany*, 11.

50. Joseph Hall, *An Humble Remonstrance to the High Court of Parliament* (London, 1640), 38.

51. Lieb, *Sinews of Ulysses*, 43–44.

52. The vestments of the priests were an object of scorn and satire by Puritans. See, for instance, William Prynne, *A Looking-Glasse for all Lordly Prelates* (London, 1636), 67–68, who spurns the ostentation of the vestments. Their "many silken, satin, scarlet, Gownes" are in contrast to the "thread-bare Coate" of Christ. See also Richard Overton, *Lambeth Faire* (London, 1641),

wherein these priestly vestments are hawked at auction, including the bishops themselves.

53. *Sermons of John Donne*, ed. George R. Potter and Evelyn M. Simpson, 10 vols. (Berkeley: University of California Press, 1953–62), 8:43–45.

54. See, for instance, James H. Hanford, "The Pastoral Elegy and Milton's *Lycidas*," in *Publications of the Modern Language Association* 25 (1910): 403–47. Reprinted in *Milton's Lycidas: The Tradition and the Poem*, ed. C. A. Patrides (New York: Holt, Rinehart and Winston, 1961), 27–55. Against this assessment, see J. M. French, "The Digressions in Milton's 'Lycidas,'" *SP* 50 (1953): 485–90.

55. See, for instance, Lewalski, *The Life of John Milton*, 70–71; Evans, *The Miltonic Moment*, ch. 3; Halpern, "The Great Instauration," 12; David Norbrook, *Poetry and Politics in the English Renaissance* (London: RKP, 1984), ch. 10; Tillyard, *Milton*, ch. 7.

56. Sigmund Freud, "Mourning and Melancholia," in *Collected Papers*, gen. trans. Joan Riviere, 5 vols. (London: Hogarth, 1957), 4:152–70; quotes from 155, 159, 154. My thanks to Christine Froula for helping me think about Milton's elegy in these terms.

57. See Hughes, headnotes 4–5 on the speech of Peter, and headnote 9 on the allusion to the myth. Cf. Natale Conti, *Mythologiae . . . Libri decem* (Frankfort, 1596), 922.

58. Cf. *PL* 4.183–93. In an epic simile, Satan leaps over the walls of paradise, "As when a prowling Wolf, / Whom hunger drives to seek new haunt for prey, / Watching where Shepherds pen thir Flocks at eve / . . . / Leaps o'er the fence with ease into the Fold: / . . . / So clomb this first grand Thief into God's Fold: / So since into his Church lewd Hirelings climb."

59. Lewalski, *The Life of John Milton*, 70.

60. On YHWH's similar "dodging" of Job's questions, see Jack Miles, *God: A Biography* (New York: Vintage, 1995), ch. 10.

61. See Rosemund Tuve, *Images and Themes* (Cambridge: Harvard University Press, 1957), 79.

62. See J. Auffret, "Pagano-Christian Syncretism in *Lycidas*," *Anglia* 87 (1969): 26–38. Auffret argues that the poem does not develop a strict Christian-Pagan opposition, but that the arcadian voices and complaints function as types or "half-truths" that find their fulfillment in the Christian mystery.

63. James K. A. Smith, *Introducing Radical Orthodoxy: Mapping a Post-Secular Theology* (Grand Rapids: Baker Academic, 2004), 76–77. See also Milbank, *Radical Orthodoxy*, 3.

64. Donald G. Marshall, "Truth, Universality, and Interpretation," in *Disciplining Hermeneutics: Interpretation in Christian Perspective,* ed. Roger Lundin (Grand Rapids: Eerdmans, 1997), 110.

65. *Sermons of John Donne,* 2:172.

Chapter 2. Infernal Prophesying

1. Thanks to Emily Bryan for noticing this typographical pun.

2. See John Leonard, "'Though of Thir Names': The Devils in *Paradise Lost,*" in *Milton Studies* 21, ed. James D. Simmonds (1985): 157–78, for a provocative essay on angelic names in *Paradise Lost.* His *Naming in Paradise* is a more extensive treatment. See also John Leonard, "Language and Knowledge in *Paradise Lost,*" in *Cambridge Companion to John Milton,* ed. Dennis Danielson (Cambridge: Cambridge University Press, 1999), 97–111, for a good introduction to Milton and his views of language.

3. See, for instance, the following contributions: Catherine Canino, "The Discourse of Hell: *Paradise Lost* and the Irish Rebellion," *Milton Quarterly* 32, no. 1 (1998): 15–23, supplies us with a fascinating glimpse into Milton's relations with the Irish after the Irish Rebellion of 1641; Todd H. Sammons, "Ciceronian Inventio and Dispositio in Belial's Speech during the Debate in Hell," *Milton Quarterly* 25, no. 1 (1991): 14–22, explores Belial as Ciceronian orator in conjunction with Thomas Wilson's *The Arte of Rhetorique* (1560); Robert Thomas Fallon, *Captain or Colonel: The Soldier in Milton's Life and Art* (Columbia: University of Missouri Press, 1984), 156–64, finds parallels with Cromwell's exchange with the Earl of Manchester; and E. H. Visiak, *The Portent of Milton: Some Aspects of His Genius* (London: W. Laurie, 1958), 116, argues that the debates in hell reflect speeches in Parliament.

4. Thomas Cogswell, "The Politics of Propaganda: Charles I and the People in the 1620s," *Journal of British Studies* 29 (1990): 187–215; quote from 196. Cogswell quoted in Jeanne Shami, *John Donne and Conformity in Crisis in the Late Jacobean Pulpit* (Cambridge: D. S. Brewer, 2003), 4.

5. Shami, *John Donne and Conformity in Crisis,* 4. For insightful readings of how Jacobean preachers "repackaged" such political incidents as the accession of James VI and the Gunpowder Plot, see Lori Anne Ferrell, *Government by Polemic: James I, the King's Preachers, and the Rhetoric of Conformity, 1603–1625* (Stanford: Stanford University Press, 1998), chs. 2–3.

6. William Perkins, *Of the Calling of the Ministerie* (London, 1605), 7.

7. Joad Raymond, *Milton's Angels: The Early-Modern Imagination* (Oxford: Oxford University Press, 2010), 84–124.

8. Lares, *Milton and the Preaching Arts,* 153.

9. Heiko Oberman, "Reformation, Preaching, and *Ex Opere Operato,*" in *Christianity Divided: Protestant and Roman Catholic Theological Issues,* ed. Daniel Callahan, Heiko Oberman, and Daniel J. O'Hanlon, S.J. (New York: Sheed and Ward, 1964), 223–39. Originally published as "Preaching and the Word in the Reformation," *Theology Today* 18 (1961): 16–29.

10. Ibid., 225; emphasis original.

11. Quoted in ibid., 232.

12. Hillier, *Milton's Messiah,* 66.

13. Donne, *The Sermons of John Donne,* 3:87.

14. Ames, *The Marrow of Sacred Divinity,* 3, 143; Perkins, *Of the Calling of the Ministerie,* 17, 10.

15. *The Sermons of John Donne,* 8:52.

16. This is, of course, the ideal. See Martha Tuck Rozett, *The Doctrine of Election and the Emergence of Elizabethan Tragedy* (Princeton: Princeton University Press, 1984), 15–25. Rozett explains that ministers, especially when confronted with preaching before a large crowd or in the open air, were often met with disruptive behavior from the audience. Business transactions were made, jokes and "water-cooler" gossip were exchanged, children were reprehended for fussing or playing noisily about, and particularly dull preachers were heckled. Far from being a sacred and transformative encounter, sermon gatherings were frequently seen as social occasions with congregants departing without substantial transformation. For preachers voicing their frustrations, see the comments of George Gifford, *A sermon on the parable of the sower* (London, 1582), sig. Avii; George Herbert, *The Priest to the Temple, or The Countery Parson* (London, 1652), 22.

17. William Haller, *The Rise of Puritanism, Or, The Way to the New Jerusalem as Set Forth in Pulpit and Press from Thomas Cartwright to John Lilburn and John Milton, 1570–1643* (New York: Columbia University Press, 1938), 258.

18. Christopher Durston and Jacqueline Eales, eds., *The Culture of English Puritanism, 1560–1700* (New York: St. Martin's, 1996), 20.

19. For more on "gadding," see Patrick Collinson, *The Religion of Protestants: The Church in English Society 1559–1625* (Oxford: Clarendon, 1982), ch. 6. For a revisionist account of "gadding," see Christopher Haigh, "The Taming of Reformation: Preachers, Pastors and Parishioners in Elizabethan and Early Stuart England," *History* 85 (2000): 572–88.

20. Bryan Crockett, *The Play of Paradox: Stage and Sermon in Renaissance England* (Philadelphia: University of Pennsylvania Press, 1995), 38.

21. For more on the shared audience of the pulpit and playhouse, see Rozett, *The Doctrine of Election*, 15–25.

22. For the classic study on the subject, consult Debora K. Shuger, *Sacred Rhetoric: The Christian Grand Style in the English Renaissance* (Princeton: Princeton University Press, 1988).

23. See John Milbank, "Suspending the Material: The Turn of Radical Orthodoxy," in *Radical Orthodoxy: A New Theology*, ed. John Milbank, Catherine Pickstock, and Graham Ward (London: Routledge, 1999), 1–20. Milbank and the other contributors to the volume reassess the doctrine of participation within postmodern categories.

24. Smith, *Speech and Theology*, 123. See also Jean-Luc Marion, *Idol and Distance: Five Studies* (New York: Fordham University Press, 2001).

25. John Spittlehouse, *The first addresses to His Excellencie the Lord General, with the Assembly of elders elected by him and his Council for the management of the affairs of this Commonwealth; as also, to all the cordial officers and souldiers under his command. Containing certain rules & directions how to advance the kingdome of Jesus Christ over the face of the whole earth* (London, 1653), 13.

26. Peter Fiore, *Milton and Augustine: Patterns of Augustinian Thought in Paradise Lost* (University Park: Pennsylvania State University Press, 1981), 11.

27. I am thankful to Scott Huelin for this point.

28. Augustine, *On Christian Doctrine*, 4.2.3; 4.15.32.

29. Bernard, *The Faithfull Shepheard*, 13.

30. Augustine, *On Christian Doctrine*, 4.30.63.

31. Ibid., 4.1.2.

32. See Augustine, *De Magistro*, in *Augustine: Earlier Writings*, trans. John H. S. Burleigh (Philadelphia: Westminster, 1953). In this dialogue with his son, Adeodatus, Augustine suggests that every word is a sign (2.3) and that speaking is the giving of signs (1.2). This conclusion, however, poses a logical puzzle for Augustine and Adeodatus that they are unable to resolve. Augustine quotes Virgil (*Si nihil ex tanta superis placet urbe relinqui*) and asks how many signs there are (eight: each word a sign), and then Adeodatus says that "*Nihil* signifies simply what is not." Augustine responds that "what is not cannot be something. So the second word in the verse is not a sign, because it does not signify something" (2.3).

33. Augustine, *On Christian Doctrine*, 2.28.

34. Bernard, *The Faithfull Shepheard*, 36, 25, 87.

35. Herbert, *A Priest to the Temple*, 10, 22–24.

36. John Preston, *Sinnes Overthrow: Or, A Godlie and Learned Treatise on Mortification* (London, 1635), 102–4.

37. Bartimaeus Andrewes, *Certaine Verie worthie, godly and profitable . . . Sermons* (London, 1586), 26–27.

38. William Dell, *Power from on high, or, The power of the Holy Ghost dispersed through the whole body of Christ, and communicated to each member according to its place and use in that body* (London, 1645), 18. Despite his reservations about university learning, Dell was master of Gonville and Caius College, Cambridge. See N. H. Keeble, *The Literary Culture of Nonconformity in Later Seventeenth-Century England* (Athens: University of Georgia Press, 1987), esp. ch. 5. Keeble points out that the impulse from Puritans was toward educational reform and not its abolition; what Dell and others like him objected to was a perceived tendency among the clergy toward a kind of Scholasticism.

39. Dell, *The tryal of spirits both in teachers and hearers wherein is held forth the clear discovery and certain downfal of the carnal and anti-Christian clergy of these nations* (London, 1653), Epistle Dedicatory, 3.

40. Samuel How, *The sufficiencie of the spirits teaching, without humane-learning: or A treatise, tending to proue humane-learning to be no help to the spirituall understanding of the Word of God* (London, 1640), sig. B2, B3, C1.

41. Shuger, *Sacred Rhetoric*, 70. For more on architecture and church aesthetics, consult Jack Bowyer, *The Evolution of Church Building* (London: Crosby Lockwood Staples, 1977). On iconoclasm, see John Phillips, *The Reformation of Images: The Destruction of Art in England, 1335–1660* (Berkeley: University of California Press, 1973).

42. How, *The sufficiencie of the spirits teaching*, sig. D2, D3.

43. William Perkins, *Satans Sophistrie Answered by Our Saviour Christ* (London, 1604), 94, 33, 72.

44. William Perkins, *The Combat Betweene Christ and the Deuill displayed: or, a Commentarie upon the Temptations of Christ* (London, 1606), 30–31.

45. John Morgan, *Godly Learning* (Cambridge: Cambridge University Press, 1986), 99; emphasis original.

46. Perkins, *Satans Sophistrie*, 15.

47. Ibid., 29.

48. Stanley Fish, *How Milton Works* (Cambridge: Harvard University Press, 2001), 122, 118–119; emphasis original. Oddly, however, Fish comments that Milton's rejecting external rhetorical rules and exempla results in an "anti-aesthetic," where "eloquence is disjoined from speech." Moreover, this eloquence

"need have no visible form at all, no particular manifestation," but exists in an "ever-present potential." But do not language and speech serve a crucial and necessary function in the preacher's "infusing" those "good things"? Does Fish lead us to conclude that Milton embraces a dualist aesthetics, wherein the beauty of the carnal and the beauty of the spiritual are in competition? If the God-man is Milton's (and Augustine's) model preacher and performer, what good is "potential" charity without "particular manifestation"? The God-man *is* God's speech in action; his interpretation, or "eloquent visible form," *is* performance; his life *is* narrative. Fish would likely agree, but he is being a little less than careful here when he "disjoins" eloquence and speech. To the contrary, Milton the "Church-outed" poet-preacher insists on and is invested in a material-spiritual aesthetic of the highest order, where the True, the Good, and the Beautiful converge and shine forth with the same integrity they do at the Incarnation.

49. Fallon, "The Metaphysics of Milton's Divorce Tracts," in *Politics, Poetics, and Hermeneutics in Milton's Prose*, 69.

50. Ibid., 75.

51. See Loewenstein, *Representing Revolution*, 180–201.

52. Lares, *Milton and the Preaching Arts*, 159.

53. See Peter Lake, *The Boxmaker's Revenge: "Orthodoxy," "Heterodoxy" and the Politics of the Parish in Early Stuart London* (Stanford: Stanford University Press, 2001), 56. Denison's flair could, at times, backfire. When he was occupied in the vestry following one of his sermons, one Mistress Rose Law assumed the pulpit to parody the preacher for her friends, causing such laughter that Denison rushed back into the sanctuary to witness her make "an immodest and unseemly gesture, not fit to be used in the church." Not surprisingly, the incident spurred a church court case in March 1617.

54. Ibid., 53.

55. Herbert, *The Priest to the Temple*, 5.

56. For more on ancient models of language theory, consult Stephen Everson, *Language: Companions to Ancient Thought*, vol. 3 (Cambridge: Cambridge University Press, 1994). Everson remarks that the "explanation of our linguistic abilities is taken to require an account of concept-possession, and this, in turn, requires a particular theory of the world which will allow the subject to acquire the concepts needed for the understanding of language" (6). Language theory is linked to epistemology and metaphysics.

This is certainly the case for Plato and Aristotle. For the former, language functions to reveal the Forms (*Phaedo* 78c–79d), and any statement, whether true or false, involves notions of being and participation. The Sophist poses such an insidious danger because sophistical language is language that discloses nothing ("no-thing") and reduces language to a game of manipulation without regard for the Truth of the Forms (*Sophist* 259e–260). Sophistical language for Plato is language suspended over the void; rather than participating in the unchanging realm of the eternal Forms, and hence meaningful and ultimately disclosive of reality, Plato argues, sophistical language is in constant flux and characterized by aggression. We might anachronistically say that in a "Platonic" version of "satanic" language, the Sophist both "says and unsays" in the same utterance; like Milton's Satan, the Sophist appears to promise disclosure, but manipulates and hides instead.

While Aristotle fundamentally disagrees with his teacher on the nature of the Forms (*Nichomachean Ethics*, 1.4.1096a), he affirms (*De Interpretatione*; *Posterior Analytics*, 92b–93a) that the proper end of language is to reveal the essence of a particular object or concept; therefore, a "satanic" rhetorician, one who does not have an understanding of a sign's existence and/or essence, thus threatens to unravel the fabric of reality. Existence and essence confer genuine knowledge, and without them names remain significant but empty. Consequently, in an Aristotelian version of "satanic" language, one in which the speaker does not have the essential knowledge of an object, we can only "say and straight unsay"; the speaker summarily invokes a name only to revoke it in the same utterance because he does not *know* it. Without this essential knowledge, argues Aristotle, the world is reduced to nothing more than a beautiful lie told by a "son of thunder" of a different sort. He is one who knows of its existence because he hears the din of its roar in the clouds above, but because he does not know its essence, he can only spin clever mythologies about it while relying on his own performance in the telling.

57. Christopher Kirwan, "Augustine's Philosophy of Language," in *Cambridge Companion to Augustine*, ed. Eleanor Stump and Norman Kretzmann (Cambridge: Cambridge University Press, 2001), 186–204; quote from 186.

58. Augustine, *On Christian Doctrine*, 1.13.12.

59. Ibid., 1.14.13; 1.15.14.

60. Ibid., 1.16.15.

61. Augustine, *The Enchiridion on Faith, Hope, and Love*, trans. J. F. Shaw (Chicago: Regnery Gateway, 1961), §22.

62. See Lares, *Milton and the Preaching Arts*, 1–15 and 56–80, for a good introduction to classical rhetoric and a treatment of Protestant sermon manuals.

63. Ibid., 61–62. Cf. William Chappell, *The Preacher, or the Art and Method of Preaching* (London, 1656). Chappell collapses correction and

instruction to maintain four categories: instruction (of doctrine), refutation, reprehension, and consolation, the latter two often twinned together.

64. Lares, *Milton and the Preaching Arts,* 146. See chs. 4 and 5 for her rendering the angelic discourses of Books 5 and 12 in *Paradise Lost* according to these sermon types, and her argument that Christ is corrective preacher in *Paradise Regained.*

65. Perkins, "A Godly and Learned Exposition Upon the whole Epistle of Jude," in *Workes,* 3:520.

66. John M. Steadman, *Milton's Epic Characters: Image and Idol* (Chapel Hill: University of North Carolina Press, 1968), 242; emphasis original.

67. Raymond, *Milton's Angels,* 218.

68. See, for instance, Raymond A. Mentzer, "The Synod in the Reformed Tradition," in *Synod and Synodality: Theology, History, Canon Law, and Ecumenism in New Contact,* ed. Alberto Melloni and Sylvia Scatena (London: Transaction Publishers, 2005), 173–86.

69. G. T., *The method of a synod, or a rationall and sure way to compose and settle the differences and controversies in religion to the contentment of honest and wise men* (London, 1642), sig. B1, B2.

70. For more on the demons as dissenters, see Bryan Adams Hampton, "'new Lawes thou see'st impos'd': Milton's Dissenting Angels and the Clarendon Code, 1661–65," in *Paradise Lost: A Poem Written in Ten Books: Essays on the 1667 First Edition,* ed. John Shawcross and Michael Lieb (Pittsburgh: Duquesne University Press, 2007), 141–58.

71. The exchange is reprinted in Patrick Collinson, *Godly People: Essays on English Protestantism and Puritanism* (London: Hambledon, 1983), 91–106; quotes from 92, 96, 99–100.

72. Quoted in Patrick Collinson, *The Elizabethan Puritan Movement* (Berkeley: University of California Press, 1967), 192.

73. Patrick Collinson, *Archbishop Grindal 1519–1583: The Struggle for a Reformed Church* (London: Jonathan Cape, Ltd., 1979), 16.

74. Collinson, *The Elizabethan Puritan Movement,* 195.

75. Collinson, *Archbishop Grindal,* 104–5.

76. Collinson, *Godly People,* 175.

77. Collinson, *The Elizabethan Puritan Movement,* 175.

78. Ibid., 179.

79. For more on the various ways in which invectives between Catholics and Protestants, and between factions of Protestants, shaped religious discourse, impacted public policy, and intensified paranoia especially during the

Jacobean and Carolingian reigns, see Anthony Milton, *Catholic and Reformed* (Cambridge: Cambridge University Press, 1995).

80. Collinson, *Godly People,* 474–77.

81. On the multivalent groups included in the terms "dissenter" and "Church of England," see John Miller, *After the Civil Wars: English Politics and Government in the Reign of Charles II* (New York: Longman, 2000), 133, 145–46.

82. Christopher Hill, *The World Turned Upside Down* (New York: Penguin, 1985), 104.

83. Dell, *Several Sermons and Discourses of William Dell, Minister of the Gospel; . . . Heretofore published at several times, . . . and now gathered in one volume* (London, 1709), 273.

84. George Fox, *The Journal of George Fox,* rev. ed. by John L. Nickalls (Philadelphia: Religious Society of Friends, 1997), 33.

85. On the numbers of ministers affected by the Act of Uniformity, see Keeble, *The Literary Culture of Nonconformity,* 31–32; Keeble acknowledges that historians have confirmed Richard Baxter's own estimate that 1800 to 2000 ministers were silenced or ejected.

86. Edwards, *Gangraena,* 1:19; for more on the "anti-scripturists," see Christopher Hill, *The English Bible and the Seventeenth-Century Revolution* (London: Penguin, 1993), 223–38.

87. Gary S. De Krey, "Radicals, Reformers, and Republicans: Academic Language and Political Discourse in Restoration London," in *A Nation Transformed: England after the Restoration,* ed. Alan Houston and Steve Pincus (Cambridge: Cambridge University Press, 2001), 71–99; quotation from 81. See also his "Rethinking the Restoration: Dissenting Cases of Conscience, 1667–1672," *Historical Journal* 38, no. 1 (1995): 53–83.

88. Ames, *The Marrow of Sacred Divinity,* 23.

89. Michael Lieb, *Poetics of the Holy* (Chapel Hill: University of North Carolina Press, 1981), 178–79.

90. F. S. Donns, *YaHWeH: The Significance of the Unique Name of God* (Berkeley: Bacchus, 1986), 3.

91. *The Interpreter's Dictionary of the Bible,* 4 vols. (New York: Abingdon, 1962), 2:408.

92. John Calvin, *Commentaries on the Last Four Books of Moses,* vol. 1 (Edinburgh: Calvin Translation Society, 1852), 73.

93. Lieb, *Poetics of the Holy,* 175–76. Cf. Henry Ainsworth, *Annotations Upon the Five Books of Moses* (London, 1639), 10; Matthew Poole, *Annotations upon the Holy Bible* (London, 1683), I:sig. P6^r; Milton, *CPW* 6:138–44.

94. See Blair Worden, "The Question of Secularization," in *A Nation Transformed: England after the Restoration*, ed. Alan Houston and Steve Pincus (Cambridge: Cambridge University Press, 2001), 20–70. Worden argues that the latter half of the seventeenth century saw an increasingly secular notion of conscience, as "less a property leased to me by God, on his terms" and "more a property of my own" (31).

95. Edwards, *Gangraena*, 1:123.

96. Chappell, *The Preacher*, 184.

97. Ibid., 182.

98. Fish, *How Milton Works*, 90.

99. Thanks to David Ainsworth for this point.

100. For more on these mechanic preachers, see Hill, *The World Turned Upside Down*, ch. 14.

101. Stanley Fish, *Surprised by Sin: The Reader in Paradise Lost*, 2nd ed. (Cambridge: Harvard University Press, 1997), 95–96.

102. Dustin Griffin, "Milton's Hell: Perspectives on the Fallen," *Milton Studies* 13, ed. James D. Simmons (1979): 237–54; quote from 238.

103. Raymond, *Milton's Angels*, 171.

104. Ludwig Wittgenstein, *Philosophical Investigations*, trans. G. E. Anscombe, 2nd ed. (Oxford: Blackwell, 2000), §19, §28.

105. Ludwig Wittgenstein, *The Blue and Brown Books* (Oxford: Blackwell, 1972), 28, 67–68.

106. Fergus Kerr, *Theology After Wittgenstein* (Oxford: Blackwell, 1986), 69.

107. See ibid., 29. Kerr notes that there is a great deal of disagreement among philosophers about what Wittgenstein means by this phrase. He suggests that in *Philosophical Investigations* §19, Wittgenstein asks us to "imagine a community in which giving and obeying orders would be the only 'system of communication' required: something much less than *we* call language." The idea that "form of life" refers to culture, continues Kerr, is again explored in Wittgenstein's earlier *Blue and Brown Books*, where Wittgenstein states, "We could easily imagine a language (and that means again a culture) in which there existed no common expression for light blue and dark blue" (134).

108. Cf. Levinas, *Totality and Infinity*.

109. Fish, *How Milton Works*, 92.

110. Ibid., 91.

111. Hauerwas, *A Community of Character*, 97.

Chapter 3. The Greatest Metaphor of Our Religion

1. Gregory of Nyssa, *Life of Moses*, 2:19–20; reprinted in Stephen E. Fowl, ed., *The Theological Interpretation of Scripture* (Oxford: Blackwell, 1997), 109.

2. Strictly speaking, John's assertion is not a metaphor, for "the Word *was made* flesh" is different from "the Word *is* flesh." While this technical distinction may be cause for demur, the debates in the Christological tradition demonstrate an overwhelming sensitivity to the structure of John's formulation and the implications of joining the two disparate terms together.

3. Stanley Hauerwas, *Truthfulness and Tragedy: Further Investigations in Christian Ethics* (Notre Dame: University of Notre Dame Press, 1977), 73.

4. *Anchor Bible Dictionary*, gen. ed. David Noel Freedman (New York: Doubleday, 1992), 961.

5. Thorlief Bowman, *Hebrew Thought Compared with Greek* (Philadelphia: Westminster, 1960), 66.

6. *Anchor Bible Dictionary*, 963. This dynamic, namely, obedience-blessing/rebellion-destruction, is of particular importance to the Deuteronomic writers, but is the subject of critique by the writers of Job and Ecclesiastes, for whom there exists no necessary relation between the one and the other.

7. Bernard J. Lee, *Jesus and the Metaphors of God: The Christs of the New Testament* (New York: Paulist, 1993), 110.

8. The classic study is C. H. Dodd, *The Interpretation of the Fourth Gospel* (Cambridge: Cambridge University Press, 1953); cf. David T. Runia, *Philo in Early Christian Literature* (Minneapolis: Fortress, 1993), 78–83.

9. Philo of Alexandria, *De Vita Mosis*, 2.127; quoted in David Winston, *Logos and Mystical Theology in Philo of Alexandria* (Cincinnati: Hebrew Union College Press, 1984), 17. For a more detailed exposition of Philo's doctrine of creation, the difficulties it presents, and Philo's debt to Plato's *Timaeus*, see David T. Runia, *Philo of Alexandria and the Timaeus of Plato* (Leiden: Brill, 1986).

10. See Winston, *Logos and Mystical Theology in Philo of Alexandria*, 28. Winston notes that in his treatise on creation, *De Opificio Mundi*, Philo calls the human mind the "imprint," "fragment," and "effulgence" of the Logos (146).

11. See ibid., 15. Winston observes that although "word" (*logoi*) and "wisdom" (*sophiai*) are not interchangeable in the Hebrew Bible, the "Jewish Hellenistic wisdom literature employed the term 'Wisdom' synonymously with the 'word of God,'" and "it was only natural for Philo to use that term too as the equivalent of Logos" (cf. Wisd. of Sol. 9:1–2).

12. Lee, *Jesus and the Metaphors of God*, 153.

13. Dodd, *The Interpretation of the Fourth Gospel*, 278.

14. Aloys Grillmeier, S.J., *Christ in Christian Tradition: From the Apostolic Age to Chalcedon (451)*, trans. J. S. Bowden (London: A. R. Mowbray & Co., 1964), 34.

15. William Shullenberger, "Doctrine as Deep Structure in Milton's Early Poetry," in *A Fine Tuning: Studies of the Religious Poetry of Herbert and Milton*, ed. Mary A. Maleski (Binghamton, N.Y.: Medieval and Renaissance Texts and Studies, 1989), 187–203.

16. Quoted in J. N. D. Kelly, *Early Christian Doctrines*, 5th ed. (London: Continuum, 1977), 140.

17. Ibid., 118.

18. See Thomas Aquinas, *Summa Contra Gentiles*, 4.28.2–5; 4.4. Aquinas argues that Paul's position "destroys the Incarnation's mystery. For according to this position, God would not have assumed flesh to become man; rather, an earthly man would have become God. Thus the saying of John (1:14) would not be true: 'The Word was made flesh'; on the contrary, flesh would have been made Word. In the same way, also, emptying Himself and descent would not fit the Son of God; rather, glorification and ascent would fit man."

19. For more on the tradition of *kenosis* and how Milton uses the metaphor of attire in his work as a *kenotic* aesthetic, see Michael Lieb, *The Sinews of Ulysses: Form and Convention in Milton's Works* (Pittsburgh: Duquesne University Press, 1989), ch. 2.

See also William B. Hunter, "Milton on the Incarnation," in *Bright Essence*, 131–48. Fascinatingly, Hunter points to the "false incarnations" of the pagan gods who "forsake their temples dim" in the "Nativity" ode (197), and Satan's inhabiting the Serpent in *Paradise Lost*, 9.165–66, where Satan is "mixt with bestial slime, / This essence to incarnate."

20. See Barbara Kiefer Lewalski, *Milton's Brief Epic: The Genre, Meaning, and Art of Paradise Regained* (Providence, R.I.: Brown University Press, 1966), ch. 6. Situating Milton's Jesus of *Paradise Regained* within the Arian variation of the Word-man framework, Lewalski asserts, "[f]or the encounter between Christ and Satan to constitute a genuine dramatic action and a real conflict, Christ's character must be conceived in such a way that the test or temptation is real: he must be able to fall, must be capable of growth, and must be genuinely (not just apparently) uncertain of himself" (135).

21. See Kelly, *Early Christian Doctrines*, 306–8. Theodore allows there to be two distinct natures, though "the two natures are, through their connexion,

apprehended to be one reality." Christ is thus two natures, but one person—a formulation that appears to be in agreement with the orthodox one decided at Chalcedon. But as Kelly observes, "By *prosopon* he did not mean Person in the full Chalcedonian sense, but rather the external presentation of a reality which might be two fold (e.g. soul and body). His doctrine was, not that Christ was a third *prosopon* effected by the union of the *prosopa* of the Word and the man, but that the indwelling Word imparted his own *prosopon* to the man in indissoluble, ineffable union." Theodore quoted in ibid., 306–7.

22. Ibid., 313.

23. Quoted in Grillmeier, *Christ in Christian Tradition*, 187.

24. Apollinarius quoted in Kelly, *Early Christian Doctrines*, 291–92. On orthodox responses to Apollinarius, see ibid., 296–301. Apollinarius's one-sided solution is precisely what the Cappadocian fathers objected to, citing that Apollinarius's "metaphor" erred too far in one direction, which resulted in several soteriological blunders. If Christ was not a real man by assuming a real human soul, they argued in response, then several consequences follow, all of which have implications for Christ's performance in the world, and hence the believer's appropriation of it. First, Christ did not really suffer in the flesh, but merely appeared to suffer, echoing the heresy of the Docetists. Second, Christ did not really exhibit free will since he could choose no other than what the Logos prompted in his flesh. Third, Christ could not be called "man" at all since he lacked the defining essence of the human creature, the rational soul—an omission that left one to think that Christ was in some way monstrous. Fourth, and perhaps most important, this lack led to the conclusion that human beings cannot be truly saved, for Christ must take upon him all the characteristics of manhood to fully redeem humanity.

25. Grillmeier, *Christ in Christian Tradition*, 483.

26. The Chalcedonian Definition is translated in ibid., 481.

27. Paul Ricoeur, "On Interpretation," trans. Kathleen Blamey, in *From Text to Action: Essays in Hermeneutics* (Evanston: Northwestern University Press, 1991), 8.

28. To be sure, the fourteenth chapter of the first book, "OF MAN'S RESTORATION AND OF CHRIST THE REDEEMER," which deals with the Incarnation, is one of the shortest chapters in the entire treatise. We are instructed, instead, to refer to the lengthy fifth chapter, "OF THE SON OF GOD," which endeavors to clarify nothing regarding the Incarnation, but rather expounds on the unequal relationship between and distinct essences of the Father and the Son.

29. Milton copiously pleads to preserve a sense of mystery: "As this is such a great mystery, let its very magnitude put us on our guard from the outset"; "We should be afraid to pry into things further than we were meant"; "We do not know how it is so, and it is best for us to be ignorant of things which God wishes to remain secret"; "As for his natures themselves, they constitute in my opinion too deep a mystery for anyone to say anything definite about them" (*CPW* 6:421, 424, 427).

30. See Ulreich, "'Substantially Express'd,'" in *Milton Studies* 39. See also Kenneth Borris, "Milton's Heterodoxy of the Incarnation and Subjectivity in *De Doctrina Christiana* and *Paradise Lost*," in *Living Texts: Interpreting Milton,* ed. Kristin A. Pruitt and Charles W. Durham (Selinsgrove, Pa.: Susquehanna University Press, 2000), 264–82. Other significant contributions to the discourse, with particular reference to *Paradise Regained,* include the following: William B. Hunter, "Milton on the Incarnation," 131–48, argues for Milton's orthodoxy in *Paradise Lost,* but asserts that the heterodoxy of the Incarnation in *De Doctrina Christiana* is Nestorian; Hugh MacCallum, *Milton and the Sons of God: The Divine Image in Milton's Epic Poetry* (Toronto: University of Toronto Press, 1986), 210–15, places Milton's Christology in the context of Reformed theology, and examines *Paradise Regained* as a "dramatic and aesthetic" adaptation of the views formulated in *De Doctrina Christiana*; Barbara Kiefer Lewalski, *Milton's Brief Epic: The Genre, Meaning, and Art of "Paradise Regained"* (Providence, R.I.: Brown University Press, 1966), ch. 6, suggests that Milton's formulation of the doctrine escapes many of the common Christological positions, but urges that Milton's doctrine has some affinity with Monophysitism, Monotheletism, and Arianism.

31. Aristotle, *Metaphysics,* trans. Hugh Tredennick, 2 vols., Loeb Classical Library (Cambridge: Harvard University Press, 1933–35), 1:5.4.7.

32. Ulreich, "Substantially Express'd," in *Milton Studies* 39, 105; emphasis original. Cf. Borris, "Milton's Heterodoxy of the Incarnation," 269. Borris concurs, but does not acknowledge, Ulreich's conclusions: "according to the Christology of *De Doctrina* . . . the Son thus partakes as fully as possible of what it is to be human being and becomes head of humankind in terms of that specific human identity."

33. Martin Heidegger, Gadamer's teacher, was much taken with this listening hermeneutic. See Heidegger, "The Nature of Language," in *On the Way to Language,* trans. Peter Hertz (New York: Harper, 1971), 57–58. See also Gerald Bruns, *Hermeneutics: Ancient and Modern* (New Haven: Yale Uni-

versity Press, 1992), ch. 7. Bruns suggests that Heidegger was influenced by Martin Luther's distinction between the letter and the spirit of the text.

34. Quoted in Ulreich, "Substantially Express'd," in *Milton Studies* 39, 109. Cf. Origen, *On First Principles*, trans. G. W. Butterworth (Gloucester, Mass.: Harper & Row, 1973), 4.4. For more on the doctrinal similarities between Milton and Origen, see Harry F. Robbins, *"If This Be Heresy": A Study of Milton and Origen* (Urbana: University of Illinois Press, 1963), esp. ch. 4.

35. Edwards, *Gangraena*, 1:21.

36. Ulreich, "Substantially Express'd," in *Milton Studies* 39, 114. For Ulreich's application of this statement with regard to Milton's Jesus in *Paradise Regained*, see esp. 114–18.

37. See Lewalski, *Milton's Brief Epic*, 153. Milton's view of the hypostatic union "assumes a unification much more complete and total than even the orthodox theory provides for." This is so because Milton rejects the orthodox position represented by Hieronymus Zanchius: "He took upon him not, strictly speaking, man, he [Zanchius] writes, but the human nature. *For when the Logos was in the virgin's womb, it took human nature upon itself by forming a body for itself out of the substance of Mary, and at the same time creating a soul for that body"* (*CPW* 6:422). Milton criticizes Zanchius for his intellectual hubris, voicing that this conclusion is nowhere stated in the Bible, and that Zanchius expounds these mysteries as if he himself were present in the womb. For Milton, one cannot abstract "man" from "human nature," and to do so constitutes an "absurd idea": "For human nature, that is, the form of man contained in flesh, must, at the very moment when it comes into existence, bring a man into existence too, and a whole man, with no part of his essence or his subsistence (if that word signifies anything) or his personality missing" (*CPW* 6:422).

38. Hillier, *Milton's Messiah*, 26–27.

39. On this point, see also Phillip J. Donnelly, *"Paradise Regained* as Rule of Charity," *Milton Studies* 44 (2004): 171–97; see esp. 183–85.

40. Jakob Böhme, *The fifth book of the authour, in three parts the first, Of the becoming man or incarnation of Jesus Christ, the Sonne of God, that is, concerning the Virgin Mary . . . and how the Eternal word is become man: the second part is of Christ's suffering, dying, death, and resurrection . . . : the third part is of The tree of Christian faith . . .* (London, 1659), 1.1.

41. See Raymond, *Milton's Angels*, ch. 5.

42. Böhme, *Of the becoming man or incarnation of Jesus Christ*, 1.12.

43. Ibid., 1.7, 14.

44. Ibid., 1.34–35, 24–25.

45. Ibid., 1.89–90, 42.

46. Stephen M. Fallon, *Milton Among the Philosophers: Poetry and Materialism in Seventeenth-Century England* (Ithaca: Cornell University Press, 1991), 102–7, places Milton's monism within the "animist materialism" of the seventeenth century, and draws a connection to Thomas Hobbes; Christopher Kendrick, *Milton: A Study in Ideology and Form* (New York: Methuen, 1986), asserts *in passim* that Milton's monism is both "static" and "open-ended"; moreover, his monism allows the soul an ultimate freedom that finds its economic analogue in the emergent capitalism of *Areopagitica*; William Kerrigan, *The Sacred Complex: On the Psychogenesis of "Paradise Lost"* (Cambridge: Harvard University Press, 1983), 193–262, explores the bodiliness of angelic beings in conjunction with knowledge as nourishing food; and John Rogers, *The Matter of Revolution: Science, Poetry, and Politics in the Age of Milton* (Ithaca: Cornell University Press, 1996), 103–76, brings Milton's monism in line with the revolutionary vitalist movement in the mid- to late 1640s, asserting that inchoate traces of Milton's monism can be detected in the divorce pamphlets (1643–45) and *Areopagitica* (1644). See also Stephen M. Fallon, "The Metaphysics of Milton's Divorce Tracts," in *Politics, Poetics, and Hermeneutics in Milton's Prose,* ed. David Loewenstein and James Grantham Turner (Cambridge: Cambridge University Press, 1990), 69–83.

47. We must be careful in our language here. I say "tendency" or "strain" because sin is always a present reality for Milton, unlike for the Ranters, for instance, for whom "all things are pure to the pure." Moreover, the author of *De Doctrina Christiana* makes a distinction between "incomplete glorification" and "complete glorification." While believers are adopted as "sons of God," and share a special kinship with the Son whose "substance" has been purified, the latter "is unattainable in this life" (*CPW* 6:514). Complete glorification "consists in eternal and utterly happy life, arising chiefly from the sight of God" (*CPW* 6:530).

48. Fox, *The Journal of George Fox,* 27–28, 367.

49. Ibid., 27–28.

50. Kendrick, *Milton: A Study in Ideology and Form,* 182–83.

51. Hillier, *Milton's Messiah,* ch. 3, esp. 61–64.

52. Thanks to Phillip J. Donnelly for pointing this distinction out to me.

53. Cf. Richard Parr, *The End of the Perfect Man* (London, 1628). In a funeral sermon delivered upon the death of Sir Robert Spenser, Parr, 9,

asserts that good works make election certain, "For howsoever good works are no meriting causes, yet they are witnessing, effects or assurances of *salvatio*."

54. See Aristotle, *Nichomachean Ethics,* trans. Hippocrates G. Apostle (Grinnell, Iowa: Peripatetic, 1984), 2.1103a–3b: "In the case of the virtues, on the other hand, we acquire them as a result of prior activities; and this is like the case of the arts, for that which we are to perform by art after learning, we first learn by performing. . . . Similarly, we become just by doing what is just, temperate by doing what is temperate, and brave by doing brave deeds."

55. Emmanuel Katongole, *Beyond Universal Reason: The Relation Between Religion and Ethics in the Work of Stanley Hauerwas* (Notre Dame: University of Notre Dame Press, 2000), 41.

56. Hauerwas, *A Community of Character,* 226. For an extended analysis on this point, see ch. 2. See also Katongole, *Beyond Universal Reason,* 30. Katongole maintains that one's moral actions are always "narrative-dependent."

57. Interestingly, although they do not believe in *creatio ex Deo,* Augustine and Aquinas voice strong inclinations toward human deification as well through the doctrine of participation, and precisely because of the Incarnation, for the Incarnation reveals a special "kinship" between the divine and the human. In Sermon CXXVIII Augustine declares that "it is not by themselves being so that men are gods, but they become gods by participation in that one God who is the true God." He echoes a common phrase, "God was made man that man might become God," found among many church fathers, and as early as Irenaeus (d. 202) in *Adversus Haereses* (4.28). Aquinas declares that the Logos "has a kind of essential kinship . . . with the whole of creation," as "all creatures are nothing but a kind of real expression and representation of those things which are comprehended in the conception of the divine word" (*Summa Contra Gentiles* 4.42.3). Similarly, Aquinas echoes Augustine when he says, "the son of man, in assuming our flesh, certainly did not come to us for any light reason, but for our very great benefit. For he, as it were, traded with us by assuming a living body and deigning to be born of the Virgin so that we may participate in his divinity. And so he became man in order to make man divine" (*Articles of Faith,* Art. 3).

58. On this point, see Roger Chartier, "Labourers and Voyagers: From the Text to the Reader." Originally published in *Diacritics* 22, no. 2 (1992): 49–61, trans. J. A. González. Reprinted in *Readers and Reading,* ed. Andrew Bennett (London: Longman, 1995), 132–49.

Chapter 4. Milton's Parable of Misreading

1. See, for example, *PL* 2.285–90, 636–40, 918–20, 1041–44; 4.159–65, 556–60; 5.264–66; 9.513–15; *PR* 3.209–10; *SA* 197–200; 1044–45; *Of Reformation, CPW* 1:596; *The Reason of Church Government, CPW* 1:753, 821; *Doctrine and Discipline of Divorce, CPW* 2:254; *The Tenure of Kings and Magistrates, CPW* 3:257; *Eikonoklastes, CPW* 3:416, 501; *The Readie and Easie Way, CPW* 7:433–34, 458.

2. For alternate readings of this epic simile, see Richard J. DuRocher, *Milton and Ovid* (Ithaca: Cornell University Press, 1985), 134–35; and Christopher Grose, *Milton's Epic Process* (New Haven: Yale University Press, 1973), 150–52. For more on how Milton personally identifies in his poetry and prose with the situations and characters in Jesus's Parable of the Talents, Parable of the Wise Virgin, and Parable of the Householder, see David V. Urban, "The Parabolic Milton: The Self and the Bible in Milton's Works" (Ph.D. diss., University of Illinois at Chicago, 2001). See also Urban, "The Talented Mr. Milton: A Parabolic Laborer and His Identity," in *Milton Studies* 43, ed. Albert C. Labriola (2004): 1–18.

3. See Jackson Campbell Boswell, *Milton's Library* (New York: Garland, 1975). Milton had an extensive and wide-ranging collection of patristic writings in his library, and the works of Origen, Basil, and Augustine in particular were prominent. While he does not allow his own interpretive authority to be eclipsed by them, Milton does not wholly reject the work of the fathers (cf. *Of Reformation, CPW* 1:560). For a study of Milton and Origen, see Harry F. Robins, *If This Be Heresy: A Study of Milton and Origen* (Urbana: University of Illinois Press, 1963); for Milton's relation to Augustine, see Peter Fiore, *Milton and Augustine: Patterns of Augustinian Thought in Paradise Lost* (University Park: Pennsylvania State University Press, 1981). Milton's connection to Basil has yet to be fully explored, but he cites Basil in his prose: *Of Reformation, CPW* 1:565; *Areopagitica, CPW* 2:510; *The Tenure of Kings and Magistrates, CPW* 3:212; *Eikonoklastes, CPW* 3:518.

4. See Henri de Lubac, *Medieval Exegesis, Volume I: The Four Senses of Scripture,* trans. Mark Sebanc (Grand Rapids: Eerdmans, 1998), esp. ch. 1. Significantly, the pre-medieval and medieval exegetes of scripture assume the need for personal virtue and discipline *before* one begins the task of interpretation. Without the necessary training, or spiritual exercise, the expositor ran the dangerous risk of running afoul in his interpretation. Thus interpretation is not so much performed *on* the text as much as it is *lived* first by the

expositor. Provocatively, Milton seems to share this view of the practice of interpretation.

5. Madeleine Boucher, *The Mysterious Parable* (Washington, D.C.: The Catholic Biblical Association of America, 1977), 23, 30; emphasis original. For key contemporary scholarship on the parable, see Frank Kermode, *The Genesis of Secrecy* (Cambridge: Harvard University Press, 1979); and *Parable and Story in Judaism and Christianity*, ed. Clemens Thom and Michael Wyschogrod (New York: Paulist, 1989). For studies of the parable and postmodern theory, see especially the works of John Dominic Crossan: *In Parables: The Challenge of the Historical Jesus* (New York: Harper & Row, 1973); *The Dark Interval: Towards a Theology of Story* (Niles, Ill.: Argus Communications, 1975); and *Cliffs of Fall: Paradox and Polyvalence in the Parables of Jesus* (New York: Seabury, 1980). For a critique of Crossan, see Lynn Poland, *Literary Criticism and Biblical Hermeneutics: A Critique of Formalist Approaches* (Chico, Calif.: Scholars, 1985).

6. Kermode, *The Genesis of Secrecy*, 3. The particular scripture that Kermode has in mind is Mark 4:10–13. See also David Stern, "Jesus' Parables and Rabbinic Literature," in *Parable and Story in Judaism and Christianity*, 42–80. Arguing that the parables of Jesus derive from the rabbinic *māshal* tradition, Stern, 58, observes that the *māshal* "tends to leave it to the audience to figure out, upon reflection for itself." Boucher, *The Mysterious Parable*, 24–25, observes that the *māshal* tradition existed from the time of the composition of 1 and 2 Samuel and 1 and 2 Kings, and cites at least three examples in the Hebrew Bible when the hearer of a parable utterly fails to comprehend it: 2 Sam. 12:1–14; 14:4–13; 1 Kings 20:39–42.

7. Boucher, *The Mysterious Parable*, 25.

8. C. H. Dodd, *The Parables of the Kingdom* (London: Nisbet & Co., 1935), 23.

9. Achinstein, *Milton and the Revolutionary Reader*, 15; Loewenstein, *Representing Revolution*, 203. For more on Milton and the relation between an enthusiastic poetics and a radical political agenda, see also Achinstein, *Literature and Dissent in Milton's England*, ch. 6 (see full citation below, 347n6). See also Fish, *Surprised by Sin*, 54–55.

10. Brian Stock, *After Augustine* (Philadelphia: University of Pennsylvania Press, 2001), 17, 12. For more on Milton's spiritual reading, see David Ainsworth, *Milton and the Spiritual Reader: Reading and Religion in Seventeenth-Century England* (New York: Routledge, 2008).

11. For more on medieval monastic reading practices, see M. B. Parkes, "Reading, Copying, and Interpreting a Text in the Early Middle Ages," in *A*

History of Reading in the West, 90–102. Parkes asserts that the "motive for reading was . . . the salvation of one's soul" (91).

12. Barbara Lewalski, *Protestant Poetics* (Princeton: Princeton University Press, 1979), 86.

13. Edmund Spenser, *The Faerie Queene,* ed. A. C. Hamilton, rev. 2nd ed. (London: Pearson Education Limited, 2007), cited parenthetically in the text by book and/or canto, followed by stanza and line number.

14. Donne, "A Sheaf of Snakes," in *Donne: Poetical Works,* ed. Sir Herbert Grierson (New York: Oxford University Press, 1967), lines 5–6, 9–10.

15. Robert Wilkinson, *The Merchant Royall, being a sermon preached in 1607 in praise of the wife, wherein she is likened to a merchant ship* (London: 1607), sig. B2. See also William Johnson, *A Sermon Preached upon a Great Deliverance at Sea* (London, 1672).

16. Francis Quarles, *Emblemes* (London, 1635), sig. A3.

17. Don Diego Saavedra Fajardo, *The Royal Politician Represented in One Hundred Emblems,* trans. Sir. J. A. Astry (London, 1700), 259.

18. For an extended treatment of Milton's doctrine of baptism and its centrality in *Paradise Regained* as foreshadowing the cross, see Hillier, *Milton's Messiah,* 187–93.

19. Origen, *Homilies on Genesis and Exodus,* trans. Ronald E. Heine, *Fathers of the Early Church,* vol. 71 (Washington, D.C.: Catholic University Press, 1982), 78–79.

20. Ibid., 86–87.

21. Basil the Great, *Address to Young Men,* 385.

22. One might recall that John admonishes "believe not every spirit, but try the spirits whether they are of God" (1 John 4:1). John's warning is directed to believers to cultivate spiritual discernment in order not to be deceived by false teachers.

23. Basil, *Address to Young Men,* 387–89.

24. Ibid., 389, 381.

25. Augustine, *Confessions,* 3.3.5.

26. On this point, see especially Camille Bennett, "The Conversion of Vergil: The *Aeneid* in Augustine's *Confessions,*" *Revue des Études Augustiniennes* 34 (1988): 47–69.

27. Cf. Augustine, *Confessions,* 4.16.31.

28. Augustine, *Confessions,* 10.3.4–10.4.6.

29. Ross Chambers, *Room for Maneuver: Reading (the) Oppositional (in) Narrative* (Chicago: University of Chicago Press, 1991), xvi.

30. Pierre Hadot, *Philosophy as a Way of Life,* trans. Michael Chase, ed. Arnold I. Davidson (Cambridge: University of Cambridge Press, 1995), 83; emphasis original.

31. See Merritt Y. Hughes, *John Milton,* 1022–23. John Aubrey, an early biographer of Milton, describes a typical day for Milton spent in contemplation: "He was an early riser, *sc.* at 4 o'clock *mane. . . .* The first thing he read was the Hebrew Bible, and that was at 4h. *mane* – 4/2h. +. Then he contemplated. At 7 his man came in to him again, and then read to him and wrote till dinner. . . . After dinner he used to walk 3 to 4 hours at a time." The classic work on Milton (and other poets) with regard to meditation is Louis Martz, *The Poetry of Meditation: A Study in English Religious Literature of the Seventeenth Century,* 2nd ed. (New Haven: Yale University Press, 1962).

32. Hadot, *Philosophy as a Way of Life,* 112n38.

33. See Plotinus, *Enneads,* 6, 9, 10, 14–17; quoted in ibid., 101; emphasis original.

34. Quoted in ibid., 132.

35. Herman, *Destabilizing Milton,* 49–50. Consult 192n15 for Herman's useful review of critics who argue for this narrative's stability.

36. Ibid., 45.

37. See James Dougal Fleming, *Milton's Secrecy and Philosophical Hermeneutics* (Burlington, Vt.: Ashgate, 2008). Fleming's overriding thesis is that Milton's work is infused with an opposition to secrecy and hiddenness.

38. On the situatedness of Milton's readers in the twentieth century, see William Kolbrener, *Milton's Warring Angels: A Study of Critical Engagements* (Cambridge: Cambridge University Press, 2008).

39. Leviathan also appears in Job 41 during God's rebuke from the whirlwind. Here Leviathan is a fearsome creature, and no one but God can control or tame him. Psalm 104 also mentions Leviathan, but in more positive terms as one of God's glorious creations. Milton echoes the Psalmist's version in his retelling of creation in *Paradise Lost* 7.412.

40. This is the sense that the *OED* captures: "leviathan" is the "great enemy of God, Satan."

41. John Calvin, *Commentary on the Book of the Prophet Isaiah,* 2 vols., trans. James Anderson (Edinburgh: Calvin Translation Society, 1851), 2:247.

42. Ibid., 246. The *OED* cites Thomas Hobbes's use (1651) of "leviathan": "used by Hobbes for: the organism of political society, the commonwealth."

43. See Bernard Capp, "The Political Dimension of Apocalyptic Thought," in *The Apocalypse in English Renaissance Thought and Literature: Patterns, Antecedents and Repercussions,* ed. C. A. Patrides and Joseph Wittreich (Ithaca: Cornell University Press, 1984), 93–124.

44. See Darren Oldridge, *Religion and Society in Early Stuart England* (Brookfield, Vt.: Ashgate, 1998). Oldridge maintains that the discourses of disobedience, persecution, and Christian militancy in Puritan preaching were some of the major factors leading to the English Civil War.

45. Bastwick, *Letany,* 10.

46. See *The Apocalypse in English Renaissance Thought and Literature: Patterns, Antecedents and Repercussions,* ed. C. A. Patrides and Joseph Wittreich (Ithaca: Cornell University Press, 1984).

47. Achinstein, *Literature and Dissent,* 159.

48. Augustine, *Confessions,* 1.1. For an insightful treatment of divine Sabbath rest in the poem, see Michael Lieb, "'Holy Rest': A Reading of *Paradise Lost,*" *ELH* 39 (1972): 238–54.

49. Augustine, *Confessions,* 2.10; 4.12.18.

50. Fiore, *Milton and Augustine,* 16.

51. Augustine, *Confessions,* 1.2.2.

52. See Regina Schwartz, "Real Hunger: Milton's Version of the Eucharist," *Religion and Literature* 31, no. 3 (Autumn 1999): 1–18.

53. See Lewalski, *Protestant Poetics,* 200–201.

54. See Rowen Williams, *On Christian Theology* (Oxford: Blackwell, 2000), 63–78. "God creates 'in God's interest,'" and God's interest is to act entirely for humanity's sake in "being for" his creation as pure gift (74).

55. Regina Schwartz, *Remembering and Repeating: On Milton's Theology and Poetics* (Chicago: University of Chicago Press, 1993), 68.

56. Treip, *Allegorical Poetics and the Epic,* 222.

57. John Preston, *The Breastplate of Faith and Love* (London, 1634), 2:224–26.

58. While Jameela Lares does not treat the exemplum tradition in her book, I am indebted to her for encouraging me to consider its possibility.

59. John Burrow, *Ricardian Poetry* (London: Routledge & Kegan Paul, 1971), 82.

60. See Larry Scanlon, *Narrative, Authority and Power: The Medieval Exemplum and the Chaucerian Tradition* (Cambridge: Cambridge University Press, 1994), chs. 4–5.

61. Ibid., 113.

62. G. R. Owst, *Literature and the Pulpit in Medieval England* (Cambridge: Cambridge University Press, 1933), 199, 203.

63. Scanlon, *Narrative, Authority and Power,* 81.

64. Lares, *Milton and the Preaching Arts,* 144.

65. Chappell, *The Preacher,* 155.

66. Aquinas, *Summa Theologica,* 2a2œ.9, 4.1. Quoted in Lares, *Milton and the Preaching Arts,* 145; see 261n18.

67. Cf. "On Regeneration," in *De Doctrina Christiana* (*CPW* 6:461): "This is how supernatural renovation works. It restores man's natural faculties of faultless understanding and of free will more completely than before." The proper "government" of oneself, it seems, hinges on conversion.

68. Achinstein, *Milton and the Revolutionary Reader,* 8.

69. See Plato, *Protagoras,* 324d–325b. Milton shares Plato's assumption, made throughout the Socratic dialogues, that the state is only as just as its citizens.

70. Plato, *The Republic,* 488d–489.

71. Robert Fallon, *Milton in Government* (University Park: Pennsylvania State University Press), 188–210.

72. John Lilburne, *Londons Liberty in Chains Discovered* (London, 1646), 6; Gerrard Winstanley, *The New Law of Righteousnes Budding Forth, to Restore the Whole Creation from Bondage of the Curse* (London, 1649). Reprinted in *The Complete Works of Gerrard Winstanley,* 2 vols., ed. Thomas N. Corns, Ann Hughes, and David Loewenstein (Oxford: Oxford University Press, 2009), 1:525. Unless otherwise noted, all citations of Winstanley's writings are from this edition, and pagination reflects this edition, not the original publication.

Chapter 5. Fashioning the True Pilot

1. Chartier, "Labourers and Voyagers," in *Readers and Reading,* 137.

2. For the best sustained discussion of early modern discourses on moderation, see Joshua Scodel, *Excess and the Mean in Early Modern English Literature* (Princeton: Princeton University Press, 2002).

3. Calvin, *Institutes of the Christian Religion,* 1:445.

4. Perkins, *Workes,* 2:127.

5. Winstanley, *The New Law of Righteousnes,* 1:502.

6. On the centrality of Aristotle's *Ethics,* see Scodel, *Excess and the Mean,* 2. See also the works that Scodel cites, 289nn2, 4. For an attempt to go beyond Aristotle's account of the virtues to those elaborated on in the work

of Thomas Aquinas, see Gerald Morgan, "The Idea of Temperance in the Second Book of *The Faerie Queene*," *The Review of English Studies*, New Series, 37, no. 145 (February 1986): 11–39.

7. Aristotle, *Nichomachean Ethics*, 1.6, 1098a, 1.2, 1095a. For more on Aristotle's notion of virtue, and a provocative contemporary reflection on virtue and moral decay in the liberal state, see Alasdair MacIntyre, *After Virtue: A Study in Moral Theory*, 2nd ed. (Notre Dame: University of Notre Dame Press, 1984), esp. ch. 12.

8. William J. Prior, *Virtue and Knowledge: An Introduction to Ancient Greek Ethics* (London: Routledge, 1991), 150.

9. Aristotle, *Nichomachean Ethics*, 1.6, 1098a.

10. MacIntyre, *After Virtue*, 154.

11. Prior, *Virtue and Knowledge*, 178.

12. Aristotle, *Nichomachean Ethics*, 3.7, 1114b; emphasis added.

13. On development of this point with regard to Spenser's Sir Guyon, the Knight of Temperance, see Paul Cefalu, *Moral Identity in Early Modern English Literature* (Cambridge: Cambridge University Press, 2004), 69–70.

14. Stephen Everson, "Aristotle on Nature and Value," in *Companions to Ancient Thought, Volume 4: Ethics,* ed. Stephen Everson (Cambridge: Cambridge University Press, 1998), 77–106; quote from 106.

15. Aristotle, *Nichomachean Ethics*, 6.13, 1144a.

16. Charles M. Young, "Aristotle on Temperance," *The Philosophical Review* 97, no. 4 (October 1988): 521–42.

17. Ibid., 528.

18. Aristotle, *Nichomachean Ethics*, 3.14, 1119a; emphasis translator's.

19. Young, "Aristotle on Temperance," 532.

20. Ernest Sirluck, "Milton Revises *The Faerie Queene*," *Modern Philology* 48, no. 2 (November 1950): 90–96; quotes from 93–94.

21. Bishop Joseph Hall, *Christian Moderation In two books* (London, 1640), 1.3–4. Quoted in C. A. Patrides, *Milton and the Christian Tradition* (Oxford: Clarendon, 1966), 115–16.

22. Albert W. Fields, "Ethics," in *A Milton Encyclopedia*, gen. ed. William B. Hunter (Lewisburg: Bucknell University Press, 1976), 72–82; quote from 78. Hanford quote from 72.

23. These harmonic interrelations are not lost on several critics. See Achinstein, *Milton and the Revolutionary Reader*, 15. She argues that Milton's overall project was concerned "not simply to pass on his revolutionary messages in code, but to mold a readership that was increasingly required to know how to

decipher conflicting interpretations." See also Loewenstein, *Representing Revolution*, 203. Loewenstein asserts that *Paradise Lost* "constantly challenges its engaged readers by showing them how to discern the treacherous ambiguities and contradictions of political rhetoric and behavior." David Ainsworth, "Spiritual Reading in Milton's *Eikonoklastes*," *Studies in English Literature, 1500–1900* 45, no. 1 (Winter 2005): 157–89, argues that critical reading is integral to Milton's evolving idea of Christian freedom. See also Rosemond Tuve, *Images and Themes in Five Poems by Milton* (Cambridge: Harvard University Press, 1957). Tuve argues that *Comus* in particular demonstrates that a virtuous disposition is not enough to "see through to the true nature of that which . . . simply says it is other than it is" (128).

24. On Milton's pastoral celebrations of temperance as an English virtue, see Scodel, *Excess and the Mean*, 102–10.

25. Tuve, *Images and Themes*, 128.

26. John Guillory, *Poetic Authority: Spenser, Milton, and Literary History* (New York: Columbia University Press, 1983), 84.

27. Comus's commodification of beauty perhaps reflects the Parable of the Talents. See Leah S. Marcus, "John Milton's *Comus*," in *A Companion to Milton*, ed. Thomas N. Corns (Oxford: Blackwell, 2001), 232–45, particularly her comments on 241. See also Guillory, *Poetic Authority*, 88–89.

28. See Hughes's footnote to line 785; he references 1 Tim. 3:16, wherein Paul is speaking of the "mystery" of the Incarnation. On Milton's Reformed notion of virginity as moral purity and its relationship to temperance, see Georgia B. Christopher, "The Virginity of Faith: *Comus* as a Reformation Conceit," *ELH* vol. 43, no. 4 (Winter 1976): 479–99.

29. Thanks to an anonymous reader for encouraging me to be more skeptical on this point.

30. For more on the Isocratic persona, see Paul M. Dowling, "*Areopagitica* and *Areopagiticus*: The Significance of the Isocratic Precedent," in *Milton Studies* 21, ed. James D. Simmonds (1986): 46–69.

31. William Haller, ed., *Tracts on Liberty in the Puritan Revolution, 1638–1647*, 3 vols. (New York: Columbia University Press, 1933–34), 1:75.

32. Lewalski sorts through the four main arguments of *Areopagitica* in *The Life of John Milton*, 193–96.

33. Nigel Smith, "*Areopagitica*: Voicing Contexts, 1643–5," in *Politics, Poetics and Hermeneutics in Milton's Prose*, ed. David Loewenstein and James Grantham Turner (Cambridge: Cambridge University Press, 1990), 103–22; quotes from 104–5.

34. See Blair Worden, "Marchamont Nedham and the Beginnings of English Republicanism, 1649–1656," in *Republicanism, Liberty, and Commercial Society, 1649–1776,* ed. David Wootten (Stanford: Stanford University Press, 1994), 45–81; Martin Dzelzainis, "Republicanism," in *A Companion to Milton,* ed. Thomas Corns (Oxford: Blackwell, 2003), 294–308, as well as his "Milton's Classical Republicanism" in *Milton and Republicanism,* ed. David Armitage, Armand Himy, and Quentin Skinner (Cambridge: Cambridge University Press, 1995), 3–24. See also Nigel Smith, *Literature and Revolution in England, 1640–1660* (New Haven: Yale University Press, 1994), esp. ch. 3. Smith adroitly concludes that the "middle ground" during the Civil War years and the Interregnum "was sacrificed to a series of increasingly confident and opposed views and rhetorics" (360). All three critics, however, neglect to identify temperance as the key virtue associated with the "middle way" of a republican agenda that sought to avoid the negative extremes of mob license and monarchical tyranny, and the virtue that is also at the core of Milton's incarnated, republican reader in the pamphlet.

35. See Fish, *How Milton Works,* 202. Fish here appears to have reconsidered his earlier position on *Areopagitica* as a self-consuming artifact. See Fish, "Driving from the Letter in Milton's *Areopagitica,*" in *Remembering Milton: Essays on the Texts and the Traditions,* ed. Mary Nyquist and Margaret W. Ferguson (New York: Methuen, 1987), 234–54. Fish argues that what many see in *Areopagitica* as Milton's argument for books is actually "an argument that renders books beside the point" because "by denying their potency in one direction [toward vice], Milton necessarily denies their potency in the other [toward virtue]" (236). This latter claim has been challenged by James Rovira, "Gathering the Scattered Body of Milton's *Areopagitica,*" *Renascence* 57, no. 2 (Winter 2005): 87–102.

36. See John D. Schaeffer, "Metonymies We Read By: Rhetoric, Truth and the Eucharist in Milton's *Areopagitica,*" *Milton Quarterly* 34, no. 3 (2000): 84–92. Schaeffer profitably suggests that Milton thus views books eucharistically because when they are consumed "their spiritual contents, human reason as image of divinity, enter the mind of the reader through the body by means of their materiality, paper, print, etc" (87).

37. Worden, "Marchamont Nedham and the Beginnings of English Republicanism," in Wootten, *Republicanism, Liberty, and Commercial Society,* 94.

38. Perhaps this is why metaphors of consumption are so prevalent in his argument. On this metaphor and competing images in *Areopagitica,* see the following: Smith, "*Areopagitica*: Voicing Contexts"; Lana Cable, *Carnal Rheto-*

ric: Milton's Iconoclasm and the Poetics of Desire (Durham: Duke University Press, 1995), 137. Smith's and Cable's conclusions that Milton's shifting metaphors in the tract are contradictory has been challenged by Schaeffer, "Metonymies We Read By," 84–85.

39. See Michael Schoenfeldt, "Reading Bodies," in *Reading, Society and Politics in Early Modern England,* ed. Kevin Sharpe and Steven N. Zwicker (Cambridge: Cambridge University Press, 2003), 215–43. Schoenfeldt comments that "A book could either stir the cauldron, applying heat and pressure to an already unstable system, or help to cool the cauldron by the addition of maxims drawn from the realm of cool reason" (216).

40. For an illuminating discussion on Milton's debt to alchemy, see Glenn F. Sucich, "'By gradual scale sublim'd': Alchemy and the Matter of Souls in the Age of Milton" (Ph.D. diss., Northwestern University, 2005), esp. ch. 3, which engages alchemy's significant conceptual and metaphorical presence in Milton's prose.

41. *The Works of John Milton,* ed. Frank A. Patterson et al., 18 vols. (New York: Columbia University Press, 1931–38), 12:81.

42. Representative discussions include Mary Ann Radzinowicz, *Toward Samson Agonistes: The Growth of Milton's Mind* (Princeton: Princeton University Press, 1978); Michael Lieb, *Milton and the Culture of Violence* (Ithaca: Cornell University Press, 1994); Loewenstein, *Representing Revolution,* ch. 9; Derek N. C. Wood, *Exiled from Light: Divine Law, Morality, and Violence in Milton's Samson Agonistes* (Toronto: Toronto University Press, 2001); and John Shawcross, *The Uncertain World of Samson Agonistes* (Rochester: D. S. Brewer, 2001). For a critique of the righteousness of Samson's action, see Joseph Wittreich, *Interpreting Samson Agonistes* (Princeton: Princeton University Press, 1986); and John Carey, "A Work in Praise of Terrorism?" *TLS* 6 (September 2002): 15–16. Along these non-orthodox lines, see also Wittreich, *Shifting Contexts: Reinterpreting Samson Agonistes* (Pittsburgh: Duquesne University Press, 2002); and Irene Samuel, "*Samson Agonistes* as Tragedy," in *Calm of Mind: Tercentenary Essays on Paradise Regained and Samson Agonistes in Honor of John S. Diekhoff,* ed. Joseph Anthony Wittreich Jr., James G. Taaffe, and Jane Cerny (Cleveland: Case Western Reserve University Press, 1971), 235–58. For a response, see Stanley Fish, "'There Is Nothing He Cannot Ask': Milton, Liberalism, and Terrorism," in *Milton in the Age of Fish: Essays on Authorship, Text, and Terrorism,* ed. Michael Lieb and Albert C. Labriola (Pittsburgh: Duquesne University Press, 2006), 243–64.

43. Michael Schoenfeldt, *Bodies and Selves in Early Modern England: Physiology and Inwardness in Spenser, Shakespeare, Herbert, and Milton* (Cambridge: Cambridge University Press, 1999), 48.

44. See Anthony Low, *The Blaze of Noon: A Reading of Samson Agonistes* (New York: Columbia University Press, 1974), 158–63, who argues that the giant Harapha is Samson's "parodic double" (162).

45. Wittreich, *Interpreting Samson Agonistes,* passim.

46. This particular scene captured the imagination of many Renaissance artists, including Andrea Mantegna, Michelangelo Merisi da Caravaggio, Peter Paul Rubens, Anthony Van Dyke, Rembrandt van Rijn, Matthias Stom, Jan Havicksz Steen, and Jan Lievens. Nearly without fail, Dalila's sexuality and Samson's helplessness or unconsciousness are prominently depicted.

47. Thanks to Michael Lieb for help with the Hebrew.

48. For more sympathetic readings of Dalila, see William Empson, "A Defense of Dalilah," *Sewanee Review* 68 (1960): 240–55; Joyce Colony, "An Argument for Milton's Dalila," *Yale Review: A National Quarterly* 66 (1977): 562–75; and Wood, *Exiled from Light,* ch. 6.

49. Lewalski, *The Life of John Milton,* 524.

50. The nuances of Dalila's veil have been keenly explored by Karla Landells in her unpublished essay, "'But who is this?': Unveiling Milton's Dalila," delivered at the 2011 Conference on John Milton.

51. Jean Baudrillard, *Simulacra and Simulation,* trans. Sheila Faria Glaser (Ann Arbor: University of Michigan Press, 1994), 3–4; emphasis original.

52. Low, *The Blaze of Noon,* 80; Abraham Stoll, "Milton Stages Cherbury: Revelation and Polytheism in *Samson Agonistes,*" in *Altering Eyes: New Perspectives on Samson Agonistes,* ed. Mark R. Kelley and Joseph Wittreich (Newark, N.J.: University of Delaware Press, 2002), 281–306; quote from 283; Stanley Fish, "Spectacle and Evidence in *Samson Agonistes,*" *Critical Enquiry* 15, no. 3 (Spring 1989): 556–86; quote from 586; Kerrigan, *The Sacred Complex,* 119; Richard J. DuRocher, "Samson's 'Rousing Motions': What They Are, How They Work, and Why They Matter," *Literature Compass* 3, no. 3 (2006): 453–69; quote from 464; Stanley Fish, "'There Is Nothing He Cannot Ask': Milton, Liberalism, and Terrorism," in *Milton in the Age of Fish: Essays on Authorship, Text, and Terrorism,* ed. Michael Lieb and Albert C. Labriola (Pittsburgh: Duquesne University Press, 2006), 243–64.

53. See, for instance, John Bunyan, *Grace Abounding to the chief of Sinners* (London, 1666), 1–25 and passim; Bunyan repeats the pattern more than once. See also Fox, *The Journal of George Fox,* 9–27; Charles Marshall, *The*

Journal: Together with Sundry Epistles and Other Writings (London: R. Barrett, 1844), 11–12.

54. A. R. Faussett, "Introduction to the Poetical Books," in *A Commentary, Critical, Experimental, and Practical, on the Old and New Testaments,* ed. Robert Jamieson, A. R. Faussett, and David Brown, 6 vols. (Grand Rapids: Eerdmans, 1945), 3:xvii. I have been unable to confirm wholly Faussett's interpretation of the analogous relationship between these wisdom books and the Temple in either the Talmud or Midrashic tradition. It is highly plausible, however, that Faussett was inferring the analogous relationship from the tradition of a common Solomonic authorship as well as Rabbi Akiba's ardent defense of the Song of Songs for inclusion in the canon. See M. Yadaim III 5, in *The Mishnah,* trans. C. Danby (Oxford: Oxford University Press, 1933), 781–82. Several rabbis had argued that Ecclesiastes and the Song of Songs left one's hands "unclean." R. Akiba, however, stated that "all the Writings are holy, but the Song of Songs is the Holy of Holies."

55. Lieb, *Theological Milton,* 153, 183.

56. For an examination of Milton's God as dread itself, see Michael Lieb, "'Our Living Dread': The God of *Samson Agonistes,*" *Milton Studies* 33 (1996): 3–25. This volume of *Milton Studies* is dedicated to *Samson Agonistes.*

57. On the cultic roots of this hermeneutical blurring, see Lieb, *Poetics of the Holy,* ch. 1.

58. For a negative assessment of this passage from *The First Defense,* see Wittreich, *Interpreting Samson Agonistes,* 301; see also Evans, *The Miltonic Moment,* 126–28. Evans rightly takes Wittreich to task on his misuse of this passage.

59. Lewalski, *The Life of John Milton,* 525; Loewenstein, *Representing Revolution,* ch. 9.

60. Bernard Capp, *The Fifth Monarchy Men: A Study in Seventeenth-Century Millenarianism* (London: Faber & Faber, 1972), "Appendix II," 272–73. There was also a group meeting in Chalfont, St. Giles, in 1669, but Milton left there in 1666 when the plague lifted in London. See also Capp, "The Fifth Monarchists and Popular Millenarianism," in *Radical Religion in the English Revolution,* ed. J. F. McGregor and B. Reay (Oxford: Oxford University Press, 1984), 165–90; and P. G. Rogers, *The Fifth Monarchy Men* (Oxford: Oxford University Press, 1966). For more on Milton's millenarianism and contemporary responses to the Fifth Monarchists, see the essays in Juliet Cummins, ed., *Milton and the Ends of Time* (Cambridge: Cambridge University Press, 2003).

61. Capp, *The Fifth Monarchy Men,* 13.

62. See ibid., ch. 2. The political and ecclesial details of what the millennial kingdom would consist vary. The most important issue here was whether Christ would reign as a physical monarch during the millennium, or if the saints would rule in his stead. For examples of Fifth Monarchists who maintain the former position, see Mary Cary, *The little horns doom & downfall or A scripture-prophesie of King James, and King Charles, and of this present Parliament, unfolded* (London, 1651), 212–13; Thomas Tillam, *The two witnesses: their prophecy, slaughter, resurection and ascention: or, An exposition of the eleventh chapter of the Revelation . . .* (London, 1651), 109–10; and John Rogers, *Othel or Beth-shemesh. A tabernacle for the sun* (London, 1653), 24. Those who maintained the latter position include William Aspinwall, *A brief description of the fifth monarchy or kingdome that shortly is to come into the world* (London, 1653), 4; Anonymous, *A door of hope: or, A call and declaration for the gathering together of the first ripe fruits unto the standard of our Lord, King Jesus* (London, 1660), 8–9. For more on the differing ideas of the "rule of the saints," see Christopher Hill, *The Experience of Defeat: Milton and Some Contemporaries* (London: Faber & Faber, 1984), 52–62.

63. See, for instance, Thomas Brightman, *Apocalyptis Apocalypseos* (Frankfort, 1609), English trans. *The Revelation of St. John Illustrated* (London, 1644); Johann Alsted, *Diatribe de mille annis apocalypticis* (Frankfurt, 1627), English trans., *The Beloved City, or The Saints Reign on Earth a Thousand Years* (London, 1643); Joseph Mede, *Clavis Apocalyptica, ex innatis et insitis visionum characteribus eruta et demonstrata* (Cambridge, 1627), English trans. *The Key of the Revelation* (London, 1643). For an analysis of the influence of the expositions by Thomas Brightman, Johann Alsted, and Joseph Mede, see Stella Revard, "Milton and Millenarianism: From the Nativity Ode to *Paradise Regained*," in Cummins, *Milton and the Ends of Time*, 42–81.

64. Aspinwall, *A brief description of the fifth monarchy*, 3, 5, 7–8.

65. See Capp, *The Fifth Monarchy Men*, 162–71.

66. Aspinwall, *A brief description of the fifth monarchy*, 8–10; John Rogers, *Sagrir. Or Doomes-day drawing nigh, with Thunder and Lightning to lawyers* (London, 1653); Rogers quoted in Capp, *The Fifth Monarchy Men*, 162; emphasis original.

67. See Capp, *The Fifth Monarchy Men*, 66–75.

68. Anonymous, *The last Speech and Prayer with other passages of Thomas Venner The Chief Incourager and Promoter of the late Horrid Rebellion* (London, 1660–61), 3–4. For more on Venner's rebellion and its aftermath, see Rich-

ard L. Greaves, *Deliver Us From Evil: The Radical Underground in Britain, 1660–1663* (New York: Oxford University Press, 1986).

69. See Henry Gee, "The Derwentdale Plot, 1663," in *Transactions of the Royal Historical Society,* Third Series, 11 (1917): 125–42; quote from 125.

70. On dating the composition of *Samson Agonistes,* see Low, *The Blaze of Noon,* 222–27; Radzinowicz, *Toward Samson Agonistes,* 387–407; and Shawcross, *The Uncertain World of Samson Agonistes,* 23–27. I am largely persuaded by Shawcross's forceful case for an early beginning (1648–49) and late revision (1667–70).

71. Loewenstein, *Representing Revolution,* 10.

72. See Revard, "Milton and Millenarianism." Revard notes that Milton removed this passage in the second edition published in April 1660 and argues that even though Milton denounced their agenda he may have continued to share their millenarian preoccupations. For speculation on Milton's motives, see Stanley Stewart, "Milton Revises *The Readie and Easie Way,*" *Milton Studies* 20 (1984): 205–24.

73. Wittreich, *Interpreting Samson Agonistes,* xii, 80.

74. See Loewenstein, *Representing Revolution,* 276–81; David Loewenstein, "Afterword: 'The time is come,' in Cummins, *Milton and the Ends of Time,* 241–49; quote from 247.

75. Evans, *The Miltonic Moment,* 126; Evans specifically responds to Ann Gossman, "Milton's *Samson* as the Hero Purified by Trial," *Journal of English and Germanic Philology* 61 (1962): 528–41; and Michael Atkinson, "The Structure of the Temptations in Milton's *Samson Agonistes,*" *Modern Philology* 69, no. 4 (May 1972): 285–91.

76. Shawcross, *The Uncertain World of Samson Agonistes,* 140–41.

77. See Low, *The Blaze of Noon,* 222. Low observes a "close compatibility between *Samson Agonistes* and the *Christian Doctrine,*" so much so that Low contends "[n]o other single prose work . . . or even perhaps all of them together, proves as widely relevant to understanding the play as the *Christian Doctrine.*"

78. John Coffey, "Pacifist, Quietist, or Patient Militant? John Milton and the Restoration," in *Milton Studies* 42 (2002): 149–74; quotes from 156. Coffey provides a roadmap to scholarship that presents Milton as pacifist or quietist and entrenches him in the cultural context of apocalypticism and violence.

79. See Wood, *Exiled from Light,* 120–22.

80. For more on this point, see Low, *The Blaze of Noon,* 187–99.

81. Michael Bryson, "From Last Things to First: The Apophatic Vision of *Paradise Regain'd*," in *Visionary Milton: Essays on Prophecy and Violence*, ed. Peter E. Medine, John T. Shawcross, and David V. Urban (Pittsburgh: Duquesne University Press, 2010), 241–65; quote from 256.

82. Ken Simpson, "The Apocalypse in *Paradise Regained*," in Cummins, ed., *Milton and the Ends of Time*, 202–23; quote from 219. Anne K. Krook, "The Hermeneutics of Opposition in *Paradise Regained* and *Samson Agonistes*," *SEL* 36 (1996): 131–36. See also Mary Ann Radzinowicz, "*Paradise Regained* as Hermeneutic Combat," *University of Hartford Studies in Literature: A Journal of Interdisciplinary Criticism* 15–16 (1983–84): 99–107.

83. See *De Doctrina Christiana*, 6:582, where Milton argues that an interpreter must possess linguistic fluency in the original languages and the abilities to discern literal from figural language, as well as to account for authorial intent, and to understand the historical and literary context.

84. For more on Milton's exegetical adherence to the rule of charity in *The Doctrine and Discipline of Divorce* and *Paradise Lost*, see Regina M. Schwartz, "Milton on the Bible," in Corns, ed., *A Companion to Milton*, 37–54; quote from 37, emphasis original. On how some of Milton's Protestant contemporaries understood the rule of charity as a hermeneutical guide for scriptural interpretation, see Dayton Haskin, *Milton's Burden of Interpretation* (Philadelphia: University of Pennsylvania Press, 1994), 54–83.

85. For a picture of Augustine himself applying and working through these two canons as he interprets Genesis 1, consult *Confessions*, 12.17.24–31.42.

86. Augustine, *On Christian Doctrine*, 1.36.

87. John Wildman, *Truths triumph, or Treachery anatomized* (London, 1648), 4; John Lilburne, *An Impeachment of High Treason against Oliver Cromwell* (London, 1649), 23.

88. Anonymous, *The Vanities of the present Churches, and the uncertainty of their Preaching discovered, &c.* (London, 1649), 25.

89. Ibid., 12, 15–18, 39.

90. See, for example, Alexander Parker, *A Testimony of the Light Within* (London, 1657). Parker avers that "there is no life in the Scriptures" and that they are only an "outward declaration" of the way to salvation. But "the Scriptures themselves, are not the Rule of Life," he remarks, "nor the way to salvation, nor the will and mind of God. . . . There is but one Rule of life, and that is the Spirit of God which is life, and gives life, and makes free from the Law of Sin and Death" (11–12). The classic work on the place of the Spirit in Puritanism is Geoffrey F. Nuttall, *The Holy Spirit in Puritan Faith and Experience*

(Oxford: Oxford University Press, 1946). See also John R. Knott Jr., *The Sword of the Spirit: Puritan Responses to the Bible* (Chicago: University of Chicago Press, 1980).

91. See Stanley Fish, "Things and Actions Indifferent: The Temptation of Plot in *Paradise Regained*," in *Critical Essays on John Milton*, ed. Christopher Kendrick (New York: G. K. Hall & Co., 1995), 74–94. Fish argues that Milton's Satan lures readers and critics into thinking that Jesus's temptations occur on an ascending scale of importance and plot, when in fact Jesus's responses "have the effect of leveling that scale by refusing to recognize it" (77). Instead, the temptations are all insidiously linked by the temptation to power apart from the Father.

92. Lewalski, *Milton's Brief Epic*, 135.

93. Stock, *After Augustine*, 10.

94. Ricoeur, "The Hermeneutical Function of Distanciation," in *HHS*, 143; emphasis Ricoeur's.

95. Ibid., 144.

96. Fox, *Journal*, 261.

97. For more on the comparisons between Samson and Satan, see Michael Bryson, "A Poem to the Unknown God: *Samson Agonistes* and Negative Theology," *Milton Quarterly* 42, no. 1 (March 2008): 22–43.

98. Aspinwall, *A brief description of the fifth monarchy*, 3.

99. On the ambiguities of Milton's "or," see Peter C. Herman, "*Paradise Lost*, the Miltonic 'Or,' and the Poetics of Incertitude," *Studies in English Literature, 1500–1900* 43, no. 1 (Winter 2003): 181–211.

100. See Stephen Greenblatt, *Renaissance Self-Fashioning: From Moore to Shakespeare* (Chicago: University of Chicago Press, 1980), 179.

101. Douglas Bush, *The Renaissance and English Humanism* (Toronto: University of Toronto Press, 1939), 125; E. M. W. Tillyard, *Milton* (London: The Diall Press, 1930), 309; quoted in Lewalski, *Milton's Brief Epic*, 282.

102. Northrop Frye, "The Typology of *Paradise Regained*," *Modern Philology* 53, no. 4 (May 1956): 227–38; quote from 236.

103. See Lewalski, *Milton's Brief Epic*, 290–302.

104. Baudrillard, *Simulacra and Simulation*, 3–4.

105. How, *The sufficiencie of the spirits teaching*, sig. B1; Winstanley, *The New Law*, 1:566. For an extended study on conflicting views of knowledge in the period, see Keeble, *The Literary Culture of Nonconformity*, ch. 5.

106. Augustine, *The Trinity*, in *Augustine: Later Works*, ed. John Burnaby (Philadelphia: Westminster, 1955), 37–181; quote from 93–94.

107. Ibid., 94.

108. Augustine, *On Christian Doctrine*, 1.27.

109. Aristotle, *Nichomachean Ethics*, 3.14, 1119a.

110. See Ryan Netzley, "How Reading Works: Hermeneutics and Reading Practice in *Paradise Regained*," in *Milton Studies* 49, ed. Albert C. Labriola (2009): 146–66. Netzley observes that when Jesus turns away from books and knowledge the epic affirms that "wise readers are themselves self-sufficient and do not gain anything from reading," and the activity of reading "can only function as reconfirmation and reaffirmation of what one already knows and possesses" (146). That may be so, but readerly self-sufficiency is not the only endgame strategy; charity toward one's neighbor must be included as well. While one's reading may not "gain anything" for the self-sufficient reader, it certainly has gainful implications for conducting oneself in the world, a point that Netzley does not ignore, but which is understated in his argument.

111. Augustine, *On Christian Doctrine*, 3.8.

112. For differing accounts of the meaning of this moment, see Lewalski, *Milton's Brief Epic*, 315–17; Fish, *How Milton Works*, 336–38; and Entzminger, *Divine Word*, 116.

113. Ricoeur, *Freud and Philosophy*, 27.

Chapter 6. The Perfect Seed of Christ

1. Ann Hughes, "Approaches to Presbyterian Print Culture: Thomas Edwards's *Gangraena* as Source," in *Books and Readers in Early Modern England*, ed. Jennifer Andersen and Elizabeth Sauer (Philadelphia: University of Pennsylvania Press, 2002), 96–116; quotes from 104, 109. Broadly, her essay provides an illuminating look at what Edwards's *Gangraena* reveals about early modern print culture. Her discussion is more fully addressed in Hughes, *Gangraena and the Struggle for the English Revolution* (Oxford: Oxford University Press, 2004).

2. See Kristen Poole, *Radical Religion from Shakespeare to Milton: Figures of Nonconformity in Early Modern England* (Cambridge: Cambridge University Press, 2000), ch. 4.

3. Edwards, *Gangraena, or A Catalogue and Discovery of many of the Errours, Heresies, Blasphemies and pernicious Practices of the Sectaries of this time* (London, 1646), 1.3.113–14. See Thomas Corns, "Milton's Quest for Re-

spectability," *Modern Language Review* 77 (1982): 769–79. While heresiographers like Edwards and Ephraim Pagitt may have intended to describe the individual sects, Corns asserts that they actually "denied any major distinctions of doctrine" in those who stood "to the left of Presbyterianism" (771). See also Colin Davis, *Fear, Myth and History: The Ranters and the Historians* (Cambridge: Cambridge University Press, 1986). Davis avers that Edwards's compendium displays an "indiscriminant jostling of different groups, sources and types of information" (127).

4. Edwards, *Gangraena*, 1.1.21; 3.1.10; 2.1.15.

5. For more on the rise of the antinomian underground in Stuart and Carolingian England, see David Como's masterful *Blown by the Spirit: Puritanism and the Emergence of an Antinomian Underground in Pre-Civil-War England* (Stanford: Stanford University Press, 2004). Disagreeing with Christopher Hill's assessment of the radicals, Como comments that "what divided antinomians from their mainstream puritan counterparts was not class, but rather differing conceptions of the godly life and differing conceptions of how a believer arrived at salvation" (28). Everard and Winstanley belong to the "category" of antinomians that believed in the earthly perfection of human beings. Como remarks that central to those in this category is the allegorical reading of scripture, "in which the literal narratives of scripture were taken to be figures for events and transformations that took place in the believer's soul" (38).

6. See David Loewenstein, "Milton Among the Religious Radicals and Sects: Polemical Engagements and Silences," in *Milton Studies* 40, ed. Albert C. Labriola (2001): 222–47. Loewenstein disagrees with the tenor of Christopher Hill's assertion that Milton was in constant dialogue with the radicals. While always defending the liberty of conscience, germane especially to the radical fringe, Milton never names or specifically defends in his prose the many sects proliferating in England, other than the Fifth Monarchists. He thus maintains both critical "distance and sympathetic engagement." Cf. Christopher Hill, *Milton and the English Revolution* (London: Faber & Faber, 1977), 5. For more on Milton among the radicals, see also these important contributions: Sharon Achinstein, *Literature and Dissent in Milton's England* (Cambridge: Cambridge University Press, 2003); David Loewenstein, *Representing Revolution in Milton and His Contemporaries*; Kristen Poole, *Radical Religion*, chs. 5, 6; Hill, *The World Turned Upside Down*, appendix 2; Hill, *Milton and the English Revolution*, ch. 8.

7. Alexander Parker, *A Testimony of the Light Within* (London, 1657), 11.

8. Geoffrey F. Nuttall, *The Holy Spirit in Puritan Faith and Experience* (Oxford: Oxford University Press, 1946), 28. See also John R. Knott Jr., *The Sword of the Spirit: Puritan Responses to the Bible* (Chicago: University of Chicago Press, 1980).

9. For a slightly different argument with respect to Winstanley, see James Holstun, *Ehud's Dagger: Class Struggle in the English Revolution* (London: Verso, 2000), ch. 9. Holstun points out that Winstanley's "very writing proceeds from hunger, for he customarily forsook his companions, his ordinary labor, and his food for days at a time in order to write. In this isolated, voluntary hunger, he adopts the traditional ascetic technic [*sic*] of the impoverished prophet seeking individual and spiritual transcendence" (374). Part of the Diggers' strategy actually encouraged voluntary hunger, as Holstun observes that this "freedom to starve," or "elective displacement," forces the landlords "to work their own fields, and the distinctions between landlord and tenant, enclosure and common field, will disappear" (406–7).

10. Poole, *Radical Religion*, 107–8.

11. My thanks to Ethan Shagan for this point.

12. Even before the First Civil War Milton had defended dissenting opinion (*Reason of Church Government, CPW* 1:786–87), and in *Areopagitica* (1644) he denounced the "fantastic terrors of sect and schism" (*CPW* 2:554). Milton's apology for religious toleration, excluding Catholics and atheists, and tenacious support for the sects finds its culmination in his late treatise *Of True Religion* (1673), where the aged poet and polemicist argues that "no true Protestant can persecute, or not tolerate his fellow Protestant, though dissenting from him in som opinions" (*CPW* 8:421). Dissenting opinion, Milton champions, works to strengthen the church and is the essence of Protestantism itself. For Milton, the punishment of heresy should not be made subject to state control, for he understood heresy by its classical definition as "choice." On the other hand, Milton did approve of the state's interference in matters of blasphemy. In his *Treatise of Civil Power* (1659) he refers to the Blasphemy Act of 1650, spurred in part by Ranter behavior, as "that prudent and well deliberated act" (*CPW* 7:246).

13. J. G. A. Pocock, *Virtue, Commerce, and History* (Cambridge: Cambridge University Press, 1985), 219.

14. Nuttall, *The Holy Spirit*, 28–33.

15. Richard Baxter, *Works*, 4:294; quoted in Nuttal, *The Holy Spirit*, 51.

16. Richard Hollingworth, *The Holy Ghost on the Bench, other Spirits at the Bar: Or, the Judgement of the Holy Spirit of God upon the Spirits of our Times* (London, 1655), 7–8, 10.

17. Rapha Harford, *The Epistle Dedicatory,* in John Everard, *The Gospel-Treasury Opened; or The Holiest of all Unvailing* (London, 1657), A5, A6. Unless otherwise stated, the italicized portions of quotations from *The Gospel-Treasury Opened* belong to their original author.

18. Ibid., A9.

19. Harford, "To the Christian Reader," in *The Gospel-Treasury Opened,* A3–A4.

20. Como, *Blown by the Spirit,* 225.

21. Everard, *The Gospel-Treasury Opened,* 47, 323–24.

22. Ibid., 336. The sermons were preached (undated) before a private audience at Kensington, and are printed in *The Gospel-Treasury Opened* as if they are only two separate sermons: *The Dead and Killing Letter; The Spirit and the Life,* 271–326, and *Shadows vanishing, Some Rays of Glory appearing,* 327–76. Given their organic relation, I cite original page numbers throughout without referring to the individual sermon.

On the revival of Catholic reading practices among the radicals, see Nigel Smith, *Perfection Proclaimed: Language and Literature in English Radical Religion, 1640–1660* (Oxford: Clarendon, 1989), 17: "Radical religious writers, especially learned ones [e.g., Everard], were using medieval and sixteenth-century Catholic, reformed and radical, mystical and spiritual writings in order to extend the boundaries of their own spiritual experiences. . . . That Catholic works were used should come as less of a surprise when it is realized that the emphasis upon direct divine inspiration put them in the same position as Catholic spiritual writers." For more on the spiritual Anabaptists on the Continent, see George Huntston Williams, *The Radical Reformation* (London: Weidenfeld and Nicolson, 1962).

23. Scott G. Huelin, "Spiritual Reading: Tropology, Discernment and Early Modern European Literature" (Ph.D. diss., University of Chicago, 2002), 9. Chapter 1 provides a cogent survey of the tradition of spiritual reading, and attempts to apply it to a general hermeneutics. For more on the development of allegorical interpretations among the early church fathers, see Anthony Thiselton, *New Horizons in Hermeneutics* (Grand Rapids: Zondervan, 1992), ch. 4.

24. Henri de Lubac, S.J., *Medieval Exegesis, Volume 1: The Four-Fold Method,* trans. Mark Sebanc (Grand Rapids: Eerdmans, 1998), 75. See also

de Lubac, "Spiritual Understanding," trans. Luke O'Neill, in *The Theological Interpretation of Scripture: Classic and Contemporary Readings*, ed. Stephen E. Fowl (Oxford: Blackwell, 1997), 3–25.

25. Quoted in Robert M. Grant and David Tracy, *A Short History of the Interpretation of the Bible* (New York: Macmillan, 1984), 85.

26. Quoted in de Lubac, *Medieval Exegesis*, 85.

27. De Lubac, "Spiritual Understanding," 13.

28. Huelin, "Spiritual Reading," 13.

29. Jean Leclerq, *The Love of Learning and the Desire for God*, trans. Catherine Misrahi (New York: Fordham University Press, 1961), 100.

30. Everard, *The Gospel-Treasury Opened*, 275, 283–85.

31. Ibid., 374, 350, 319.

32. De Lubac, *Medieval Exegesis*, 16, 27.

33. Thiselton, *New Horizons*, 170; emphasis original.

34. Jeremiah Ives, *Innocency above Impudency: or, The Strength of Righteousness exalted Above the Quakers* (London, 1656), 23.

35. Leo Damrosch, *The Sorrows of the Quaker Jesus: James Nayler and the Puritan Crackdown on the Free Spirit* (Cambridge: Harvard University Press, 1996), 100.

36. John Saltmarsh, *Sparkles of Glory: Some Beams of the Morning Star Wherein are many discoveries as to Truth, and Peace* (London, 1647), 5.

37. Everard, *The Gospel-Treasury Opened*, 341, 349, 343, 363–64.

38. See Smith, *Perfection Proclaimed*, ch. 3. Everard translated the perfectionist occult work *Theologia Germanica* in 1628, for which he was brought before the Ecclesiastical Commissioners Court at Lambeth, and subsequently ordered to issue a recantation and fined £1000—both of which he failed to accomplish, as he descended into the radical underground.

39. See Hill, *Milton and the English Revolution*, 73, 294. Hill notes that a Latin translation of the catechism was burned in London in 1614; additionally, he speculates that John Bidle, the infamous anti-Trinitarian and "father of English Unitarianism," was responsible for the English translation. For more on the ambiguity of Milton's licensing the catechism, see Stephen B. Dobranski, "Licensing Milton's Heresy," in *Milton and Heresy*, 139–58, as well as his book, *Milton, Authorship, and the Book Trade* (Cambridge: Cambridge University Press, 1999), ch. 6. See also Sabrina Barton, "Licensing Readers, Licensing Authority," in *Books and Readers in Early Modern England*, 217–42. Barton briefly mentions Milton's licensing of the *Racovian Catechism* and points out that it was published by the official state printer, William Dugard, who was

also the publisher of Milton's *First Defense* (1651). More broadly, Barton discusses Milton's relationship to various London printers, and addresses *Areopagitica* within the context of anonymous and unlicensed printed books. See also Michael Lieb, "Milton and the Socinian Heresy," in *Milton and the Grounds of Contention,* ed. Mark R. Kelley, Michael Lieb, and John T. Shawcross (Pittsburgh: Duquesne University Press, 2003), 234–83. Lieb discusses the *Racovian Catechism,* cautions that scholars ought to avoid attaching Milton too closely to any single heresy, and examines how Milton responds to the Socinian heresy in his work.

40. See John Owen, *Diatriba de Justitiae Divina . . . contra Socinianos* (Oxford, 1653).

41. On this point, and the difficulties of identifying Milton's Arianism or Socinianism, see Hillier, *Milton's Messiah,* 13–15.

42. *The Racovian Catechism* (Amsterdam, 1652), 27–29.

43. Ibid., 58–60, 141, 101.

44. Everard, *The Gospel-Treasury Opened,* 284.

45. Saltmarsh, *Sparkles of Glory,* 10–11, 138, 187.

46. James Nayler, *What the Possession of Living Faith Is,* in *A Collection of Sundry Books, Epistles and Papers, Written by James Nayler, Some of which were never before Printed. With an Impartial Relation of the Most Remarkable Transactions Relating to His Life,* ed. George Whitehead (London, 1716). Republished in 2 vols. (Cincinnati: R. C. Stanton, 1829), 2:422–43; quote from 423. Subsequent quotations from the *Sundry Books* are taken from this latter edition.

47. Everard, *The Gospel-Treasury Opened,* 345–46, 287–88.

48. Ibid., 323–24.

49. Smith, *Perfection Proclaimed,* 232; Nuttall, *The Holy Spirit,* 28.

50. Everard, *The Gospel-Treasury Opened,* 374, 325.

51. See Graham Ward, "The Displaced Body of Jesus Christ," in *Radical Orthodoxy,* 163–81.

52. Everard, *The Gospel-Treasury Opened,* 277, 334, 361, 335, 324.

53. Ibid., 346, 368, 370, 374–75.

54. Harford, "To the Christian Reader," in *The Gospel-Treasury Opened,* A3–A4.

55. Hillier, *Milton's Messiah,* 57, 61, 88.

56. Winstanley, *The New Law of Righteousnes Budding Forth,* 1:507. Cf. Edwards's cataloguing the "common treasury" heresy in *Gangraena,* 1.1.34: "All the earth is the Saints, and there ought to be a community of goods, and the Saints should share in the Lands and Estates of Gentlemen, and rich men."

57. Winstanley, *A Watch-Word,* 2:80.

58. David Underdown, *Pride's Purge: Politics in the Puritan Revolution* (Oxford: Clarendon, 1971), 284. Despite numerous projects proposed for relieving poverty, little large-scale action was taken. High food and coal prices led to an increase in vagrancy, and the fiscally impoverished Rump's refusal to abolish the excise tax contributed to the dilemma of the poor.

59. The geographical extent of the Digger experiment continues to be a subject of research. After being violently expelled in Surrey by the locals, Winstanley and his immediate group moved to Little Heath in the parish of Cobham. See David Taylor, "Gerrard Winstanley at Cobham," in *Winstanley and the Diggers, 1649–1999,* ed. Andrew Bradstock (London: Frank Cass, 2000), 37–46. See also G. E. Aylmer, "The Religion of Gerrard Winstanley," in *Radical Religion in the English Revolution,* 91–120. Aylmer indicates that we might consider Wellingborough in Northamptonshire and Iver in Buckinghamshire as Digger communities based on the publication of Digger manifestos, and communal experiments were initiated in as many as seven sites in five different counties (102). Cf. Underdown, *Pride's Purge,* 267. Underdown confirms Aylmer's findings, but overstates the perception of the Diggers, who "appeared menacingly on St. George's Hill." See John Gurney, "'Furious divells?' The Diggers and Their Opponents," in *Winstanley and the Diggers,* 73–86. Gurney notes that early news accounts, and even the letters to Fairfax from the Council of State, portrayed the Diggers as "harmless or deluded . . . rather than as a threat to the social order" (73). See also Brian Manning, *1649: The Crisis of the English Revolution* (Chicago: Bookmarks, 1992), 121–23.

60. For more on the social and economic factors that contributed to the Digger movement, consult the following: Gerald Aylmer, "The Diggers in Their Own Time," in *Winstanley and the Diggers,* 8–18; Brian Manning, *1649,* chs. 2–3; Manning, *The English People and the English Revolution, 1640–1660* (London: Heinemann, 1976), 292.

61. Christopher Hill, "The Religion of Gerrard Winstanley," *Past and Present,* Supplement 5 (1978): 29; Nigel Smith, "Gerrard Winstanley and the Literature of Revolution," in *Winstanley and the Diggers,* 51.

62. Winstanley, *The New Law,* 1:513.

63. Hill, "The Religion of Gerrard Winstanley," 22.

64. Michael Lieb, *The Visionary Mode: Biblical Prophecy, Hermeneutics, and Cultural Change* (Ithaca: Cornell University Press, 1991), 217.

65. Winstanley, *The New Law,* 1:513.

66. The date of *Fire in the Bush* cannot be precisely determined. The title page of the only edition of the pamphlet is dated 1650, but scholars are divided about whether it was published before or after *The New Law* in that year.

67. Heiko A. Oberman, *The Harvest of Medieval Theology: Gabriel Biel and Late Medieval Nominalism* (Grand Rapids: Baker Academic, 1983), 252. As Oberman relates, this theory was rejected in 1177 because of its Nestorian undertones describing an accidental, and not essential, hypostatic union in Christ. Cf. Ulreich, "'Substantially Express'd,'" 103–4. Ulreich notes that in the early poetry Milton often uses the language of the *habitus* theory, but rejects it in the *De Doctrina Christiana* (*CPW* 6:426).

68. Winstanley, *Fire in the Bush*, 2:176.

69. Ibid., 2:172–73.

70. Ibid., 2:177. Cf. Joseph Salmon, *Antichrist in Man: or, A Discovery of the Great Whore That sits upon many waters* (London, 1648): "This *Garden of Eden* in the mystery, O man! is in thee, in whom God hath placed the manifestation of himselfe, and hath brought forth the buddings of his glory" (4).

71. For more on the metaphoric dimensions of enclosure in the period, see *Enclosure Acts: Sexuality, Property, and Culture in Early Modern England*, ed. Richard Burt and John Michael Archer (Ithaca: Cornell University Press, 1994).

72. Holstun, *Ehud's Dagger*, 402.

73. Winstanley, *Truth Lifting Up Its Head Above Scandals* (London, 1648–49), 1:415.

74. Winstanley, *Fire in the Bush*, 2:176.

75. Winstanley, *The New Law*, 1:478.

76. Joseph Salmon, *Heights in Depths and Depths in Heights, or Truth no less Secretly then Sweetly sparkling out its Glory* (London, 1651). Reprinted in *A Collection of Ranter Writings*, ed. Nigel Smith (London: Junction, 1983), 203–23; quote from 218.

77. Jacob Bauthumley, *The Light and Dark Sides of God* (London, 1650). Reprinted in Smith, *A Collection*, 227–64; quote from 232.

78. See Sallie McFague, "Human Beings, Embodiment, and Our Home the Earth," in *Reconstructing Christian Theology*, ed. Rebecca S. Chopp and Mark Lewis Taylor (Minneapolis: Fortress, 1994), 141–69. McFague offers us a "bush" paradigm of creation: "A bush does not have a main trunk, a dominant direction of growth. There is no privileged place on a bush; rather, what a bush suggests is *diversity* (while at the same time interconnectedness and interdependence since all its parts are related and all are fed by a common root system)" (163).

79. See, for instance, Winstanley, *The New Law,* 1:478; *Fire in the Bush,* 2:176.

80. Winstanley, *The New Law,* 1:481.

81. Winstanley, *Truth Lifting Up Its Head,* 1:423.

82. Loewenstein, *Representing Revolution,* 61. The classic study on the purge of Parliament is David Underdown, *Pride's Purge: Politics in the Puritan Revolution* (Oxford: Clarendon, 1971).

83. Winstanley, *The Saints Paradice,* 74.

84. Loewenstein, *Representing Revolution,* 63; see also "Introduction," George Sabine, in *Works of Gerrard Winstanley,* ed. George H. Sabine (Ithaca: Cornell University Press, 1941), 32.

85. See, for instance, *Truth Lifting Up Its Head,* 1:418–19, 425–27; *The New Law,* 1:515–16; *Fire in the Bush,* 2:180–88.

86. Winstanley, *Truth Lifting Up Its Head,* 1:415, 420.

87. Manning, *1649,* 121–23.

88. Winstanley, *A Letter to the Lord Fairfax and His Councell of War* (1649), 2:49.

89. Ibid., 44.

90. See G. E. Aylmer, *Rebellion or Revolution? England, 1640–1660* (Oxford: Oxford University Press, 1986), 136–37.

91. Salmon, *Antichrist in Man,* 28, 34.

92. T. Wilson Hayes, *Winstanley the Digger: A Literary Analysis of Radical Ideas in the English Revolution* (Cambridge: Harvard University Press, 1979), 70.

93. Hill, "The Religion of Gerrard Winstanley," 29–30.

94. Everard, *The Gospel-Treasury Opened,* 59, 78–79.

95. See Bernard Capp, "The Fifth Monarchists and Popular Millenarianism," in *Radical Religion in the English Revolution,* 165–189. Capp shows that many Fifth Monarchists like Thomas Venner and Vavasor Powell were readily engaged in promoting changes in the army, elections, and the Rump Parliament, and Cromwell feared assassination plots fomented by members of the Fifth Monarchists.

96. Winstanley, *The New Law,* 1:498.

97. Ibid., 1:483–84, 491.

98. Hayes, *Winstanley the Digger,* 72.

99. Winstanley, *The New Law,* 1:489.

100. Aquinas, *Summa Theologica,* 1.16a.1.

101. John Milbank and Catherine Pickstock, *Truth in Aquinas*, 11; emphasis original.

102. Daniel L. Migliore, *Faith Seeking Understanding: An Introduction to Christian Theology* (Grand Rapids: Eerdmans, 1991), 83.

103. Winstanley, *A New-Yeers Gift for the Parliament and the Armie* (London, 1650), 2:142.

104. Winstanley, *The New Law*, 1:567.

105. Ibid., 1:566, 524.

106. Ibid., 1:530.

107. Ibid., 1:508.

108. Winstanley, *Truth Lifting Up Its Head*, 1:435.

109. Cf. Augustine, *On Christian Doctrine*, 1.39.43. Speaking of interpreting scripture, Augustine suggests that those who embody the theological virtues of faith, hope, and charity no longer need the scriptures.

110. Winstanley, *The Saints Paradice*, 64–65.

111. Winstanley, *The New Law*, 1:494–95, 504.

112. Gregory of Nyssa, *The Life of Moses*, in *The Theological Interpretation of Scripture*, 109–10.

113. Hill, *The English Bible*, 20.

Chapter 7. Pageant and Anti-Pageant

1. Accounts of the incident from contemporary but hostile recorders occur in John Deacon, *The Grand Impostor Examined, or The Life, Tryal, and Examination of James Nayler, the Seduced and Seducing Quaker* (London, 1656); Ralph Farmer, *Sathan Inthron'd in his Chair of Pestilence, or Quakerism in its Exaltation: Being a true Narrative and Relation of the manner of James Nailer (that eminent Quaker's) entrance into the City of Bristol the 24 day of October, 1656* (London, 1657); and William Grigge, *The Quaker's Jesus: or, The unswadling of that Child James Nailor, which a wicked Toleration hath midwiv'd into the World* (London, 1658). For a sympathetic defense of Nayler, and a critical response to Farmer's pamphlet, see George Bishop, *The Throne of Truth Exalted over the Powers of Darkness. From Whence is Judged The Mouth of Ralph Farmer (an Unclean and Blood-thirsty Priest of Bristol* (London, 1657). On the millenarian fervor surrounding the year 1656, see William G. Bittle, *James Nayler, 1618–1660: The Quaker Indicted by Parliament* (York: William Sessions Ltd., 1986), 94.

2. See Emilia Fogelklou, *James Nayler: The Rebel Saint, 1618–1660,* trans. Lajla Yapp (London: Ernest Benn Limited, 1931), 175–76; Leo Damrosch, *The Sorrows of the Quaker Jesus,* passim.

3. My thanks to Jeffrey Masten for encouraging me to think about Nayler's entry at Bristol in this context.

4. Farmer, *Sathan Inthron'd,* 20; Thomas Burton, *Diary of Thomas Burton, Esq.,* ed. John Towill Rutt, 4 vols. (London, 1828). Reprinted in 4 vols. (New York: Johnson Reprint Corporation, 1974), 1:72.

5. Stephen Orgel, "Making Greatness Familiar," in *Pageantry in the Shakespearean Theatre,* ed. David Bergeron (Athens: University of Georgia Press, 1985), 19–25; quote from 23.

6. Hans Urs von Balthasar, *Theo-Drama: Theological Dramatic Theory,* trans. Graham Harrison, 5 vols. (San Francisco: Ignatius, 1988), 2:54; 1:26, 264.

7. See ibid., 1:136–37, 160, 33.

8. Farmer, *Sathan Inthron'd,* 28–29.

9. Bittle, *James Nayler,* 108–9; Bishop's testimony cited, 104. Farmer confirms the presence of Samuel Cater in *Sathan Inthron'd,* 17.

10. Farmer, *Sathan Inthron'd,* 6–7, 13, 8.

11. Fox, *Journal,* 34; George Fox and James Nayler, *Saul's Errand to Damascus* (London, 1653), 10. For more on the relationship between early modern enthusiasm and the impetus toward democracy, see Rufus M. Jones, *Mysticism and Democracy in the English Commonwealth* (New York: Octagon, 1965), esp. ch. 3 on the Seeker movement.

12. Bittle, *James Nayler,* 102.

13. Bishop, *The Throne of Truth,* 10.

14. See George Fox, *Journal,* 133–35. Fox was himself interrogated in October 1652 at Lancaster before the Sessions to answer similar charges, and Fox's answers indicate a similar shrewdness.

15. For instances of Fox's experiences with refusing the right of "hat honor," see *Journal,* 36–37, 387–88.

16. Thomas Weld et al., *The Perfect Pharisee under Monkish Holinesse, Opposing the Fundamentall Principles of . . . Quakers* (London, 1653), 33–34.

17. Nayler, *A Discovery of The Man of Sin . . . ; or, An Answer to a Book set forth . . .* (London, 1654), 42–43.

18. Farmer, *Sathan Inthron'd,* 17.

19. Grigge, *The Quaker's Jesus,* 10.

20. Farmer, *Sathan Inthron'd,* 19.

21. Ibid., 15.

22. Nayler, *A Discovery*, 6.

23. Nayler, *A Few Words, Occasioned by a Paper Lately Printed, Styled A Discourse concerning the Quakers* (London, 1653), reprinted in *Sundry Books*, 1:142–48; quote from 149.

24. Fox, *Journal*, 135, 368.

25. Damrosch, *The Sorrows of the Quaker Jesus*, 105; see his excellent extended discussion on Quaker ideas of perfection, 97–107.

26. Nayler, *A Discovery*, 4; Fox and Nayler, *Saul's Errand*, 13.

27. Deacon, *The Grand Impostor Examined*, 26–27.

28. For more on each of these processions, see David M. Bergeron, *English Civic Pageantry 1558–1642* (Columbia: University of South Carolina Press, 1971). Bergeron indicates that there was a steady decline in the number of royal pageants. Unlike Elizabeth, James I was largely passive in such matters and preferred the private masques; Charles I, in fact, refused to indulge in a coronation pageant into London. Lord Mayor's Shows, however, continued to flourish, and many of them were written by prominent dramatists such as Thomas Middleton, Thomas Dekker, and Thomas Heywood. For more on the Lord Mayor's Shows, see Anne Lancashire, *London Civic Theatre: City Drama and Pageantry from Roman Times to 1558* (Cambridge: Cambridge University Press, 2002), ch. 10.

29. Alice S. Vernezky, *Pageantry on the Shakespearean Stage* (New York: Twayne, 1951), 90–91. See also Bergeron, *English Civic Pageantry*, 19–23.

30. Vernezky, *Pageantry on the Shakespearean Stage*, 174–75.

31. Ibid., 78–79.

32. David Scott Kastan, *Shakespeare After Theory* (New York: Routledge, 1999), 113, 117–18; Stephen Greenblatt, *Shakespearean Negotiations: The Circulation of Social Energy in Renaissance England* (Berkeley: University of California Press, 1988), 64. See also his "Performances and Playbooks: The Closing of the Theatres and the Politics of Drama," in *Reading, Society and Politics in Early Modern England*, 167–84.

33. Steven Mullaney, "Civic Rites, City Sites: The Place of the Stage," in *Staging the Renaissance: Reinterpretations of Elizabethan and Jacobean Drama*, ed. David Scott Kastan and Peter Stallybrass (New York: Routledge, 1991), 17–26; quotes from 18–20.

34. Farmer, *Sathan Inthon'd*, 3. See Barry Reay, *The Quakers and the English Revolution* (New York: St. Martin's, 1985). Reay indicates that both Bristol and London were geographical centers for Quaker expansion. He estimates that Bristol had perhaps one thousand Quakers, or 5.6 percent of the

population, and London had perhaps eight thousand to ten thousand Quakers, or 1.5 percent of the population (27–29).

35. There appears to be no data on which almshouse this was. See Bruce Williams, "The Excavation of Medieval and Post-Medieval Tenements at 94–102 Temple Street, Bristol, 1975," *Transactions of the Bristol and Gloucestershire Archaeological Society* 106 (1988): 107–68. Williams provides a map showing the locations of the principal pre-Reformation almshouses in Bristol, and there are no indications that an almshouse existed outside Redcliff Gate; just inside Redcliff Gate, however, is Richard Foster's Almshouse, and Redcliff Almshouse was located about 300 meters to the east, near Temple Gate, which was the other major entrance from the south (23). On the almshouse as the predecessor to the hospital, see Walter H. Godfrey, *The English Almshouse* (London: Faber & Faber, 1955).

36. Deacon, *The Grand Impostor Examined*, 2.

37. Christopher Hill, *The World Turned Upside Down*, 49; for more on the threat of the "masterless men," see esp. ch. 3.

38. D. Stephen Long, *Divine Economy: Theology and the Market* (New York: Routledge, 2000), 4.

39. Ibid., 228–29. Cf. Aquinas, *Summa Theologica*, 2a.2ae.57–59.

40. Long, *Divine Economy*, 28.

41. See ibid., 232–40.

42. Deacon, *The Grand Impostor*, 17–18.

43. Fogelklou, *James Nayler*, 163.

44. See Long, *Divine Economy*, 186.

45. For more on the financial condition of Nayler's family at his death, consult Mabel Richmond Brailsford, *A Quaker from Cromwell's Army: James Nayler* (London: Swarthmore, 1927), 197–98. In her third appendix, Brailsford reproduces John Nayler's account of his late father's assets and liabilities. One daughter, Sarah, is willed forty pounds as a legacy, leaving "eight pence to be devided amongst the mother [Ann Nayler] & five children—according to the devise of the will, & nothing for the Executor but his labour for his paines."

46. On Colonel Fiennes and the imprisonment of beneficed clergy, see John Latimer, *The Annals of Bristol in the Seventeenth Century* (Bristol: William George's Sons, 1900), 168–70. Latimer further notes that the Reverend Matthew Hazard, while vicar to St. Ewen's, initiated one of the first dissenting congregations in England in 1640. This congregation oftentimes met in All Saints in the mid-1640s under the preaching of a Mr. Ingello.

47. See Bergeron, *English Civic Pageantry,* 26–27. Bergeron observes that archival receipts for Elizabeth's march through Bristol in 1574 indicate that the High Cross was painted and gilded for the occasion; moreover, standing at the High Cross was a boy dressed in the figure of Fame, who welcomed the queen. The welcome oration by the boy is preserved in Thomas Churchyard, *The Firste Parte of Churchyardes Chippes* (London, 1575), 100–101. See Robert Naile, *A Relation of the Royall Magnificent, and Sumptuous Entertainement, given to the High, and Mighty Princesse, Queene Anne, at the renowned Citie of Bristol* (London, 1613). There is no explicit mention of Queen Anne's passing by the High Cross in 1613, for the focus of her entertainment was a spectacular mock water battle. At the very end of his account, Naile simply comments that after the entertainment the queen's train went through the streets of Bristol, but given the monument's central location along the main thoroughfare of the city, it seems likely she passed by. For a short discussion of Anne's entry at Bristol, see Bergeron, *English Civic Pageantry,* 98–99.

48. For more on Milton's "paradise within," see Loewenstein, *Representing Revolution,* ch. 8; John C. Ulreich Jr., "A Paradise Within: The Fortunate Fall in *Paradise Lost,*" *Journal of the History of Ideas* 32 (1971): 351–66. Loewenstein in particular draws explicit connections between Milton and the Quakers.

49. Fox and Nayler, *Saul's Errand,* 17–18.

50. Latimer, *Annals,* 125, 230.

51. Francis Higginson, *A Brief Relation of the Irreligion of the Northern Quakers* (London, 1653), 22.

52. Fox and Nayler, *Saul's Errand,* 19.

53. Latimer, *Annals,* 275.

54. See Grigge, *The Quaker's Jesus,* 3.

55. Fogelklou, *James Nayler,* 177–78; Bittle, *James Nayler,* 104.

56. John Gough, *A History of the People called Quakers. From their first Rise to the present Time. Compiled from Authentic Records and from the Writings of that People,* 4 vols. (Dublin, 1789–90), 1:56. Quoted in Bittle, *James Nayler,* 5.

57. This public incident is discussed in Bittle, *James Nayler,* 97–102.

58. My thanks to an anonymous reader for offering this point for consideration.

59. For more of these indictments against the stage, see Jean E. Howard, *The Stage and Social Struggle in Early Modern England* (London: Routledge, 1994), ch. 2.

60. Nayler, *To the Parliament of the Commonwealth of England,* in *Sundry Books,* 2:718–19.

61. Farmer, *Sathan Inthron'd*, 25, 39, 29.

62. See Kastan, *Shakespeare After Theory*, 112.

63. Farmer, *Sathan Inthron'd*, 34–35.

64. Deacon, *The Grand Impostor Examined*, 4, 44; Farmer, *Sathan Inthron'd*, 27.

65. Quoted in Damrosch, *Sorrows of the Quaker Jesus*, 204. See Burton, *Diary*, 1:52.

66. Deacon, *An Exact History of the Life of James Naylor* (London, 1657), 35–37; pages 36 and 37 are misnumbered as 44 and 45.

67. See Damrosch, *Sorrows of the Quaker Jesus*, 225. The relevant portions of Jacob Millerd's map are reprinted in Donald Jones, *Bristol Past* (Shopwyke Manor Barn, West Sussex: Phillimore & Co., Ltd., 2000), 38–40.

68. Thanks to John Morrill for this clarification.

Epilogue. Milton and the Limits of Incarnation in the Seventeenth Century

1. Steiner, *Real Presences*, 8, 11.

2. Howgill quoted in Bittle, *James Nayler*, 103.

3. George Lindbeck, *The Nature of Doctrine* (Philadelphia: Westminster, 1984), 16.

4. Richard Hooker, *Of the Laws of Ecclesiastical Politie* (London, 1593), preface, 8.7.

5. See Jean-François Gilmont, "Protestant Reformations and Reading," in *A History of Reading in the West*, 213–37. For more on the evolution, politics, and uses and abuses of reading and interpreting scripture in the seventeenth century, see Hill, *The English Bible*.

6. Dora Neill Raymond, *Oliver's Secretary: John Milton in an Era of Revolt* (New York: Minton, Balch & Company, 1932), 191.

7. Burton, *Diary*, 1:24–26. For discussion on other contemporary perceptions of the Quaker threat, and the danger of other dissenting movements, see Barry Reay, "The Quakers, 1659, and the Restoration of the Monarchy," *History* 63 (1978): 193–213. Reay argues that these fearful perceptions of the Quakers and Baptists in particular in 1659 contributed to the Restoration. See also Greaves, *Deliver Us From Evil*, passim; and Capp, "The Fifth Monarchists and Popular Millenarianism," in *Radical Religion*, 175.

8. Burton, *Diary*, 1:47, 65, 56, 61, 27.

9. Ibid., 1:96, 98, 101.

10. Ibid. Articles from the *Instruments of Government* reproduced in the footnotes by the editor, 1:50. For more on Cromwell's concerns for the establishment of the godly commonwealth and Protestant unity, see Barry Coward, *Cromwell* (New York: Longman, 1991), ch. 5. For more on the development of the liberty of conscience, see Gary S. De Krey, "Radicals, Reformers, and Republicans: Academic Language and Political Discourse in Restoration London," in *A Nation Transformed: England After the Restoration,* ed. Alan Houston and Steve Pincus (Cambridge: Cambridge University Press, 2001), 71–99. See also his "Rethinking the Restoration: Dissenting Cases of Conscience, 1667–1672," *Historical Journal* 38, no. 1 (1995): 53–83.

11. Burton, *Diary,* 1:38, 50–51.

12. Ibid., 1:38, 50–51, 28–29, 34.

13. My thanks again to an anonymous reader for helping me sharpen up this point. See, for instance, the essays collected in *The Tudor and Stuart Town: A Reader in English Urban History, 1530–1688,* ed. Jonathan Barry (London: Longman, 1990).

14. David Harris Sacks, "The Corporate Town and the British State: Bristol's Little Businesses 1625–41," *Past and Present* 110 (1986): 69–105. Reprinted in *The Tudor and Stuart Town,* 297–333; quote from 304. See also Sacks, *The Widening Gate: Bristol and the Atlantic Economy, 1450–1700* (Berkeley: University of California Press, 1993).

15. Sacks, *The Widening Gate,* 310–11.

16. Everard, *The Gospel-Treasury Opened,* 301, 30.

17. Burton, *Diary,* 1:48.

18. Ibid., 1.47–48; Nayler, *An Answer to the booke called the perfect Pharisee* (London, 1653), 28.

19. Achinstein, *Literature and Dissent,* 169.

index

Page numbers for definitions are in boldface.

BRYAN ADAMS HAMPTON

is the Dorothy and James D. Kennedy Distinguished Teaching Associate Professor of English at the University of Tennessee at Chattanooga.